LULA!

LULA!

The Man, The Myth and a Dream of Latin America

RICHARD LAPPER

BLOOMSBURY CONTINUUM
LONDON · OXFORD · NEW YORK · NEW DELHI · SYDNEY

BLOOMSBURY CONTINUUM
Bloomsbury Publishing Plc

50 Bedford Square, London, WC1B 3DP, UK
Bloomsbury Publishing Ireland Limited,
29 Earlsfort Terrace, Dublin 2, D02 AY28, Ireland

BLOOMSBURY, BLOOMSBURY CONTINUUM and the
Diana logo are trademarks of Bloomsbury Publishing Plc

First published in Great Britain 2026

Copyright © Richard Lapper, 2026

Richard Lapper has asserted his right under the Copyright,
Designs and Patents Act, 1988, to be identified as Author of this work

For legal purposes the Acknowledgements on p. 310
constitute an extension of this copyright page

All rights reserved. No part of this publication may be: i) reproduced or transmitted in any form, electronic or mechanical, including photocopying, recording or by means of any information storage or retrieval system without prior permission in writing from the publishers; or ii) used or reproduced in any way for the training, development or operation of artificial intelligence (AI) technologies, including generative AI technologies. The rights holders expressly reserve this publication from the text and data mining exception as per Article 4(3) of the Digital Single Market Directive (EU) 2019/790

Bloomsbury Publishing Plc does not have any control over, or responsibility for, any third-party websites referred to or in this book. All internet addresses given in this book were correct at the time of going to press. The author and publisher regret any inconvenience caused if addresses have changed or sites have ceased to exist, but can accept no responsibility for any such changes

A catalogue record for this book is available from the British Library

Library of Congress Cataloguing-in-Publication data has been applied for

ISBN: HB: 978-1-3994-1358-9; eBook: 978-1-3994-1360-2; ePDF: 978-1-3994-1355-8

2 4 6 8 10 9 7 5 3 1

Typeset by Lumina Datamatics Ltd
Printed and bound in Great Britain by Clays Ltd, Elcograf S.p.A.

To find out more about our authors and books visit www.bloomsbury.com
and sign up for our newsletters

For product safety related questions contact productsafety@bloomsbury.com

To my wife Fátima Carvalho who has made our home in London's docklands a little corner of Brazil.
To my former teacher Colin Henfrey (1941–2025), who originally introduced me to Latin America more than half a century ago.

Contents

	Introduction	1
1	A Man from the Backlands	15
2	The City and the Factory	29
3	Soldiers and Guerrillas	43
4	The Reluctant Trade Unionist	61
5	All Out	75
6	The Workers' Party Arrives	89
7	The Odd Couple	103
8	The Tide Turns	119
9	2002: A Decisive Year	133
10	The Rise of Lulismo	149
11	Green Brazil	165
12	The Dilma Dilemma	181
13	The Fall	197
14	The Fall 2: Lula Bites the Dust	213
15	Bolsonaro	233
16	Lula 3 Takes Shape	247
17	'Welcome to the sacred land of the working class'	263
18	The Seductions of Celebrity	283
	Conclusion	299
	Acknowledgements	310
	Notes	314
	Index	346

Introduction

Shortly before 8 o'clock on the evening of Brazil's presidential election at the end of October 2022[1] the tension around Avenida Paulista suddenly lifted and the air was filled with noise. Motorbikes roared past. Convoys of celebrating drivers blared their horns, their passengers perched perilously on the outside of the vehicles, waving red flags. All along the six-lane highway in the centre of São Paulo, knots of giddy Lula supporters danced in front of TV cameras. Others were rendering the old familiar football-style chant of 'Olé, Olá, Lula Lula!', as samba rhythms thumped from giant speakers. Someone in a Spiderman costume covered in Lula stickers careered among the makeshift stalls selling beer and caipirinhas cocktails.

I'd witnessed these scenes in Latin America's most populous city before, most memorably in late 2002 when Luiz Inácio Lula da Silva was elected Brazil's first working-class president. Now it was happening again. And for his supporters this new victory, 20 years on, was especially sweet because their man had defeated Jair Bolsonaro, a former army captain, political outsider, close ally of Donald Trump, and fervent admirer of his country's military governments. Only four years before, Lula – president of Brazil for eight years from January 2003 – had watched Bolsonaro win the presidency from his prison cell. In any case, relief featured prominently among the emotions of those celebrating. The final count had been closer than many had expected. 'We have suffered a lot tonight, just like all progressive and left-wing Brazilians,' Telma

Clemente, a 64-year-old pensioner, told a reporter as she waited to greet Lula outside his headquarters at the Hotel Intercontinental. 'We thought the victory would be by a bigger margin. Thank God we have won.'[2]

Lula's political comeback was remarkable in many ways, not least because his original journey to the presidency had been such an odyssey. He was born on 27th October 1945 into a poor farming family from the north-eastern state of Pernambuco. With his mothers and siblings he had migrated south as a child to the rapidly industrialising city of São Paulo, where he became a lathe operator and gradually got involved in a growing labour movement during the late 1960s. After forming and then leading the trade union-based Workers' Party (PT), Lula ran for president three times in the 1980s and 1990s but was defeated on each occasion. At the time, many had written Lula off, dismissing him as an old-style labour leader entirely out of touch with the new, more liberal and market-friendly public mood. But Lula had surprised his critics. He had moderated his goals, dropped the rabble-rousing tone that had marked his first forays into politics, and then surged to success. After winning the presidency twice successively in the 2000s, Lula left office in January 2011 with his popularity sky-high and as something of an international star. His success in maintaining economic stability, reducing poverty, and improving living standards was seen as a model for other countries to follow. Lula – famously – was lauded by President Barack Obama as 'my guy'. His political fortunes, though, had dipped dramatically in the 2010s. He watched helplessly as Dilma Rousseff, his hand-picked but headstrong successor, blundered politically and mismanaged Brazil's economy into recession.

Rousseff floundered so badly that congressional leaders agreed to impeach her, cutting her second term short. Two years later, in 2018, the courts had sentenced Lula himself to a 12-year prison term on corruption charges. That year had also seen the election of Bolsonaro, but in the new decade Brazil's political pendulum had then swung back to the left. Bolsonaro's government lost its way during the COVID pandemic. His denialism, refusal to follow international guidelines, and delay in the development and import of vaccines cost the country heavily, with death rates from the disease among the highest in the world. Lula had been released from jail after 18 months in November 2019 – initially on a technicality – and allowed to take part in elections. Bolsonaro raged against his loss of popularity, questioned the integrity of Brazil's electronic voting system, and threatened not to accept the results. Famously, he told supporters that he would only leave office either dead or under arrest. As the campaign proceeded, Lula emerged as the head of a broad democratic alliance, winning the support of erstwhile foes such as Fernando Henrique Cardoso, Brazil's former president, now in his nineties, whose successful counter-inflationary reforms Lula had at first opposed 28 years before.

Later that night towards the end of October 2022, when Lula addressed his supporters, he was flanked by Geraldo Alckmin, his newly elected deputy, a colleague of Cardoso's who had run against Lula in 2006. Lula presented himself as the leader 'of a democratic movement that [transcends] political parties, personal interests, and ideologies. The Brazilian people are the big winners. It suits nobody to live in a country in a permanent state of war.' The grizzled old trade unionist – who had marked his 77th birthday a few days before – also knew how close he had come to being a casualty himself. He claimed to have been 'resurrected. [They] tried to bury me. But here I am. Here I am.'[3]

Political comebacks often go wrong. Think of the most celebrated example – that of Britain's Second World War leader, Winston Churchill. Ousted at the polls in 1945, Churchill regained the prime ministership in 1951 only to retire due to ill-health four years later. For 11 years, India's Iron Lady – Indira Gandhi – was known as one of the most powerful women in the world, but then lost office. Following her return to government in 1980, she was then assassinated in 1984, a fate that also awaited Olof Palme, the Swedish prime minister whose second period in government was cut short by his murder in 1986. Tragedy has also stalked the two most famous cases of political resurrection in Latin America. Juan

Domingo Perón, who returned to the presidency in Argentina in 1973 after 18 years of exile in Franco's Spain, led a chaotic left-wing government briefly before dying of a heart attack less than a year later, leaving competing factions of his Justicialist party at war over his legacy. A spate of killings paved the way for a military coup in 1976 and one of Latin America's bloodiest ever episodes of repression.

In Brazil, Getúlio Vargas led a military coup in 1930. He headed an authoritarian government modelled in part on Mussolini's Italy, was forced to step down in 1945, only to return in 1951 as a left-wing father-of-the-people figure. Three years later, though, with right-wing politicians and the army top brass plotting his overthrow, he shot himself.[4]

The prospects for Lula's comeback did not look good. He had won by a whisker, defeating Bolsonaro by only 2.1 million votes (from a population of over 200 million). Bolsonaro's performance was the strongest ever by a runner-up in a Brazilian election. Lula had carried the day largely because of the extent of his support in the poorer north-east, where people had benefited most from the social policies introduced during his first two governments and that of his successor, Dilma Rousseff.

Overall, Bolsonaro won 14 of Brazil's 27 states, dominating a swathe of territory stretching from the Atlantic coast to the savannah lands of the centre-west. Lula's Workers' Party and its left-wing allies had performed poorly in congressional elections, leaving the newly elected president dependent on centre and right-wing parties that had been willing to lend support to Bolsonaro over the previous four years. Everywhere you looked there was evidence of the enduring strength of social conservatism. In the words of one of the PT's most important political strategists, the election had been won by a 'miracle. A miracle called Lula.'[5] Lula was (and in 2025 remains) effectively the leader of a minority government. Back in 2003, he took office backed by an alliance that controlled more than 360 of the 513 seats in the lower house of Congress. In 2023 his government could rely on no more than 200 votes (and frequently far fewer) in the same chamber. The PT's own representation had fallen from a maximum of 93 deputies and 14 senators in 2003 to only 67 deputies and 9 senators in 2023. Conservative parties and politicians dominated the legislature.

The same right-wing congressional lobbies – popularly known as Beef, Bible, and Bullets – that backed Bolsonaro still held enormous sway. Many farmers – big and small – clashed with the Lula government over environmental conservation and indigenous rights. Faced with high levels of violent crime, many policemen, soldiers, and ordinary Brazilians still railed against restrictions on their ability to defend themselves, championing instead an old-fashioned 'iron fist' approach, even if it meant innocents got caught up in the crossfire. Evangelical Christians and many Catholics remained angry about social liberalism in areas such as sexuality, education, and the family. Finally, another long-term social trend was still pushing Brazil to the right. The manufacturing industries that had fuelled the rise of Lula's trade union movement had long been in decline. In the 1980s, roughly a third of the labour force was unionized. By 2022, only about 9 per cent of the population were members of unions. Services dominated employment opportunities in cities. Thousands of Brazilians were working in the new individualized digital economy as drivers for taxi companies such as Uber and the delivery platforms. Just as the liberation theologists and radical left-wing clerics helped the growth of the unions and the Workers' Party in the 1970s and early 1980s, so the right-wing Pentecostal sects with their creed of restraint and individual responsibility supported poor Brazilians as they negotiated the uncertainties of what was often labelled *empreendedorismo*, or entrepreneurship. Evangelicals had grown from just under 7 per cent of the population in 1980 to 27 per cent in 2022. As one sociologist put it, they were 'the elephant in the room and the most important mass phenomenon of recent decades'.[6]

These conservative forces seemed to be quite consolidated. In the words of Felipe Nunes and Thomas Traumann, Brazilian political attitudes had hardened to such an extent that they had become 'calcified' and impossible to change.[7]

Nor was the international horizon much more promising for Lula. The world had changed dramatically since he had first taken office. Back in 2002, there were undoubtedly significant economic challenges. Still, there was then at least a residual belief in the potential offered by the progressive recipe of stable, well-regulated markets and steady social reform. China's entry into the world trading system was just beginning, offering a new source of economic growth to countries traditionally dependent on North America and Europe.

Twenty years on, China and Russia were increasingly authoritarian, with their own expansionary ambitions. Europe and the United States were heavily indebted, with the difficulties exacerbated by the costs of the COVID-19 pandemic. The world was more individualistic, more obsessed with sectoral identities, and more intolerant. There was also increasing desperation about significant issues, such as climate change. It seemed that a global war, triggered by the conflict in Ukraine or the Middle East, or potential Chinese action over Taiwan, might happen. In Latin America, the pink wave of centre-left governments had receded. Poverty had returned with a vengeance. Brazil's northern neighbour, Venezuela – which had suffered from the most radical social experimentation – was in ruins. Two other strident leaders of Latin American radicalism – Argentina's Cristina Kirchner and Bolivia's Evo Morales – were discredited.

It was not surprising then that Lula's first three years in office did not go particularly well. The president struggled to implement reforms. His government was fractious and far less popular than those of his first two periods in office. Whether or not – after Jair Bolsonaro was handed a prison sentence of 27 years and 3 months in September 2025 for plotting a military coup – the Bolsonaro family managed to retain its power and influence, right-wing populism still seemed strong.

This book, however, takes a longer-term view of the country's development, seen through the prism of Lula's life story and political career, as well as the stories of those who have been close to him. It is subtitled *The Man, The Myth and A Dream of Latin America*.

Although Lula himself – as he frequently reminds interviewers – is a convinced pragmatist, more radical ideas about social transformation have played a big part in his story. In the late 1960s and early 1970s several of Lula's closest lifelong political associates were members of armed guerrilla groups. A dozen members of his first cabinet that met in 2003 had in their youth been activists in revolutionary Marxist organizations, most of which had either supported or been sympathetic to the idea of armed struggle.[8] Catholic social activists played a central role in forming Lula's own Workers' Party.

The radical Catholic experiments of the 1960s and 1970s built on a long tradition of Utopian thought in Latin America, nowhere more so than in Lula's native north-east of Brazil. Even before its colonization from the sixteenth century onwards, indigenous philosophies of community, collective well-being, and harmony with nature were deeply rooted. The Christian powers that colonized the Americas brought their own visions. The same conquistadors whose search for mineral riches brought devastation were inspired by their own ideas of ideal societies, based on the concept that a Kingdom of God would be realized on earth. From the early 1500s the Jesuits, Franciscans, Dominicans, and other orders set up to revive and renew the Catholic Church, established missions across Latin America, aiming to convert and protect indigenous populations.[9] Among isolated and marginal rural communities in eighteenth- and nineteenth-century Brazil, messianic and utopian Christian schemes flourished. Sebastianism, a folk creed based on the idea of a returning king, thrived in Lula's native north-east. In Ceará a dissident Catholic priest, Father Cícero, converted the town of Juazeiro into a holy city. In the remote north of Bahia an even more radical rebel cleric, Antonio Conselheiro, and his followers set up an egalitarian peasant city at Canudos. In a grim and bloody precursor of the military dictatorship's destruction of the twentieth-century guerrilla groups, the defenders of Canudos were eventually crushed by the Brazilian army in 1897 and the city's inhabitants massacred.

Utopias of one kind or another frequently influenced the way outsiders see Latin America. Again, this idea has deep roots.

Utopia, written in 1516 by the English theologian Sir Thomas More and detailing perhaps the West's most celebrated fictional paradise, was based in the mid-Atlantic, its location influenced by the then recent discoveries of the age of exploration. The myth of the golden city of El Dorado sprung from early Spanish encounters with Latin American indigenous groups. For Enlightenment thinkers such as Voltaire the New World was seen as a place where ideas could be tested, a site for experiments such as the (disastrous) Darien scheme in modern-day Panama, set up by Scottish settlers in the late 1690s and financed by the Scottish Crown. Against this background it is perhaps not surprising that to outsiders Latin America has often been something of a political theatre, where ideas that might be considered too extreme or too impractical in more complex developed societies seem viable.

In the 1970s – when I first learned about Latin America – British right-wingers preoccupied with Britain's industrial stagnation and recalcitrance looked sympathetically upon the brutal methods of Augusto Pinochet. Margaret Thatcher nurtured a close friendship with the Chilean dictator. Equally, left-wing politicians and political activists like me saw the martyred left-wing Chilean president, Salvador Allende, as a moral exemplar. As air-force jets bombed the presidential palace in Santiago, Allende had died with a sub-machine gun in his hands (a weapon that had been given to him by Fidel Castro) and became a symbol of heroic resistance to the military dictatorships sweeping the region. Like Che Guevara, the Argentinian doctor turned Cuban guerrilla commander, he was seen as a leader with moral authority.

I have to admit that this kind of vision influenced my own early interest in Latin America. At Liverpool University where I studied sociology, I was taught a course on Latin American social structure by Colin Henfrey, an Oxford-educated social anthropologist who had a strong sympathy for the underdog. Henfrey's course, heavily influenced by dependency theory – the idea that Latin America's economic development was constrained by its ties to the imperial powers of North America and Europe – was colourful, introducing me to the writing of authors such as Gabriel García

Márquez and Mario Vargas Llosa. And it was a course that seemed relevant to what was happening in the world now, a long way from the dry theoretical texts that dominated other degree work. Within weeks of the bloody Chilean coup of September 1973 that brought General Pinochet to power, Henfrey had introduced a course unit looking at how the left-wing Popular Unity government had been destroyed.

In 1974, when I began a postgraduate course under Henfrey's direction, dozens of Chilean left-wing refugees were settling in Liverpool. I shared an office with a young left-wing exile from Concepción. My PhD thesis, which remained unfinished, focused on how unplanned migration to Latin American cities was creating a new underclass. One of the first papers I studied was by Fernando Henrique Cardoso, the Brazilian sociologist who would become president of Brazil in 1994, and as a friend and then political rival of Lula, plays an important part in this story. As the 1970s progressed, I secured a position at a small London-based research centre called The Contemporary Archive on Latin America and then with the *Latin American Newsletter*, a specialist publication that, in the more closed world of the 1970s and 1980s, was an essential source of information about the region. I learned Spanish and worked as a correspondent for nearly two years in El Salvador, Guatemala, Honduras, and Nicaragua, attracted by the excitement of the revolutions sweeping through those countries. By the mid-1980s, though, back in London, the economic and political realities that I was discovering as a journalist were at odds with my left-wing politics and my stance shifted towards the centre.

I first began covering Brazil regularly as part of my broader Latin American responsibilities at *The Financial Times* in 1998. I was the paper's Latin America editor for 10 years, lived in São Paulo between 2003 and 2008, and I concluded my 25-year career at the newspaper, heading up an *FT* research project on Brazil, China, and other developing countries. After I met my wife, Fátima, one of my teachers on a Portuguese language course I took in 1998, I got to know her family and friends in Salvador, São Paulo, and Uberlândia, in the central Brazilian state of Minas Gerais. Since leaving the *FT*, I have continued to visit Brazil regularly, spending up to a quarter of the year there. I interviewed Lula when I was with the *FT*. During the reporting trips to Brazil for this book, in 2023 and 2024, I met many senior and not-so-senior figures in the PT who know or have worked closely with Lula, both in the union movement, the Workers' Party, and the government. I also spoke with reporters, diplomats, and businesspeople who know or have met Lula.

Hopefully my own journey from Marxism, academia, and left-wing activism to journalism and *The Financial Times* has given me some insights into how Lula and his party have evolved. Although many PT politicians and activists retain a commitment to the hard-line statism and anti-Americanism of their youth, others, most notably Fernando Haddad, the Finance Minister, and Marina Silva, the Environment Minister, are pragmatic reformists who – like Fernando Henrique Cardoso – have come to recognize the realities of markets and the necessity to adopt a patient and long-term approach to social change. Lula, perhaps, sits somewhere in the middle, often appeasing his own left-wing supporters by adopting radical rhetoric, but generally in the end tending to favour moderation. Although, as we'll see, it's complicated.

Chapters 1 and 2 recount Lula's early childhood on a smallholding in a remote area in the state of Pernambuco and the family's flight following a prolonged drought to São Paulo, where on a public apprentice scheme Lula learned how to operate a lathe, then secured regular relatively well-paid skilled employment in the metal-bashing industries of the so-called ABC towns of São Paulo's southern periphery (Santo André, São Bernardo do Campo, São Caetano and Diadema).

Chapter 3 examines the 1964 military coup and the left-wing guerrilla movement established in an ultimately disastrous attempt to overthrow the dictatorship. It's important because many of the most significant figures in the Workers' Party cut their political teeth in that movement and learned from their mistakes.

Chapters 4 and 5 chronicle Lula's emergence as a trade union leader and the strikes of the late 1970s that brought him to national and international attention, establishing him as a media celebrity. Chapter 4 focuses on Lula's relationship with one of his older brothers, Frei Chico, a Communist Party member who persuaded Lula to become a trade unionist.

Chapter 6 covers the formation and rise of the Workers' Party, as well as the 1989 presidential campaign that, although unsuccessful, consolidated Lula's reputation as a national political leader.

Chapter 7 explores the relationship between Lula and Cardoso, examining how former political allies became rivals. The core issues that separated the PT and Cardoso's Social Democratic Party of Brazil (*Partido da Social Democracia Brasileira* or PSDB) are in many ways still at the heart of Brazilian politics, with the PT resisting calls to restructure the state and make it more flexible.

Chapters 8 and 9 look at how Cardoso's governments eliminated hyperinflation and stabilized the economy through the *Plano Real* (*Real* Plan) of 1994 and the adjustment packages of the late 1990s. The changes made Brazil attractive for foreign capital. But, the financial crises of 1999–2002 triggered rises in unemployment and a fall in Cardoso's popularity, paving the way for Lula in 2002 to win the presidency at the fourth attempt.

Chapter 10 discusses Lula's successes during his first two mandates. China's entry into the world economy led to a commodity boom, which enabled Brazil to strengthen its balance of payments. This 'China dividend' in turn helped finance an expansion in wages, credit, and social welfare. However, the chapter also examines the way in which the PT became part of a political system that it had once bitterly criticized and was ensnared by corruption. As a result of these developments, the geographical and sociological base of its support shifted away from the south-east, where it had been founded, towards the poorer north-east, which had benefited most from social programmes and rising living standards.

Chapter 11 traces the origins of another perhaps less heralded success. Marina Silva, Minister of the Environment and Climate Change for the first five and a half years of Lula's presidency, was the daughter of a rubber tapper, whose background was every bit as poor and deprived as Lula's own. She became the standard-bearer of a green politics originally pioneered with PT support by the rubber tappers' leader, Chico Mendes, which helped protect the Amazon Rainforest and significantly reduced deforestation between 2004 and 2012.

Chapter 12 charts the rise of a different figure. Dilma Rousseff was, in some ways, the antithesis of Marina Silva, being charged with developing infrastructure, including several massively controversial Amazon-based projects, from 2007 onwards. Anxious to create jobs and win votes, Lula made her his heir apparent, and with his backing Rousseff won a landslide victory in 2010. Rousseff, who had never before won an election for office, proved to be temperamentally ill-suited to the complexities of party politics. She encouraged an anti-corruption campaign that eventually led to the Lava Jato investigation of 2014.

Chapter 13 revisits the disintegration of the Rousseff administration and her impeachment by Congress in April 2016.

Chapter 14 unpicks how Lula himself became entangled in the Lava Jato investigation and was eventually sentenced to a lengthy prison term. The corruption inquiry devastated the entire political establishment, creating a vacuum that paved the way for the 2018 election of a political outsider, Jair Bolsonaro.

Chapter 15 evaluates the fortunes of Bolsonaro's government and explains the tensions that emerged between his far-right supporters and more traditional conservatives, primarily in response to Bolsonaro's denial of the COVID-19 pandemic.

Chapter 16 reviews the political instability surrounding the transition and the failed attempts by Bolsonaro supporters to launch a right-wing coup. It also examines more subtle, longer-term changes, including the growing dominance of a physiological politics of self-interest, the rise of the parties of the Centrão or big centre, and the increasing economic power of the legislature. In Lula's third term the executive has been weaker and its ability to govern has been dependent on its capacity to strike deals with legislators. Fernando Haddad, Lula's moderate Finance Minister,

INTRODUCTION   13

has become the dominant figure in the government, despite being disliked by the left-wing leaders of the Workers' Party.

Chapter 17 analyses the rise of individualism among poorer Brazilians. It is divided into two parts. The first looks at the decline of trade unionism in urban Brazil and the way that digitalization has opened new self-employment opportunities in the informal sector, highlighted by the rapid increase in the number of workers dependent on digital platforms, such as ride-hailing and delivery apps, including Uber and iFoods. The withdrawal of legislation designed to limit working hours and improve working conditions in 2024 highlighted the inability of Lula's Workers' Party to deal with this trend.

The second part of this chapter deals with the rise of individualism in the Amazon and the collapse of the PT's efforts to introduce a forest-based economy in Acre state. Like their counterparts in urban areas, people with low incomes in rural areas have been increasingly drawn towards small-scale agribusiness, especially cattle-raising and away from environmentally sustainable activities such as the harvesting of rubber and fruits.

Chapter 18 considers the foreign-policy agenda pursued by Lula and Brazil's interest in championing the concerns of the Global South. Led by China's breakneck expansion, the BRICS group formed by Brazil, Russia, India, and China in 2009 is becoming a powerful force in the global economy. Brazil's weight within it, however, has declined, with the recent accession of Egypt, Ethiopia, the United Arab Emirates, and Iran highlighting a growing trend towards anti-Western authoritarianism. The weakness of Lula's soft-power approach to international relations has been underscored by the failure of his efforts to prevent blatant electoral fraud in neighbouring Venezuela.

In the conclusion I offer an assessment of the future. Lula's third presidency has in general not gone well, and by June 2025 his popularity ratings were drifting lower and the chances that he would not contest a new election were rising. Lula – approaching 80 – looked to be a fading star. However, the decision by President Trump, in July 2025, to impose 50 per cent tariffs on

Brazilian exports to the United States has given him a new lease of life. And a nationalist leader, reinvigorating the broad alliance that brought him back to office in 2022. It is a tentative judgement though. As the former Brazilian President Tancredo Neves once famously warned, Brazilian politics can change as quickly as the clouds.

I

A Man from the Backlands

Shortly before Christmas 1952, a bullnose Mercedes lorry revved its engine and edged noisily out of the dusty village of Caetés to begin a 1,600-mile journey south to the city of São Paulo. On board, crammed tightly and sitting upright on hard wooden benches, were some 60 passengers, including the 37-year-old Eurídice Ferreira de Melo, better known simply as Dona Lindu, with seven of her children – among them the seven-year-old Luiz Inácio Lula da Silva.

The slow journey, mainly over dirt roads, was an epic of endurance that would take 13 days and nights, as arduous in some ways as the transatlantic migrations that had brought hundreds of thousands of European, Middle Eastern, and Japanese migrants to Brazil from the 1850s onwards. Desperate to escape the poverty that had been exacerbated by two years of drought, Dona Lindu was eager to rejoin her husband, who had abandoned his family to make the same trip seven years earlier. So she had sold the family's plot of land, the primitive shack, the cow and the donkey to join the throngs of poor north-easterners attracted by the possibility of work in the country's growing manufacturing heartland.[1]

For nearly a fortnight, the family lived off their diminishing stores of bananas, chicken, *farofa* – a rough cassava flour fried with oil – and black sugar cake called *rapadura,* all assembled by Dona Lindu in advance. Bread bought at occasional stops was something of a luxury. Hygiene was non-existent, and many passengers fell ill as a result. The lorry stopped every few hours, when men and women would peel off to separate sides of the road to relieve themselves. At night, the lorry would halt and they would sleep haphazardly, some under the vehicle.

'It was a terrible journey, with all these children,' said the 91-year-old Jorge de Né, who had made the trip alongside his brother Zé, the owner of the Mercedes lorry.² Like hundreds of similar lorries deployed for these journeys, it had been adapted by the addition of primitive seats, an improvised timber frame, and a tarpaulin sheet that could be drawn down in bad weather. It was a bus of sorts, a vehicle that Brazilians called a *pau de arara* or parrot's perch, on which each passenger had to make do with about a foot of seat space. Jorge's family made a decent living running migrants south and returning with merchandise bought in São Paulo's markets, but it was hard work, especially on the way south. 'The roads were unpaved, and the gas stations, such as they were, few and far between. It was no joke; I can tell you. Thirteen difficult days,' recalled Jorge de Né in December 2022.³

Vavá, one of Lula's older brothers who died in 2019, remembered the trip as an adventure, partly because the children were seeing cars, lorries, stretches of water, and so much else that was new to them. But 'for older people it must have been awful, a horrible business,' he told the historian Denise Paraná.⁴ Accidents on the unpaved roads were frequent, as drivers negotiated sinuous bends and natural obstacles at speed, with tired and aching passengers clinging precariously to the lorry's sides.

At Paulo Afonso in Bahia the two De Né brothers had had to strap their vehicle to a raft to cross the wide São Francisco River. The road south from the city of Feira de Santana, which now forms part of the BR-116 highway, was littered with makeshift crosses, according to one reporter who made the same journey three years later. 'It is a cemetery. Every cross tells a story. A lorry whose brakes have failed, some that careered off the road into ditches, others that caught fire and exploded,' wrote Mário de Moraes in a celebrated piece of photo-journalism for the magazine *O Cruzeiro*.⁵

When Lula's family set off on their trip, the route was at its busiest. The significant movement of people south had begun in the early 1940s. During the Second World War, with Brazil cut off from its traditional sources of imports, new manufacturing industries grew rapidly, and business owners began searching for labour. Lula's father, Aristides, left shortly before his son's birth in October 1945; he was one of nearly 150,000 north-easterners who migrated south each year. During the second half of the 1940s the numbers increased to an annual average of more than 380,000. And, with drought contributing additional pressure, the numbers doubled again to more than 760,000 a year at the start of the 1950s. In the 1940s many migrants had travelled by infrequent and painfully slow trains or even slower coastal ships. By the 1950s, the parrot's-perch lorries had started to dominate. One day in November 1952, a month before the Da Silvas departed Caetés, 139 lorries had been recorded on one stretch of road in the state of Bahia.

For a country whose population hit 50 million only in 1950, these were big numbers. The movement south had become so large that it had become a subject of national controversy, prompting bitter political debate. Ignoring the economic factors underpinning the migration, conservative politicians and newspaper editors warned about the social problems and the potential spread of disease. Notionally, the parrot's-perch lorries were banned. Columnists condemned operators such as Jorge and his brother as people smugglers. The trade was a 'gold mine', wrote João Martins in *O Cruzeiro*. Typically, he claimed, lorry owners could cover their costs five or six times over, and were easily able to pay any fines levied by the police.[6]

Lula's mother and father had grown up in farming families based in the *agreste*, a transition zone separating the humid coastal strip from the semi-arid interior, or *sertão*, of the impoverished north-eastern state of Pernambuco. Aristides' father, João Grande, owned a sizeable farm near Cajerana, eight miles or so to the east of Caetés. Lindu had grown up on a neighbouring property, but her father died when she was young, leaving her dependent on her dressmaker mother, Otília Ferreira de Melo. Otília, or Tíli, whose own family had originally come from Italy, was skilled at what she did but spent a significant portion of her earnings on *cachaça*, Brazil's famous sugar-cane alcohol. Aristides and Lindu married in 1935 and set up their home at Várzea Comprida near Caetés, a few miles nearer the bleaker and drier *sertão* to the west.

Their first child, José Inácio da Silva (nicknamed Zé Cuía), was born in 1936. From then until Aristides' departure in 1945, there was a steady stream of births: Jaime arrived in 1937, Marinete in 1938, Genival (Vavá) in 1939, José (Frei Chico) in 1942, Maria (known in the family as Maria Baixinha or little Maria) in 1943, and Luiz (or Lula) in 1945. Two other babies born in 1940 and 1944 died before they were a year old. And after Aristides returned on holiday to Pernambuco in 1950, accompanied by a new partner Moçinha, a young relative of Dona Lindu who surreptitiously he had taken with him five years previously, as well as two children from this latest relationship, Lindu gave birth again, this time to another girl, who went by the name of Tiana, short for Sebastiana (although she had been baptized as Ruth).

Life for this growing family was hard. At Várzea Comprida, Aristides grew all the basic crops and produced cassava flour on a commercial basis. With the proceeds he was able to purchase items such as salt, bananas, biscuits, and *rapadura*, as well as other essentials like soap and kerosene. He also owned a horse and a shotgun, which he used to hunt birds, goats, and guinea pigs to supplement their meagre diet. When the weather was kind, there was at least plenty to eat, but with its fierce sun and high evaporation rates, this was an area notoriously prone to drought. In rural Brazil, such hardship is typically alleviated at intervals by traditional festivals. Still, in the interviews with Denise Paraná, Lula and his relatives made no mention of any such celebrations.

The family's house, long since demolished, was a simple affair. Against a straight back wall, Aristides, with the help of one of his brothers, had built from wood and plaster a dwelling that contained two rooms and a tiny kitchen. A sloping roof had been covered with thatch. The walls had been smoothed neatly with whitewash and the floors laid with beaten earth, although red cement was used in the room where Aristides and Lindu had laid a bed and a straw mattress. The children slept in hammocks. There were three wooden stools and a simple bench to sit on, and Lindu cooked on a stove fuelled by firewood.

Water was scarce. The nearest source was a mile or two away in a dam whose contents were brackish, muddy, and yellow. Vavá, whose memories of the family's life are the most vivid in the interviews with Denise Paraná, says that the children carried water in cans back to the house. Lindu would allow the liquid to settle and strain it before use, with frogs and grasshoppers sometimes jumping out. Some two hours' walk away was a river where Lindu would go once a week to wash clothes.[7] The dry conditions meant that the house was sometimes infested with poisonous yellow-bellied puff adders. 'Often we would wake at night and there they were curled up on the roof,' said Vavá. 'We had to kill them.'

For breakfast, the family ate a cassava mash flavoured with coffee. Beans, sweet potato, and *farofa* were staples. Fruits such as cashews (which have an edible pulp) and custard apples grew plentifully nearby. Pineapples were bought from the market. Meat was eaten only occasionally, and even rice was a luxury reserved for weddings or other celebrations. Relatives were sometimes less than generous. Aristides' father, João Grande, grew watermelons but never offered any to his grandchildren and used his shotgun when they tried to help themselves. 'He was the sort who kept all his money under the mattress,' recalled Lula in 1993. 'He was such a miser.'[8]

No one had many clothes, and none of the children wore shoes. And better-off members of the family could again be stingy about helping. Vavá recalls borrowing a pair of shoes from a cousin so he could attend a church service and receive communion for the first time. 'I walked five or six miles barefoot to their house to borrow the shoes, but my cousin said I could only wear them after I got to the door of the church. I had to take great care not to damage them.'[9] Health assistance was precarious. Lula, like his six brothers and sisters, had been born at home with the help of an unqualified local midwife who had been brought to the house on a donkey by one of Lindu's brothers. Lula's delivery proceeded without mishap, but he was lucky. In the north-east of Brazil infant mortality was then roughly ten times the rate it is today, with 113 per 1,000 births not surviving infancy in 1950. In remote rural areas the rate could be three times higher still,[10] and, partly influenced by those high numbers, life expectancy in the north-east was only 35. Lindu was resourceful and knowledgeable about natural cures, and she was able to ensure that her children did not suffer from the parasites that swelled the abdomens of many of their peers. Even so, one of her babies died from dysentery caused by dehydration. Trained medical help was more than ten miles away in Garanhuns, a bigger and greener town to the east. When Lindu or one of her children was ill, Sérgio, one of her older brothers, would walk to the town, consult the doctor, and return with the prescribed remedies.[11]

The area, too, was something of an educational and cultural desert. In 1950, when Lula was five, only a quarter of the inhabitants of the north-east states of Brazil could read. Both Aristides and Lindu were illiterate, and Lula's father shored up his ignorance with a violent vindictiveness towards anyone who exposed it. By the 1940s, a school had opened near Caetés, providing basic arithmetic and reading instruction to children up to the ages of nine or ten. Vavá said that the female teacher was 'a God' and he and his brothers took care to learn their lessons, often studying by candlelight late into the night. But her methods were crude. The emphasis was on learning by rote, and by the classroom door the teacher hung a *palmatória*, a spanking paddle with which those who made mistakes were beaten. By the age of 11, after Aristides had left for São Paulo, Zé Cuía and Jaime were working all day alongside their mother on the family's land, while the eldest of their sisters, Marinete, was looking after her younger siblings. Neither the parents nor their offspring knew much about the outside world. None had travelled beyond Garanhuns. Information and news about events further afield was sparse in the extreme. Lula's older brother Frei Chico recalls hearing the commentary of the famous 1950 World Cup Final in Rio de Janeiro, in which Brazil lost to Uruguay 2–1, in a general store in Caetés. However, he told his interviewer in 1993 that his youngest grandchild aged two knew more about life than he did when he was living on the farm. Lula's siblings remember climbing the *mulungu* (a tree producing brilliant red blossoms) next to the house, in their brief respites from drudgery, and using slings and primitive traps to kill wildlife. Vavá recalled catching guinea pigs and birds such as doves and even tiny hummingbirds, which were slaughtered by the dozen and roasted on spits.

A LAND OF DROUGHT AND PROPHETS

To understand the dynamics of this world, you have to go back more than four centuries, to the birth of the Portuguese Empire in the Americas and the flourishing of an economy based on sugar and slavery. The Portuguese were skilled and innovative navigators, and they were prominent in Europe's fifteenth- and sixteenth-century expansions to the east and west. In 1494, Spain and Portugal agreed to divide their western discoveries by the rulings of Pope Alexander VI. At the Spanish town of Tordesillas, the countries' monarchs drew a north-south line of demarcation in the Atlantic Ocean, about 1,100 miles west of the Cape Verde Islands, which Portugal then controlled. To the west of the line, territories previously unknown to the European powers were to be claimed by Spain for the Christian world. To its east, all were Portugal's. In 1506 the line was redrawn further west, allowing the Portuguese, who had first set foot in what is now Brazil in 1500, to establish their new colony. Portugal lacked the resources to do much with its additional lands, partly because it was focused on what were then seen as more attractive territories in Asia. So, in 1534, King John III divided the territory of Brazil into fifteen gigantic strips of land known as captaincies, carved out perpendicular to the coast. These captaincies were handed out to members of the aristocracy. Few of the new owners did much with the largesse received. A few didn't even visit, but one or two opted to cultivate sugar, which was becoming increasingly popular in the European market, and that proved to be a crucial decision.

Portuguese planters had already mastered the techniques of sugar cultivation and production in their territories of Cape Verde, the

Azores, and Madeira. The settlers then repeated the experiment in Brazil by forcing enslaved indigenous people to cut the cane, finding success initially only in the captaincy of Pernambuco. However, in 1559, the Portuguese Crown, anxious for a source of revenue that could pay for the defence of its distant and expensive new possessions, stimulated the business by encouraging the import of a new and more reliable source of labour: enslaved Africans. In the late sixteenth and early seventeenth centuries Brazil became synonymous with the production of sugar.

The plantation owners prospered, but by the beginning of the seventeenth century their American colonies had begun to attract the attention of Spain and Portugal's European rivals. France tried to establish a colony in Brazil. Holland went one step further and, for over a quarter of the seventeenth century, took over Pernambuco and its lucrative sugar trade. When they were expelled in 1654 by Portuguese settlers, the Dutch established rival plantations and sugar factories in the Caribbean, offering financial support and technical assistance to English planters who had recently settled on islands such as Barbados. Sugar production increased, and as it became more plentiful, prices fell. By the end of the century, the profitability of the Brazilian sugar trade had begun to decline quite dramatically. That, at least, is a rough outline of what happened. The early eighteenth century saw a new commodity boom, this time based on gold and silver discovered in central Brazil (in the state that is now Minas Gerais). The exploitation of precious minerals went hand in hand with that of African slaves. That cycle was, in turn, replaced in the nineteenth century by one based on coffee in the state of São Paulo, which, like the previous exploitation, was equally dependent on slave labour.

But to return to the north-east. During sugar's heyday in the sixteenth and seventeenth centuries a curious relationship had developed between the hot and humid narrow coastal strip, dominated by the plantations, and the semi-arid interior. Because sugar was so profitable, there was an economic imperative to 'specialize'. It was not only that it made no financial sense for the planters to use their land for anything but sugar. The Portuguese authorities, anxious to maximize the Crown's revenues, did not allow this relatively expensive land to be used for anything else. Instead, food crops such as beans and cassava to feed the slave population were grown on cheaper properties inland. A royal decree in 1701 prohibited the raising of cattle within 30 miles of the coast. These were needed not only for meat, milk, and leather but also for power, as oxen turned the giant stones used to grind sugar cane in the mills. And because coastal forests had been rapidly depleted during the sixteenth and seventeenth centuries, there was a shortage of wood for building and fuel. All these ancillary supplies came from the interior.

By the middle of the seventeenth century, the north-east of Brazil had become, in the words of the economic historian Celso Furtado, a 'dual economy': on the one hand, the densely populated, productive slave plantations on the coast; on the other, the cattle farms and subsistence plots of the interior. There was almost always an opportunity to expand into the west, so that when the sugar economy started to decline in the eighteenth century, the local economy was able to adapt. It developed, for example, an artisanal leather industry to replace the manufactured products that the estate owners could no longer afford to import from abroad. But over the longer term, in Furtado's view, the economy of the interior first stagnated and then began to 'atrophy'.[12]

There was a short-lived period of prosperity during the American Civil War in the mid-nineteenth century, when local farmers began to cultivate cotton to fill the gap left by the planters of the warring Southern states. There were other exceptions, too. Garanhuns, for example, experienced a brief boom at the end of the nineteenth century when the railway arrived from Recife, enabling local beef, dairy, and coffee farmers to access markets further afield. But following the recession of the early 1930s, the forces that had led to the region's stagnation and slow decline reasserted themselves. Around Garanhuns many farms were broken up. Between 1927 and 1950 the number of small farms quadrupled.[13] There was another overwhelming problem: much of the interior was vulnerable to drought. As part of a tropical region, the semi-arid *sertão* and even the slightly wetter *agreste*, where Lula was born, are subject to intense heat for most of the year. High rates of evaporation rapidly return moisture to the atmosphere. Two other geological features also play a role. The landscape is flat and lacks a mountain range to meet the winds moving south-east. There is nothing to force air upwards, to cool and condense. In addition, an impermeable layer of crystalline rock underpins much of the terrain, and soils are frequently shallow, so when it does rain, water does not soak into the ground sufficiently to accumulate.[14] In December, when the rainy season typically begins, a shift in wind patterns can trigger drought. Historically, these have taken place at regular intervals across the north-east, occurring in partial form as frequently as every four to five years. Historians record particularly devastating droughts in the periods 1710–1711, 1723–1727, 1744–1745, 1777–1778, 1808–1809, 1824–1825, 1835–1837, and 1844–1845. More than 5,700 people died and 125,000 were forced out of their homes by the three-year drought that began in 1877, when – perhaps apocryphally – many north-easterners resorted to cannibalism. In the 1915 drought 30,000 people died, and 680,000 cattle were lost. The population of the state of Ceará was herded into massive refugee camps built to contain the impact of migration to urban centres. There were also severe droughts in 1919, 1920, and 1932, and, as we shall see, between 1951 and 1953.[15] Furthermore, there have been frequent, and longer-lasting, droughts since, the most recent being the longest on record, lasting from 2011 to 2019.

This withered economy was always austere. Euclides da Cunha, the author of *Os Sertões* (*The Backlands*), one of the most celebrated pieces of Brazilian literature,[16] describes 'scorching heat and scarce rain, dwarfed and stunted vegetation and stony cracked ground'. Other writers have explored the same theme. 'The backlands have become completely unsuitable for life,' wrote Roger Bastide, a French sociologist and ethnographer. He described a landscape that is 'hard, angular and tragic' and a 'civilisation with the hardness of bone . . . The man of the caatinga has nothing before him but an immense implacable sky over his leather hat and the rare clouds are quickly eaten up by insatiable sun.'[17]

But it is what Da Cunha variously and graphically describes as the 'frightful spasm' or 'terrible scourge' of drought that brought this shrivelled world to the point of crisis. It is not surprising that the north-east has provided such fertile ground for self-styled prophets and messiahs offering to lead desperate displaced rural communities towards precious water sources. Bastide describes the inhabitants of the semi-arid zone as a 'race of nomads always ready to follow a prophet in search of the marvellous city'.[18] It is in a broader sense the tradition of messianism draws on the indigenous beliefs of the Tupi Guarani (the largest indigenous group at the time of Brazil's settlement), as well as strands of mainstream Christianity.

One potent myth that took root in north-eastern Brazil was Sebastianism. Back in 1578, during a war between Portugal and a Sultanate then in charge of what is modern-day Morocco, Dom Sebastião, the king of Portugal, disappeared after the battle of Alcácer-Quibir. His body was never conclusively identified, giving rise to a legend that he would be reborn, save the nation, and herald the second coming of Christ. In the first half of the nineteenth century, at a time when the myth was becoming resurgent in Portugal itself, two Sebastianist movements emerged in Pernambuco, not far from where Lula was born many decades later. In 1965, Maria Isaura Pereira de Queiroz, a Brazilian sociologist who was one of the most assiduous chroniclers of Brazilian messianism, described both movements.[19] In the first, in 1817 Silvestre José dos Santos, an illiterate former soldier, set up an independent community in the Rodeador hills 40 to 50 miles north-east of Garanhuns. Dos Santos's 'City of Earthly Paradise' emerged around a chapel built next to a slab of 'enchanted' rock. From there he introduced his own version of Catholic rites. His promise that Sebastian's return would 'make the poor rich' attracted hundreds of followers from neighbouring villages. But these radical ideas bothered the local elite. Deeming the new settlement's brotherhood a threat, in 1820 Pernambuco's governor dispatched troops. Ninety-one people were killed and several hundred others carted off to prison.

Twenty years later, another young preacher called João Ferreira founded a similar settlement at Pedra Bonita, 180 miles or so to the north-west of Lula's birthplace, and made similar promises of return and redemption. 'If you are black, you will return white as the moon, immortal, rich and powerful; if you are an old woman, you will become a young girl, and in the same way, rich, powerful and immortal,' preached Ferreira from a sacred cave positioned between two giant rocks.[20] Hundreds of people were seduced by the fantasy, but the self-appointed king's rule became increasingly repressive and eventually ended in bloodshed. Hallucinating on the effects of a drink made from two local psychoactive plants (*jurema* and *manacá*, which had the impact of a mixture of opium and alcohol), Ferreira decreed that only mass sacrifice could bring back Sebastian. And after killing dozens of his followers, he himself committed suicide.

Across rural Brazil throughout the nineteenth and early twentieth centuries, similar figures continued to emerge, but the north-east always retained a particular susceptibility to the appeal of mystics. Near Juazeiro in Ceará (now Juazeiro do Norte to distinguish it from a city of the same name in Bahia state), in 1850, a group known as the Serene Ones demonstrated their religious devotion through rites of self-flagellation at a desert crossroads. But they also alarmed the public by conducting large-scale robberies, developing along similar lines as the Robin Hood-style rural thieves known as *cangaceiros*. A few years later, Father Cicero, a quiet, austere and highly dedicated priest launched a 'holy city' in Juazeiro. The priest provided food and public works programmes for the dispossessed in the drought of the late 1870s. And his social work and well-publicized miracles – whose authenticity was disputed by the church hierarchy – made him popular across the north-east, attracting thousands of pilgrims, and propelling him into politics.[21]

By far the most celebrated of these millenarian figures was Antônio Vicente Mendes Maciel. who became better known as Antônio Conselheiro. Like the Sebastianist settlements of the early part of the nineteenth century, the community that Conselheiro established in 1893 at Canudos in northern Bahia was also seen as a threat to the established order. During 1896 and 1897 the recently created federal republic launched four military expeditions to quash it, eventually resorting to artillery to crush the city's heroic defence and massacring hundreds of its 10,000 or so inhabitants. The story of those battles is the subject of Da Cunha's *The Backlands*, and a cause of enduring political controversy. Left-wingers have drawn attention to the fact that the ancestor of one of the judges involved in sentencing Lula to prison commanded government troops at Canudos, and from his cell Lula himself closely followed an online left-wing education class that stressed the parallels between the way Brazil's elites had repressed the two leaders.

In the ten years before he set up Canudos, Conselheiro and his followers had criss-crossed the north-east, their numbers augmented by refugees from the drought of the late 1870s. Increasingly confident, he began to oppose the authorities, especially after 1889 when the 'king', Emperor Pedro II, went into exile and Brazil became a republic. For example, he persuaded communities to reject the taxes being charged by newly autonomous municipalities, and his followers clashed with federal forces. In 1893 after discovering an abandoned farm at Canudos, then a settlement of 500 mud-and-thatch shacks, Conselheiro instituted a form of primitive communism. Everyone who went to the city was obliged to give up some of their possessions, creating a common fund, from which less well-off people were supported. Even so, the parallel between the 19th century prophet and Lula, highlighted in a book published in 2020,[22] is a bit of a stretch. Conselheiro seems to have been a tortured soul. His childhood in Quixeramobim, in the state of Ceará, was scarred by a bloody struggle between his relatives and a rival family of cattle ranchers. He dedicated himself to a life of prayer and extreme self-abnegation. Like Father Cicero, he claimed to work miracles, a divine facility that helped his followers in the main practical task that they had set themselves – building and repairing churches. 'Blessed by his prayers, men could lift huge pieces of wood as if they were feathers.' For his desperate followers, 'miracle cures, a hair from Conselheiro's beard or a bit of fingernail, protected against all evils'.[23]

Da Cunha described a gaunt, shrunken figure, his flesh bruised by the use of abrasive hair shirts and driven to the edge of exhaustion by prolonged fasting. 'His face was like a death mask, unseeing and unsmiling: he had the repugnant appearance of a disinterred corpse, his long robe resembling a black shroud; his matted, dirty hair fell to his shoulders and entangled with the stiff hair of his unkempt beard, which hung to his waist,' he wrote. 'He had suffered the brutal tyrannies of hunger, thirst, exhaustion, anxiety, and deep distress. There was no torture he had not experienced. His dried-out skin was a broken and withered shell over his lifeless flesh. Pain itself had become his drug.'[24]

In any event, by the time Lula was born, in 1945, the popularity of such messiahs was waning. Rather than looking to preachers, bandits, or miracle workers for redemption, the poor were voting with their feet. Dona Lindu's decision to leave her home in Pernambuco was not inevitable. However, conditions in the little house at Várzea Comprida had seriously deteriorated since Aristides' visit in 1950 and the birth of Ruth, Lula's youngest sister. By now, Aristides was back in the south, working regularly as a stevedore, heaving heavy bags of coffee into a warehouse at the port of Santos. However, the money he sent back to his family in Pernambuco proved essential to their survival. The year 1950 had been a relatively dry one, and very little rain at all fell in 1951 and 1952. 'If it hadn't been for the money my father sent, we wouldn't have survived,' said Vavá.[25] A curious piece of benign duplicity triggered Dona Lindu's decision to leave. Lula's second-oldest brother, Jaime, had accompanied his father two years before but had an unhappy time in Santos and was missing his mother. Unlike his father, Jaime was literate and responsible for penning their letters, which enabled him to trick Aristides into inviting Lindu to sell up and head south. After the fortnight's ordeal, there was at least a relatively comfortable end to their journey. When the parrot's perch deposited its passengers in the São Paulo suburb of Bras, Dona Lindu had enough cash left over to hail a taxi, a 1950 Chevrolet, that took them all to Santos, where an angry Aristides awaited. At the port, the view of the Atlantic Ocean was a shock. 'I had never seen so much water in my life,' said Vavá. A new chapter in Lula's life was beginning.

2

The City and the Factory

When Lula stepped into the bulky 1950 Chevrolet that took him the 45 miles to the port of Santos, it was the first time he – or anyone in his family – had been in a car. As they drove through the bustling city of São Paulo, everyone must have looked out of the windows, wide-eyed. On the arduous trip south, the attention of the seven-year-old Lula had been drawn by the enormous lorries that lumbered along the narrow highways. 'I saw one of those Shell [fuel] tankers and was fascinated. I wanted to be a truck driver,' he confessed to Denise Paraná. In São Paulo there were new sights and sounds to discover. 'The city was so modern. It was quite a thing. It was as if I had come out of hell and gone to heaven.'[1]

That modernity was to shape Lula's life over the next decade, transforming him from a quiet, poorly educated rural boy into a streetwise and ambitious adolescent. And the car, the bus, and the lorry were emblematic of that newness. The urban landscape of sprawling highways, bridges, and viaducts was where Lula grew up, and the growing car industry was at the centre of the city's heavy manufacturing complex, where he came of age and started his long, eventful career in trade unionism. However, there was some business from the past to be cleared up first.

Aristides, now ensconced in Santos with his new family, was surprised to see his wife and children arrive and angry that they had not been able to bring Lobo, the family's dog, which had necessarily been left behind in Pernambuco. Even so, he managed to find them a house, and for a few months he lived between the two families. For Lindu's household, his presence alleviated their material worries since Aristides ensured there was always food on the table. Every Wednesday, without fail, the greengrocer's cart would stop outside the house, loaded with enough fruit and vegetables for the week, all paid for by Aristides. But his support came at the cost of arbitrary domestic tyranny and frequent episodes of drunken violence.

At the end of 1952, Lindu and her children began living in Itapema, across the estuary from Santos and just a few miles north of Guarujá, a seaside resort connected by a steam train at the time, where Lula and his siblings sometimes went on weekends. (Sixty years later, Guarujá would become infamous as the site of an alleged property scam for which Lula was given a 12-year prison sentence.) Their rented wooden house was a decent size, but at least 40 years old and in a state of disrepair. Worse, the land around it flooded regularly with the tide. 'We used to joke that we had a swimming pool at home,' Vavá told Denise Paraná.[2]

All the children worked, and when they were at home, they were at Aristides' beck and call. The girls were forbidden to attend school, let alone go out to dance or meet their boyfriends. No one could smoke, and Lula and the older brother closest to him in age, Frei Chico, were often sent off to fetch water or gather firewood from a nearby mangrove swamp. There were frequent clashes, with Frei Chico being the primary target for Aristides' anger. 'My father was a monster,' said Frei Chico, who remembers being beaten so severely that he wet his pants. Lula escaped the worst of his father's rages but began to hate him all the same. 'He was very ignorant, a deep well of ignorance,' Lula remembered in 1993,[3] recalling that for show the illiterate Aristides regularly bought a newspaper but was often mocked by workmates who caught him staring intensely at pages held upside down. Later, in 2001, Lula said grudgingly that he forgave his father. 'At least he provided the sperm that brought me about.'[4]

Finally, though, at some point in 1953, Lindu had had enough. After Aristides had raised his hand to hit her, she told him she was leaving. The next day, with the help of nearby relatives, she organized alternative accommodation, first in Itapema, and then in 1955 in Vila Carioca, a low-lying, insalubrious working-class district in the south of São Paulo, where one relation owned a bar. It was not ideal. The family shared a single room and a kitchen that contained putrid toilet facilities, which were also used by the bar's customers.

The neighbourhood was bleak; unpaved roads lay over poorly drained land settled by many of the north-eastern migrants who had come to work in the embryonic industrial zone a few miles to the south. 'After heavy rain, it was like a marsh and full of croaking frogs,' Sebastião Zanone, one of Lula's former neighbours, told a newspaper reporter.[5] 'The stink was unbearable. A mixture of chemicals and waste products dumped by nearby factories formed a hellish cauldron,' wrote one contemporary observer.[6]

But for Lindu and her family, at least this grim corner of São Paulo offered a refuge from Aristides' manias. The family moved to a bigger property a few hundred yards away and then again shortly afterwards. It wasn't an easy time for Lindu. She was frequently bewildered by the scale and complexity of São Paulo and easily got lost. But when interviewed, Lula has always been quick to praise her stoicism. 'She never felt sorry for herself. If you complained, she always used to say, "there are people who are worse off than you",' he told Denise Paraná in 1993.[7]

The family's circumstances were extremely Spartan. Lula remembers, day after day, wearing the same short trousers made by his mother out of odd bits of rough brown cloth and held up by yellow and green braces.[8] Even the tiny signs of improvement that had accompanied their successive moves were evidence of penury. When they left Aristides in 1953, Lindu had taken with her just a knife and a can of milk powder. By 1956, she owned some second-hand beds and a gas cooker. And things gradually improved. As they grew older, Lindu's children found jobs. Work, at least in the expanding economy of the late 1950s, was plentiful. Vavá, who had served coffee in a bar in Santos, soon found employment in a textile mill, for example. Lula – who, along with Frei Chico, had sold peanuts, oranges, and a coconut sweet called *cocada* on the street in Santos – started to shine shoes. In his early teens, still at school, Lula found a part-time position as an office boy for a company that dyed fabrics.

At his poorest, he had been reduced to asking friends to give him used gum, which, after cleaning and sprinkling with sugar, he was happy to chew. Now he could afford occasional trips to a cinema in nearby Vila Bueno, where he would watch films starring heroes such as Tarzan, Zorro, Buffalo Bill, and Roy Rogers. He even had enough left over to buy a baguette and a few slices of mortadella.[9]

It was about this time that Lula started to play football regularly and developed his lifelong passion for Corinthians, the São Paulo side, who – somewhat bizarrely – took their name from England's most aristocratic amateur team Corinthian Casuals. The Anglo-Brazilian connection dated back to a 1910 tour by the Casuals, but Corinthians had built a reputation as the city team that counted with the most working-class support. Lula took to them in 1954 when they won a string of championships. In addition, freed from Aristides' incessant demands, Lula could also take part in games more often. He played as a defender or midfielder, and his skill earned him respect among his friends. 'It was in football that Lula showed the first signs of his leadership capacity,' wrote his biographer Fernando Morais.[10] 'He was the guy who organised the team, arranged to get the ball and the pitch and set up championships between teams from different localities.' These regular kickabouts would sometimes end up in fights, and the Da Silva boys would stick together. 'Lula was invariably something of a ringleader, but he knew he would have Vavá – who had always been quite a big guy – and Frei Chico – who had taken up weightlifting – at his side.'[11]

In 1958, then just 13, Lula completed the fourth grade of primary school, an achievement which at the time only one in five Brazilian children managed. It also marked him out in his own family. The schooling of his brothers and sisters had been cut short by the pressing need for money. According to his siblings, Lula was something of a favourite of Dona Lindu, and she made extra efforts to help him do well. Having passed his exams, Lula was now eligible to enter the government's National Service of

Industrial Apprenticeships, an institution supported by contributions from the manufacturing sector and usually known by the acronym Senai. This was a passport to the world of well-paid, skilled manual work. Lindu went out of her way to push her son's case, making endless trips to the institute's offices in the Ipiranga district, even though it was five miles from Vila Carioca. 'Mum said that Lula had to be something in life,' said Maria Baixinha, one of Lula's two older sisters. 'She didn't rest. She made that journey I don't know how many times.'[12] For Lula, too, there was now a clear and realizable goal in life. He wanted the security and money of factory work. The blue overalls – the *macacão* – would come with it, serving as a badge of status among neighbours, friends, and potential girlfriends.

'No one saw the employment card in his pocket, but the overalls showed that he had a job and a future,' wrote Morais.[13]

The industries now rapidly setting up in the suburbs of São Paulo offered a passport to relative prosperity, especially the foreign-owned motor companies like Volkswagen and Mercedes. Between 1957 and 1960, the number employed in the motor industry more than tripled from 9,653 to 32,576, with the bulk of the new jobs concentrated in Santo André, São Bernardo do Campo, and São Caetano, the so-called ABC towns, about 12 miles to the south of São Paulo's city centre. The employment boom triggered rapid urban growth. São Bernardo's population rose from just under 30,000 to more than 80,000 during the 1950s, for example.

A job in the ABC belt was much sought after. As Lula himself recalled some years later: 'The people in the car industry got something like ten wage increases each year. They were the elite – they had houses, they were the first to buy televisions, the first to buy cars . . . they would pass by at Christmas loaded with boxes of toys for their kids.'[14] And as Lula described it to Denise Paraná, 'The dream was to work for Vemag, Willis [the two local Brazilian carmakers], Volkswagen, Mercedes [the German companies], or Simca [from France] – because you earned better. The wife of a metalworker took her shopping bag home full of pineapple, papaya, melon, oranges.'[15]

Finally, towards the end of 1960, shortly after his fifteenth birthday, Lula did get a job. It was with a company based nearby. Parafusos Marte was a small family-owned business making screws that had advertised for an apprentice turner. It wasn't the much-desired position with a motor company, but it did offer a technical education course at Senai. For the next three years Lula attended classes at the institute's two-storey branch in Ipiranga. It would be a transformative experience, throwing him entirely into the emerging industrial world and providing him with the skills and self-confidence that allowed him to rise further.

BRAZIL'S LATE INDUSTRIALIZATION

As Lula grew up, Brazil was undergoing rapid changes. To understand why, we must revisit its history. The country had abolished slavery and overthrown the monarchy by the end of the 1880s, but many features of its social and economic model remained essentially unchanged. The landed elites, who produced coffee, sugar, and beef, were still in charge, and politics reflected their interests. Under what came to be known as the First Republic, power was devolved to what were then twenty states, each of which could raise taxes, borrow money, and maintain a well-armed and equipped military police force that was often better equipped than the federal army. From the 1890s through to the 1920s, conservative political factions linked to the economically powerful regions of São Paulo, based on coffee, and Minas Gerais, based on cattle ranching, alternated in power in an alliance known as *café com leite* (coffee with milk). The franchise was extremely limited anyway, but political bosses known as *coroneis* (colonels, as many held that rank in the powerful local security forces) protected the interests of landowners. The colonels delivered votes for candidates in return for federal, state, and municipal appointments.

The deprivation and inequalities were immense. By the 1920s, less than 25 per cent of the population of 30 million was literate. Poverty was widespread, but those in power cared little about it. President Washington Luís (1926–1930) was said to have called the social question a police matter.¹⁶ Societal conflict frequently threatened stability, not least when, in the mid-1920s, Luís Carlos Prestes, an army captain from Brazil's most southerly state, Rio Grande do Sul, led an unsuccessful armed revolt. By 1930, the São Paulo-Minas alliance began to fray, and the result of that year's election won again by São Paulo's Washington Luís was disputed. Alleging their candidate had been defrauded, the supporters of Getúlio Vargas, the son of a landowner and governor of Rio Grande do Sul, refused to accept the result. Backed by the military, Vargas became president in 1930. He was to dominate Brazilian politics for the next 25 years. He was a contradictory figure. Good-natured, pragmatic, and authoritarian, he described himself as a 'progressive conservative'. His presidencies, between 1930 and 1945 and from 1951 until 1954, saw sharp increases in military numbers and were punctuated by periodic coups. Having come to office on the back of one coup, he then led what amounted to a second in 1937, when he closed down Congress and centralized power. Political parties were abolished, censorship decreed, and civil rights circumscribed. Vargas's Estado Novo (New State) bore similarities to Mussolini's Italy, and his Defence Minister and right-hand man was an admirer of both Adolf Hitler and the Italian dictator. Vargas was a nationalist who drew inspiration from figures such as Kemal Atatürk in Turkey and Poland's Józef Piłsudski. He crushed a regional revolt in São Paulo in 1932 and then cracked down on the Communist Party, which in 1935 had launched a poorly organized insurrection.

After sitting on the fence during the Second World War for three years, Vargas cast his lot with the Allies, declaring war on Germany in 1942 and sending troops to Italy two years later to fight alongside the Americans and British. Vargas, who had built up support among trade unions and formed a Labour Party, shifted to the left but was himself blocked by a military coup from taking part in the 1945 election. Five years later, though, he returned to power after winning an election with an appeal to poorer Brazilians. In a 1949 interview with *O Journal*, he had promised to come back 'not as a political leader but as a leader of the masses'.¹⁷ Vargas, though, then clashed with Brazil's business elite, and in 1954, with the threat of a military coup against him looming, he shot himself through the heart. Yet just a year later, backed by the same political parties that had supported Vargas and promising to build on his predecessor's legacy, Juscelino Kubitschek, the charismatic governor of the state of Minas Gerais, was elected.

Throughout this volatile period, several consistent trends emerged. The federal state and its institutions, especially the armed forces, grew stronger. The military's share of the federal budget increased from 20 per cent in 1930 to 36.5 per cent in 1942, with army enrolment rising from 38,000 in 1928 to 75,000 in 1937 and 160,000 in 1944. Under Vargas, Brazil developed a notion of itself, a more genuinely national culture with ideas that almost all Brazilians identify with. Football was promoted as a national sport. Also elevated was the country's Carnival tradition. Thinkers close to the government, such as Gilberto Freyre, a renowned historian, anthropologist, and writer, developed the concept of racial democracy, which contrasted Brazil's history of miscegenation and supposed racial fluidity with the sharp divisions and open discrimination in the United States or South Africa.

More importantly, in these years Brazil began to industrialize. Initially, the shift away from exports of raw materials occurred by accident. As a result of the Great Depression of the early 1930s, the price of coffee – Brazil's overwhelmingly dominant export – collapsed, and the country simply lacked the foreign exchange to pay for imports. Domestic production of iron, steel, and cement surged in the early 1930s, and Brazilian businesses began to manufacture what could no longer be imported. Towards the end of the decade, Vargas began to place a much greater emphasis on planning. Brazil established a bureaucracy, and a proliferation of technical councils, commissions, and federal-state agencies emerged, all of which played an increasingly significant role in the country's development. These trends accelerated during the Second World War, when Brazil was compelled to place a new emphasis on import substitution. The other key element of this was the organization of a labour regime, designed to ensure the provision of enough workers to these emergent industries. This framework of employment regulations was inspired by the Polish and Italian labour codes and was specifically designed to calm any potential class conflict and bind workers into the new, rapidly urbanizing society. As Vargas himself put it: 'The labour laws are laws of social harmony. The state does not want and does not recognise class struggle.'[18] To that end, single state-controlled unions, financed by mandatory contributions from each worker, were established in all industries.

A national minimum wage was established, and provisions were made for regular increases. A system of arbitration involving regional offices was in place in the event of a dispute, and if that was unsuccessful, there were a series of labour courts. Provision was also made for workers to be trained through the establishment in 1942 of Senai, the agency that, as we have seen, the young Lula was to attend less than two decades later. All this was made law in May 1943 through the decree of a consolidated labour code. Most rural workers were outside this system, but for those urban workers who were inside it there were pensions, medical care, and limited social welfare benefits. Unions, as one observer put it in the 1970s, were 'bureaucratic welfare agencies'.[19] And as Leslie Bethell explained in his analysis of the Vargas regime, 'Brazilian workers under the Vargas dictatorship – at least those that were unionised – had rights not enjoyed by workers in many democratic countries, including Great Britain.'[20]

During the early 1950s, after Vargas returned to office, Brazil more explicitly promoted developmentalism by building up its road and energy infrastructure, as well as through tax, credit, and foreign-exchange policies that favoured the expansion of the internal market and the attraction of foreign capital into manufacturing. In 1952, Vargas created the state-owned National Bank for Economic and Social Development (*Banco Nacional de Desenvolvimento Econômico e Social* or BNDES) and a national oil company, Petrobras, the following year. By the mid-1950s, Brazil was already producing a significant amount of its consumer goods, including food, drinks, and clothing. Under Kubitschek, Brazil stepped up the pace of its industrial advance, with the new president promising '50 years in five'.

The highlight of his five years in office (1956–1961) was the construction of Brasília, a new modernist capital that was designed to turbocharge the development of Brazil's interior. Just as important, however, were the financial incentives, import tariffs, and new planning mechanisms chosen to attract foreign capital to national industries and reduce the dependency on imports. As Kubitschek himself put it in 1958, 'all planning studies made in Brazil show us clearly that the investment needed to accelerate our development greatly exceeds our capacity to save. . . . The collaboration of foreign capital is thus not material for emotional debate; it is a technical necessity.'[21]

The motor industry was at the forefront of this drive. Eleven companies – three controlled by Brazilian capital – had established truck, van, and car plants, several of them in the ABC towns near where Lula and his family were living. For example, in the second half of the 1950s, Mercedes-Benz and Volkswagen both began to build vehicles at plants in São Bernardo do Campo. Toyota and Scania followed suit in 1962. Volkswagen started building its iconic Beetle saloon car there in 1959 and dominated the Brazilian market throughout the 1960s. During Kubitschek's five-year term, Brazil's car production increased sevenfold. And the efforts were more broadly successful. Manufacturing as a whole grew by 11.2 per cent annually during Kubitschek's term in office, with its share of economic output reaching 34 per cent by 1961.

LULA ENTERS THE WORKFORCE

In 1963, Lula received his diploma from Senai and was now a skilled worker, aged 18, able to operate an industrial lathe on which he worked metal parts. It was a moment of triumph. 'Senai was the best thing that happened in my life,' he reflected thirty years later. 'Because I was learning a trade [and] it was the first time I had contact with decent people. You know that thing where you're at a good school, where you have lunch and can take a coffee? It was the first time, really.' At Senai, 'they looked after us. We had meals at set times. We had coffee, we played five-a-side football, and we played basketball. It was a great thing for me. For someone who had worked from the age of eight, to get to this level, to be a skilled man was a dream.'[22]

Lula was the first of Lindu's children to become a skilled worker and earn more than the minimum wage. It was a propitious time to enter the workforce. The rapid growth of industries in the ABC region continued during the early 1960s. For much of this period, those with qualifications were in short supply. As one worker put it, 'the car industry has grown so explosively that they are hunting for potential recruits. They are almost lassoing them in.'[23] In his early years of work, Lula was able to increase his wage simply by changing jobs.

He soon quit the screw company Parafusos, his first employer, to get a job in 1964 at Metalúrgica Independência, a family-owned business that machined parts for metal safe boxes, and then in 1965 at Fris Moldes Car, an Ipiranga-based outfit that made mouldings for cars. There were some setbacks. At Metalúrgica, where he worked nights, Lula lost part of the small finger of his left hand when a dozing colleague accidentally allowed a piece of heavy equipment to fall on him. At Fris, he was sacked for refusing to work weekend overtime, and then in 1965, during a temporary downturn in trade, he spent several months out of work.

There were also some domestic difficulties. Lindu and her family moved to São Caetano in 1963. Like Vila Carioca, this low-lying district on the southern periphery of São Paulo was subject to flooding. Lula was forced to move home more than once. His oldest sister Marinete, who had married in the late 1950s, was particularly unlucky, losing successive homes and sets of possessions in the regular deluges. It was all an ironic contrast to the extensive and regular droughts the family had suffered in Pernambuco.

By the mid-to-late 1960s, however, life was becoming easier for Lula. This, as we shall see in our next chapter, was a terrible time for Brazil politically. Still, the country's broader problems were of only limited interest to a comparatively well-off worker in his early twenties. In January 1966, Lula found a job at a large and profitable company that had a reputation for paying good wages. This was Indústrias Villares, a Brazilian-owned engineering giant that made elevators, excavators, cranes, locomotives, train carriages, and giant engines for ships. Like the car companies that dominated the region, Villares had benefited from the tariff protections, and subsidies, introduced by the developmentalist governments of the 1940s, 1950s, and early 1960s. Each day, Lula travelled down to São Bernardo and worked alongside 530 other workers at a plant on Rua Vergueiro, producing motors and other parts for escalators and trains. At Indústrias Villares, Lula earned a reputation as a diligent and reliable worker, eventually rising to become a foreman.

Lula took pride in his skills as a machinist. Sometimes, when he was shaping a piece of metal on his lathe, he felt like a sculptor crafting a work of art. While the monotony and relentlessness of factory work could be unforgiving, as a skilled man Lula enjoyed a little more autonomy and control than others. Like his colleagues, he valued the ability to plan and dictate the pace of his activities. 'We needed to analyse the drawing of the part to be machined and then decide about every small detail involved in the job,' he explained to a journalist in 1979. 'There was the question of how to set the lathe up, and then which precise tool to use and in what order.'[24]

Lula was a relatively well-off single man, but his finances were kept on a tight rein by the shrewd and careful Lindu. 'Lula would hand over his earnings to Lindu, who looked after household expenses, and would hand out pocket money and funds for bigger items to those who needed them.' His ambitions were modest. 'My dream was to live near a bakery, near a bus stop, near a chemist's. These were the three fundamental things,'[25] he told Denise Paraná. He kept a close eye on his beloved Corinthians, reading the daily column of the *Diário da Noite*, São Paulo's main evening paper, and he played football regularly. 'I just didn't have a head for anything else' at the time, he admitted.

In 1965, with his hand still in plaster after the loss of part of his little finger, Lula struck up a friendship with his next-door neighbours, who had also made the long journey down from the north-east on a parrot's-perch bus. Jacinto Ribeiros dos Santos, nicknamed Lambari, a young man of his age who had found work at the nearby Volkswagen plant, became his best friend. The pair, often accompanied by a third friend, a Japanese Brazilian named Olavo, spent their leisure hours together. Weekends often found them at the cinema, a local café, or simply hanging out at home, smoking cigarettes, drinking *cachaça*, and listening to music from a newly acquired transistor radio. Lambari taught Lula to dance, but says Lula was shy and the butt of the small group's jokes. 'He was the most gullible of our group and didn't flirt at all,' said Lambari.[26] Lula, though, had developed a soft spot for Lambari's younger sister, Lourdes. The two started seeing each other regularly at impromptu Sunday afternoon parties that Erminia, Lambari's mother, held at their house. They would dance to the records of Roberto Carlos and Ray Conniff, an American band leader whose albums *Exclusivamente Latino* and *Amor Amor* had made him a popular figure across Latin America. And at a dance hall in São Caetano, Lula – his courage reinforced by several glasses of local brandy – asked Lourdes out. Within three years, in 1969, they were married and had moved to a home of their own. Their honeymoon had been in the spa town of Poço de Caldas in Minas Gerais. The grainy black-and-white picture of them in a country club gondola surrounded by swans evokes the romanticism of French New Wave cinema or British films of the era such as *Saturday Night and Sunday Morning* or *A Kind of Loving*. A cultural world similar in many respects to that of the European working class of the period: stable, communitarian, ordered, and slowly improving. It couldn't have been more different to the bleak sparseness of Pernambuco. But it was not to last long.

3

Soldiers and Guerrillas

There was little opposition when late on the afternoon of 31 March 1964 a military rebellion clicked into gear and 4,000 rebel troops from the Fourth Infantry Division marched into Rio de Janeiro. The soldiers proclaimed an end to the 'chaos, corruption and communism' of the left-wing administration of João Goulart, who had taken over the presidency three years earlier. Most Brazilian military commanders quickly threw their support behind the plotters, and within 24 hours Goulart had left office and was heading into exile in Uruguay. Threats to resist from the Third Army garrisoned in the southern state of Rio Grande do Sul failed to materialize, and Brazil soon established a military government, which won widespread support from the political and business establishment and was welcomed by the United States.

For the 18-year-old Lula, just then beginning his first job as a recently qualified turner at a tiny screw-making company on the outskirts of São Paulo, it was something of a non-event. 'When the coup came, I hadn't got the faintest idea what it meant,' Lula told his biographer Fernando Morais. 'I was 18 or 19, and what we heard in our lunch break was that the army was going to sort things out, without knowing exactly what was to be sorted out. The armed forces had a lot of credibility among workers. It was surprising.'[1]

Like most conservative or apolitical Brazilians, Lula viewed the military's action not as something arbitrary but as a democratic revolution, implemented to free Brazil from the threat of a communist takeover. Business and church leaders, as well as influential voices in the conservative-dominated Congress, had been egging on the military to act for weeks. Just 12 days before the coup, 200,000 people had demonstrated in São Paulo in favour of the family, God, and liberty, their banners urging Jango – as Goulart was nicknamed – to 'go now' and reminding him that 'red was only a colour for lipstick'.[2]

Neither Lula nor his colleagues paused much to reflect on what had happened. 'Lula was proud of the armed forces and the way they were beginning to sort out Brazil's problems,' wrote his biographer.[3] But just as it is today, the country was divided. Goulart's supporters and many others were alarmed by the way democracy had been overthrown and wanted to act. They may have passed Lula by at the time, but the events of this period would eventually catch up with him.

Indeed, some of those responsible for the most radical, audacious, and ultimately disastrous responses to military government were activists who would, from the 1980s onwards, become the most important of Lula's political allies. José Dirceu, the most influential political strategist in the Workers' Party, and Dilma Rousseff, Lula's designated successor as president in 2010, were the two most prominent participants in a short-lived, ill-thought-out, and tragic guerrilla war. But in their younger days many other Workers' Party supporters spent their time running clandestine safe houses, organizing bank robberies or kidnappings, or forming generally ill-equipped units of partisans in remote areas of the Brazilian countryside. A good number of them had been exiled or ended up in prison, and many, including Rousseff, suffered grievous torture there. The emotional scars of those experiences continue to influence Workers' Party politics to this day.

A COLDER COLD WAR

To understand what happened in Brazil in the 1960s, it is essential to consider the international context and the impact of the Cuban Revolution of 1959 on intensifying the Cold War in Latin America.

US domination in the hemisphere was well established. From the late nineteenth century through the twentieth, the United States regularly intervened in a region, especially in the small countries of Central America and the Caribbean, close to the strategically vital Panama Canal and deemed to fall within its direct sphere of influence. Since the end of the Second World War, a series of particularly controversial interventions has been driven by a forthright anti-communism. In 1954, America had sponsored the overthrow of the mildly reformist government of Guatemala simply because its labour policies had depressed the profits of United Fruit, a US-owned banana company, and an agrarian reform had nationalized some of the company's land. Although, at least on paper, Washington supported elected rulers, in practice, it had begun to back authoritarian military regimes. As McCarthyism raged at home, American foreign policy prioritized the war against communism. The Republican President Dwight D. Eisenhower (1953–1961) supported military dictators in Cuba, Nicaragua, the Dominican Republic, Peru, Paraguay, and Venezuela. Eisenhower's vice-president, Richard Nixon, had praised the Cuban autocrat Fulgencio Batista as 'Cuba's Abraham Lincoln'. When Nixon visited Venezuela in 1958 his car was attacked by protesters.

The Cuban Revolution ratcheted up tensions. Noting high levels of poverty and growing discontent in Latin America, in 1961 the newly elected President John F. Kennedy launched a significant aid and development plan called the Alliance for Progress, which aimed to provide billions of dollars in assistance. Much of the programme ran aground and promises to fund land reform did not materialize. Instead, Cuban alignment with Moscow gradually shifted the American emphasis back towards security. Stopping communism in whatever way possible became the top priority.

Several Cuban revolutionaries, most notably Che Guevara, who had spent nine months in Guatemala in 1953 and 1954 and witnessed the US-backed invasion, were always convinced that Cuba had to follow a communist path if it was to free itself from American domination, achieve any development, and provide basic welfare for its citizens. After the partisans took power in 1959,

Cuba's first radical economic measures, including the nationalization of US energy plants and the first tentative trade contacts with Moscow, alarmed Washington. In 1961 a US-backed invasion force was routed by Cuban defenders at the Bay of Pigs. A year later, Kennedy imposed a full economic embargo on the island.

Cuba's alignment with the Soviet Union soon became complete when Fidel Castro formally announced that the country would become a socialist republic. To defend Cuba from a full invasion, the Soviet Union installed medium-range nuclear missiles on the island, triggering a crisis that took the world to the brink of nuclear conflict before the Soviet leader Nikita Khrushchev backed down. (Kennedy, as a quid pro quo, had also stepped back from confrontation by removing atomic weapons stationed in Turkey.) By 1964, US suspicion of the Soviet Union and China was leading towards intervention in Vietnam. As for Latin America, the Secretary of State for Inter-American Affairs, Thomas Mann, was now explicit about the shift in policy. The US would no longer seek to punish military juntas that overthrew elected governments.[4]

This fervid atmosphere began to influence Brazil's politics. As we have seen, Getúlio Vargas, during his second, more left-wing government (1951–4), and his successor Juscelino Kubitschek (1956–61), had pursued policies designed to promote economic development and social reform. After Jânio Quadros, Kubitschek's short-lived and eccentric successor, resigned in 1961 barely seven months into his term, his vice-president, João Goulart, continued in a similar vein to Vargas and Kubitschek. Goulart had been Kubitschek's vice-president and had rewon the office due to the unpopularity of Quadros's running mate and the eccentricities of the Brazilian electoral system. He was now the head of the moderate Brazilian Labour Party (*Partido Trabalhista Brasileiro* or PTB), which Vargas had formed. Goulart alarmed conservatives by his adventurous land and tax reforms, as well as by markedly strengthening relations with China, the Soviet Union, and Cuba. He had also provided federal support for a literacy programme based on the ideas of the radical educationalist Paulo Freire (who will figure again later in our story). Initially, a legislature dominated by conservative opponents had fettered Goulart, but in 1963 a plebiscite called by him resulted in a vote to end the parliamentary experiment. The curbs on his power were lifted, putting him on a collision course with the right.

Concern about Goulart's intentions in the United States had been growing steadily. In the 1962 Brazilian congressional elections, America, through a democracy promotion agency (the Brazilian Institute for Democratic Action), spent $5 million to promote opposition candidates. Lincoln Gordon, the US ambassador to Brazil, worried about instability and potential gains by the left in 1962 and had even discussed military intervention with Kennedy. In March 1964 the US had watched opposition military officers make their plans and worried more about the potential impact of failure than any breach of the democratic order. President Lyndon B. Johnson approved Operation Brother Sam, a plan that involved the despatch of a fleet carrying tons of munitions and squadrons of helicopters and fighter aircraft to Brazil. This hardware was never needed and, as Elio Gaspari points out in his monumental history of the dictatorship, no Brazilian 'took part in the overthrow of Goulart because the US wanted it'.[5] Even so, the US stance reaffirmed left-wing suspicion of American motives and gave a nationalist anti-*yanqui* character to radical politics. In a memoir José Dirceu is emphatic that in 'its efforts to isolate the Cuban Revolution and stifle the innumerable revolts and rebellions popping up all over the region', the US had sought to attract all Latin America to its 'political, military and ideological camp'.[6]

The Cuban Revolution also had a significant impact on the left, decisively shaping radical politics in Brazil and other Latin American countries, where many socialists had been confused by developments in the once monolithic communist camp. In 1956 the Soviet leader Nikita Khrushchev had shocked the communist world with his vehement criticism of the regime of Joseph Stalin, who had died three years previously. Khrushchev was not prepared to tolerate a democratic experiment, as he demonstrated by sending Russian troops and tanks to crush an anti-communist revolt in Hungary later the same year. However, he did attempt to pursue a less confrontational approach towards the United States, arguing that capitalist and socialist countries should 'peacefully co-exist' and compete. Supremacy for either system would only be determined in the long term. This shift in stance introduced an element of pragmatism to foreign policy, illustrated by the Russian leader's decision to withdraw his missiles from Cuba. The policy, however, directly precipitated a split with China's Mao Zedong, who was perplexed by the Soviet critique of Stalin and believed that a true revolutionary should have been prepared to risk nuclear war. Fidel Castro and Che Guevara shared similar mindsets. Informed that Khrushchev had secretly negotiated a deal with Kennedy, Castro was so angry that he smashed a mirror with his fist. Sam Russell, a correspondent for the *Daily Worker*, the newspaper of the British Communist Party (later renamed *The Morning Star*), interviewed Guevara shortly after the crisis blew over and said he 'thought [Che] was crackers for the way he went on about the missiles'.[7] 'To Che, the term peaceful co-existence was anathema, mere appeasement of the imperialist system, dressed up in diplomatic language,' wrote Jon Lee Anderson.[8]

BRAZIL'S LEFT DIVIDES

When Luís Carlos Prestes, a former army captain and leader of the Brazilian Communist Party, visited Moscow only a month before the 1964 coup, he had told Khrushchev that the local party had significant support among the high command of the armed forces and that fears of a coup were unjustified. 'If the right raises their head, we will cut it off,' he told the Soviet leader.[9] The approach was part of a risk-averse strategy that involved patiently working through the system, building contacts with trade unions and what the party saw as progressive, nationally minded business groups that it labelled a 'national bourgeoisie'. It was a long game, influenced in part by Moscow's greater caution, as well as Prestes's personal experience, which was briefly referred to in the last chapter. Twenty-nine years prior in November 1935, at a time when Stalin and the Communist International (Comintern) were engaged in their so-called left turn, Prestes, together with his German wife, Olga Benário, had participated in a disastrously unsuccessful insurrection which had served to trigger Vargas's move to the right and his flirtation with Mussolini-style fascism. Prestes spent much of the rest of the decade in exile, while Benário was repatriated to Germany in 1936, transferred to Ravensbrück concentration camp three years later, and gassed in the Bernburg Euthanasia Centre in 1942 with hundreds of other female political prisoners.

Prestes's overconfidence and the failure of the party's plan to stop the 1964 coup led to a significant split on the left. Many younger activists railed against the party's passivity. José Dirceu, who was 18 at the time of the coup, started university in 1965 and had immediately joined up. However, after attending meetings and discussing the ideas of Marx, Engels, and Lenin in educational groups, Dirceu quickly grew frustrated. The Communist Party not only failed to react to the coup, but it was also incapable of proposing any idea of resistance at all. 'For us, it was all too much,' he wrote in his memoir. It was also an error to show 'blind faith' in the institutional loyalty of the military, and the party should have done more to mobilize its supporters and distribute weapons so that 'we could resist the coup'.[10]

There were also wider cultural changes, of the kind that were sweeping through Europe and North America at the same time. Urbanization and the growth of youth culture were eroding allegiance to traditional social values. Many young Brazilians were feverish with impatience. Fernando Gabeira, then in his early twenties and working at the Rio de Janeiro newspaper *Jornal do Brasil*, devoted all his free time to revolutionary activism.

In his memoir, written in 1979, he describes the impassioned atmosphere perfectly. 'There was a discussion that fascinated us. Was the road to power peaceful or not? This was more than a discussion. It was an obsession . . . . It was necessary to do something. How many times did you hear that phrase? And how many times was it the beginning of great mistakes?'[11] Later in the book, reflecting on his decision to join The Revolutionary

Movement 8 October (MR8), one of a plethora of guerrilla groups that sprang up, Gabeira writes, 'for many of us our dream was to join an armed organisation. . . . It was leaving a third-division team to play in the premier league.'[12] For Gabeira and Dirceu's generation, resistance to the dictatorship was intrinsically linked to new cultural, social, and sexual freedoms. When the police raided left-wing events, they confiscated contraceptives as well as books. Arriving early in 1965 at the Catholic University in São Paulo, Dirceu expected to find a 'free, open and equal atmosphere but the reality was completely different. The dictatorship had imposed silence and fear,' he wrote. 'The cinema and theatre had been closed down; students were forbidden even to get together to play games and . . . most of the teaching staff were authoritarian reactionaries who collaborated with the dictatorship. A good few were members of an ultra-conservative Catholic society called Tradition, Family and Property.'[13]

Other young people had been influenced by liberation theology and the grassroots radicalization of the Catholic Church. Although more conservative clerics, including Brazil's most senior bishops, initially supported the coup, many priests were unhappy with this stance. In the years leading up to the coup, a cultural shift had occurred in Rome. Since 1958, a newly elected Pope, John XXIII, had done much to promote the Church's pastoral role and make it more relevant and these initiatives continued after his death in 1963. Between 1962 and 1965 theologians, officials, and bishops met in Rome, in what became known as the Second Vatican Council, and began to reassess the Church's role, revising antiquated rules and rituals and developing new ways to communicate their message. The changes included, for example, the end of the exclusive use of Latin for the celebration of Mass and greater attention to the study of the Bible in local languages. More generally, the Church began to give more attention to the secular world, and its officers looked at ways they could alleviate poverty and deprivation. The Church's youth movement started to set up literacy and other social projects in poor areas, and from 1960 onwards its leadership became increasingly left-wing. Significant numbers of university students were members of the movement, and because it shifted ever further leftward as the decade progressed it soon provided recruits for guerrilla organizations.

In practical terms, though, weaponry and know-how for these armed groups came from the more radical communist regimes, especially China and Cuba. Beijing offered training to several activists from a radical Catholic group called *Ação Popular* (Popular Action), who we will return to in future chapters, and to members of the *Partido Comunista do Brasil* (a Maoist Communist Party formed in 1962).

It was Cuba, though, that provided the most extensive and reliable assistance to Brazil's armed rebels. Fidel Castro and Che Guevara insisted that other Latin American leftists should follow their example, regardless of local conditions and whether they had any popular support. Guevara outlined a clear and categorical position. 'The line in Latin America is the armed struggle: the imperialists and their puppets make it necessary,' he said.[14] In 1964, under pressure from Moscow, Castro had agreed with Latin America's mainstream communist parties to put the brakes on their support for guerrilla insurgencies. However, he did nothing to implement this accord; instead, he promoted revolutionary wars in Latin America and elsewhere.

To back this strategy in Brazil, Cuba initially extended support to Leonel Brizola, a leader of Goulart's Brazilian Labour Party, who had risen to the governorship of the southern state of Rio Grande do Sul. Brizola, who was married to Goulart's sister, was disgusted by his brother-in-law's meek acceptance of the coup. He had unsuccessfully urged loyal soldiers to launch a counter-coup and then tried and failed to establish a resistance militia, whimsically organized into groups of 11, a number apparently based on the size of football teams. Subsequently, from self-imposed exile in neighbouring Uruguay, Brizola had organized a guerrilla movement along lines adopted by the Cubans. As we will see, the National Revolutionary Movement (*Movimento Nacional Revolucionário* or MNR) – as the experiment was known – was a resounding failure, but there was no shortage of other candidates willing to take on the revolutionary mantle. Cuba opted to double its bet.

In the mid-to-late 1960s dozens of young would-be revolutionaries from Brazil and other parts of Latin America visited Cuba, and many stayed on to receive training in guerrilla warfare. Cuban leaders insisted on action, whatever the cost. 'Sooner or later revolutionaries will realize that all peoples will be obliged to take up arms to secure their freedom,' a typically verbose Castro told what was labelled the 'Tri-Continental Conference' in January 1966. 'We need to spend less time theorizing and more time on the practical business of politics.'[15]

After Brizola's failure, Cuba backed Carlos Marighella, a hardened 54-year-old leader of the mainstream (Moscow-aligned) Brazilian Communist Party (*Partido Comunista Brasileiro* or PCB), who had been imprisoned four times and had unsuccessfully pressed his fellow leaders to change course. In Havana for the Latin American Solidarity Conference of August 1967, Marighella wrote a letter to Castro condemning the Brazilian party for its 'imbecilic fear of revolution. There is another alternative, the armed struggle.' A month later, he had been expelled from the party and had received pledges of support from Cuba. Within a few weeks of the conference the first batch of Marighella's militants were being trained in Cuba.[16] According to Gaspari the Cubans pledged $25,000 to make that possible.[17] Marigehella's National Liberation Action (Ação Libertadora Nacional or ALN) was formally established in February 1968. And over the next three years the ALN sent a steady flow of young members to the Cuban camps. By July 1971, 92 Brazilian guerrillas – mainly from the ALN – had received instruction. At an army barracks near Havana, they learned how to use explosives and take their weapons apart, and they practised shooting. Then they went to camps in the mountainous countryside in Pinar del Rio to the west. There were marches and survival drills, and the training ended with military exercises which pitched them against regular Cuban units. 'People who went to Cuba thought they would come back like guerrilla commanders. There was so much mythology about this because the Cubans conveyed the idea that you went and spent some time there and came back like Che Guevara,' a former ALN member told Denise Rollemberg.[18]

Another guerrilla leader, a former army captain named Carlos Lamarca, then emerged to head up a separate group called the Revolutionary Popular Vanguard (*Vanguardia Popular Revolucionária* or VPR. Although from mid-1969 following a merger with another organisation Lamarca's group became the *Vanguardia Armada Revolucionária - Palmares* or VAR-P, the extra word a homage to the eighteenth century rebel state created by escaped slaves). Lamarca had been radicalized by his experiences during a United Nations peace mission in the Middle East. He had deserted the army in 1969, stolen a lorry full of rifles and submachine guns, and joined the Vanguard's ragtag mix of Brizola survivors and Trotskyists. Lamarca's group had the same idea as Marighella's, and a few of its members also went to Cuba. 'Everyone wanted to go,' Mário Japa, the code name of Shizuo Osawa, one of its members, told Rollemberg. 'It was almost a baptism of fire: you had to take part in a military action, and you had to go and train in Cuba.'[19]

Almost before they had begun, however, all the groups were on the defensive. In mid-1969 the armed forces centralized the political police units responsible for monitoring 'subversion', for interrogating and usually torturing those who were detained. Even though the notorious Doi-Codi (Department of Information – Centre of Internal Defence Operations) was not established until a year later, the guerrilla organizations quickly began to disintegrate. It was now that extensive human rights abuses took place, as in their relentless quest for information police officers routinely beat prisoners, hung them upside down or subjected them to electric shocks. During 1969 and 1970 more than 2,200 detainees were tortured, up from an average of 61 a year in the period between 1964 and 1968. The savagery quickly paid off. In just five months towards the end of 1969, the police busted 66 safe houses, arrested 320 people, and captured more than 300 weapons. By May 1970 half of the VPR's militants had been picked up, including the woman who, forty years later, would be Lula's successor as president, Dilma Rousseff. Marighella was hounded down and slain late in 1969. Brizola was in exile. Lamarca was on the run and was eventually tracked and killed in 1971. By the end of 1970, about 400 guerrillas were in prison, many of them serving long sentences. A further 200 were exiled, mainly to Cuba, Algeria, France, or Chile, where the socialist president, Salvador Allende, had recently been elected. Some of these exiles had been freed from jail in exchange for the release of kidnap victims. No more than a hundred militants were active in Brazil, struggling to survive in a seemingly endless, nightmarish flight from police pursuers and sorely tempted by the idea of desertion. As Elio Gaspari points out, it was an agonizing dilemma since giving up now would mean letting down their imprisoned friends or betraying those who had died.

To this sequence of disaster there was now a bizarre coda. In 1972 the Maoist Communist Party of Brazil launched a fruitless and very bloody guerrilla campaign in the Amazonian region of Araguaia. However, by the time the group got its activities off the ground, its main support came not from Beijing, but from Albania's Enver Hoxha, who, following China's adoption of a more cautious position, was seen as the bearer of the true revolutionary flame. Led by their stoic and frugal veteran secretary general, João Amazonas (nicknamed Uncle Sid), the party made more progress than rivals in setting up bases and connecting with the rural poor. For a year or so, the few dozen guerrilla fighters would pause their labours every night to listen to Radio Tirana's Portuguese-language service, which broadcast the achievements of Brazil's peasant revolutionaries. However, the group was poorly equipped – it had just four submachine guns and minimal quantities of ammunition – and by 1975 it had been wiped out, although one fighter, José Genoino, survived to become an important member of the PT.[20]

WHAT WENT WRONG?

Part of the problem was that the concept at the heart of the strategy was flawed. In Cuba, between December 1956 and the beginning of 1959, a small group – known as a *foco* – of motivated and committed irregular fighters had taken on an established army and emerged victorious. Che Guevara, who had been one of a handful of armed rebels who had landed in the Granma fishing boat on the

Cuban shore, now believed that his example could be mechanically repeated elsewhere. Through commitment, organization, and sheer willpower, he believed that revolutionaries could achieve radical change, irrespective of local conditions and political circumstances. Guevara did much to popularize the idea by writing extensively about his experiences in the early 1960s. Then, between 1965 and 1967, he went off to lead guerrilla wars in other countries, starting in Congo. After the abject failure of this attempt, he led a similarly unsuccessful effort in Bolivia.

The problem was that in Cuba, Castro and Guevara's guerrilla army had been part of a much broader trade union and nationalist movement. Che Guevara and Fidel Castro could survive in the mountains only because they received supplies from a well-organized network of activists in the cities. And they were fighting against a dictator, Fulgencio Batista, whose close links to the United States made him a target of deep-rooted nationalist passions. Cuba had fought for its independence from Spain and then been occupied by American troops and very nearly annexed by Washington. North American business interests on the island were extensive and very controversial.

In this context the idea that a group of guerrillas had single-handedly taken on the Batista regime was, in the words of one American writer, 'a founding fathers myth' deliberately promoted by Che Guevara, who had clashed with the urban underground and criticized what he described as a lack of political ambition.[21] As with much else to do with Guevara, form triumphed over substance. According to one prominent Cuban revolutionary leader, 'Che didn't know what he was talking about [on this subject].'[22]

Brazil was very different. American economic influence was far more diffuse, and for the Brazilian population at large the United States was much more popular. The left might rail against US imperialism, but for the average Brazilian, US lifestyles and popular culture were aspirational. The military dictatorship was accepted, especially when the economy began to grow rapidly at the end of the 1960s and Brazil experienced what became known as its economic miracle. GDP expanded by 9.5 per cent in 1969, with the dynamic industrial sector, where Lula had now found regular work, up by 11 per cent. Opinion polls that year showed that seven of every ten Brazilians were optimistic about the economy. Better-paid workers were able to buy televisions and even cars for the first time. Some 4.68 million TVs were sold, nearly three times the figure for 1964. As one British academic noted, 'paradoxically under military rule, the minimum wage was always higher than it was for the first two decades of the post-1985 democracy. It is alarming to recognise and even more painful to say so in print, but the military dictatorship vastly improved the material conditions of most Brazilians even while depriving them of the right to change their government.'[23]

However, not only did Brazil's guerrilla movements lack grassroots support for their ideas, but their leaders also made little effort to develop a presence in the areas where they planned to establish their rural operations or *focos*, assuming perhaps that poor farmers and rural labourers would automatically give their backing. Leonel Brizola had been a charismatic speaker in the style of his mentor, Getúlio Vargas, and took a top-down approach to politics. So, not surprisingly, his guerrilla experiment seemed particularly quixotic. From his Uruguayan exile, Brizola practised shooting and using his bayonet and read endlessly about North Vietnam (then beginning its long war against the United States). He was prone, wrote one activist, to exaggerating the capacities of his fighters. 'There were these two guys who had come back from Cuba, [and he said they were] so well trained that they were like monkeys and could stay in the trees for a week.'[24]

Even though Brizola could rely on trained soldiers and sailors and count on Cuban support, his attempt in 1967 at a *foco* was over almost as soon as it had begun. Brizola chose to base his MNR column in the Serra do Caparaó, a remote mountainous area of Minas Gerais in central Brazil; however, nothing had been done to prepare the ground, and there was no history of social conflict in the area. 'I felt as if I had been parachuted in,' said one former fighter, recalling the experience more than three decades later.[25] 'There was simply no political basis for what we were trying to do.' Isolated and without food, the guerrillas began to steal to survive. They were denounced by local farmers and arrested.

A similar story unfolded with the other groups. Their political ideas were primitive and crassly oversimplified. 'They came back from Cuba with a one-eyed vision of reality. They were impregnated with the idea of disembarking from Granma and beginning the revolution in the following weeks, even without knowing who they were going to fight against,' said one former member of the ALN.[26] The spate of bombings, bank robberies, and kidnappings that shook Rio de Janeiro and São Paulo during the late 1960s, and the hapless rural campaign in the Amazon launched by the Maoist Communist Party, attracted some international attention. However, they never involved more than a few dozen people, most of whom were politically inexperienced university students in their twenties and thirties, seduced by romantic and utopian ideas. Reading the accounts of people like Dirceu and Gabeira, you get the sense of an endless cycle of activity in which the groups and their hapless members are forever running harder to stand still.

The 1969 abduction of the American ambassador Charles Ebrick, in which Gabeira participated, won the release of fifteen imprisoned guerrilla fighters, including Dirceu, but brought the guerrillas no nearer to any definable long-term objective and did nothing to promote popular support. After being released from jail in 1969, Dirceu was flown to Cuba, where he was trained as a guerrilla. Subsequently, he made two epic journeys back to Brazil, circuitous adventures involving long bus trips to regional airports, flights to Lisbon and Rome, and stays in Moscow and Prague. He carried false passports and changed his identity and appearance through plastic surgery. He even launched a business (improbably a menswear shop in a small town in Paraná in southern Brazil) and married his co-owner to keep the security forces off his tracks. But the results of all these efforts were negligible. By 1975, when the last Maoist fighters were killed in the Araguaia, Brazil's guerrilla movement was as isolated and remote from most Brazilians as it had been ten years before.

The international image that the groups and their supporters attempted to project at the time, and continue to claim, was disproportionate to their actual impact in Brazil. Handsome and moustachioed Marighella was every left-wing student's idea of a revolutionary leader. In an interview published in the French magazine *Action* shortly before he died in late 1969, Marighella boasted that Brazil would become a new Vietnam. By then, his portrait was everywhere: on the cover of Brazil's new weekly magazine *Veja*, on police posters as Brazil's most wanted terrorist, and in the pages of *Les Temps Modernes*, the prestigious publication of the French left founded by the then fashionable philosophers Jean-Paul Sartre and Simone de Beauvoir. Jean-Luc Godard, the French filmmaker, gave the entire proceeds of one of his films, *Wind from the East*, to the ALN. Joan Miró, the Catalan artist, also provided money to the group.

By the early 1970s a string of books extolling the virtues of the foco and of revolutionary war in Latin America could be found in the bookshops of Europe and the Americas. Prominent among them were *Revolution in the Revolution* by the French philosophy teacher Régis Debray, who had accompanied Che Guevara in Bolivia and been captured and imprisoned, and Marighella's *For the Liberation of Brazil*, a text that included the Brazilian revolutionary's 'Manual of an Urban Guerrilla', mimeographed copies of which had first appeared a few months before his assassination in 1969.

In 1972 the British publisher Penguin also had available under its Pelican Latin America library imprint Che Guevara's *Guerrilla Warfare*; *Fidel Castro Speaks*; *Cambão – The Yoke* by the Brazilian peasant leader Francisco Julião; *Brazil: The People and the Power* by Miguel Arrães, another radical Brazilian political leader from the north-eastern state of Pernambuco; and *Guatemala – Another Vietnam* by Thomas and Marjorie Melville. Marighella's 'mini manual' is a 50-page booklet divided into 14 chapters. Reading it today, it seems less a practical guide than a wholly delusional anarcho-militarist tract. Triumphalist and disordered, it proposes the creation of groups of five people capable of acting autonomously. According to Elio Gaspari, the kind of guerrilla fighter

Marighella was hoping to train would be 'somewhere between a boy scout and a secret agent'. And his ideas about organization are completely unrealistic. For example, there are no suggestions as to how practitioners are to find hiding places or safe houses, which contemporary accounts show was a constant preoccupation. The manual also informs its readers that helicopters are useless for counter-insurgency, as it is difficult for them to land in urban areas, a dubious premise that ignores their self-evident value as tools for observation.

These rose-tinted European and American visions contrasted sharply with the dour reality in Brazil, where guerrilla leaders such as Marighella had radicalized to such an extent that they had become closed off from society, trapped in a world of their own, and in Gaspari's words, 'absorbed with the daily reality of survival'. None of this came as a surprise to members of the Brazilian Communist Party, who were no doubt quick to talk about the perils of ultra-leftism. In a brutal dismissal, Luis Carlos Prestes, now approaching 80, described the armed movement as a 'petty bourgeois scab'.[27] Meanwhile, many of its grassroots members, whose efforts were so contemptuously dismissed by the radicals, continued with their humdrum activities in trade unions and community groups. Among them was Lula's older brother, Frei Chico, who joined the party in 1971. He was to have a significant influence on our story.

4

The Reluctant Trade Unionist

In his younger days, Lula's brother José Ferreira da Silva worked in factories in the ABC towns at the heart of São Paulo's industrial belt. With his leather apron and his hair prematurely thinning, from a distance the stocky young welder had the appearance of a priest. And as a political activist close to both the Communist Party and the far-left Catholic Ação Popular (AP), the nickname – Frei Chico (Brother Chico) – seemed appropriate. All the more so, since, as we saw in the last chapter, the priests of the Franciscan and Dominican orders were among the staunchest opponents of the dictatorship. 'The union's lawyer called me this after I'd given a particularly aggressive speech one day,' Frei Chico told an interviewer. 'I was an atheist, but the nickname stuck.'[1]

More naturally outspoken than his youngest brother and much more rebellious, Frei Chico had taken to radical politics in his adolescence. Some neighbours from Bulgaria were an early influence and when he joined the trade union at Pontal, the agricultural implements factory where he first worked, Frei Chico met several more members of the party. 'The Communists were very strong in the region where we lived and I got to know a few and really admired them. There were two or three at the factory . . . and it was through them that I joined the union when I was 18.'[2]

By the mid-1960s Frei Chico was very active in the metalworkers' union and close to the party. As Lula himself later pointed out, 'Frei Chico was the kind of guy who would go to the union all the time, the kind of person who had lunch there, took coffee there.'[3] Not only that but in the political turbulence of the late 1960s, Frei Chico started to campaign for left-wing opposition candidates who were challenging the more moderate figures who ran things.

Growing up together, and three years apart, Frei Chico and Lula as the youngest of the five brothers had been inseparable. Moreover, predictably perhaps, the older brother tried hard to get his younger sibling politically involved. It was hard work though.

Lula, as we have seen, was totally disconnected from the big events of the 1960s that excited his elder brother: the 1964 coup, the beginning of armed left-wing resistance and the military's Institutional Act Number Five of 1968, which radicalized the regime, led to the closure of the national Congress and the repression of opposition. Lula instead was obsessed with football and Lourdes, the next-door neighbour who had become his new girlfriend and would soon be his first wife, and more interested in the *novelas* – the popular soap operas that were beginning to dominate national television – than the endless meetings that seemed to absorb his elder brother. Their always influential mother, Dona Lindu, was suspicious of unions and left-wing politics in general and favourably disposed to the army, which she believed was going to fix the country's problems. Lula's other brothers and sisters were similarly minded.

In fact, as Lula pointed out in a 1981 interview, 'the whole family, apart from Frei Chico, were anti-union. We believed . . . that the union was full of thieves and people you couldn't trust and that our brother was a bit of a fool [for going along with it all]'.[4] Lourdes was worried too, concerned that if Lula got involved it might blemish his reputation as a good worker, and that this might make it more difficult to secure a job in the future. Lula remembers quite angry encounters at home where everyone would gang up on Frei Chico. 'We would be having a family get-together or just sitting around drinking a cachaça, and he'd come in with: "because the union" . . . And once he went on like this, we'd all let him have it because we didn't want to hear about the union.'[5]

Fernando Morais says that conversations between the two brothers always followed a similar pattern. 'You need to get to know the union. Go to a meeting and see,' Frei Chico would insist. 'No way, I'm not going. They are all robbers,' Lula would reply. 'Come on, just see what it's like,' rebutted his brother. 'No, I don't want to. I'm not going. I've seen that these are the guys who are on those wanted posters. The terrorists the police are after are all involved.'[6]

Frei Chico was nothing if not persistent, though, and finally, in August 1968, he did manage to persuade Lula to go to a meeting, even though he was obliged to pay the bus fare to get him there. The gathering sparked Lula's interest, less perhaps because of its content than because of the violence of the factional disputes between the union's moderate leadership and left-wing opponents. As a vocal opposition supporter, Frei Chico was at the centre of a relatively minor social welfare controversy. When some members threatened to beat him up, Lula felt he had to be prepared to defend his sibling.[7] Within a few weeks, Lula was drawn in more deeply and then, for entirely circumstantial reasons, more deeply still. Every three years – according to labour law – union officials had to submit themselves for re-election. For the contest scheduled to take place in February 1969, Frei Chico, by now an active and popular figure among both colleagues at work and friends in the Communist Party, was under pressure to participate. But workers at Carraço, where he was employed, already had a delegate representing them. As Frei Chico and others discussed what to do, it became clear that Lula would be a good choice. After all, the politically innocent younger brother got along well with everyone he worked with at Indústrias Villares, and even though he was inexperienced, both the union's leadership and Frei Chico's party contacts thought he was somebody they could influence.

As John French explains, Lula's obvious lack of political involvement was a significant advantage, as the military, who had already intervened extensively in the unions, were unlikely to raise objections. Since the coup, more than 750 trade unions had been subjected to intervention by the regime, 300 or so of them in the more industrialized south-east. 'We had to find individuals who had no links to the left or who were not publicly known as leftists . . . sometimes, given the difficulties of the period, we took someone who wasn't even a left-winger but who was honest and hardworking,' one of Lula's predecessors as metalworkers' leader told French.[8]

The 23-year-old Lula took some convincing. Both Lourdes, to whom he was by now engaged, and his mother were unhappy. Lula too feared that to stand for office would 'invite persecution'. Slowly, though, Frei Chico and the union leaders won Lula round to their way of thinking. Their arguments were persuasive. It would be an opportunity to be helpful to colleagues and win status. There were material benefits. Officials had access to cars and could travel elsewhere in Brazil or abroad to attend conferences. The position was stable because the union owned property and had significant regular income guaranteed by the government.[9] And Lula would not need to give up his job at the factory because he would stand for a position as one of the seven reserves or *suplentes*. After several rounds of *cachaça*, Lula bit the bullet and decided to ignore the worries at home. In February 1969 he was voted in. His career as a trade unionist had begun.

He quickly began to enjoy his new activities. 'These controversies began to fascinate me,' he told Denise Paraná in 1993. 'Colleagues started to ask me for information and when I didn't know . . . I would go down to the union in the evening and return with the answer the next day.'[10] It was at this point that Lula got to know Paulo Vidal, the incoming president of the union, a moderate and modernizer who wanted the union to be able to negotiate directly with local employers rather than via slow-moving state-appointed mediators. Vidal favoured an approach towards labour relations more typical of Europe or North America. He was pragmatic and level-headed, committed to defending his members rather than pursuing any broader political agenda. The union, he argued, should be more efficient and communicate more effectively. In 1971 the union launched a free newspaper, *Tribuna Metalúrgica*, which soon developed a distinctive style, including a popular cartoon that attracted a strong following among workers.

As left-wing activists stepped up their campaign against military rule, tensions within the union grew. The practical Vidal had little patience for 'gestures of protest that endangered the union,' wrote French. '[To him] it seemed suicidal to chant down with the dictatorship in union meetings full of police informers.'[11] Left-wing organizers attacked Vidal, labelling him a *pelego* or bosses' man, or even a police agent.[12] Late in 1971, as the date for new union elections came closer, they began to draw up their slate of candidates. A group of left-wing workers at the Ford plant in São Bernardo do Campo who were close to the Communist Party sounded out Lula, suggesting that he break with Vidal and join their bid to take control. Frei Chico, who, after many years hovering on its fringes, had secretly joined the party recently, threw his weight behind these efforts.

Lula though was already a committed member of Vidal's camp. Vidal had become a mentor. Lula confessed in 1993 that Vidal 'was advanced and progressive in terms of achieving things. He was very intelligent and competent.'[13] Moreover, the bond between the two men tightened following the sudden and unexpected loss of Lourdes, his young wife who died in the eighth month of her pregnancy. The death of Lourdes and his unborn young son hit Lula hard emotionally, and he started drinking more and took to sleeping on a mattress at the union. Vidal invited him to stay at his home. 'I thought it was best to take him to stay with us. It was three weeks staying in my sons' room. My wife washed his clothes,' Vidal told an interviewer in 2018.[14]

Early in 1972, Lula took an active role in Vidal's re-election campaign and himself stood as candidate for first secretary, a position that would put him at the heart of the union organization. He not only rebuffed the left's approach but deliberately undermined their efforts. Fernando Morais describes how, when supporters of the opposition's slate distributed leaflets at the factory gate, Lula would follow them and use a stick capped with a nail to spear the propaganda off the ground before anyone could read it. Now one of Vidal's most loyal lieutenants, Lula helped the union expand and gain influence. When Vidal asked him to set up a new division of the union's legal department dedicated to social welfare, Lula took the opportunity to attend courses on union and social welfare legislation, mastering the rules of redundancy and pension payouts. As more workers came to him for advice, Lula's reputation grew. 'Everything relating to pensions and welfare went through his hands,' wrote Morais.[15] Lula kept on top of the complex paperwork and developed a following among members and their families. There were some political tensions, of course, but Lula was on friendly terms with everybody. Conversations in his office were frequently smoothed by the bottle of *cachaça* always close at hand.

Vidal's leadership had been successful. The union more than doubled in size between 1969 and 1974 and a new concrete and glass headquarters, opened in 1973, symbolized its progress.[16] But in 1975 elections for the union's committee took place again. Vidal unexpectedly had to step down as president, and Lula was elected to replace him.

The politics surrounding this switch were complex. Vidal's employer, Molins, the machinery manufacturer for which he had originally been elected as a representative, was moving, so theoretically he was no longer eligible as a representative.[17] The union could have found a way to surmount the difficulty, but Vidal's success had created friction between him and other colleagues on the committee. What's more, Vidal had become a prominent member of the local section of the Brazilian Democratic Movement (MDB), then the main opposition party to the military government, and nurtured political ambitions. For union moderates, backing Lula was simply a safer and less complicated option.

As Lula emerged onto the national scene for the first time it was hard to pin down exactly what he represented and where he was coming from. The Communist Party had supported his candidacy, but he had made it clear repeatedly that he would have nothing to do with their plans for Brazil. Early on in his period as a full-timer he had angrily rejected an approach from the party orchestrated by the ever-persistent Frei Chico. Lula had agreed to meet a senior party member on a park bench in São Bernardo. Pretending to read a newspaper, the communist, Emilio Bonfante Demaria, a prominent organizer in the seamen's union, had whispered his intentions. But the form of the contact had simply enraged Lula, who stormed off, told his brother that he had nothing to hide and should be contacted in his office. He would not, he said, 'take part in this ridiculous theatre', nor have anything to do with clandestine organizations.[18] At his inauguration as union president Lula openly criticized Marxist ideas. In a speech apparently drafted by the union lawyer, he said people were 'crushed by the state, enslaved by Marxist ideology, and denied the right to think and express themselves freely'.[19]

With Vidal's help, Lula had developed friendly relations with senior establishment figures. Military and business leaders saw Lula as a man they could deal with. Paulo Egydio, the conservative governor of São Paulo who was close to the military government, attended Lula's inauguration ceremony as the newly elected president on the grounds that Lula had 'defeated the communists'. 'Lula wasn't a communist [then] – just as he is not [today]. I would dare to say that . . . he doesn't have an ideological matrix,' said Egydio 30 years later.[20]

The American consul in São Paulo reckoned Lula's independence was genuine, noting that the union rejected the presence at its meetings of activists from the main opposition party, the MDB, and refused to participate in student demonstrations against the government. Many on the left were convinced at that time that Lula was working for the intelligence services. For example, Gilberto Carvalho, one of the founders of the PT, said the radical priests that he knew thought Lula was an agent. Lula later told Denise Paraná that he and his union colleagues simply disliked the Soviet model, which he referred to as 'actually existing socialism', a term used by the East German dissident Rudolf Bahro in his 1977 book *The Alternative in Eastern Europe* and associated with a left-wing critique of centrally planned development in the Soviet Union and Eastern Europe.

Yet, some right-wingers were suspicious. A report by Brazil's then military intelligence agency, the *Serviço Nacional de*

Informações (National Information Services or SNI) noted that Lula had been 'projected from out of nowhere to be some sort of media star' and that 'people outside the union were manipulating him'. The journalist Elio Gaspari felt there was at least the appearance of inauthenticity. 'His age, his background, and his inexperience make him seem like a bear at a circus, sympathetic and obedient,' he wrote. 'He had no boss or roots, no connections with anyone other than the workers of São Bernardo. He had no political project, didn't want to overthrow the government, much less the regime, and didn't even talk about a socialist society.' Lula was certainly dismissive of the limited party politics allowed by the military government in the 1970s. The two legal parties, the pro-regime *Aliança Renovadora Nacional* or The National Renovation Party (Arena) and the opposition MDB, were "flour from the same sack. (It is) a game between two teams that I don't support," he said.[21]

RADICALIZATION

Two things would give a radical edge to Lula's stubbornly independent approach. They both played a significant role in Brazil's political and economic dynamics during this period. First, there was a military crackdown on the Communist Party, during which Frei Chico was kidnapped, tortured, and then released. Second, the sharp increase in oil prices following the Yom Kippur War of 1973 led to higher inflation, lending a new urgency to the unions' wage battles.

During the crackdown against the guerrilla left, hard-line anti-communist soldiers had enjoyed free rein to come down heavily on subversion. In 1974, however, with the armed opponents of the regime vanquished, the pendulum within the military government swung back towards the centre. More far-sighted generals, who wanted to see the return to a kind of limited or managed democracy, began to gain the upper hand, successfully guiding General Ernesto Geisel to the presidency, and starting to rein in right-wing radicals. Geisel sought to restore the authority of the top brass, and begin a 'slow, gradual and safe' return to civilian rule. It was, wrote Leslie Bethell and Celso Castro, a process designed to return Brazil to its pre-1968 state, before the imposition of radical restrictions with Institutional Act Number 5. As part of that process limited media freedoms were introduced and legislative elections held in somewhat more open conditions than before.[22]

This process, however, soon got out of hand when the MDB, the only opposition party allowed to participate, inflicted a heavy defeat on Arena, which had hitherto had overwhelming control of the legislature. The MDB, which was supported by many on the left, including the Communist Party, won 14.5 million votes to Arena's 10.1 million, took 16 of the 22 Senate seats, and 161 of the 364 lower house (Chamber of Deputies) seats in Congress, a performance that was far better than had been expected. Alarmed by these developments, military right-wingers led by General Silvio Frota pressed for a crackdown on the apparent growth of left-wing influence in the media, trade unions and the MDB itself. Frota was eventually sacked by Geisel two years later, but the repression of late 1975 was significant. The most well-known piece of brutality was the murder in police custody of Vladimir Herzog, editor-in-chief of a popular television channel called TV Cultura. Financed by a non-profit foundation linked to São Paulo's state government, the station was a beacon of independent and socially conscious journalism at a time of heavy censorship, and Herzog's killing led to some of the biggest anti-government protests since the coup. But as Frota and his allies flexed their muscles, dozens of far less well-known political activists and labour organisers were also rounded up. Among the victims of these actions was Frei Chico.

Now deputy president of the São Caetano metalworkers, Frei Chico had played an active role in the MDB's 1974 campaign, assisting the election of a fellow Communist as a federal deputy. One Saturday he returned home to find an unmarked Chevrolet station wagon parked outside his front door. Moments later a group of armed plainclothes men grabbed him, put a hood over his head, threw him into the back of the station wagon, and took him to the headquarters of the political police, Doi-Codi. Within hours, Frei Chico was stripped naked and strapped to a dragon's chair, a metal seat to which a simple generator and a hand crank had been attached. As the investigators interrogated their prisoner, they applied increasing amounts of electric current, frequently throwing cold water over their victim and applying salt to his mouth to intensify the pain. For 15 days Frei Chico was dragged back and forth from his cell to this agony before being eventually moved to another military detention centre.[23]

Testifying many years later to a truth commission set up by the government of Dilma Rousseff, Frei Chico said he had got off lightly because, as a member of the Communist Party's tiny municipal committee in São Caetano, he was a relatively unimportant figure. He had not been 'penetrated by a billy club', or 'had his teeth broken'. The experience, though, was 'mad', said Frei Chico, describing how prisoners were dragged back and forth from the cell they shared with 18 or 20 others. 'It was 24/7. There were three teams of torturers and a medical guy with a white coat to examine you and make sure it was safe to continue.' Regaining consciousness, Frei Chico said he would wake up to the radio playing the country music of Zé Betty (a *sertanejo* star of the 1970s) loud enough to drown out the screams.[24]

When all this was happening, Lula was in Tokyo, at an international conference organized by union colleagues at Toyota. He was unhappy anyway, suffering from a throat infection, not enjoying the local food, and understanding next to nothing about the debates. The call he received from an official of the São Paulo Metalworkers Federation about his brother's detention only made his misery complete. Advised to lie low for his own safety, Lula did the exact opposite. He cut short his stay and as soon as he had returned to Brazil, Lula set out to find Frei Chico. Visiting the police detention centre was like walking into the lion's den. It seemed a bad idea, particularly so in retrospect since it has emerged that Frei Chico's torturers were focusing their interrogation on what they erroneously imagined were the real motives of Lula's journey by way of Tokyo: the delivery of a letter to Luís Carlos Prestes, the Communist Party's leader who was living in exile in Moscow.

When hearing the news of Frei Chico's kidnapping and detention, the 'average Joe' would have 'tried to hide,' wrote John French.[25] For Lula to do otherwise was brave, though, and went some way to mending relations with his brother that their spats about union politics had damaged. Frei Chico himself later praised his brother's 'courage'. And Lula has made the episode something of a turning point in his biography. The torture was 'bad for [his brother's] body but extremely good for my head . . . [and] contributed to an extraordinary leap in the quality of my political activities,' he said in a 1993 interview. 'I stopped being frightened. If I were to be imprisoned for what I thought, then so be it. It was essential because I stopped trying to moderate my language in mass meetings. We said what had to be said.'[26]

This clarity, however, brought Lula no closer to Frei Chico's Communist Party, and political friction between the two brothers continued well into the 1980s. Frei Chico disagreed with the direction in which Lula was taking the union, arguing against the creation in 1980 of the Workers' Party (see Chapter 6). In 1986 Frei Chico stood against his brother in the election for the constituent assembly, which would steer the country's return to democracy.[27]

But Lula was emboldened and, in the mid-1970s, began to negotiate changes that would widen his room for manoeuvre as head of the São Bernardo metalworkers. He trimmed the sails of Vidal, who, despite the difficulties that had prevented his re-election as president, had managed to retain a place on the union's committee and the associated political influence. Brazil's economic difficulties afforded Lula the chance to strengthen his hand even further.

Soon after Lula began working in the mid-1960s, Brazil's economic performance began to improve. By 1970, output was growing at a rate of more than 10 per cent per year. As we have seen, the expansion helps explain why the military government was relatively popular, but during the mid-to-late 1970s the success soured.

An important trigger for the downturn was the Middle East war of October 1973, in which Israel overcame an Arab coalition led by Egypt and Syria. Angered by the defeat, the Arab exporters, which dominated the OPEC cartel, reduced their output of oil. Prices surged, quadrupling in less than a year, and countries such as Brazil, which were heavily dependent on imports, were hit hard. The government took steps to diversify its energy sources, building huge hydroelectric dams and launching a programme to use ethanol made from sugarcane as a fuel for cars. And it borrowed in a bid to sustain growth. Even so, growth slowed, and inflation started to increase. From an annual rate of about 15 per cent in 1973, inflation rose to 30–34 per cent in 1974–5, 46 per cent in 1976, and 39–41 per cent in 1977–8, before leaping to 77 per cent in 1979 and 110 per cent in 1980.[28] Wages in the ABC industrial belt had been relatively high in the 1960s, especially for skilled workers like Lula. But in the first years after the coup, salaries were squeezed through what John French describes as an 'ingenious formula of adjustments that was based on a frequently underestimated estimate of future inflation'. According to a confidential labour ministry briefing prepared in 1968, the policy sought to avoid 'compensating workers for past losses in purchasing power due to inflation', which had been the practice of elected governments before the coup.[29] Antônio Delfim Netto, the Finance Minister between 1967 and 1974 and the politician most closely associated with the achievements of the 'miracle', had been particularly insistent on breaking the bad habits of the past and ensuring that real increases in wages were linked to productivity improvements.

Unions, therefore, had good reason to complain and were suspicious of government data. Back in the late 1950s, unions from São Paulo state had formed a think tank – known by its acronym Dieese – whose research challenged questionable official data. In 1977 a group of researchers led by Walter Barelli discovered documents in the basement of the Ministry of Labour building that, when compared with official figures collected by Brazil's statistics institute, suggested the Treasury had been manipulating the numbers. 'There was,' as Fernando Morais put it, 'nothing complicated about it. No complicated economic theory nor anything plotted in Moscow, just simple arithmetic. In 1973, prices had risen at double the rate claimed by the treasury, and unions demanded a wage rise to compensate.'[30]

Delfim Netto altered the inflation numbers by, for example, instructing the Getúlio Vargas Foundation, a business school and think tank that calculates several pieces of official economic data, to use wholesale rather than retail prices for certain items. This sleight of hand depressed the official inflation rate, on which wage adjustments were based, and left workers out of pocket. João Ferrador, the cartoon character created by *Tribuna Metalúrgica*, was, as union leaflets distributed at the factory gates put it, 'not happy'. Ultimately, it was this untruth about inflation that fomented a wave of militant strikes that catapulted Lula onto the national political stage.

5

All Out

A greying, thickset man in his late seventies, Juno Rodrigues Silva, looked wistful as he recalled the moment nearly half a century ago when his lifelong friend Lula launched Brazil's 'new' trade unionism. 'It was like this. He was like a singer. He had no notes. The arguments just came to him in the spur of the moment,' recalled Rodrigues Silva, who is widely known as Gijo – or Big Ears – a nickname given to him back in the 1960s by fellow workers at the Volkswagen plant in São Bernardo do Campo.[1]

The restaurant where Gijo and his wife, Divina, now make their living is not far from the house where the president lived with his second wife, Marisa Letícia, until she died in 2017. Back in the day, Lula was often to be found there eating his favourite dish of *chuleta*, a sirloin steak topped with roasted potatoes. Framed photographs of Lula, Marisa Letícia, of PT, trade union, and government colleagues, cover nearly every inch of the wall in the dining area. And in a small private office, at the back of a storeroom next door – where we talked – there is a kind of shrine. The shelves are full of books, pamphlets, and albums, innumerable snapshots, newspaper cuttings, trade union pennants, and other memorabilia detailing the political rise of Gijo's one-time neighbour.

As Gijo recalled, the decisive point came on a rainy afternoon in March 1979. Lula, then, in his fourth year as president of the Metalworkers Union, had to roar to get his message across. More than 60,000 workers from the motor factories and the engineering plants of the ABC towns had gathered in São Bernardo do Campo's Vila Euclides football stadium, and Lula was speaking to them without sound equipment, not even a megaphone.

Union colleagues had put a wooden table in the centre of a pitch where the legendary Pelé had performed just a few years before. But now Lula was at the centre of everybody's attention. 'Every time he made a point, he would tap his foot, and the table he was standing on would sink lower into the muddy ground,' laughed Gijo, who was one of half a dozen union colleagues desperately holding on to the makeshift stage. As Lula spoke, the workers nearest him chorused the message to those more distant, with those, in turn, repeating it until the sound boomed out high in the stands. 'It was like a chain or a network that gave a voice to the workers,' Gijo told me. 'We called it *Radio Peão* [poor man's radio].' 'Comrades, comrades, comrades,' echoed the speech. 'We are here to decide whether to take on the bosses, we are here to decide whether to take on the bosses; again, they want a bit of our wage, but this time we are going to bite the bullet, again they want a bit of our wage . . .'[2] Lula urged his members 'not to go to the factory, not to use the company buses, not to fall victim to the plot that the bosses were preparing'. He told the workers to 'hold their heads up high' and – using religious imagery that was to crop up again and again in this movement – said that the mass meeting was 'a consecration of working-class power'.

The strike of 1979 brought to a head a union campaign that had begun in 1976 and had led to industrial action the previous year. It included, as the conservative *O Estado de São Paulo* was to remind its readers in its report, the deployment of pickets at factory gates for the first time since 1968. As we saw in the last chapter, the union had been looking for some time to break out of the straitjacket of corporatist labour law. Prices were rising in the wake of the 1973 oil shock. By manipulating the figures, the government was keeping wage increases below the inflation rate, and workers were getting poorer. Now, having established complete control over the union leadership, Lula was conducting a very aggressive campaign to regain the ground that had been lost. Gijo had witnessed it all firsthand.

Gijo had met Lula in 1968 when he had started a job as a welder at the factory where Volkswagen was making its Karmann Ghia car. Holding a die-cast model of the sleek Italian-designed coupé, Gijo said he was proud to have been a car worker. Getting the job had been an achievement. Volkswagen had allowed him to train on a day-release basis, and the wage rates for skilled workers were good. The factory where Gijo worked was enormous, so big in fact that – with its 30,000–40,000 workers – it was hardly a single factory at all.

Gijo and Lula, then a lathe operator at Indústrias Villares, had joined the union at the same time. Gijo's wife Divina had known Lula's first wife, Lourdes, and the couple were among those consoling Lula after Lourdes died in hospital in 1971 from hepatitis that doctors had failed to diagnose during the eighth month of her pregnancy. After the tragedy, in which Lula had also lost an unborn child, the two men became neighbours. Divina had been a childhood friend of Marisa, the young school administrator and widow who became Lula's second wife in 1974. Gijo and Lula would drink together and play football and cards. 'We'd often be at the union until 10 or 11 at night,' recalled Gijo, who said that his friend was then just beginning to broaden his horizons away from the football columns of the sports paper, *Gazeta Esportiva*, and was becoming less shy about speaking in public.

Ever since he had been elected a reserve member of the union's committee in 1968, Lula had always been a good listener, receptive to the grumbles of fellow workers, and always happy to help if he could. Once active, he persuaded many colleagues to join up. 'If there were something wrong, he'd say, "Let's go and talk to the president of the union." He would open doors,' explained Gijo.

And metalworkers in the ABC towns had plenty to grumble about. For one thing, there was almost constant low-level harassment and regular arbitrary searches. 'The military was on top of us all the time,' Gijo recalled. 'Even if you went to see your mum, you'd need all your documents. You couldn't leave the house without your papers. The police were all over us. You'd be having a beer with a few mates, and they'd be there, or they'd make you get off the bus. It happened to me several times. You couldn't do this. You couldn't do that. It was all "yes, sir" and "no, sir". We were fed up.'

That was enough to create simmering discontent, but it was the rising cost of living that triggered things, Gijo told me. 'We earned well, but prices started going up. Rice cost 10 *cruzeiros* one day, 11 the next. Milk was three *cruzeiros*, and then the next day, it was four.'[3]

The São Bernardo metalworkers had long been keen to negotiate directly with employers rather than rely on the highly convoluted official procedures dominated by pro-government union bureaucrats, in which their interests were bundled together with those of less well-organized workers from small towns and rural areas of São Paulo state. But from 1976, Lula and his fellow leaders began to press this demand with much greater audacity.

'Lula didn't follow the playbook of Paulo Vidal (his predecessor as union president). He developed his own style,' said Gijo. In short, Lula was prepared to speak with anyone to convey his point: both pro-government politicians and top executives of major companies, as well as rank-and-file workers. Rather than waste time in routine meetings with officials from the regional federation, Lula preferred discreet encounters with the heavy hitters of Brazilian industry or influential politicians such as Paulo Egydio, the conservative governor of São Paulo state who, as mentioned in the last chapter, had attended his inauguration as union president, brokered contacts with military commanders, and even helped the union build a holiday camp on the São Paulo coast. At the same time, Lula wanted to persuade his members of the justice of the union's wage campaign. *Tribuna Metalúrgica*, the union's newspaper, published the numbers to back up the union's case. Every issue showed wage levels factory by factory across the ABC towns. The prices of 28 food items – which made up the so-called basic 'basket' – were there, too. And so were the blatant injustices: the increased salaries paid to senior executives who were advocating wage restraint for those lower down, for example. As always, João Ferrador, the newspaper's cartoon character, wittily reinforced the message.

Lula didn't always manage to make this balancing act work. One leading São Paulo industrialist who met Lula at this time told me (on condition of anonymity) that Lula had been civil in conversation, but that immediately afterwards and in the hearing of the executive had publicly criticized him in an off-the-cuff speech made to workers at the same factory. 'He is a complete joker, not at all serious, and I never spoke to him again,' said the executive.[4]

But Lula was steadily building a rapport with the rank and file. Whereas other officials could sometimes become entangled in bureaucratic language and procedures, Lula was widely perceived as always retaining the same honest and direct approach with fellow workers, no matter how high he rose in the hierarchy. 'As the pressure grew from below he spoke and acted identically. It won people over,' said Gijo.

At about this time, Paulo Okamotto, a young toolmaker who had recently completed his apprenticeship at Volkswagen, was astonished to find Lula outside the factory gates, handing out copies of the *Tribuna Metalúrgica*. (Okamotto, who had begun to work at Brastemp, a manufacturer of fridges and ovens whose factory was a stone's throw from the union headquarters, would subsequently become a stalwart in the union and the Workers' Party.)

'We'd read in the papers that Lula was doing this and that. Anyway, I went to the factory one morning and there was Lula at the gate giving out copies of *Tribuna Metalúrgica*. I said to myself, fuck, the president of the union is here at the gate of the factory,' Okamotto told me in 2023.[5] 'Imagine that. The president himself [being there] first thing in the morning. I remember feeling a little bit silly: it was as if you were a big admirer of Pelé, and suddenly you're in a restaurant or something, and Pelé is there in front of you. It caught my attention. I thought to myself this guy is really something.' Okamotto had grown up seeing union bosses as unapproachable and unreachable, but here was somebody different. 'Lula was practising what he preached,' he told me. 'We had never seen this before. I thought it was impossible to see a trade union leader at the factory gate.'

SCANIA TRIGGERS A STRIKE WAVE

Arriving at the factory early on the morning of Friday, 12 May 1978, Alcides Klein, the commercial director of Scania, the Swedish lorry-maker, was surprised by the silence. Typically, there would have been an incessant clatter, but no one had turned on the machines that made that din. Scania's 3,000 workers were hanging around chatting, reading the papers, or smoking cigarettes. 'Nobody expected this. I am shocked,' Klein told Valdir dos Santos, a reporter from *O Estado de São Paulo* who was part of a bureau set up to cover the rapidly growing ABC towns. Later that day, Lula met Scania executives at the local Holiday Inn. He told them that he supported the strikers and refused to intercede. In his report, Dos Santos said that Lula 'seemed visibly nervous'.[6] It was understandable. After all, the Scania stoppage was the first strike in a decade. But the repressive climate that marked labour relations in the late 1960s and early 1970s had eased. Although the Metalworkers Congress of 1974 had been tightly policed, by 1976 the situation was changing. Union members grilled government officials attending that year's conference. Wage deals edged upwards. Ford had conceded an agreement to improve medical insurance, and Scania had just agreed to give a measure of job security to the shop-floor union.

It was the kind of reform that Lula was particularly keen to see extended because, as things were, there was nothing to stop managers from sacking the activists helping the union leadership strengthen links with rank-and-file members. As one contemporary observer pointed out: 'Experience has shown that when the union attempted to develop its activities [on the shop floor], activists were fired because they had no protection against dismissal.'[7]

The broader political moment, too, seemed favourable for the union's campaign. Following the oil price hikes of 1973 and 1974, military leaders became less confident, and relatively moderate figures, such as Ernesto Geisel, who sought a controlled return to democracy, gained prominence. The 1976 US election brought Jimmy Carter to office, and his administration was trying to keep its distance from hard-line military regimes and had begun to criticize human-rights abuses.

Even so, it was hard to read how the security forces in Brazil would respond. There were plenty of right-wingers who thought that the country should crack down on upstarts like Lula. One was General Otávio Medeiros de Aguilar, the head of military intelligence, who said, 'Lula should have been looked after a long time ago.' And there were employers, too, who favoured confrontation, such as a Volkswagen executive who thought it 'was high time rebellious workers were taught a lesson'.[8]

News of the Scania stoppage came as a surprise to Lula and his colleagues. 'It happened earlier than [we] expected,' said Walter Barelli, director of the Dieese trade union think tank, who had been in a meeting with the metalworkers' leadership that morning. 'We knew the strike atmosphere was building, but we wondered whether we were going to be thrown out, fined, or sent into exile.'[9]

The Scania strike began in the tool room, where skilled workers such as Paulo Okamotto created the implements required for the assembly line, and where management control was weakest. In April 1978, when the wage increase promised for the year was due, it had not been delivered in full. 'The whisper had gone round. We are going to stop tomorrow; we will stop. Nobody is going to work. We'll clock in as usual, but we will not turn on the machines,' a worker had told the reporter for *O Estado*.[10] Workers elsewhere were soon following suit. By the end of May 1978, 28,000 workers from 62 companies in São Bernardo do Campo and the nearby town of Diadema were on strike, including those from motor manufacturers such as Ford, Chrysler, and Mercedes-Benz. 'Everywhere the story was the same,' wrote one eyewitness. 'Workers reported for work each day, taking the company bus into the factory, eating in the canteen, and even staying in the factory during the normal overtime period. But they did not work.'[11]

By the middle of June 1978, approximately 100,000 workers from 55 companies had stopped work across Brazil. Barely a month would now pass without stoppages – everyone from teachers, hospital and bank workers to gravediggers and police officers, even the actors who specialized in dubbing foreign films were out. In Itu, a small city near São Paulo, some 2,000 pottery workers went on strike for two weeks. 'After a decade of government dictated wage deals, everyone looked to a strike to improve their life,' wrote Elio Gaspari.[12] As Lula himself recalled in 1993, a 'kind of fever had taken hold'.[13]

For years the word 'strike' had been studiously avoided by government officials; now, however, it was impossible to deny the new reality. As the left-wing social scientist Paul Singer put it: 'Not only had the stoppage established the right to strike, but also the right to meet and hold assemblies, to represent and be represented and the whole set of democratic rights that are part of a strike movement.'[14]

Over the next 24 months, the strike movement escalated. Lula had had the idea of holding the 1979 gathering at Vila Euclides – which Gijo recalled so well – just a few months before as the union leadership was preparing for another round of negotiations. In November 1978 he was with friends watching his beloved Corinthians take on the Campinas team Guarani at São Paulo's vast Morumbi stadium in the south of the city. Corinthians had won 3-2 with Socrates, the legendary midfielder well-known for his left-wing political stance, scoring one of the home team's goals. 'Seeing that sea of people, Lula had said to a friend – fuck it. The day we get a crowd of workers together even half this size, we will turn Brazil upside down.'[15]

Lula and his colleagues soon put the idea into action, persuading the mayor of São Bernardo to let them use the municipally owned football stadium for their next rally. And Lula's forecast was not far off the mark. On that wet March afternoon recalled by Gijo, Lula had barely finished speaking before workers due to start night shifts downed tools, kicking off a new round of strikes. By the end of 1979 there had been 113 strikes. According to one of Lula's biographers, 3.2 million workers had been involved.[16] During those nearly two years the union and its leader made progress. The mood was optimistic. 'There was a real fighting spirit,' recalled Okamotto. 'We knew it could be framed as a challenge to national security [and was therefore a risk] but there was a real effervescence about it. It wasn't everybody who threw shit at the dictatorship.'

Greater freedom to organize was the most significant gain. Unions were able to bargain directly with employers. Some workers also won the right to establish factory commissions, on which representatives from the rank and file, such as Okamotto, were elected. The commissions gave the union a much closer connection with the mood on the shop floor. 'What happened was that we called meetings to explain where we were with the wage negotiations. The workers of each factory elected a representative. Then we'd all meet together and discuss whether the workers were angry or not, whether they wanted to go on strike or not.'[17]

Slowly, within the trade union movement, leaders who had been pressing for autonomy from the state structures were gaining ground at the expense of more conservative colleagues. These so-called independents or autonomists began to meet regularly, challenging the prohibition of confederations.

During the strikes, unions also started to make connections with the wider community. Many workers were poor and ill-educated recent arrivals from the north-east who were already living at the limit of their means. No one expected the strikes to last long since families had no reserves to fall back on and would soon be unable to buy food or pay their energy and water bills. In 1979 and 1980 the government declared the strikes illegal and sent in troops to occupy the union's headquarters. It banned further use of the Vila Euclides stadium. In 1980 the metalworkers' leadership, including Lula, were arrested and imprisoned for offences against national security laws. Lula spent much of that year's strikes in his prison cell.

Yet the 1979 strike in the ABC towns lasted for just over two weeks, and the one in 1980 for 41 days. The union established a strike fund, which enabled it to provide its members with food parcels and assistance with their bills. Lula and his colleagues raised money by organizing concerts featuring popular singers such as Chico Buarque, a star of the New Brazilian Music (Música Popular Brasileira or MPB) scene. Above all, the union won support from the Catholic Church, in which, in the late 1970s, the influence of liberation theology doctrines was at its height. With its headquarters occupied, São Bernardo's main Catholic church, Nossa Senhora da Conceição da Boa Viagem, served as the site for regular union meetings, and the union subsequently relocated its headquarters to a church property next door. Both the São Paulo archbishop, Evaristo Arns, and the bishop of Santo André (whose diocese covered the ABC region), Cláudio Hummes, supported the strikers. Both disliked the military government. Gijo remembered Hummes ordering the police out of the church. 'He said, "Colonel, in the house of God, God decides. You can order people about outside."' Another cleric, Frei Betto, a Dominican priest, moved to São Bernardo in early 1980 and became a close friend of Lula. He lived with the family during the strike and was there when the police arrested Lula.[18]

Despite this, judged purely on economic grounds the strikes were a failure. The wage increases secured were, in the main, little better than those offered to their more passive colleagues, and frequently workers received no compensation for the days they spent on strike. And the union could do little to stop employers from dismissing strikers, so that many workers, including Gijo, lost their jobs in the aftermath of the actions. As Elio Gaspari bluntly puts it: 'They returned to work having won nothing', and as he caustically noted, 'there was no strike the following year'.[19] Some of the organizational gains proved short-lived. By 1980, most of the central features of the labour laws remained intact. It would be another eight years before even partial change came, when the new constitution removed the labour ministry's extensive powers to intervene in union affairs and relaxed the legal requirements for founding a trade union. Even today Brazilian industrial relations are bedevilled by an anachronistic legal framework, which includes at its heart the expensive and painfully intrusive system of labour courts.[20]

THE MYTH OF LULA

The strikes started something, nevertheless. It was during these actions when Lula really began to establish himself as the pre-eminent popular leader and a kind of media myth was created. Whether speaking at Vila Euclides, Samuel Sabatini Square in front of São Bernardo's town hall or anywhere else for that matter,

Lula attracted crowds. Tens of thousands of people always turned up. Researching the period of the strikes, one image stays with me. Lula, wearing a dark, open-necked shirt with a polka-dot pattern, stands and chats briefly with Djalma Bom, the union's treasurer at the time and something of a right-hand man. Lula pauses to take a drag from his cigarette and walks determinedly towards the edge of a platform overlooking the crowd gathered in São Bernardo's main square. 'Right, you all know what you have to do,' he shouts, with a downward drive of the fist that still grips the lighted cigarette. 'We have to go to the barrios, go to the bus stops and tell people that it is important they do not go to the factories.'

The footage is from 1979 and can be found in Leo Hirszman's *ABC da Greve* (shot during that year), as well as in both *Peões*, made by Eduardo Coutinho in 2004, and *Chão da Fábrica*, a trade union documentary produced in 2018. (All these films are available on YouTube.) It is a powerful image liked by these left-wing filmmakers because it showcases Lula's charisma and asserts his 'brand' as Brazil's preeminent left-wing leader.

In the films Lula's rapport with the crowd is evident. Groups of workers are constantly punctuating his speeches with choruses of 'The Workers United Will Never Be Defeated', a chant popularized a few years before during the Popular Unity government of Chile's Salvador Allende. Supporters needed no excuse to carry Lula shoulder-high out of the stadium. There was a kind of hero worship. Many regarded him in almost religious terms.

A banner filmed by Hirszman shows a roughly painted image of Jesus Christ on the left and Lula on the right and reads, 'Union is progress, and we are united. They represent the people and will never be forgotten.' 'He was a second father to me,' Joaquím de Souza Lima, a former car worker, told Coutinho in 2004. 'We had this man we admired so much to push and guide us. He was on our side no matter what.'[21]

Noting Lula's easy speaking style, the way in which he spoke "working from a few notes scribbled on the back of his hand" and the close attention with which his audience followed his words, one writer suggested a connection to the messianic traditions of his native north-east. 'Lula had been drawing on something he'd absorbed as a child, maybe through his mother, on memories of the wandering preachers and ballad-composing troubadours who worked the north-eastern interior, men who knew their audience, knew their lives, knew how to transfix a crowd and make time stand still'.[22]

Maybe, but there was also something much more contemporary about the growing buzz surrounding Lula. His compelling performances and the scale and bravery of the actions he inspired won him growing media attention, at a point when the shackles that had constrained reporters since the late 1960s were being removed. In the still buttoned-up political climate Lula was something of a phenomenon. He took little care with his appearance, guesting on TV shows in the same clothes with which he would have gone to work in. Lula's rough, occasionally ungrammatical Portuguese and directness also marked him off from the politicians who featured. So did his life story, which as Ricardo Kotscho, a journalist who went on to become Lula's spokesman noted in his memoirs, Lula was always eager to recount. Sometimes, it seemed he deliberately cultivated the image of a rebel. In January 1979, for example, against the wishes of his wife, he acquired a thick black beard. He was, wrote Kotscho, 'his own hero, [someone] without idols or models'.[23] By July 1979, Lula was important enough to warrant an interview conducted by the Brazilian edition of *Playboy*. In it, Lula appears almost deliberately to cultivate an image of political naivety. He joshes with Marisa about posing in the nude and happily confesses to having lost his virginity in a São Paulo brothel. He admits to admiring Mahatma Gandhi, Che Guevara, Mao Zedong and Tiradentes (the dentist executed for his role in Brazil's eighteenth-century independence movement), but also, somewhat bizarrely, Adolf Hitler. 'Even though he was wrong, he expressed his ideas forcefully and in a dedicated way,' he told his interviewer.[24]

An incident during the 1979 strike, when Lula was negotiating a deal and an end to strike action with an employer's representative, underlined his media fame. Cláudio Bardella, the industrialist with whom the talks had taken place, asked Lula for his autograph on behalf of his teenage son. As Elio Gaspari put it: 'It was a paradox.

The unions had lost in terms of the deal. The unions who didn't strike had done better. [But] politically, the boss's son was asking for Lula's autograph.'[25]

Lula was also quickly becoming a subject worthy of international media attention. Back in 1975, when he was elected union president, almost all mentions of the name Lula in the press outside Brazil referred to the footballer Luiz Ribeiro Pinto Neto, a winger who played for the national side. By the middle of 1978 it was the trade union leader whose name was registering with alert correspondents based in Brazil.

In June 1978, Juan de Onis, a correspondent for *The New York Times*, wrote that the strikes had made Lula 'a national figure overnight. He appears on television programs, is interviewed by national news magazines, and businessmen, politicians, and foreign labor attachés visit him.'[26] On the same day, in a despatch for the Toronto-based *Globe and Mail*, the Swedish reporter Björn Kumm noted similarly that 'Lula has made a meteoric career. He is the darling of the Brazilian mass media.'[27]

Beyond the creation of a new media celebrity, something else was also happening in these years. In the intricate and complex politics of the Brazilian left, Lula was quickly gaining ground against rival leaders as Brazil's military prepared for a return to democracy. General João Baptista Figueiredo, who became president in 1979, pushed ahead with plans to restore democracy, opening the party system and divesting the pro-military Arena and the opposition MDB of the duopoly they had enjoyed since the mid-1960s. Shortly after Lula gave his *Playboy* interview, Brazil's political exiles were allowed back into the country. Their number included the most prominent surviving left-wing politician of the 1960s, Leonel Brizola. Lula told *Playboy* that he had already begun to plan for the formation of a workers' party.

Within the trade union movement, the metalworkers' union was at the head of an increasingly influential independent – or 'authentic' – tendency, battling against the traditional pro-regime bureaucrats and the ideological left led by the Communist Party. A loose group of 'authentic' leaders were beginning to play a wider role. In August, after thousands of striking construction workers clashed with police in the city of Belo Horizonte, local union leaders asked Lula to help them advance their case. Lula and fellow *autênticos* flew into the city, met with the workers, and suggested the best way to proceed with their strike. With the state governor's blessing, they also arranged for the free distribution of milk to strikers' families. *Latin American Newsletter* astutely summed up the significance of the action. 'By discouraging the workers from further undisciplined violence, Lula and the other leaders took the risk of being accused, if the strike had failed, of playing into the hands of the government. In the event, the leaders were able to give the government a lesson in how a national workers' confederation could work, and they all emerged with their prestige greatly enhanced,' wrote its correspondent. 'It has become crystal clear that Lula will have to be taken into serious consideration by any group wishing to form a workers' party. Indeed, more and more observers believe that Lula, rather than the populist politician Leonel Brizola, will be calling the shots in the approaching power struggle.'[28]

On trips like these, Lula always attracted big crowds, unlike his more moderate and Communist Party rivals. In September he told the news weekly *Isto É*, 'Our concern is to avoid radicalization and guarantee that things remain peaceful so that there is no tightening in the political sphere.'[29] A week or so earlier, Brizola had returned from exile, perhaps hoping for an impact similar to that made by the left-wing populist leader Juan Domingo Perón in neighbouring Argentina a few years earlier. Perón, who had been in Spain since being deposed by a right-wing military coup in 1955, was greeted by vast crowds of more than three million people when he returned to Buenos Aires in June 1973 and was elected president three months later. Brizola's return was a flop, however, with no more than 3,000 people turning up to welcome him home to São Borja, a small town in the interior of his home state of Rio Grande do Sul, where both Getúlio Vargas and João Goulart lie buried. Brizola's hopes of becoming a kind of Brazilian Perón had been dashed. Lula's growing media prominence and celebrity meant that Brizola had been upstaged.

6

The Workers' Party Arrives

Gilberto Carvalho remembers 1979 as a magical time. Then 28, Carvalho, recently graduated in philosophy, had abandoned his plan to become a priest, was living in a shack in a *favela* in the southern city of Curitiba, and was training to be a welder. He was one of the organizers of the strikes that had swept through Curitiba and other Brazilian cities, and he was among those advocating the creation of a party. 'It was total immersion [but we realized] trade unionism had its limits. We needed an influence in the state, and we needed to take the next step,' Carvalho told me as he reflected on the 'fervid atmosphere' in which the Workers' Party was created. 'We believed we were going to change Brazil.'[1]

Now widely regarded as one of the party's most significant thinkers, Carvalho was a pivotal figure in the first two Lula governments as well as a senior player in the administrations of Dilma Rousseff, Lula's successor. We met in his spartan office in Brasília. Carvalho is a short, affable man who still has the air of a priest or lay preacher. And he was one of those present at the launch in February 1980 of the Workers' Party in the unlikely setting of the Colegio Sion, a private school based in the leafy São Paulo suburb of Hygienópolis.

The idea of a new left-wing party had been circulating for two years before that. The bruising industrial battles of the late 1970s highlighted the need for a fresh approach. The unions were growing; their example was encouraging workers elsewhere in Brazil, and their links with the Church and its 'base communities' had made them resilient and broadened their appeal for many in the middle class. Even so, at the end of the day – as we saw in the last chapter – they had made only modest economic gains. Many of the strikers, including Carvalho, had lost their jobs, and the institutional machinery that constrained their independence remained largely intact. As the Figueiredo government began to relax controls over party politics, Lula began to talk about a new party that could effectively represent popular interests and push forward a broader agenda change.

In July 1978, Lula told an oil workers' conference in the north-eastern state of Bahia that it was time for the workers to have their own party. One of his colleagues on the platform, Almino Afonso, a senior left-wing politician who had served as Minister of Labour in the Goulart government of the early 1960s, also liked the idea, and the two men began to meet regularly. They both thought it was essential that any new workers' party involve its grassroots much more. Giving members a voice would make the new party a very different proposition from the party launched by Getúlio Vargas and, in its most recent incarnation, led by Vargas's acolyte Leonel Brizola.

Several other left-wing activists, mainly members of a small Trotskyist party known as Convergência Socialista (Socialist Convergence), took the idea further. They had their union contacts, including Benedito Marcílio, a leader of the metalworkers in a town neighbouring São Bernardo and, in a minor way, a rival to Lula. In February 1979, at a conference organized by Socialist Convergence, Marcílio announced plans to launch a party. Lula had not been consulted and would have preferred to wait, but faced with the prospect of potential confusion, he threw his support behind it. 'The Trotskyists had forced his hand,' wrote Celso Rocha de Barros in his history of the Workers' Party.[2]

Just four months later, at a meeting at the Hotel Pampas in São Bernardo, Lula was elected its first leader. 'Union leaders who support the formation of the PT concluded that they had to participate in politics because, within the current union structure, they have already tried everything possible to improve conditions for workers and failed,' said Lula at a meeting in August 1979.[3]

In October of that year the military government's new political-party law took effect, and within weeks Lula, Carvalho, and thousands of other people had signed up as members. Soon, activists had completed the onerous paperwork required to register the new organization with the electoral authorities. In February 1980, a few days before the annual Carnival celebrations, the party was formally unveiled.

The independent or autonomous trade unionists were joined by left-wing militants and intellectuals who had either been active in or sympathetic to the fateful guerrilla campaigns of the 1960s and early 1970s but had now realized that it would be impossible to achieve radical change without building grassroots support. Perhaps even more significant, however, was a third ingredient: radical Catholics such as Carvalho. Maybe nowhere else in the world did the transition from Catholic liberation theology to left-wing Catholicism develop as powerfully as in Latin America. As Celso Rocha de Barros put it: 'The importance of the Catholic left for the Workers' Party is immense. The Catholic Church reached places where no other left-wing organization had ever set foot.'[4] Carvalho himself described the connection between left-wing politics, the 'new' unionism, and the 'base communities' as 'an incredible marriage. Make no mistake about it. For 80 per cent of people who joined the PT [at this time], it was a question of faith.'[5] Carvalho had grown up in the Catholic Church, was steeped in its traditions, and had become an enthusiastic exponent of its new radical creeds. As an altar boy from a 'very religious' immigrant family in the southern town of Londrina, he had learned the Mass by heart and become obsessed with the ritual of the eucharist and other ceremonies. 'It was all so glorious,' he told me. Growing up in modest circumstances – his father had been a cobbler and his mother a dressmaker – Carvalho had enrolled in a seminary at the age of 11 and set his heart on becoming a priest. He studied philosophy at the Federal University of Paraná and lived at the Theological College of the Pallottine Order in the nearby city of Curitiba. But it was at this point that his course in life began to change.

'There were some French Benedictine monks that were very progressive, and they helped open my mind to a different way of thinking,' recalled Carvalho. 'Next to the seminary, there was a *favela*, and I started to make friends there. I used to help them, take people to the hospital, for example, and I became aware of how their lives differed from my much more middle-class existence.'

At university, Carvalho studied Marxism as part of his philosophy courses. Even though there was censorship, writing by radical priests such as Pedro Casaldáliga, Fredy Kunz, and Carlos Alberto Libânio Christo, better known as Frei Betto, whom we encountered in the last chapter, circulated among fellow students. These were clerics who had been influenced by the French worker priests of the 1940s and whose efforts were encouraged in the 1950s by a hierarchy worried about the rising tide of secularism and the inroads that evangelical Protestantism was making. Inspired by the doctrine of St Thomas Aquinas about the 'right to rebellion', Frei Betto, who was a Dominican, supported the ALN guerrilla group, suffered two periods of imprisonment as a result, and subsequently headed the workers' mission in São Bernardo.

Originally from Spain, Casaldáliga had been a priest in Araguaia when the Communist Party of Brazil (*Partido Comunista do Brasil* or PCdoB) launched its fateful armed campaign. He had protested the military's repression and taken a beating for his pains. But it was Kunz, a Swiss priest, who had the most significant influence on Carvalho. He had survived a German concentration camp, emigrated to Canada, and then, in the 1960s, moved to Brazil, where he lived and worked in a *favela* in the north-eastern town of Crateús. *Balaam's Donkey: An Experience of a Brazilian Favela*, a book jointly written by Kunz and Joseph Bouchard and published in 1968, reflects on the biblical story of an Old Testament prophet to whom God and his angels are revealed by a talking donkey.

Carvalho bought into the story to such an extent that he not only translated it from the original French but also followed Kunz's example, opting to quit his conservative order and embrace poverty – and, like the Balaam of the allegory – conform to the supposed purpose of God.[6]

With two fellow students, Carvalho bought a shack in Vila São Paulo, one of the several improvised settlements that had grown up around Curitiba since the 1940s. 'We got rid of everything. I used to wear jeans, a T-shirt and flip-flops. It was a radical kind of poverty, but I took to it.'

The decision plunged him into grassroots politics. Carvalho remembered how he had blithely brushed aside objections both from the seminary fathers and his parents. As his father prospered with a recently launched events business, Carvalho joined campaigns to demand local authorities provide piped water, electricity, and a local clinic for his new neighbours.

These meetings of the base community would typically begin with hymns and lunch, followed by members discussing their day-to-day problems and how the Bible's teachings could help resolve these concerns. The New Testament's evangelists – Matthew, Mark, Luke, and John – were a big focus. So were Old Testament books like Exodus, which involved the search for the promised land and the idea that it might require a long period of sacrifice – a painful and uncomfortable 'long march through the desert' – to arrive there.

These scenes were repeated throughout Brazil. Frei Betto's claim that there were 700,000 such communities in the country may be an exaggeration. Still, the support of local bishops meant that in some parts of Brazil the network was dense. Late in 1978, Thiago Ryan, the Irish American bishop of the city of Santarém, told an interviewer from *O Estado de São Paulo* that 600 base communities were active in the area of the Amazon for which he had responsibility.[7]

In the ABC towns, the PT's grassroots cells in neighbourhoods and factories – which the party called their nuclei – took the same approach to organization as the base communities, sharing a similar decentralized approach and, in principle, at least, seeking to involve even the humblest recruit in discussion. The party's slogan – 'Our turn, Our voice' (*Nossa Vez, Nossa Voz*) – expressed this idea in opposition to the prevailing approach in which party organizers were simply interested in amassing votes.

The disastrous failures of the 1960s and 1970s also meant that there was a pragmatic aspect to the new party's ideas. Many former guerrillas were among those encouraging a rethink. 'I knew many comrades who were Marxists and convinced atheists, but they used to pray alongside us. It was the best way to try and build something,' Carvalho told me. The former guerrillas had abandoned their former commitment to the *foco* or 'prolonged popular war' in favour of a more patient long-term approach to change. For the more theoretically inclined Marxists, the writings of the Italian communist Antonio Gramsci were very influential. Gramsci, who died in 1937, spent the last ten years of his life in captivity, after the Fascists banned the Communist Party that he co-founded, pondering the failure of European revolutions and the rise of fascism. In *Prison Notebooks and Letters*, Gramsci argued that the states of Europe, North America, and other developed societies had established control not simply through repression, as the Russian Tsars had done, but by winning the consent of their citizens. To combat the dominant groups in these countries, Gramsci argued that they needed to place greater emphasis on the battle of ideas and establish what he called 'a cultural hegemony'. Many in the PT argued that this same approach was also well-suited to Brazil. As one of the party's founders, Francisco Weffort, put it, 'Gramsci came to save us.' In exile in Chile, Weffort had prepared for guerrilla warfare by engaging in target practice with birds. By placing Gramsci's ideas at the centre of the political debate, he believed that one could 'integrate the PT, its social movements and the emerging democratic culture without letting go of the idea of social transformation'.[8]

Another thinker who proved enormously important was the Brazilian educationalist Paulo Freire, whose ideas had influenced the Goulart administration and provided the basis for a literacy campaign that did not survive the 1964 coup d'état. Gramsci had said that education should play a crucial part in left-wing strategy. Given Brazil's high rates of illiteracy, Freire's methods seemed like a good starting point, particularly since they seemed to dovetail neatly with the work of the Church's base communities. Freire's teaching methods expressed in books such as *The Pedagogy of the Oppressed*, published in Brazil in 1968, depended on intensive and attentive teaching. In sharp contrast to the passive learning-by-rote style of mainstream schools, the student played a much more active role in Freire's classes. The starting point was the everyday words, broken down into syllables, with which they were already familiar. Freire's colleagues in the base community were enthusiastic about their method, which allowed them to teach their Bible classes more effectively. 'We were passionate about Freire and his books,' Carvalho told me. '[He] was critical because he had this idea that you can only get change by working at the grassroots. So, we developed a methodology of popular education in these movements of the church.' There was another benefit, too. In the 1970s illiterates in Brazil – then amounting to 18.7 per cent of the population[9] – were still not allowed to vote. Promoting literacy would directly help the political cause, not just by 'raising consciousness' but by harvesting electoral support. Another significant influence came from abroad. During 1978 and early 1979 the Sandinista guerrilla movement in Nicaragua stepped up its offensive against the corrupt and authoritarian regime of Anastasio Somoza. Back in the 1930s, the United States had supported Somoza, a former National Guard commander, as an alternative to César Augusto Sandino, a nationalist and anti-American revolutionary. The Somoza family had been in power ever since, gradually turning the tiny country into a fiefdom. However, after Jimmy Carter took office at the beginning of 1977, he cut aid to Somoza and pressed the dictator to reform his ways. The Sandinistas had also drawn support from the two Latin American countries that benefited most from the oil boom, Mexico and, especially, Venezuela. The neighbouring country of Costa Rica, whose leaders had long detested Somoza, offered logistical support. In June 1979 the Sandinistas launched their final offensive, and within weeks Somoza was in exile. For the first time since 1959, in the Americas, a revolutionary government had been brought to power by force of arms.

For the Brazilian left, this was important for several reasons. For those former guerrillas who had been imprisoned or tortured, it suggested that they hadn't been entirely misguided. If only, like the Sandinistas, they had linked up more effectively with other opposition groups and drawn greater international support, might they not have won too? More importantly, the Sandinista Revolution, like the Workers' Party, shared an ethical imperative rooted in the ideas of liberation theology. Many Nicaraguan clerics, including the Jesuit poet Ernesto Cardenal, had been active supporters of the guerrillas. Early in the 1980s, as Nicaragua began to rebuild its economy, Jesuit aides such as Xavier Gorostiaga had advised the young revolutionary leaders on how to do so.

I remember Gorostiaga's didactic style vividly as he explained to me (then a young correspondent covering the Central American wars for *Latin American Newsletter*) how revolutionary Nicaragua could develop a mixed economy and 'walk on four legs', balancing its dependency on the socialist countries by drawing support too from Western Europe, Latin America, and the Washington-based multilateral banks. Brazilian activists were excited by all this. News and analysis from Nicaragua circulated widely. In October 1979, Paulo Freire travelled there and assisted the new government in launching its literacy campaign. Soon, Brazilian leftists volunteered to pick coffee or work as teachers. 'Nicaragua was a beacon for us,' Carvalho told me. 'We collected money for them. We did everything that we could to help.' More importantly, perhaps, for a moment at least, Nicaragua seemed to demonstrate the possibility of a third way, between pro-American capitalism and Soviet or Cuban-style socialism.

TEETHING TROUBLES

Armed with these new ideas and perspectives, the immediate prospects for the *Partido dos Trabalhadores* seemed encouraging. Thousands of people were joining unions and as the military prepared to withdraw from the centre of the political stage, it was becoming easier to organize. The ideas of Gramsci and Freire, along with the experiences of Nicaragua and other Central American revolutions, provided new inspiration. The Brazilian economy was struggling. Oil price hikes following the 1979 Middle East War had increased the cost of imports. The military government's borrowing spree of the 1970s had left behind an enormous debt burden. Unable to repay its creditors, Brazil had been cut off from sources of fresh credit. Although it seemed the new party, the PT, might take advantage of the situation, things soon started to go wrong for it. Its financial difficulties were immense. It may have had the backing of trade unionists. However, Brazilian law forbade the unions from providing financial support, ruling out the kind of union-sponsored social democracy that had been developed in Germany, Sweden, and Britain early in the twentieth century. Activists managed to gather the necessary members to meet the electoral authority's stringent legal requirements – a remarkable achievement in the circumstances – but the PT lacked the funds to register candidates for every location and level of government. Election rules obliged voters to vote for only one party, implicitly favouring established catch-all opposition groupings such as the MDB (which became the Brazilian Democratic Movement Party – PMDB – in 1979), which already had a national network and could afford to run candidates in every state and municipality. The state provided some financial support, but only to parties such as the PMDB, which were already represented in the legislature.

Indeed, financial difficulties hobbled early campaigning. Until well into the 1990s, the PT was run from the legal offices of one of its better-off members, Ayrton Soares. To create the banner for the 1982 election campaign, Marisa Letícia, Lula's wife, personally sewed the first five-pointed red star onto a piece of cloth she had kept. 'It was completely miserable in my time,' Weffort told Rocha de Barros.[10]

At the same time, the grassroots organizations forged during the late 1970s began to show their weaknesses. Few of the neighbourhood cells worked properly. Successive conferences lamented the decline of these nuclei. As early as 1982, only 5 per cent of members participated in this kind of structure, according to one internal party document.[11]

The party's performance in the 1982 legislative and local elections was disappointing. The PT won the mayorship of Diadema, the town adjacent to São Bernardo do Campo. However, despite his rallies attracting large crowds, Lula failed in his bid to become governor of São Paulo state. Although the party won its first seats in Congress and the local state legislature, it fell well short of the number that would have allowed it to access public funding. Soon, another problem was looming large: the utopian and frequently naive visions of many activists were clashing with the practical demands of day-to-day politics.

During the 1982 campaign, the PT boasted that many of its candidates had served prison terms because of their involvement with the armed resistance. But what its leaders saw as a credential was not seen so positively by the average voter. In the Diadema city hall, the party was frequently divided, with five of the PT's six councillors often voting against the party's elected mayor. 'Conflicts between the community groups represented by the party and the municipal authorities it now controlled were frequent,' wrote Rocha de Barros.[12]

The PT administration of Fortaleza, the first large city controlled by the party, was similarly ill-starred. Maria Luiza Fontenele, the mayor, sent out leaflets to people telling them to protest against the private company that the municipality had itself contracted to provide bus services, and she was eventually expelled from the party after being accused of giving city hall jobs to her tiny faction.[13] Neither she nor Gilson Menezes, the mayor of Diadema, finished their mandates as party members, so neither municipality was much of a shop window.

Part of the problem was that, in many cases, the most active PT members also belonged to smaller left-wing parties. In the early days of the PT these small, energetic, and dedicated activist groups exercised an influence disproportionate to their size, and their loyalties were often divided. Members of such groups engaged in endless discussions about whether membership of the PT was strategic – in which case you worked to win representation in government and bring about democratic change – or merely a tactic designed to win recruits, a stepping stone in a broader plan to bring about more radical change. In other words, the members of the group had to decide whether they were committed to the PT to advance the party's long-term goals or were merely temporary passengers. Within the Trotskyist movement, whose various factions were strongly represented within the PT, this approach was known as entryism.

José Genoíno, who had survived the defeat of the pro-Albanian PCdoB's guerrilla movement and joined the *Partido Revolucionária Comunista* or Revolutionary Communist Party (PRC) in the late 1970s, told Rocha de Barros that all these tiny parties were obsessively ideological, participating in what he described as a kind of 'enlightened dogmatism'.

The PRC believed that the PT was a front or coalition and was happy to allow its members to join other parties, depending on local circumstances. As a result the PRC's members joined the PMDB in Rio Grande do Sul and Brizola's *Partido Democrático Trabalhista* or Democratic Labour Party (PDT) in Rio de Janeiro. As Genoino joked, during this early phase of its existence the PT was the only party in which all the very different socialist internationals were present: the anarchists of the first, the social democrats of the second, the communists of the third, and the Trotskyists of the fourth. 'The Brazilian political tradition of improbable consensus had crossed over into the history of socialism,' wrote Rocha de Barros.[14]

But for their critics – whose number included Lula himself – these so-called entryists were simply parasites. 'I don't understand this at all,' Lula said. 'I just want to create a party to elect deputies, elect a president of the republic, elect governors, and win elections to do [in office] what we have always dreamed of doing. Others just want to make a revolution. If a guy wants to make a revolution, they shouldn't be worried about creating a party; they'll need a fucking army.'[15]

José Dirceu, who had himself been trained in Cuba and participated in armed actions, was one of the most serious about developing a new and more hard-headed approach to electoral politics. If the party was serious about government, it needed to let people know what it planned to do once it won. It needed policies and its own programme. The failures of the 1960s and 1970s had, as Dirceu put it, 'vaccinated' the PT against groups that claimed to be vanguards and who believed in organization for organization's sake *(vanguardismo e aparelhismo)*. He proposed to unify all those sections of the party that favoured this new approach.

'At the end of the day, the dispute was about what the PT was about. The tendencies were parties inside the PT and we had to sort it out,' wrote Dirceu in a memoir published in 2018. 'Was the PT a party or a front? That was the question we were asking.' Those who signed the 'Articulation of the 113'[16] wanted a proper party. Formed in 1983, the Articulation was renamed 'Building a New Brazil' in 1995. Its members, including Lula, wanted to differentiate the party from the smaller entryist parties.[17] 'It was also a reaction to the idea of meetings for meetings' sake and excessive internal disputes that consumed so much energy and meant we had less time to connect with people.'[18]

The PT's far-left factions were unhappy about the changes, which also downplayed the role of nuclei, the party's community or grassroots groups. Even today, many of them remain as bitter as ever. In 2023, Walter Takemoto, a PT organizer from Bahia, told me that the nuclei had provided a connection with the base that no longer exists and that the party and union structures had become bureaucratized. 'The Articulation ended the nuclei. The PT no longer works with the population in the same way,' said Takemoto, whose MEP faction had gone through various fusions and name changes. Takemoto had spent most of his political career in the PT. In the 1980s, living in São Paulo, he managed first creche provision and then a municipal bus service after the PT's Erudinha da Silva became the city's mayor. Subsequently, he worked in the education sector. When I saw him, he was still a card-carrying member of the PT but, describing himself as a 'Leninist', expressed profound disillusion about the party's drift to the centre. 'There is no difference from a political and ideological point of view between [the PT's leaders and the opposition]. PT federal and state deputies make agreements with anyone.'[19]

By the mid-1980s, the PT had modernized and become more centralized, but its basic approach to politics was rooted in a purist belief in direct democracy. Members were often suspicious of elected bodies and prone to oppose the decisions of governments or other authorities. This kind of 'oppositionalism' made it a relatively marginal player in the re-establishment of democracy. PT activists had been prominent in the enormous demonstrations of 1984 and 1985 that supported demands for direct presidential elections. However, when the campaign failed to meet its immediate objective, the party's legislators refused to participate in the congressional vote, even though it ultimately led to a significant defeat for the military by bringing the democratic candidate, Tancredo Neves, to office. The party even expelled three of its eight deputies who voted for Tancredo against the military candidate. Two years later the PT won only 16 of the 559 seats in an assembly set up to draft a new constitution. The PT's representatives did play a role in drafting the final document. However, that, too, was a double-edged achievement since the approved constitution, which incorporated many ideas put forward by the PT, has since been widely criticized as being too lengthy, over-analytical, and inflexible. In any event, for Celso Rocha de Barros, the debates in the constituent assembly marked a decisive point. It was during these discussions that Lula's party finally became convinced about the need to push for change through established institutions. Rocha de Barros states that many of the PT leaders he interviewed for his book view these debates as a pivotal moment in the party's life. 'After the constitutional assembly, the PT became more comfortable about taking part in institutional life. It was what Gramsci called big politics, the dispute about general visions of society and a real opening of opportunities.'[20]

From then on the party's electoral performance improved. Further economic deterioration in the wake of a series of failed counter-inflationary plans helped the PT. By late 1988, inflation was running at a rate of 1,000 per cent a year and rising. In 1989 a two-day general strike in March shut down most of the country, and a new strike wave, similar to that of the late 1970s, got underway. The PT won control of 37 cities in the 1988 municipal elections, including three of the largest, São Paulo, Porto Alegre, and Vitória, the capital of Espírito Santo state. Its campaign for the 1989 presidential election was unexpectedly successful. It perhaps marked the high point of Lula's high-energy tub-thumping style launched ten years earlier in São Bernardo do Campo. Peter Robb, the Australian writer whose account of the campaign and the subsequent scandals that engulfed the government of Fernando Collor de Mello forms the core of his classic *Death in Brazil*, carefully watched Lula. 'Sometimes, around Brazil, he spoke to seven meetings a day. In September, fifty thousand people saw Lula in São Paulo, the biggest crowd yet. Sixty thousand in Belo Horizonte, and there was a month to go until the vote. Brizola, the honey-tongued old rabble-rouser, faded on TV. Lula, the week before the vote, drew crowds of a quarter of a million in Rio and São Paulo.'[21]

To the surprise of his supporters, Lula came second in the first round, defeating Brizola and a raft of other more established Brazilian politicians. 'At the end of the first round, the enthusiasm of PT members [Petistas] was indescribable,' wrote Rocha de Barros some three decades later. 'Leaders and activists who had never believed in a victory now faced a real possibility that Lula da Silva – only 11 years after the strike at Scania – could be elected president. Even today the chant of 'Olé Olá Lula Lula' excites Petistas. The party had beaten all the big parties with a campaign that was much cheaper . . . nothing like this had ever happened before in Brazilian politics.'[22]

With the establishment and the media empire of *O Globo* opposing him, the obstacles were considerable. Even so, amid a storm of misinformation and with a radical programme promising greater state intervention and debt default that would have frightened off many middle-class voters, Lula won 31 million votes, 45 per cent of the total. He and his party had definitively arrived.

7

The Odd Couple

As the campaign to restore democracy in Brazil gained momentum in the late 1970s, Lula began to form a close friendship with one of the country's most internationally renowned intellectuals. Fernando Henrique Cardoso participated in the first discussions that led to the formation of the Workers' Party. A few months later in 1978, Lula had thrown the weight of the Metalworkers Union behind Cardoso's successful campaign to win a Senate seat for the opposition, the Brazilian Democratic Movement (MDB), the catch-all party that united politicians opposed to military rule.

The two men campaigned together in São Bernardo do Campo, chatting with voters and handing out leaflets. 'We shared numerous long lunches, late-night *cachaças*, and no small amount of coffee,' Cardoso recalled in a 2007 autobiography. 'We became friends.'[1]

A few months later, Cardoso recommended that the Workers' Party select Lula as its leader. And in the early 1980s the two men became the most well-known leaders of the Direct Elections Now Movement (*Diretas Já*), which was pressuring the military government to allow Brazilians to directly elect their president rather than relying on a Congress dominated by military appointees.

The relationship proved to be pivotal in Brazil's modern political history. As the military ceded power to the democrats, Cardoso and Lula became famous political rivals: Lula as leader of the left-wing Workers' Party and Cardoso as chief of the social-democratic

PSDB. Twice in 1994 and 1998, Cardoso comprehensively defeated his left-wing rival, winning an overwhelming first-round triumph. Then four times, in 2002, 2006, 2010, and 2014, Lula and his designated successor, Dilma Rousseff, overcame the presidential candidates of Cardoso's party.

Cardoso, Lula, and Rousseff all depended on broad coalitions to govern Brazil, but for more than two decades the battle between Cardoso's liberal pro-market social democracy and Lula's more traditional state-centred leftism was the axis around which the country's politics turned.

In Europe and North America, these different political strands had remained within the mainstream left-of-centre opposition parties, such as the Democrats in the United States, Germany's SPD, or Britain's Labour Party. In Brazil it was as if – as Rocha de Barros suggested[2] – America's Bill Clinton or Britain's Tony Blair had attracted the support of moderate Republicans or Conservatives and headed centrist alliances whose main adversaries were left-wing parties led by a Bernie Sanders or a Tony Benn.

It wasn't surprising, though. After all, Cardoso and Lula came from radically different backgrounds. Whereas Lula grew up in obscurity and poverty, Cardoso's family was deeply entrenched in Brazil's traditional elite and played a central role in the decisive political events of the past century. His great-grandfather had been the governor of the rural state of Goiás, and both his grandfather, Joaquim Inácio Batista Cardoso, and his father, Leônidas Cardoso, had been prominent army generals. Batista Cardoso was one of the three soldiers who persuaded King Dom Pedro II to abdicate in 1889, ushering in the country's first republican government. Subsequently, as an adviser to President Floriano Peixoto, Batista Cardoso lived in the presidential palace in Rio de Janeiro. Fernando Henrique's father, Leônidas, was close to President Vargas and a deputy for the populist president's labour party (the PTB). Cardoso's great-uncle was Augusto Inácio do Espírito Santo Cardoso, who was Minister of War under Vargas. He had arrested members of his own family who had taken part in the 1932 São Paulo rebellion and had them sent to prison.

Born in 1931, Fernando Henrique Cardoso had grown up in a rarefied and elite atmosphere. Precociously, he learned to read at the age of three, soon after which he began studying French with the aid of a personal tutor and listened to political debates at his family's dinner table. He was soon taking part. As a schoolboy he was an oddity and a bit of a crank. While his schoolmates spent their time playing football, the young Cardoso preferred to write poetry and even launched a literary magazine. When he travelled from his home in São Paulo to visit his grandparents in Rio de Janeiro, he insisted – despite the sapping heat – on wearing a smart suit, waistcoat, and tie, even when going to the beach. During the Second World War – while still a teenager – Cardoso remembers 'staying up late at night listening to the radio and tracking the movements of the Allied and Axis armies on a large map in my parents' bedroom, using buttons to pinpoint troop locations'.[3]

As a university student and academic, that otherworldliness continued. As young sociologists at the University of São Paulo, Cardoso and his colleagues wore white lab coats around campus to demonstrate their scientific credentials. Researching race relations in southern Brazil, Cardoso would appear at the houses of interviewees in the same outfit, clutching a clipboard. Cardoso, however, had, through osmosis, almost adopted the same progressive nationalist politics as his father and grandfather. His grandfather had been a prominent disciple of positivism, the nineteenth-century philosophy that viewed science, rather than religion, as the solution to the world's problems.

Very quickly, though, as a budding sociologist Cardoso became increasingly aware of his country's sharp socio-economic and racial divides. Marxism held an enormous appeal. So did communism, which, Cardoso reflected more than four decades later, initially 'offered an alternative to an existing scheme that we all believed had failed. It promised to level the flagrantly unfair playing field and create a society based on need and merit.' But like many left-wing intellectuals of his generation, it was the socialism of the new left rather than the orthodoxies of the *Partidão* (the big party, the nickname Brazilians gave to the Communist Party) that exercised the most significant pull. Cardoso was 25 when Nikita Khrushchev sent Russian troops and tanks into Hungary in 1956, an act of repression that proved to be the final straw for tens of thousands of Communist Party fellow travellers.

However, as a left-wing academic at the University of São Paulo, Cardoso lived a life generally quite remote from the city's industrial neighbourhoods, where Lula grew up. Nothing perhaps epitomizes Cardoso's rarefied position more than the way that he came to national prominence for the first time. In 1960 the radical French philosopher and writer Jean-Paul Sartre and his feminist partner, Simone de Beauvoir, travelled to Cuba to meet with the revolutionaries who had seized power at the beginning of the previous year. On the way back, they visited Brazil and participated in a televised philosophical debate. When the designated translator struggled to deal with Sartre's abstract formulations, Cardoso, then 29, volunteered his services and completed the task with aplomb.[4]

Cardoso never had high expectations for the left-wing government of João Goulart, withdrawing for a while into his academic shell. However, his left-wing sympathies were well known, and as the military crackdown began he found himself a marked man. The day after the takeover, soldiers detained one of Cardoso's university colleagues after mistaking him for the sociologist. Cardoso immediately went into hiding, and within a few days friends helped smuggle him out of the country, first to Buenos Aires and then to Santiago. Based in the Chilean capital, the United Nations Economic Commission for Latin America and the Caribbean (ECLAC) had offered Cardoso a job.

In Chile, Cardoso shared a house with other prominent Brazilian exiles, among them Francisco Weffort, a political scientist who, as we saw in the last chapter, was to become one of the founders of the PT. Cardoso circulated smoothly among Chile's left-leaning political elite. He got to know Salvador Allende, who would soon become president in 1970, and taught Allende's daughter, Isabel (not to be confused with the novelist), who went on to become a significant politician in her own right. Returning to Brazil, he worked for a think tank whose efforts garnered support from the

Ford Foundation, and in 1978 he was elected a senator for the opposition PMDB party.

At this point in his career, Cardoso was very much part of the new left, distant from the old-fashioned and inflexible pro-Soviet Communist Party but very much part of a new body of more imaginative left-wing thinking represented by philosophers such as Sartre or Latin American politicians such as Allende, or even Castro and Che Guevara.

He was soon, though, to begin an academic journey that would take him into quite new political territory. As a sociologist, Cardoso gained recognition for his writings on development. His work explained the problems of poorer countries such as Brazil by the way they had become integrated with the 'metropolitan' heartlands of the United States and Europe. The idea first emerged in the 1940s during post-World War II discussions at the United Nations about Latin America. Two development economists, Britain's Hans Singer and Argentina's Raúl Prebisch, argued that Latin America's dependence on the exports of primary commodities meant it consistently lost out in its trade with the richer industrialized countries. This disadvantage arose because, the two economists claimed, in real terms, the prices of their mineral and commodity exports, such as copper or coffee, fell compared to those of the manufactured goods they imported. Prebisch, who in 1950 became the executive director of ECLAC, proposed that Latin American governments should strengthen their economies by protecting their own industries and reducing their dependency on imports. As we saw in Chapter Two, Brazil had established manufacturing along these lines since the 1930s, and for the next two or three decades many other developing country governments sought to do the same.

However, what became known as 'dependency theory' was a much more radical variant of the idea, popularized in the 1960s by Marxists such as Paul Sweezy, Paul Baran, and particularly André Gunder Frank. The radicals argued that international companies had taken advantage of the new import substitution arrangements by dominating businesses such as Brazilian car production. Gunder

Frank's *Capitalism and Underdevelopment in Latin America*, initially published by Sweezy and Baran's Monthly Review Press in 1967, was hugely popular at the time.[5]

Perhaps the most influential of Frank's followers was the Uruguayan journalist Eduardo Galeano, whose hastily written *The Open Veins of Latin America* was published in 1970. 'Latin America's backwardness and poverty are merely the result of its failure. We lost; others won. But the winners happen to have won thanks to our losing. The history of Latin America's underdevelopment is . . . an integral part of the history of world capitalism's development. Our defeat was always implicit in the victory of others; our wealth has always generated our poverty by nourishing the prosperity of others – the empires and their native overseers,'[6] wrote Galeano.

In later years, Galeano revised many of his views, but the book remains significant. As Isabel Allende, the Chilean novelist, claims in her recent foreword to *The Open Veins of Latin* America, 'That book with the yellow covers, however, proved that there were no safe islands in our region, we all shared 500 years of exploitation and colonization, we were all linked by a common fate, we all belonged to the same race of the oppressed.'[7]

These ideas carried very radical political implications. Trade and investment with rich countries was making Latin America poorer. In particular, there was a danger that by passively accepting multinational capital the region could slide into ever greater backwardness. It was only by breaking with world capitalism, as the Cuban revolutionaries had done, that it could hope to resolve its growing social and economic problems. As the title of a second Gunder Frank volume (*Latin America: Underdevelopment or Revolution*), also published by Sweezy and Baran's Monthly Review Press, made explicit, Latin Americans had to choose between underdevelopment and revolution.[8] It was a binary view of the world that blamed all the problems of poor countries on the imperialist powers, the countries that dependency theorists liked to call the metropolis. It was the reworking of an older and equally apocalyptic Marxist idea that the world faced a similarly stark choice. As the German

Marxist Rosa Luxemburg had famously put it in 1915, it was either 'socialism or barbarism'.

Cardoso was critical of this notion, arguing that the developing world's options were by no means so constrained or clear-cut. *Dependency and Development in Latin America*, which he wrote in 1969 with the Chilean sociologist Enzo Faletto, was far less dogmatic and much more nuanced than the Gunder Frank theory.[9] In a 1972 piece for the *New Left Review*, a British left-wing journal that serves as a showcase for new-left thinking, Cardoso argued that Frank's formulation of the 'development of underdevelopment' was fundamentally flawed. 'Dependency, monopoly capitalism, and development are not contradictory terms,' he wrote. Reflecting on the growth of the south-eastern so-called Tiger economies such as South Korea and Taiwan, as well as the industrialization achieved by Brazil, Mexico, and Argentina in the post-war period, Cardoso claimed that there had occurred 'a kind of dependent capitalist development'.[10]

THE ROAD TO SOCIAL DEMOCRACY

This perspective opened political ground quite distinct from the radical anti-capitalist perspective influential in academia, on the Latin American left, and with intellectuals who were to form the Workers' Party. By the early 1980s, Cardoso, who had been elected to the Senate in 1978, was now more engaged in the business of practical reformist politics. His style, language, and – indeed – his whole political approach were beginning to change. As a young student, Andrés Velasco, a Chilean economist and politician who in the 2000s became Finance Minister in the left-of-centre government of Michelle Bachelet, remembers seeing Cardoso speak at Yale University in the early 1980s to a crowd radicalized by the policies of the Reagan administration in Central America and Grenada.[11]

'His attire was the first shock. Cardoso . . . showed up wearing an impeccable blue suit, not the fatigues half the attendees were expecting,' wrote Velasco. After a short speech on Brazilian politics, a woman in a poncho asked Cardoso whether democracy could mean anything in Brazil without socialism. Cardoso replied that it did and that the issue now was how to make capitalism work. 'Students sitting at his feet stared in disbelief and soon began milling out,' recalled Velasco.

Even the milder version of dependency theory was also being seen as something of a cul-de-sac. Empirical research began to show that the terms of trade faced by developing countries did not necessarily decline. The tariff barriers or import quotas and other policies introduced to defend embryonic domestic industries from competition could work for a time. However, protection could also stifle innovation and lead to significant inefficiencies, especially during periods of rapid technological change. During the 1970s, for instance, when Brazil attempted to develop a computer industry, the effort was ultimately unsuccessful. Throughout Latin America in the 1970s, 1980s, and 1990s, overstaffed state-owned industries ran telecommunications networks that became completely dysfunctional.

By the early 1990s, Cardoso had revised his old ideas and denied that peripheral countries were doomed to develop in 'distorted' ways. 'Today we know that it is not true,' he wrote in 1995. 'Countries that were able to manage their economies sensibly . . . have had more favorable trajectories than others. The case of the Asian Tigers is well-known. . . . The level of influence of political choice over the economic structure is greater than it appeared to us in the 1960s.'[12]

At the same time, Cardoso focused more on the domestic barriers to economic development. That focus became especially sharp in 1987 and 1988 during the debates surrounding the approval of Brazil's new constitution. With the military now taking a back seat, elected representatives came under pressure to concede privileges to one group or another. In an atmosphere of what political scientists have described as a 'post-authoritarian over-reaction to the institutional framework of military rule' or 'democratic libertarianism',[13] constituent assembly members gave serious consideration to any demand whatsoever, irrespective of its practicality. 'As politicians jockeyed for favour, a new rule began to operate in Brazil: Never say "no" to anyone. . . . No matter how ridiculous the request, Congress was never able to turn it down. It reminded me of 1968 in Paris, when it was "prohibited to prohibit",' wrote Cardoso two decades later.

Cardoso acknowledged that the 1988 constitution helped 're-democratize the country'. Still, the final document was, in effect, 'a completely unrealistic wish list, guaranteeing "unrealistic rights" and creating laws and expectations that would haunt the country's politicians for years thereafter'.[14]

Part of the problem was that well-organized public-sector workers had won benefits completely out of proportion to those available to their peers in the private sector. Public-sector workers were often offered lifetime employment contracts after just two years of service and could retire in their late forties. The better off, such as top judges, academics, administrators, and soldiers, for example, were able to maintain luxurious living standards. 'These privileges were absurd, especially in a country where the minimum wage was $25 a month and half the population suffered from malnutrition,' wrote Cardoso.[15]

Brazil had long suffered from the power of economic and social elites to secure preferential access to public services. For example, resources in education were heavily skewed towards public universities, but privately educated middle- and upper-class students secured most of the places on offer. Two Brazilian historians, Sérgio Buarque de Holanda and Raymundo Faoro, suggested that private and public interests were not as clearly delineated as in the more mature democracies of Europe and North America, a phenomenon that, borrowing from the ideas of the German sociologist Max Weber, they described as 'patrimonialism'.[16]

Along with many other left-wing opponents of the military government, Cardoso had been elected to Congress as a member of the anti-military (PMDB). However, this party soon won a reputation for caring more about its access to jobs and funds than for the social reforms advocated by Cardoso and close associates such as José Serra, another former student radical who had also been exiled to Allende's Chile. Late in 1988, about 100 disaffected left-of-centre members formed the Social Democratic Party of Brazil (PSDB). This party was influenced by the kind of reformist ideas being developed by Felipe González in Spain, as well as by Bill Clinton, who took office in the United States in 1993, and Tony Blair, leader of Britain's Labour Party and prime minister from 1997 to 2007. In what came to be known as the third way between statist socialism and a conservative commitment to the free market, the PSDB – nicknamed the Tucanos (Toucans) because of the bright yellow and blue party colours – advocated a blend of free-market reform and social responsibility.

As all this was happening, Lula – who had served an unhappy and uncomfortable term as an elected congressman – was embracing a politics that was more decidedly left-wing and anti-business. For the PT, as we saw in the previous chapter, Lula's 1989 campaign was a success, reinforcing him solidly as a national figure, even though he had lost the final count to the advocate for free-market reform, Fernando Collor de Mello. Cardoso had travelled widely in Eastern Europe and the Soviet Union and had not been surprised by the collapse of socialism. He reckoned that Lula had failed to adjust to the times. Rather than looking to the markets, Lula wanted to nationalize the banks, default on overseas debt, and redistribute wealth. In his campaign speeches, 'Lula seethed with a red rage that was almost adolescent . . . Instead of mellowing with age, he had become much more radical than he had been during his union days. The gentle, sweet man I had once known now screamed and sobbed on the podium during rambling speeches about the injustices of Brazil.'[17]

TACKLING INFLATION

These differences between the two men grew even sharper in the 1990s when Cardoso played a central role in resolving a problem that had long undermined Brazil's economic performance: inflation. Inflation had first begun to rise in the late 1950s when President Kubitschek borrowed heavily to finance his ambitious public-works plans. By the time he left office, the country's foreign debt had tripled, and prices were rising at an annual rate of 43 per cent. During the following two decades, yearly price rises averaged about 40 per cent. In the 1980s, following the oil shock of the late 1970s and the 1983 debt-rescheduling agreement, the annual increase reached as much as 605 per cent. In the first four years of the 1990s it doubled again, reaching a yearly rate of 1,270 per cent.[18]

For much of this period, Brazil had learned to live with constant upward adjustments in prices. The wealthy still did OK. Businesses began to manage the changes. Accountants developed new techniques to help companies adapt to changing circumstances. Supermarket checkers grew accustomed to frequently changing price stickers. Banks made huge amounts of money simply by delaying transfers of electricity or water bills paid by their customers for a few days. 'In a stable country, such a delay would be insignificant,' wrote Cardoso. 'But in Brazil, with inflation running as high as 80 per cent per month, it was an absolute scandal. At that rate, a bank could pocket an easy 8 per cent profit in real terms by waiting just three days to make the transfer, since the money was losing its value at such a rapid pace.'[19] Up to a quarter of bank profits – billions of dollars every year – came from this manoeuvre.

But there were some huge costs. Inflation made corruption much easier since balance sheets were so unreliable that a little missing cash usually went unnoticed. Moreover, investors, especially from outside Brazil, were less likely to commit money to a country where nobody could predict what assets would be worth in a year or two's time. Those in the formal economy – like property owners or trade unions – could protect themselves by indexing contracts such as wages and rents to price rises. But the poor, whose only asset was the cash in their pocket, were plunged into even deeper poverty. It was no coincidence that the period between 1980 and 1994 was a bleak period for the economy. Brazil was cold-shouldered by investors and cut off from banks and capital markets. The economy stagnated, and the poor grew poorer.

In the 1980s fiscal and external deficits were a constant concern. Monetary instability was chronic, with the Central Bank regularly printing money to cover spending commitments. Under José Sarney, the vice-president-elect who took over as president in 1985 following the unexpected death of Tancredo Neves, Brazil introduced one currency after another in unsuccessful efforts to engender confidence. The country transitioned from the *cruzeiro* in 1986 to the *cruzado* in 1988, followed by the even more short-lived *cruzado novo* (1989–90). It was all to no avail.

With national economic anxieties mounting, Brazil turned to an iconoclast for salvation. Fernando Collor de Mello came to the presidency in 1989, promising to slay the 'inflationary tiger' with a single shot. Collor de Mello, a young conservative politician from the impoverished north-eastern state of Alagoas, epitomized the free-market enthusiasm that had grown in the wake of the collapse of socialism in Eastern Europe and the growing stresses of the Soviet Union. Tall, handsome, and rich, Collor wore expensive double-breasted Italian suits, smoked 12-inch Cuban cigars, and had a penchant for riding motorbikes and piloting jet aircraft. He was a figure who seemed as if he had walked out of one of the soap operas that the Globo TV network had made famous.

Collor promised to sort out Brazil's problems with a dose of liberal shock therapy, opening protected sectors to competition and selling off state companies. He slashed tariff barriers, froze bank accounts, brought in yet another new currency – the *novo cruzeiro* in 1990 – and sacked thousands of civil servants. Prices initially fell, but without congressional backing Collor's reforms soon ran into obstacles.

In classic populist fashion, Collor was long on rhetoric but short on practicalities, always eager to scapegoat others – Congress, business, civil servants, or trade unions – for the failures of his ill-conceived and poorly executed plans. To paraphrase one foreign correspondent's assessment at the time, Collor would announce a deadline, provoke a confrontation, declare victory, and then hastily move to the next problem.[20] Sure enough, with confidence depressed and the economy sinking into recession, the inflationary 'tiger' was soon on the prowl again. By February 1991 – with the

Plano Collor less than a year old – prices were rising by 20 per cent a month.[21] When the middle class eventually got their money back out of their frozen accounts, the value of their savings had been significantly eroded, and opposition was growing.

Appropriately though for a man whose presidency resembled a melodrama, the denouement of Collor's presidency was triggered by family rivalries. In a sensational series of interviews, his younger brother Pedro Collor had accused him of benefiting from a multi-billion-dollar graft scheme. In June 1992, a week before the first revelations were published, Collor – without a trace of irony – told *The Financial Times* that Brazil had 'caught the last train to modernity'.[22]

Within days, though, Collor's train had come off the rails. Thousands of Brazilians, who had flocked to vote for this celebrity president three years before, took to the streets, painting their faces black or in the national colours of yellow and green. By August 1992, Collor's disapproval ratings stood at 84 per cent. Congressmen seeking to capitalize on the president's growing unpopularity launched impeachment proceedings. By the end of the year, however, Collor had resigned, leaving only 24 hours before the Senate voted 76 to 3 to ban him from public office for eight years. During his three years in office, economic output per capita had declined by 10 per cent. Ever given to hyperbole, Collor flanked by his wife Rosane and his lawyers denounced the Senate ruling as a 'summary execution' and blamed Brazil's business class for mounting a 'coup' against him. 'I am a victim of a campaign without precedent in the history of this nation. I have been publicly lynched,' he claimed.

THE *PLANO REAL*

Cardoso had initially been sympathetic but had kept his distance from Collor, and now he came to the centre of the political stage. Collor's deputy, Itamar Franco, who acceded to the presidency in December 1992, first asked Cardoso to take over the Ministry of Foreign Affairs and then, within a few months, offered him the job of Finance Minister, a position that many consider, even at the best of times, to be the most testing in Brazil. In 1993, with prices rising at an annual rate of 2,500 per cent, it was, to say the least, a formidable challenge. The speed of price rises dominated daily life in a way that was difficult to imagine for people who had not lived through it. Businesses and public-sector officials spent all their time administering their budgets. On payday, consumers lined up outside supermarkets, desperate to spend their money before it lost value. Cardoso's three immediate predecessors had survived only a matter of weeks, before they were burned up in what Cardoso himself described afterwards as 'an economic hell'.[23]

To determine what to do, Cardoso assembled a powerful team of economists. As they began to meet in 1993, the omens were not good. President Franco had a weak mandate. As the former deputy of a deeply unpopular president, he was now effectively a lame-duck leader whose term was due to end within 18 months. Lula was now waiting in the wings. He had criticized Collor from the outset, claiming in 1990 that his promises were illusions and dreams, and he had been proved right. What's more, he was way ahead in the opinion polls. After the failures of no fewer than six previous adjustment plans since 1986, business leaders were sceptical and saw no reason why another one would be any more successful. As Edmar Bacha, one of Cardoso's new economic team, put it, 'the mood of Brazil's economic elite was one of total incredulity that an effective anti-inflation policy could be implemented during President Itamar Franco's half-term'.[24]

Two of the measures that formed part of the *Plano Real* – budget cuts and the introduction of a strong new currency – had been tried before and failed. The new team was unwilling to accept the advice of the International Monetary Fund (IMF), which essentially amounted to much more aggressive reductions in public spending. Instead, during a series of late-night meetings, Cardoso's team engineered an innovative approach.

The plan contained some features typically associated with adjustment efforts elsewhere. The central bank would support the new currency. Interest rates would have to remain high for some time. Public spending would be cut. Cardoso persuaded congress to sacrifice control of a R$15bn in constitutionally earmarked spending. But in sharp contrast to the plan adopted by Collor and reforming presidents elsewhere, the architects of the Real plan emphasized the importance of complete transparency. Surprises – such as Collor's unexpected decision to freeze bank accounts – were to be avoided. Spending reductions had to be politically realistic. Above all Cardoso's team emphasized the importance of winning public confidence, preparing the population for change and gradually shifting expectations. For four months from March to the end of June 1994, a unit of account – the unidade real de valor (URV) in Portuguese – would be introduced alongside the actual currency, which was the *cruzeiro real*, following the most recent currency reform of 1993. The value of the URV would be indexed daily to the US dollar. During this transition period, all contracts, from wages to rents and school fees, would gradually be switched into the new unit of account. On 1 July the URV would be replaced by the new currency, to be known simply as the *real*, and the old currency, the *cruzeiro real*, would be withdrawn. In short, the architects of the *real* needed people to become familiar with the steadier value of the new currency before it was introduced in bills and coins. It was an ambitious experiment and something of a gamble. In Cardoso's own words, it was a 'combination of half-measures and wishful thinking . . . a kind of permanent work in progress'.[25]

Cardoso doubled down on his gamble by resigning from the Ministry of Finance to contest the October election a few weeks before the actual launch of the new currency. At the time he was well behind in the opinion polls, but the plan's impressive initial successes soon boosted his standing. During the second half of 1994, inflation, which had been running at nearly 5,000 per cent a year in June, was down to 916 per cent. In 1995 prices rose by only 22 per cent. Every month the rate fell from an average of 43 per cent in the first half of 1994 to 3.1 per cent in the second half of the year and 1.7 per cent in 1995. In real terms, wages started to rise. The poor, who had suffered the most from high inflation, benefited the most, with the worst-off 30 per cent of the population seeing an increase in their incomes of more than 9 per cent. Despite high interest rates, the extra spending power helped businesses increase sales and the economy started to pick up.

The improvement was dramatic. Cardoso wrote later that 'it was like living in a different country'. And the mood of confidence soon began to affect the election campaign. At Cardoso's rallies, supporters started waving the newly issued real notes. Lula had condemned the plan, which, he insisted, 'would only cause more misery' and continued to disparage the new currency despite all the visible evidence. 'The Real is not a dream,' he declared. 'It is a nightmare! It is based on massive propaganda that says the workers are going to be in heaven if inflation falls. That's just not going to happen. This plan will only freeze the misery in Brazil!'[26]

Cardoso had tried to win Lula round to the new approach but found his old friend unresponsive. 'Lula was less interested in economic consequences of the success of my plan for his voters than that it might bring political defeat to him,' wrote Cardoso. 'I was deeply disappointed with Lula, for I believed that he was placing his interests above those of the country. He knew that if the economy were in bad shape, the instability would bolster his campaign. Five years would pass before I had another significant, face-to-face conversation with Lula.'[27] By then Cardoso was well into his second term as president, having inflicted two overwhelming defeats on his rival. Although new financial problems were looming, inflation was no longer at the core of everyone's concerns. Brazil was living a new reality, and Lula was beginning to change his tune.

8

The Tide Turns

In the Spring of 1998, as a journalist at *The Financial Times*, I began travelling regularly in the region. Since I had last worked there as a correspondent in Central America in the early 1980s, the mood had changed dramatically. Rather than wars and revolutions, the Latin Americans I met were discussing privatizations, foreign investment, and social reform. One by one the military dictatorships that had seized power in most countries had been replaced by elected governments. The collapse of socialism in the Soviet Union and Eastern Europe had left the United States and its model of free-market capitalism very much in the ascendant. From Argentina and Mexico to Bolivia, Peru, and Venezuela, governments were seeking to sell off state companies to private investors. In these first few months, however, there were occasional glimpses of the changes that were on the horizon.

Almost on my first day on the job, I met Venezuela's Hugo Chávez, who was to become one of the most radical Latin American leaders of the so-called Pink Tide of the 2000s. But as we drank tea together late one May afternoon high up in an executive room at the then *Financial Times* headquarters in London, he was a rank outsider in an election that was due to take place at the end of the year. When I went to Caracas a few weeks later, I remember meeting the commercially minded executives of the state-owned oil company, who had no inkling of the dramatic change in fortunes that would befall them when Chávez was elected to office in

December. Other leaders I met at this time, such as Ernesto Zedillo of Mexico, Carlos Menem of Argentina and Gonzalo Sánchez de Lozada of Bolivia, were market-friendly reformers, looking to implement their version of the so-called Washington Consensus of reforms designed to make markets work more effectively and increase the low savings and productivity rates that were seen as the principal obstacles to democratic prosperity.

Fernando Henrique Cardoso was of the same ilk. Chile began its privatizations in the 1980s under the Pinochet dictatorship. Peru, Mexico, Argentina, Venezuela, and Brazil had followed suit in the 1990s. Brazil's sell-off had begun modestly under Collor, but in 1997, Cardoso's government privatized the large state-owned mining company, then known as CVRD (Companhia Vale do Rio Doce) – now Vale. In August 1998 I recall writing a story for the *FT*'s weekend edition about the $19 billion sale of the telecoms company Telebras. It was one of the largest sell-offs in the world and was seen as a symbol of the liberal transformation then underway. During my first trip to Brazil in July of that year, Cardoso was still enormously popular due to the achievements of the *Plano Real*.

Lula was still a candidate for the upcoming October 1998 elections, but the political commentators I spoke to saw the result as a foregone conclusion. Cardoso's lead in the opinion polls had shrunk to seven points briefly in June 1998, but for the most part he enjoyed a comfortable double-digit advantage. Just as in 1994, neither of the other major parties that had fought against the dictatorship – Brizola's PDT and the PMDB – bothered to put up candidates. As a news story, the election was something of a non-event, with Cardoso cruising to a first-round victory with 53 per cent of the vote compared to 32 per cent for Lula. It was a narrower margin than in 1994, but it still represented a comprehensive and humiliating defeat for the PT leader. On three occcasions Lula had put himself forward as a presidential candidate, and three times the voters had rejected him.

On the surface, things could not have been more promising for the market-friendly social democracy that Cardoso represented. However, even before the October election, cracks had begun to appear, and by early 1999, Cardoso found himself in the middle of a full-blown financial crisis.

The difficulties were twofold. First, the *Plano Real* had tamed inflation by linking Brazil's new currency to the dollar, a move that occurred during a period of great optimism among investors. The plan had succeeded in shifting expectations, and for a time capital flooded into Brazil. However, the country had not been able to bring a large fiscal deficit under control. Indeed, by sharply raising interest rates to keep prices low and defend its currency, the government had increased the cost of servicing the debt it owed to domestic institutions.

Second, the mood in international markets had begun to shift. For much of the decade, investors had been ebullient and triumphalistic. Some commentators were now blithely assuming that a rising global capitalism, led by powerful new multinational investment banks, would sweep all before it.

This notion was less outlandish than it now seems in retrospect. In the 1980s and early 1990s changes in the way financial markets functioned had underpinned investor confidence. Until the late 1970s, governments in developed countries had retained control over domestic capital markets, either through taxation policies, as in the United States, or systems of exchange controls, as in the United Kingdom, Japan, and continental Europe. To obtain funds from abroad, governments and large companies had been dependent on syndicated lending by international banks (where banks join forces to contribute to a large loan) and to a limited market in so-called Eurobonds (effectively international bonds denominated in dollars) established in the City of London that was free from national regulation. The US, Japan, Britain, and much of the rest of Europe abolished capital controls in the 1980s. The liberalizing Reagan and Thatcher administrations of America and Britain fuelled the pace of change by removing many restrictions, propelling the growth of international capital markets.[1]

With capital more mobile, countries were no longer so dependent on their national savings for investment. They could look to exploit on other economic strengths, such as dynamic manufacturing bases (as in the case of Southeast Asia) or their wealth of minerals, oil, or food products (as in the cases of Latin America and Africa). What's more, in the 1980s, the United States had set an example. Even though its savings rates were falling, and the government had been running large deficits, it had been able to grow the economy by importing capital.

Liberal economists in Latin America and elsewhere in the developing world now saw the more widespread availability of capital as offering potential opportunities for them as well. During the 1980s, Chile and Mexico had begun to open their economies to foreign investment and started to privatize. Under President Menem, Argentina followed suit. In Brazil, Collor had pursued a similar strategy. Now Fernando Henrique Cardoso was trying to do the same. In the Spring of 1998, there seemed every chance that on the back of the well-executed *Plano Real*, he would succeed.

As a reporter at the *FT* in the mid-1990s, I had become aware of how fragile this process could be. One afternoon before Christmas in 1994, Mexico, which had controlled high inflation by tying its *peso* to the dollar, was suddenly hit by frenzied selling of its dollar-linked bonds, as investors no longer felt confident that the country could meet its interest payments. By the turn of the year, the newly elected government of Ernesto Zedillo was dealing with a dramatic devaluation and had to slash spending to restore some stability.

In the second half of the 1990s these kinds of crises became more commonplace, partly because as the United States began to increase its interest rates, the attractions of holding high-yielding assets in Russia, Brazil, or Thailand began to pale. Starting in 1997, one country after another came under pressure. First Thailand, then Indonesia, then South Korea and in the summer of 1998, Russia. Everywhere, the story was similar. Currencies pegged to the dollar came under speculative pressure as investors took fright. Each of these crises sent shivers through all emerging markets. The way fears spread from one emerging market to another reflected the way institutional investors, such as pension funds and life insurance companies, operated.

They viewed their holdings in Asian, Latin American, and East European securities as part of a category or class of emerging market assets that moved in tandem. As a Deutsche Bank executive told me in August 1998, 'When things go badly in Asia, you don't buy Latin America, you sell it.'[2]

In other words, investors who had lost billions of dollars in Russia were more likely to cut their losses by selling other high-risk investments than expose themselves to the possibility of further losses. During that July trip to Brazil, I had met Cardoso's Central Bank chief, Gustavo Franco, an economist who had been one of the architects of the *Plano Real*. He had told me how this 'financial contagion' was making his job harder. 'People in Brazil may never have heard of Indonesia, but it is affecting us,' he said. Market turmoil in Asia and elsewhere was presenting Latin America with 'new and disturbing pressures'.[3] In the wake of Russia's default and devaluation in August, Brazil became the focus of concerns. A couple of weeks afterwards, I recall interviewing one Friday afternoon the then Mexican Finance Minister, José Ángel Gurría. As the losses spread from Brazil and Argentina to Mexico and elsewhere in Latin America, we watched together as a sea of red light spread on the bank of Bloomberg screens perched on his desk. Investors were rushing to sell. Stock market declines were so great that so-called circuit breakers were triggered, and market authorities in several countries suspended trading. The emerging markets seemed to be in the midst of a complete meltdown.

Back in Brazil, the political mood was changing. Cardoso secured his election victory in October 1998 and used his authority to relaunch a programme of fiscal reforms in a bid to restore confidence. But he met intense opposition from Congress and Brazil's powerful state governors. In December, with investors panicking about the growth of the government's deficit, Cardoso proposed that the best-paid government workers should make higher pension contributions. This measure would have generated R$5 billion in revenues and cemented an agreement to draw down money from the IMF. The government got little support for its cautious approach. Representatives of the PT and other left-wing parties viewed such proposals as neo-liberalism. Other members of Congress were happy to defend their interests, and the Chamber of Deputies voted down the proposal by a margin of 205 to 187. The next day, the São Paulo stock market fell by another 10 per cent. 'The vote was read correctly,' said Cardoso in his biography, 'as a sign that Brazil was not willing to swallow the tough medicine of fiscal austerity.'[4]

As we put it in the introduction to a *Financial Times* special survey on Brazil published ten days before the inauguration of his second term at the beginning of 1999, 'Cardoso's new administration [was] looking a little bedraggled even before it [had] officially begun.'[5]

Early in January 1999, Brazil plunged into another crisis. Shortly after Cardoso was sworn in as president for his second term, the governor of Minas Gerais announced that his state was bankrupt and was defaulting on its debt of $13.5 billion. Fears that the federal government would have to pick up the tab led to another sell-off, and with money leaving the country at a rate of $1 billion a day, Cardoso had no option but to devalue.

Gustavo Franco, the Central Banker I had met again a month before, had left as soon as the exchange-rate mechanism he'd designed – what economists call a crawling peg – proved unsustainable. His immediate replacement, Francisco Lopes, a Central Bank official who had opted for a slightly more flexible version of the same scheme, proved to be ill-adept at easing the worries of investors and the currency was eventually allowed to float. At the beginning of February, Cardoso controversially invited Armínio Fraga, a former Central Bank official who had been working in New York for the previous six years, to take over.

It was a difficult moment, and the initial omens were not auspicious. At the end of January 1999, amid rumours of a debt default, the currency had dropped to R$2.15 against the dollar, a 79 per cent decline over the previous two and a half weeks. There were also rumours that the government was about to freeze bank accounts, and some Brazilians, mindful of what had happened less than a decade before, started to queue up outside banks to withdraw their savings.

As we wrote from São Paulo at the beginning of February 1999, Brazil was 'showing the early signs of financial meltdown. What began as an attempt at a controlled devaluation is turning into a panic.'[6]

SHOCKS AND REFORMS

Reflecting on this period a decade later, Cardoso insisted that the strength of political opposition had thwarted his plans to gradually transform the economy's structure, above all by making the state work more efficiently. He was far from an advocate of the kind of shock therapy that had been tried on various occasions over the past decade or so in Russia, Eastern Europe, and most notably, perhaps in Latin America, in the poor republic of Bolivia, Brazil's neighbour to the west. Towards the end of 1985, the newly elected Victor Paz Estenssoro (his third term) closed 17 of Bolivia's 21 mines overnight, throwing 21,000 of the country's 26,500 miners out of work. The country's population was then approximately six million, and when the government cut spending and reduced subsidies, nearly 10,000 other public-sector workers lost their jobs.

Bolivia's problems had been considerable. During 1985 inflation was running at 24,000 per cent a year, and people began to contract eye infections from the mites that inhabited the enormous blocks of *peso* notes needed to pay for the simplest item. Shock therapy certainly brought inflation down. However, it didn't yield long-term solutions to the country's problems. In fact, in Bolivia, the shocks produced new and ever more complex problems since thousands of the sacked miners migrated to the countryside, where they started to grow coca leaves, contributing to the early growth of the cocaine trade, which to this day continues to undermine stability across the region.

Nevertheless, as Brazil grappled with its problems more than a decade later, some of the government's critics argued that similar drastic surgery was exactly what was needed. In January 1999, Paulo Leme, a Brazilian economist working for Goldman Sachs, then the most powerful of the new investment banks, was in the country to recommend Brazil take 'measures that can have a big impact'. Leme and Goldman Sachs eyed Brazil's crown jewels, arguing that the sale of the state oil company Petrobras and the two publicly owned banks, Banco do Brasil and Caixa Econômica, would raise significant sums and send a message to investors that the country was serious about tackling its problems. 'The Brazilian government has two options to confront the crisis. Either it accepts the challenge and takes audacious measures, or it succumbs.'[7]

Measures like that were unlikely to command political support, however. During an earlier phase of the crisis, Leme had suggested that Cardoso should assume decree powers and ignore Congress, following in the footsteps of the Venezuelan leader Rafael Caldera, even though that experiment had ended in a landslide election victory for Hugo Chávez a few months later.[8] Cardoso rejected these options. 'The irony of my being so widely labelled a neoliberal in Brazil was that my reform agenda often did not move fast enough to please the IMF or the World Bank,' he wrote later.[9] 'I found myself explaining on numerous occasions that I was not a dictator.'

Indeed, six months before the end of his second term, in an interview with *The Financial Times*, Cardoso distinguished the more radical liberal reforms introduced by Argentina in the 1990s from the more moderate approach taken by the Chilean government during the same period. Argentina, said Cardoso, had sold virtually all its state companies, whereas in Chile and Brazil the reform process had been much more modest. 'Brazil has left key banks and oil companies in state hands. There was never any chance of neo-liberalism here. Brazil is a relatively poor country, and the state will always play a crucial role in mitigating social disparities. We liberalized, but we didn't make a clean sweep of everything that existed before. In Brazil, state spending has increased as a percentage of economic output.'[10]

Nevertheless, the set of measures introduced by the Cardoso government in 1999 was radical enough. For many critics the choice of Armínio Fraga as the new president of the Central Bank suggested Brazil had submitted to the dictates of the international markets. Born in Rio de Janeiro, the son of a dermatologist, Fraga grew up in a well-off family, studied economics at the conservative Catholic University in the same city, and earned a doctorate at Princeton University. He had worked as head of international affairs at the Central Bank under Collor, where he had overseen debt-restructuring talks with government and private creditors, as well as helping negotiate a deal with the IMF.

But Fraga had spent most of the last six years working in New York for none other than George Soros, whose hedge fund was one of those many blamed for the travails of the emerging markets during the late 1990s. For the previous 18 months – until the end of January 1999, in fact – Fraga had been in the eye of the storm, managing the $1.8 billion Quantum Emerging Market Growth Fund.

Even before formal confirmation of his appointment in March 1999, Fraga was busy, initially as an informal adviser to Pedro Malan, the Finance Minister. Opposition politicians were furious, seeing Fraga's appointment – straight out of Soros' office – as evidence of the government's complete subjugation to American interests. 'We are going to have to improve our English a little bit, but it will be useful for negotiations,' said Itamar Franco, the former president and then governor of Minas Gerais whose debt default had triggered the latest phase of the crisis in January. Antônio Carlos Magalhães, the governor of the north-eastern state of Bahia, was probably the most powerful conservative politician in the country and had become an essential ally of President Cardoso. But he, too, lashed out at the influence of 'speculators', describing them as 'greedy economic agents, run by financial institutions, who are acting irresponsibly and criminally to devalue the real'.[11]

For the left, of course, Fraga's appointment was anathema. 'For the last four years, his job has been to maximise the profits of a mega-fund. Is he the right person to judge how to preserve the stability of the currency?' asked Eduardo Suplicy, a senator for the PT.[12] Lula, too, was quick to condemn the appointment, arguing that Lopes' sacking showed that the Central Bank had been 'completely under the control of international loan sharks'. Brazil had given up its sovereignty by asking this 'citizen, an employee of the mega-investor George Soros, to direct the Central Bank', chided Lula. 'Fernando Henrique has shown himself to be weak, impotent and submissive to international bankers. It is embarrassing. The president is only interested in getting external credibility back so that they can raise money abroad and Brazil can pay them back what it owes.'[13]

At Lula's side was his long-time economic adviser, Guido Mantega, a left-wing economist who – as Finance Minister in Lula's second administration and in Dilma Rousseff's government – was to become something of a bête noire among financial-market investors. Echoing a cliché heard from across the political spectrum in the previous few days, Mantega said the government had 'put a fox in charge of the chicken coop. The replacement of Lopes by Fraga Neto is a disaster for the country.'[14]

Fraga seemed to have an immediate impact, and things began to calm down. Part of the reason, though, was that the bank raised overnight interest rates to an astronomical 45 per cent, making it more attractive to hold the local currency. Under Francisco Lopes' short stint at the Central Bank, the rates had been increased to over 30 per cent, although the process of setting them remained complicated. The Central Bank began to simplify the process of bringing capital into Brazil. Fraga, Malan, and their teams worked closely with the IMF, which had shored up the country's accounts with a $41 billion emergency loan. The exchange rate was floating, but to reinforce confidence in June the government introduced an inflation-targeting regime, establishing strict annual targets for price rises along the lines successfully deployed in the late 1980s and 1990s, first in New Zealand and then in Great Britain, Israel, and Chile, among other countries.

In addition, there were targets for the fiscal deficit, with the government committed to raising enough money from taxes and other revenue sources to comfortably meet its debt obligations. If necessary, so-called primary spending – that which took place after the government had paid its interest bill – would be cut to the bone to balance the books. The overall arrangement – known in Brazil as the *tripé* (or tripod) – was seen as providing a more sustainable alternative to the foreign-exchange pegs that had initially, but as it proved rather precariously, underpinned stability within developing countries in Asia and Latin America in the 1990s. In short, Brazil, like Mexico, would replace the foreign-exchange anchor with one based on deep fiscal adjustment. Fraga had also quickly established a rapport with investors and creditors, persuading banks to maintain trade credit and inter-bank lines.

By mid-March, when investors and Latin American ministers were in Paris for that year's annual meeting of the Inter-American Development Bank, a modest revival of confidence was evident. By April, Brazil had raised $1 billion on the international capital markets, and the *real* was strengthening against the dollar. For Cardoso, the worst was over. The country had survived 'the most intense speculative attack' in its history, and the *Plano Real* was still intact.

For the next two years, the markets could not get enough of Brazil. 'Once a near-pariah, Brazil has become a market darling thanks to tough fiscal measures,' began a November 2000 piece by the *Institutional Investor*. Credit agencies such as Moody's and S&P began upgrading their ratings. Foreign direct investment reached a record $30.5 billion in 2000. 'Not even the most optimistic analyst could have predicted this recovery,' said one observer.[15] Even so, although the headlines focused on Brazil's rehabilitation, at the grassroots and in the more remote corners of Brazil, the policies of monetary and fiscal austerity were taking a heavy toll.

The bank gradually lowered rates, but between 1999 and 2001 they remained above 15 per cent. That helped keep inflation under control, but it also meant that businesses and consumers found credit prohibitively expensive. Through tight controls on spending, Pedro Malan, the Finance Minister, and his team got public accounts into shape. In 1999, Brazil achieved a primary surplus of 3.1 per cent of GDP, and the approval of a fiscal responsibility law in May 2000 brought greater discipline to the local governments of states and municipalities, which had been notorious for overspending, especially on payroll. But job cuts contributed to mounting unemployment in the late 1990s. Wage levels stagnated after 1995. 'Brazil's citizens aren't cheering their president nearly as loudly as the financial markets are,' noted the *Institutional Investor*. 'Cardoso's approval ratings hover at about 23 per cent, less than half what they were when he was elected [two years previously].'[16]

This malaise deepened a year later when prolonged electricity shortages hit Brazil. At least 85 per cent of power came from the giant hydroelectric dams built by the military government in the 1960s and 1970s; however, sparse rainfall had left the dams at very low levels, and by May 2001 managers were regularly closing down about a third of public lighting and beginning to ration electricity.

In one way the crisis, which was to last until the first half of 2002, was a matter of bad luck. There was nothing the government could do about the weather. However, problems had been building for some time, exposing some of the shortcomings of the government's economic approach. The debt crisis in the early 1980s had cut off foreign financing for the sector, while the fiscal problems that came with rampant inflation in the late 1980s and early 1990s constrained the state's ability to invest. The deregulation of the Brazilian energy sector had been a halfway house that pleased neither supporters nor critics. While most electricity distribution companies were sold off, primarily to American and Spanish companies, the bulk of generation capacity – where most new investment was needed – remained in public hands. Plans to sell off big generators fell victim to political disputes. At the same time, the fiscal austerity drive, agreed upon and painstakingly monitored by the International Monetary Fund, had tied the government's hands and prevented it from making the necessary new investments. Transmission, too, remained inadequate.[17]

The crisis in power generation further hit the government's popularity, denting its hard-won reputation for competence. Power cuts became so widespread and prolonged that they featured in the popular soap opera *Porto dos Milagres* (*Port of Miracles*), further reinforcing the sense of crisis.[18] The shortages added to pressures on the job market, and by 2001 unemployment began to rise. In the second half of that year, sales of consumer durables and cars collapsed. September was the worst month since 1994. Fiat, Scania, and Daimler put workers on short time. Volkswagen sacked a fifth of its workforce. Sales of fridges and cookers – whose buoyancy had been emblematic of the Cardoso government's success – dipped by more than 50 per cent. Philips sacked a third of its workforce. Brastemp, the local company where Paulo Okamotto had worked in the 1970s, finally closed its plant in São Bernardo do Campo, resulting in the loss of 1,000 jobs. According to Mario Pochmann, labour secretary in the PT municipal administration of São Paulo, the unemployment rate in the city had climbed to more than 17 per cent, leading him to warn that Brazil faced a depression as severe as that which hit the United States in the 1930s. Small businesses were in no position to fill the gap. 'What we are seeing now is small and micro-businesses either letting people go or shutting down altogether,' wrote Lucilene Cardoso, the boss of Vidraçaria Copa Leme, a glassware outlet then based in the Botafogo district of Rio de Janeiro, in a letter to a local business newspaper. 'I have been at this company for 17 years, and I have never seen so many people closing their doors because of the economic crisis. It is such a big crisis, and the electricity rationing is making things worse.'[19]

Outside Brazil, President Cardoso enjoyed a reputation as a successful 'third-way' leader in the style of Bill Clinton or Tony Blair. Armínio Fraga and Pedro Malan were still popular figures among the world's financial elite. But at home the problems were mounting. In local polls, Lula was capitalizing on the economic dissatisfaction and building a steady lead. On his path to the presidency over the next 12 months, however, as we will see in the next chapter, he stumbled into a new and even bigger crisis.

9
2002: A Decisive Year

At 2.30 on Friday afternoon, 1 March 2002, eight federal police agents drove up to a four-storey building in a plush neighbourhood of the north-eastern Brazilian city of São Luís. For the next few hours the officers rummaged through documents belonging to Lunus, a property company that had been set up by the husband of Roseana Sarney, the state's conservative governor and a candidate for the upcoming October election. Attractive, glamorous, and wealthy, Sarney was running neck and neck with Lula in opinion polls and was seen as well-positioned to win the upcoming presidential election.

However, in the company's safe, police agents found more than half a million dollars in banknotes, evidence that implicated Lúnus in a massive fraud at a government development agency. That same evening, images of the banknotes were shown on national television. Within weeks, Sarney was forced to withdraw from the race, and her father, the former President José Sarney, was claiming they were victims of a conspiracy designed to boost the chances of Cardoso's designated successor, José Serra.[1]

Serra, a competent politician who, as Minister of Health, had led the establishment of a basic health service that was perhaps the most significant social reform of the Cardoso years, was a demanding technocrat but a notoriously uncharismatic campaigner. Heavily intellectual and with a penchant for detail, Serra's style was at odds with Brazil's cultural lightness. Nevertheless, rather than boost Serra, Sarney's withdrawal helped Lula increase his lead in the polls.

Until then many conservative Brazilians still thought that a Lula presidency was unlikely. His three defeats in 1989, 1994, and 1998 had been decisive after all. Since the approval of the *Plano Real* in 1994, support for the kind of radical economic alternative favoured by the PT had faded. Even though, as we saw in the last chapter, there was widespread popular concern over electricity shortages and rising unemployment, many commentators – especially those more connected to the financial markets – thought Brazilians were just too worried about the possible return of inflation to elect a left-winger who might jeopardize preciously won economic stability. But as the Lunus scandal unfolded it really did look as if Lula could become the country's next president. As Armínio Fraga, the Central Bank governor at the time, told me in July 2023, these weeks in March, April, and May 2002 were crucial. 'It was when [Sarney] pulled out of the race and Serra did not move that we knew we were in for a heck of a ride. I had my finger on the pulse of the market more than anyone in our team, and I could see what was going to happen. I knew we were going to run into a panic.'

As had been the case in the late 1990s, it was events outside Brazil that were contributing significantly to the nervous mood on financial markets. Just four months before the Sarney episode investors had been stunned by the economic collapse of Argentina, Brazil's southern neighbour and then its second-biggest trading partner. It is worth going into the story in a bit more detail. Like much of the rest of Latin America, Argentina had prospered in the first half of the 1990s when the leader of its traditionally nationalist and statist Peronist party had adopted a liberal and free-market approach.

With his flamboyant macho style, bushy, grey-tinged sideburns, and swept-back long hair, Carlos Saúl Menem sometimes appeared like one of the country's nineteenth-century caudillos. His parents had emigrated to Argentina from Syria, then part of the Ottoman Empire, in 1910, and Menem had grown up as a Muslim in the impoverished and sparsely populated north-west province of La

Rioja. Visiting Buenos Aires as a 21-year-old law student, he met Juan Domingo Perón and his already totemic wife, Eva Perón, and became a devoted follower of the populist leader.

Like Perón himself, who was overthrown in a coup in 1955, Menem had veered between the right and left of the political spectrum, becoming a trade union adviser and eventually governor of his home province. Arrested in 1976 by the military leaders of another coup, he had spent time in prison and several years in internal exile but always maintained incestuous ties with business leaders and the military top brass. After the return of democracy in 1983, he quickly regained control of La Rioja for the Peronists and then, six years later, won the presidency, triumphing in a contest against Raúl Alfonsín, the leader of Argentina's moderate left.

Menem had had to deal with the same kind of hyperinflation that had faced Cardoso in Brazil but had opted for an even more radical solution. Under Menem, Argentina – like Brazil and Mexico – had slashed spending and sold off its loss-making state companies. But Argentina adopted a draconian currency regime. As we saw in Chapter 7, Brazil had initially tied its currency to the dollar through a crawling peg arrangement but in early 1999 had devalued. Under Menem, Argentina seemed to completely rule out that option, adopting an extraordinarily rigid system. Menem's Minister of Economy, Domingo Cavallo, had not only fixed his domestic currency against the dollar but also completely sacrificed national control over monetary policy by establishing convertibility, a system whereby the Central Bank was legally obliged to retain a dollar in reserve for every *peso* in circulation.

In the early 1990s, when the mood on financial markets was triumphalistic and international capital generally plentiful, the system worked well, with Argentina growing at an average rate of 6 per cent a year. Later in the decade, though, convertibility proved to be a straitjacket. As investors became more nervous, the dollar strengthened and Argentina's *peso* rose with it, inflating the costs of local businesses and depressing overall productivity. The volatile Cavallo began to frequently clash with fellow cabinet members, and in June 1996 he resigned amid clear evidence that his policy was starting to go badly wrong.

Forced to cut costs to compete, company executives slashed wages and sacked workers. Recession deepened. With prices falling by 2 per cent in 1999, it was deflation rather than inflation that was on people's minds. How Argentina might rekindle growth without reviving inflation dominated my conversations with officials, politicians, and business executives as I started to visit the country regularly. By October 1999, when Argentina voted out Menem's Peronists and elected a new president, Fernando de la Rúa, there was growing disillusionment about the economy. The staid and cautious De la Rúa, leader of the liberal Radical Party, was a very different kind of politician to the flamboyant Menem.

But not for a minute did De la Rúa contemplate any changes to the rigid exchange-rate system that seemed to be suffocating the country. Radical Party politicians were prone to discuss the possibility of devaluation in private, but it was never publicly contemplated. 'This is like questioning the virginity of the Virgin Mary,' said one pro-government senator. As De la Rúa approached the end of his first year in office and Argentina was about to complete its second year of recession, confidence – both at home and abroad – was beginning to evaporate. In the words of one commercial developer, the country was in a 'pessimism trap'. De la Rúa pressed on regardless, with, as the same senator explained, an almost 'biblical conviction' in his orthodox strategy. In April 2001 the government doubled down on its bet by inviting the architect of convertibility, the self-same Domingo Cavallo, back as Minister of Economy. Cavallo reinforced the system, but it was now becoming apparent that the kind of drastic public-spending cuts required by the policy was simply beyond De la Rúa's capacity to impose.[3]

It was evident that the country needed a complete change, but Argentina's establishment was loath to contemplate it. Events, though – in the shape of a slow but inexorable decline of bank deposits – were to force their hand. With their bigger and more sophisticated financial system, Brazilians had traditionally tended to keep their savings at home, but Argentinians have a long history of holding their savings in dollars and transferring money abroad.[4] Indeed, Argentinian dollars deposited in Uruguay have bolstered the banking system of the tiny country on the other side of the River Plate.

As the recession deepened and uncertainty grew in the second half of 2001, many savers, realizing that there were not enough dollars in the system to cover all deposits, again raced for the exits. Some 15 per cent of deposits had been lost since June, when Cavallo actually told people on 30 November that 'their savings [were] safe', blaming 'irresponsible people for talking about devaluation'. A day later, sweeping controls were introduced, preventing bank customers from taking out more than $250 a week or $1,000 a month from their accounts.

Richer Argentines were circumventing the controls – nicknamed the *corralito* or little fence – with elaborate transactions that involved buying stocks listed in Buenos Aires and then selling the same shares in New York. But most Argentines were gripped by anxiety. I was in Buenos Aires at the time reporting on the crisis and remember explaining the ABC basics of convertibility to comfortably-off left-wing friends who were now worried about their mortgages. For small traders and shopkeepers or anyone trapped in the informal economy, these were even more desperate days. They couldn't get the cash they needed to continue working, and economic activity was starting to collapse. Ever more frantically seeking a way out, Cavallo was again arguing with his colleagues, but by now he had been transformed into a hate figure, with angry demonstrators regularly surrounding his house in Buenos Aires. On 19 December, less than three weeks after the fateful *corralito* controls had been introduced, unemployed workers were ransacking supermarkets and clashing with police. Cavallo resigned. A day later, with tear gas and smoke from burning cars engulfing the centre of Buenos Aires, De la Rúa fled from the roof of the presidential palace in a helicopter. A chaotic couple of weeks ensued in which three interim presidents came and went, before Congress invited Eduardo Duhalde, the defeated candidate in the 1999 election, to take over. Under Duhalde, Argentina then formally devalued the *peso* and ceased making payments on its $155 billion external debt. It was the largest debt default in history.

After the regular financial panics of the late 1990s, the Argentinian default punctured the optimism of emerging market investors, partly because of its size, partly too perhaps because many small investors – from as far afield as Italy and Japan – had been tempted to dabble in high-yielding Argentinian debt securities. And it had a massive impact on Brazil. At the time Argentina was Brazil's second-largest export market. Like Argentina, Brazil too was heavily indebted and dependent on the inflows of capital provided by the big institutions that bought its bonds. As Brazil's bond prices dived to ever lower levels, financial news wires constantly reminded their readers of Brazil's vulnerability. Fraga, Malan and other members of the Cardoso government's economic team insisted how much stronger Brazil was than Argentina. The country had control over its monetary policy. Nationally owned banks, such as Banco do Brasil, and local pension funds were significant institutional investors, so it was easier for the government to borrow money. Moreover, the banking system was solid and well-capitalized. But it was a hard sell. In the wake of the Argentine collapse, many commentators felt that Brazil was bound to follow suit, especially with a firebrand like Lula waiting in the wings. By mid-year – as we shall see – investment banks were advising their clients to sell their holdings of Brazilian assets. Yields on Brazilian bonds shot up to levels that suggested a debt default was on the cards.

LULA'S RIGHT TURN

It was against this background that Lula and his Workers' Party colleagues shifted their strategy, dropping many of the radical policies that worried better-off voters and frightened investors, and moderating their style and language in order to win over the middle ground. The process was already well under way having started in the wake of Lula's electoral defeat in 1998. Although the PT remained critical of the kind of structural reform and privatization that had featured so prominently in the two Cardoso administrations, the party recognized that the decline in inflation had boosted the living standards of its poorer supporters. In the second half of the 1990s – in spite of their electoral competition – there was considerable overlap between the political thinking of the PT and Cardoso's PSDB, so much so that one of the PT's founders, Francisco Weffort, became Minister of Culture in Cardoso's government.

Another factor driving moderation was success in local elections which put the party much more in touch with nitty-gritty economic issues. In Porto Alegre to the south and Belo Horizonte in the centre of the country, as well as a handful of other towns and cities, a new breed of PT mayors had developed innovative ideas to manage local resources, ranging from micro-credit programmes to school-meal plans and other incentives to encourage children to attend school. Voters were offered the opportunity to shape spending plans through what were known as participatory budgets. But these local leaders had also begun to learn to work with local businesses and often found themselves at odds with the ideological critiques of their left-wing comrades. Two leaders in particular, Celso Daniel, who was first elected mayor of Santo André, a town in the ABC belt, and Antônio Palocci, mayor of Ribeirão Preto, a prosperous agribusiness city in São Paulo state, played an essential role in this change within the party, acquiring a kind of celebrity status. Daniel, who had initially been a militant with the MEP, one of the numerous Marxist factions that joined the PT in the early 1980s, was now a fan of 'public-private partnerships' and said the government was better at regulating rather than owning businesses, an idea that had become popular in the 1990s among social democrats around the world. He said that the PT had to make the state, including those employed within it, work more effectively, an approach that Cardoso's PSDB was also developing.

Ironically, several former left-wing guerrillas had been among the most senior figures in the party, pressing for a more moderate strategy that focused on electoral success rather than socialist transformation. José Genoíno, who had survived the military's brutal repression of the Araguaia guerrilla campaign, had linked up with centre-left thinkers from the old Communist Party and Cardoso's PSDB to explore the possibilities of a Brazilian version of Eurocommunism. But one man above all others played a fundamental role: José Dirceu. As we saw in earlier chapters, Dirceu was a former student leader and guerrilla leader who spent much of the 1970s either in exile or clandestinity. During the 1980s he persuaded the party to reject the far left and isolate the Trotskyist entryist groups, which enjoyed an influence disproportionate to their numbers. In the late 1990s, after Lula's third successive defeat in nine years, the party's majority – united in a faction initially known as Articulation – rejected left-wing calls for a grassroots campaign to force Cardoso from office. 'Not only was the idea that we could bring down the Cardoso government on the streets just not viable, it was also an adventure that would set back the country's democratic development by two decades,'[6] wrote Dirceu in his memoirs.

For Dirceu, elected party president in 1995 and again in 1997, the result of the 1998 elections marked the end of the party's idealistic adolescence. It was time to get real about winning office. 'The 1998 elections closed a cycle,' Dirceu told Celso Rocha de Barros in his history of the PT. 'From here on, there [was] going to be an alliance, and we [were] going to win. We decided to get our act together.'[5]

At a party conference in Belo Horizonte in December 1999, Dirceu allied with Genoíno's moderate Radical Democracy grouping and routed the left. A year later, a good performance in the local elections reaffirmed that the party was on the right track. The PT won control of 187 municipalities, including three of Brazil's biggest cities – Belo Horizonte, Porto Alegre, and São Paulo. Dirceu now stepped up efforts to build links with business, and as Brazil's economy struggled after the devaluation crisis, there was no shortage of potential allies. The conservative Liberal Front Party (*Partido da Frente Liberal* or PFL), which had firm business support in the north-east, had broken with Cardoso in the wake of the Sarney scandal. Elsewhere, many industrialists were fed up with high interest rates and believed that privatizations did little to benefit their companies. Part of the catch-all Brazilian Democratic Movement Party (PMDB), which had built close links with businesses, still backed Cardoso, but other factions were seeking alternatives.

Eventually, Dirceu was able to persuade José Alencar, a conservative self-made multimillionaire who had been elected as a senator for the PMDB in Minas Gerais, to run as Lula's deputy. Alencar was an unlikely ally in some ways. From a poor family, he had dropped out of primary school to work in a modest family-owned clothing store. Over the years he had transformed it into Coteminas, one of Brazil's largest textile manufacturers, displaying the kind of entrepreneurial drive and upward social mobility that PT leaders had previously found hard to relate to. At first Lula had not been enthusiastic about the idea. Dirceu wrote in his memoir that he had to fight hard to persuade him to accept an invitation to the business congress where the first connections were made, and that he had had to 'drag' Lula to embrace Alencar at the end of the meeting. Many party members were also initially unhappy about the choice, mainly because by the time Alencar accepted the offer, he had joined an even more conservative smaller party (the *Partido Liberal* or PL, which was quite distinct from the Liberal Front Party or PFL) and well known for its links with one of Brazil's most dynamic neo-Pentecostal churches, the Universal Church of the Kingdom of God. The PT's local leadership in five states – Paraiba, Rio Grande do Sul, Santa Catarina, Rondônia, and Roraima – rejected the alliance. But Dirceu knew the link would help make Lula palatable to voters who had not backed him in his three previous campaigns. 'He was exactly the vice president that Lula needed,' he wrote. 'The worker and the businessman, allies, not the same, not with the same programme but united against Fernando Henrique Cardoso and neo-liberalism and in defence of Brazil, production, fairer distribution and the internal market.'[7]

To sell this new political offer to the Brazilian people, the PT contracted the services of Duda Mendonça. Again, the connection was an unlikely one that gave rise to considerable grumbling from rank-and-file Workers' Party members. Mendonça was a publicist known for his work with conservative politicians, such as Paulo Maluf, a corrupt politician and former mayor of São Paulo, about whom it was famously said, '*Rouba mas faz*' (he steals but he gets things done). Another of Mendonça's clients, Mário Kertész, was originally a close associate of Antônio Carlos Magalhães, the conservative political chieftain whose family had run Mendonça's native state of Bahia for decades.

Mendonça and his business partner João Santana resorted to sales techniques that had hitherto been anathema to the PT. Focus groups were set up to help work on the PT's image. Identifying Lula as symbolic of all the party's virtues and defects, the marketeers concluded that the PT needed to stress their leader's experience, openness, and negotiation skills. They sought to win over voters who might be drawn to Lula's message of social justice but had been deterred by the image of radicalism that the PT leader sometimes conveyed. 'The target,' wrote the journalist Paulo Markum, 'was voters who were a little bit Petista [pro-PT]. The people who hadn't voted Lula in the past but wouldn't rule it out.'[8]

Mendonça brought a calmness to proceedings that had been absent in the barnstorming campaigns of the past. On the walls of the campaign headquarters in a two-storey building on São Paulo's Avenida Nove de Julho was a phrase from Paulo Coelho. The Brazilian novelist had written, 'Nobody escapes defeats. It is better to fight for your dreams than to suffer defeat without even knowing you are fighting.' Mendonça's team conducted meetings in spaces organized according to the rigorous Eastern principles of Feng Shui. As they talked through their conclusions, the scent of joss sticks filled the air.[9]

The team also worked to change Lula's style. Mendonça coached Lula relentlessly, persuading his client to use a teleprompter.

Speeches were taped and practised repeatedly. The team talked Lula into wearing smart suits and ties. Mendonça hired a personal stylist, Nazareth Amaral, who discovered that standard off-the-rack suits didn't quite work for their candidate. Lula's arms were relatively short, and his body quite long. A dozen new suits – each costing around $2,000 – were ordered from an up-market tailor who had dressed top TV celebrities and business leaders. Shirts came from another fashion designer who counted Antônio Carlos Magalhães and the head of the Odebrecht clan, Norberto Odebrecht, among his customers. Mendonça chose a simple slogan for the campaign, 'Agora é Lula' (Now it's Lula), stressed the closeness of Lula's marriage and presented him as a strong family man. The team also addressed head-on their candidate's lack of education, emphasizing the qualifications of Lula's advisers. 'He is the head of the team that is jam-packed with doctorates.' Marisa, Lula's wife, was also persuaded to submit to the dictates of a stylist and appeared more elegant and rejuvenated as a result.

THE LETTER TO THE BRAZILIAN PEOPLE

This shift in strategy and style was matched by the emergence during 2002 of a new and much more market-friendly idea about how the economy should be managed. It was a change that in some ways had seemed unlikely in December 2001, when at the party congress in Olinda, a radical economic programme had been agreed. Members voted in favour of an agenda which included capital controls and opposed the planned privatization of the electricity sector. The party was critical of the agreement that Cardoso had signed with the International Monetary Fund and blasted the alleged corruption of the administration, suggesting groups close to it had benefited from the privatizations. Above all, it argued for a 'necessary rupture' with 'neo-liberalism', a left-wing term – which, in the context of the chaos underway in neighbouring Argentina, did little to ease any nervousness that investors might feel about a Lula government. But the document seemed more radical than it was. The rhetoric disguised important policy changes. Commitments to a debt default and renationalization – which had figured in previous programmes – were dropped. As Rocha de Barros put it: '[the new programme] was very much pro-state and not market-friendly but not remotely socialist'.[10]

In addition, Lula and Dirceu chose one of the new breed of pragmatic local politicians to coordinate the party's economic policy proposals ahead of the election. Celso Daniel, who was beginning his third term as mayor of Santo André,

The assassination of Daniel in January 2002 generated a considerable controversy about corruption. It gave rise to some complex conspiracy theories, which we will examine in greater depth in a subsequent chapter. Still, on the economic front, it did not significantly alter the situation. Lula replaced Daniel with Antônio Palocci, like Daniel, a former far-leftist turned moderate pragmatist. Palocci's rise to prominence had been meteoric. His parents were both on the left, and as a medical student at the Ribeirão Preto campus of São Paulo University he had joined the Organização Socialista Internacionalista or Socialist Internationalist Organization (OSI), a tiny Trotskyist grouping which became part of a large left-wing PT faction called Liberdade e Luta or Libelu (Liberty and Struggle). Libelu had initially derided Lula as a yellow unionist (or *pelego*) and the PT as the 'fifth wheel of the bourgeoisie'. However, it had eventually been subsumed within the party. In 1988, at the age of 28, Palocci was elected a councillor for the PT in his home town. Within two years he was a state deputy for São Paulo, and by the time he was 32 he was mayor of Ribeirão Preto. Like Daniel and other moderate mayors, Palocci had quickly abandoned his university Marxism as he grappled with the challenges of city management. In the early 1990s, when privatization was still considered heresy within Lula's party, Palocci sold off part of the municipal telephone company and called on private investors to build a water-treatment system.

In spite of these changes Lula and the party remained under immense pressure from the markets to clarify their approach. In May, Goldman Sachs recommended that its clients reduce their holdings in Brazil and transfer them to Mexico, where, under the conservative government of Vicente Fox, the government was seeking ever-closer economic integration with the United States. As Lula's ratings climbed, other investment banks followed suit.[11] In June, George Soros, the billionaire hedge-fund manager, came out with a particularly blunt warning, arguing that 'Brazil is condemned to elect Serra or to sink into chaos if a Lula government takes over.'[12]

When Soros made that statement, work was already under way to produce a document designed to reassure edgy investors. Early in May, together with José Dirceu, the party president, José Genoíno, his economic adviser, Guido Mantega and his publicity team, Lula had travelled to Palocci's home town of Ribeirão Preto to speak at an agricultural show that the Brazilian farmers' association holds each year. During a lunch at one of the city's Portuguese restaurants, the PT leaders had discussed how they might start to reassure sceptical markets. Lula had been resolutely opposed to suggestions from, among others, the publicist Mendonça that he should pre-announce his choice of Finance Minister and head of the Central Bank, and even maintain the Cardoso administration incumbents in their jobs. However, Lula accepted the need to respect legal contracts, ruling out, therefore, any default on debt. In addition, he also recognized that the macroeconomic policies introduced by Malan and Fraga, designed to keep inflation low and bring a growing debt burden under control, had to be maintained.

After the meeting Palocci was dispatched to gauge the views of business leaders and was told that investors were particularly keen on the idea of a specific target for a primary fiscal surplus. He had been told by João Roberto Marinho, the president of Globo, the powerful media empire which had opposed Lula in the past, that 'the crisis is much greater than you think. There is a lot of insecurity about the future, and for that reason, I think you ought to draw up a manifesto. You have to talk about a figure because that is what the market is most worried about.'[13] The final document – entitled 'A Letter to the Brazilian People' and announced at a press conference on 22 June 2002 – was looser than Lula's critics would have liked. Even so, Lula reiterated the commitments on contracts and provided a more personal reassurance about inflation. 'No one needs to teach me the importance of fighting inflation. I began my union career angry about the way [it was eroding] the value of our wages,' Lula insisted.[14]

There was some resistance in the PT (Dirceu himself was sceptical of the letter), but in the months leading up to the election the even more moderate voices decisively won the upper hand. One crucial figure who now came to national prominence was Luiz Gushiken, a bank workers' leader and a founder of the PT, who Lula asked to coordinate the election campaign. Gushiken's parents had emigrated from Japan in the 1920s, and he combined his Marxism with Zen Buddhism. Gushiken had shared the same Trotskyist affiliation as Palocci and had made an identical shift towards a more social-democratic perspective. Crucially, he was able to match the influence that Dirceu, Genoíno, or any other senior PT figures had over Lula.

There were some anxious days though. Throughout the southern hemisphere winter, investors continued to unload Brazilian assets, eroding the value of the country's reserves and making it harder for the government to raise money on the bond markets. This sell-off forced the government to borrow money over shorter periods. The yields offered by Brazilian 10-year paper had risen sharply since April, reaching a high of more than 30 per cent in early September. In 2001, Brazil had comfortably raised $12 billion on the world's debt capital markets. However, after April, when it struggled to place an eight-year issue of $1 billion with investors, it became increasingly difficult to raise any money at all.

Reflecting on all this more than two decades later, Armínio Fraga conceded that the Cardoso government's economic team itself was beginning to doubt very much whether an incoming administration could avoid default. 'We were saying to ourselves, how are we going to make it? We couldn't sell a treasury bond that matured past the end of the year. Investors would tell us, "You guys are fine. But come January, you won't be around. So, we have to protect ourselves. I'm so sorry." Yeah, that's what we were hearing all the time.'[15]

Initially, even the prospect of a multi-billion-dollar IMF deal had failed to quell nerves. But after a $30 billion bailout package was agreed in September, two factors bolstered confidence. First, the government team worked with opposition candidates on the transition. In August, Cardoso met with Lula, and two other centre-left candidates – Ciro Gomes and Anthony Garotinho – to tell them, in Fraga's words, that 'look, this is the situation. We have cut this deal with the IMF, and things don't have to be so bad.'[16] Second, the moderate Palocci began to play a decisive role. By this stage he was the most influential PT voice on economic matters. Backed by Guskihen he had gained a clear ascendancy over rivals such as Aloizio Mercadante and Guido Mantega, who enjoyed greater support among the PT grassroots, had known Lula for longer, and worked with him in the past much more.

After Lula's election triumph in October 2002, Palocci was named coordinator of the transition and began meeting regularly with Fraga and Pedro Malan, the Finance Minister. Palocci was now sure to become Finance Minister in turn. 'For us on the inside, Palocci was a game changer,' Fraga told me.[17] After Lula won the first round of the election, the connection between the outgoing Cardoso team and Lula's new administration began to tighten. Several senior officials inside Palocci's team – Bernardo Appy, Murilo Portugal, Marcos Lisboa, and Joaquim Levy, among them – had all worked under Malan and were closer to the PSDB's social-democratic approach than to the PT's more orthodox leftism. 'We made some suggestions about people he should bring in,' said Fraga. 'Palocci had some authority to make appointments, and he brought them all in.'[18] This steady shift underway had impressed Cardoso. At the end of 2001 he had been bitterly critical of the PT and its leader, arguing that Lula and his party had learned nothing from the previous 20 years and that a win for them would be a big step backwards for Brazil. By the autumn of the following year, the president's tone had changed. Recognizing that his candidate Serra was unlikely to win, Cardoso said Lula would be preferable to either Garotinho or Gomes, and resolved to help the PT candidate. 'Even though he is a bit corporatist, a bit backward about certain things, as far as public morality and fiscal responsibility are concerned, he is much more positive,' wrote Cardoso in his diary.[19] By the time the outgoing leader passed on the green and yellow presidential sash, the two men had recovered some of the mutual affection lost in recent political battles. As Cardoso waited at the elevator to leave the presidential palace for the last time, they embraced.

10

The Rise of Lulismo

I watched the Lula government take shape from close at hand because after covering the 2002 election campaign in Brazil, I began to live in São Paulo. In the run-up to Lula's victory, there were fears that the PT's more radical supporters from grassroots organizations, such as the Landless Workers' Movement (*Movimento dos Trabalhadores Rurais Sem Terra* or MST), would push the new government to the left. They certainly seemed to be a force to be reckoned with. I'd travelled several times to the MST's well-organized camps, consisting of improvised tents made from bamboo stakes and sheets of black polythene and typically found on the edges of Brazilian towns and cities. During 2002 the MST had undermined Lula's claims of moderation by invading the Cardoso family farm in Goiás. The MST's founder, João Pedro Stédile, had warned foreign investors not to come to Brazil, 'because they will lose money'. And the mood in the settlements, whose number grew quite quickly during 2002, was similarly uncompromising. When in October 2002 I visited an MST camp in a former cocoa estate a few miles from Itabuna in Bahia, an MST organizer had told me: 'We will support Lula, but we have to press him to meet our demands. The [economic] model that the elite have been advocating is in decline. The conjuncture is very favourable for change.'[1]

But as I travelled around Latin America in the early 2000s, Brazil seemed to be an island of stability as a left-wing tide rose elsewhere. Hugo Chávez, the president of Venezuela, was the man who captured the mood. He'd been elected in a landslide in December 1998 and, following a failed right-wing coup against him in April 2002, began to develop his vision of what he called twenty-first-century socialism. 'If we don't put an end to neo-liberalism,' he boasted in January 2003, 'neo-liberalism will put an end to us.'[2]

Chávez's belligerence could not have been in sharper contrast with Lula's cautious pragmatism. The letter to the Brazilian people had not been campaign rhetoric. Lula delivered. Palocci, the privatizing mayor of Ribeirão Preto, was named Finance Minister. Henrique Meirelles, who, until his retirement in 2002, had held top executive positions at BankBoston in the United States, was appointed president of the Central Bank. Far from 'ending neo-liberalism', this team was committed to the tightest and most orthodox fiscal and monetary policies. As Palocci put it in a memoir, 'It was a plan of responsibility designed to balance the books.'[3]

Palocci and his team pared back public spending. With interest rates exceeding 25 per cent in the first half of 2003, the administration adopted the most extreme austerity measures to convince investors that it was serious about stability.[4] Local businesses started to grumble. Even Lula's deputy, José Alencar, was unhappy with the policy. But the new president stuck with it. Palocci was at the centre of the new leader's inner circle, joining the president on his morning walks. Lula stayed close to Meirelles, too, taking no important economic decision without the approval of the Central Bank chief. '[Lula] was proud of the plan' and 'showed an iron determination in tackling the economic issues', wrote Palocci.[5] The new president sometimes insisted on even more conservative objectives than Palocci himself.

The economy struggled in 2003, but slowly the commitment to stability was yielding dividends. The *real* was strengthening against the dollar. Foreign investment was coming in. The economy began to grow, and unemployment fell. During the handover, Palocci discussed with Fraga and the outgoing Cardoso team a series of relatively minor technical changes that could help improve productivity. Macroeconomic instability had been too great in the run-up to the election, but as calm returned, Palocci pushed ahead with this agenda. The new government made it easier to open a bank account, reformed antiquated bankruptcy laws, and made it possible for banks to increase consumer lending by allowing people to secure loans against their paychecks. Publicly owned banks also began to lend aggressively.

Following the austerity of the first two years of the government, an 8.2 per cent increase in minimum wages took effect in May 2005. A year later, the rise was a more generous 13 per cent. A series of social benefits, introduced first by one or two Brazilian local governments and then at the federal level by the Cardoso administration, had been conditional on recipients sending their children to school or getting them vaccinated at local clinics. The Lula administration unified these payments and extended them to millions more people. When Cardoso left office, three million families had received the benefit, which came to be known as Bolsa Família or Family Allowance. By 2005 the government was assisting more than 12 million families, making direct payments to mothers to ensure that funds were spent as intended. Underpinning everything was a startling improvement in Brazil's trade and current account, which was fundamentally related to China's emergence on the world economic stage.

In 2001 the World Trade Organization welcomed China as a member. The accession had opened up markets for its manufacturing exports, paving the way for an export-led boom that, in turn, fuelled faster economic growth. The competition from Beijing had hit Brazilian manufacturers, but China's expansion had a much more significant impact on Brazilian exports. The growth of demand from China for soya and iron ore, Brazil's two most important exports, was transformative. Attracted by the manufacturing boom, China's urban population was growing rapidly and becoming increasingly prosperous. Demand for chicken and pork skyrocketed, and although chickens and pigs were reared in China, soya was required to feed them and Brazilian farmers cashed in. As it battled to meet the burgeoning demand from builders, China's steel industry sucked in vast quantities of iron ore, benefiting mining companies such as Brazil's Vale. Farmers producing everything from beef to pork, oranges to sugar, were thriving. Helped by the more flexible exchange rate, manufacturing also did well. Embraer, which manufactures medium-sized jet aircraft, began to capitalize on the deregulation of the aviation industry in the developed world and the launch of dozens of new short-haul routes. Marco Polo, a bus manufacturer which I remember visiting in April 2004, also typified a new sense of economic optimism. Soon, with the discovery in 2006 of vast oil reserves from the so-called pre-salt oil deposits offshore from Rio de Janeiro, there would be an additional leg to Brazil's export base.

These stories of business success translated into healthier economic performance. For decades, Brazil had paid more for imports of goods and services than it earned from its exports. Debt had been one result. During the 1980s and 1990s the country had stumbled from one IMF agreement to another. However, from 2004 onwards, buoyed by this tremendous trade with China, Brazil began to record trade surpluses so large that, rather than relying on capital investments and borrowings to make ends meet, it was building up reserves. Shortly before Palocci left office in 2006, Brazil was able to repay the billions of dollars it owed to the IMF. 'When as a Trotskyist student leader, I used to chant "IMF out", I could never have imagined that 25 years later I would be in a room negotiating with these "demons of the left" or that the eventual departure of the IMF would be calm and carefully negotiated without any bravado,' wrote Palocci in 2007.[6]

This improvement in Brazil's standing, combined with continued stability, made the country much more attractive to foreign investment, compensating for the low savings and capital shortages that had been one of the constraints holding back development. The social policies started to have an impact. The two sets of policies – stable prices and more generous minimum wages, along with extensive social benefits – both helped ease the lives of the poorest Brazilians.

THE MENSALÃO

Two and a half years into the administration, however, Lula encountered turbulence, with a corruption scandal that very nearly brought his period in office to a premature end. The crisis had its origins in the fragmented nature of Brazil's political party system and the opaque nature of its financing.

The triumph of the Workers' Party in 2002 brought them into contact with this complexity at a federal level for the first time. The party had ambitious plans to transform Brazil. Lula had won comfortably, but the PT had secured only 83 of the 513 seats in the lower house and 14 of the 81 seats in the Senate, so it was bound to rely on support from representatives of allied parties. A similar challenge had faced every president elected since the return to democracy in 1985, and it had been solved by the party of the elected president forming an alliance with the parties closest to its views and handing cabinet seats to these allies to cement the arrangement. Fernando Henrique Cardoso's PSDB had formed a coalition with parties from the centre and the right of the political spectrum who were most committed to maintaining its far-reaching counter-inflationary plans. Political scientists labelled these arrangements 'presidential coalitionism'. In 2002 the PT's moderate wing, led by figures such as Palocci, shared many similarities with the PSDB. However, the left wing of the party had demonized Cardoso and had been fiercely critical of privatizations. Despite the similarities between his government's fiscal and monetary policies and those of Cardoso, Lula opted to establish a distance from the Tucanos. Party activists despised the politics of the third-largest party, the Brazilian Democratic Movement (PMDB), and opposed making a deal with them. So, under a scheme devised by the party's strategist José Dirceu, the PT mounted an original, highly controversial, and ultimately quite disastrous approach. Lula awarded 16 cabinet positions to his party – a far larger quota than warranted by its congressional showing – and paid its allies for their votes, making regular monthly disbursements from a slush fund.

Disbursements were administered by Delúbio Soares, the party treasurer, and Silvio Pereira, the party's general secretary, and were financed by fraudulent payments to Marcos Valério, a friendly publicist. When it came, the denouement was remarkably rapid. One of the beneficiaries of this arrangement was Roberto Jefferson, leader of the Brazilian Labour Party (PTB). This name might suggest that he was a natural ally of the PT. However, Jefferson had gained national prominence as a cheerleader for former President Fernando Collor. Although PT managers had enlisted his support in the cash-for-votes scheme, it would be fair to say that Jefferson and the PT had a strained relationship. In his memoir written in 2006, Jefferson wrote that the decision to support Lula and the PT made him 'want to vomit'. As Rocha de Barros wrote in his history of the PT, the sentiment was mutual. One minister in Lula's administration told the PT historian that every time he shook Jefferson's hand, 'I felt physically ill. . . . He [Jefferson] was a symbol of the most sordid bloody-minded approach to politics that there was.'[7]

Jefferson had exposed the scheme in an interview published in *Folha de São Paulo* on 6 June 2005. A week later, in a follow-up, the newspaper reported that Dirceu and Genoíno, as well as Pereira and Soares, were all involved. Genoíno had simply signed some of the paperwork involved without apparently reading it,[8] but he was forced to resign anyway. Dirceu left the government. Along with him went Luiz Gushiken, the architect of the successful 2002 election campaign and Palocci's leading supporter. At a parliamentary inquiry established at the behest of the opposition, PT deputies were filmed in tears. 'It was so sad and painful,' said Chico Alencar, a left-wing PT deputy. An ex-minister defended the scheme, arguing that it was the price the party had to pay to win approval for its progressive social policies. 'We needed these guys – these right-wing allies – to approve pro-Uni (student grants) and Bolsa Família. We knew they would do their thing in the ministries and state companies, but we closed our eyes to it and looked after the essential thing (the social policies of the party), which was the battle against hunger.'[9]

The affair, which prefigured what would prove to be even more disastrous for the PT, the Lava Jato scandal of 2014–18 (Operation Car Wash), highlighted a deeper problem. Traditionally Lula's Workers' Party had been fiercely critical of the corruption embedded in Brazilian party politics. The PT disliked the close connections established by elected politicians with the private sector. Members of the PT typically donated significant amounts of their own income to support political activities. They were active in pressing for greater accountability. During the constituent assembly elected in 1987, PT leaders had presided over the commission that gave autonomy to the public ministry, creating an institution theoretically capable of cracking down on abuses of power. Subsequently, two PT deputies, José Dirceu and Eduardo Suplicy, spearheaded the congressional investigation that exposed the extent of President Collor's malfeasance, paving the way for his impeachment and dismissal.

Gradually, though, the messy business of government had led the PT to dirty its own hands. In the late 1980s, Luiza Erundina, the PT's elected mayor of São Paulo, had broken with her deputy, Luiz Eduardo Greenhalgh, over accusations that he had agreed to license a property development in exchange for a contribution to party funds from the construction company that had benefited. Similar accusations plagued PT city and state administrations throughout the 1990s, nowhere more so than in Santo André, a city in which an up-and-coming PT mayor, Celso Daniel, won successive elections from 1990 onwards.

Political financing has always been a tricky problem in Brazil because the way the electoral system has been designed makes it expensive. Its architects chose an unwieldy mix of an open-list system and extensive districts that elect multiple representatives. The open list means that voters can cast their ballot not just in favour of a party but also for individual candidates, irrespective of their position on the list. In a closed list, by contrast, party headquarters decide which candidates have the most chance of getting elected. Effectively, this means that individual candidates have more work to do in a campaign because they are competing against both party colleagues as well as political rivals. And because election districts are large, candidates must conduct these campaigns over a geographically wide area. The system offers voters a wide range of choices, but it comes at a significantly higher cost than the closed-list system and narrower voting districts favoured in Great Britain, the United States, and much of the developed world.

To fund campaigns, parties in Brazil frequently resorted to illicit financing arrangements with local companies. These were typically referred to as 'second accounts' (*caixa dois*) to distinguish them from contributions declared to the electoral authorities. For decades, politicians across Brazil – not only from the PT – had drawn on money from private companies, initially from construction companies and then, from the 1990s onwards, as public-works programmes shrank, from businesses operating refuse services or bus operators.

Under Brazil's electoral law, parties are obliged to declare such contributions to the authorities, but enforcement is weak. In any event, the practice was commonplace. Antônio Palocci, who had won several elections before becoming Finance Minister, claimed that it would have been impossible to finance his campaigns without a second account. Gilberto Carvalho, chief of staff to Lula and Dilma Rousseff, acknowledged in a 2022 documentary that the use of parallel accounts had been widespread. As Celso Rocha de Barros puts it, 'Candidates that didn't do *caixa dois* had a lot of difficulties in getting elected. It was possible to have a system in which politicians agreed not to steal but not one where they agreed never to win elections.'[10]

The investigation into Celso Daniel's assassination in January 2002 did little to clarify controversies surrounding such arrangements. The police found that Daniel was a straightforward victim of a criminal gang. But a separate probe by officials from São Paulo's public ministry thought the crime was the responsibility of Daniel's bodyguard and right-hand man, Sérgio Sombra, who, they alleged, was skimming off money donated to the local party's 'second account' for his own purposes, effectively – in a byzantine twist – creating a '*caixa tres*' or 'third account'. According to this version of events, Sombra had ordered Daniel to be killed because the mayor had been planning to clamp down on this private scheme. In the heated atmosphere of Brazilian politics ahead of the 2002 election, critics of the PT – including Daniel's family members – had even alleged that national PT leaders had colluded in the assassination. But as Rocha de Barros concludes, it is hard to see how this would make any sense, and no evidence has ever been produced. 'Even if we attribute the worst intentions to the PT leadership, it is difficult to imagine that they would kill to have less money in the campaign.'[11]

Nevertheless, for conservative anti-Lula voters, the Daniel affair confirmed their prejudices. For them, the PT's ethical stance was hypocritical. The *Mensalão* – or monthly-backhander scandal – news of which broke in June 2005, was further proof of PT duplicity. The *Mensalão* battered Lula's popularity. During July and August 2005 opposition parties had considered the possibility of impeaching him because of his alleged involvement in the backhander scheme. They desisted from this partly because there was every likelihood that had they done so, their own *caixa dois* activities might have come under scrutiny, threatening their sources of campaign financing. Moreover, in 2005, opposition candidates were polling well, whereas Lula was polling poorly. It was simply necessary to keep up the pressure, and they would surely defeat Lula at the polls. 'It was,' as the editor of one of the São Paulo daily newspapers told me at the time, 'a question of allowing Lula to bleed.'

These opposition plans came unstuck, however. In 2006 the clouds that had gathered over Lula's future suddenly lifted. Until the end of 2005, José Serra, then considered the most likely candidate for Cardoso's PSDB, maintained a steady lead in opinion polls ahead of the October 2006 election. But by the beginning of February 2006, Lula was level-pegging and, by the end of that month, seemed to have shrugged off the adverse effect of the *Mensalão* and was back in the lead. This change in fortunes was puzzling at first. But as the year progressed it became apparent that Lula was beginning to reap the benefits of stability, wage increases, and the dramatic expansion of popular credit and social welfare that had begun towards the end of his first mandate. Marcelo Neri, a Princeton-trained economist then working at the Social Affairs Unit of the Getúlio Vargas Foundation, a business school, claimed that the overall impact of these changes would be as beneficial for Lula as the *Plano Real* had been for Cardoso.

Visiting poor areas in the north-east of Brazil ahead of the election it was easy to find enthusiastic support for Lula. 'Lula is the only one who's done anything for the poor,' Ivandro Santos, a 33-year-old street trader told me, as he sold fruit juice and *coxinhas* – a minced chicken savoury – in a run-down corner of Itapuã, a suburb of Salvador. He, his wife, and their two children were receiving monthly payments under Bolsa Família and other income-transfer programmes. Helenita Santana, who earned a couple of hundred dollars a month working as a domestic servant, had been convinced to support Lula because of the broader availability of credit. She proudly showed us around her humble house in a down-at-heel neighbourhood adorned with new items: a flat-screen TV, a fridge, and a DVD player that she had been able to buy in the previous couple of years. 'All of us here have made up our minds,' said David Sebastião Costa, a 45-year-old who was one of 3,800 members of the Itapuã fisherman's co-operative, hardly pausing to add that he and his colleagues would vote for Lula. 'Everything's much easier for us since he's been in power.' For them, the promise of a R$40,000 loan to help renovate the boats and tackle had been a crucial factor.[12]

With the higher minimum wage and enhanced social benefits, north-easterners were benefiting disproportionately from Brazilian growth. In the election year, sales in Sergipe and Paraiba, two of the poorest states, rose by more than 28 per cent, compared to a national average of 5 per cent. Income levels per head advanced more quickly than in richer states, and more jobs were being created. Overall, between 2001 and 2005 the average income of the poorest 10 per cent of the population increased by 35.9 per cent, equivalent to nearly 8 per cent a year. Effectively, some parts of the north-east were experiencing growth nearly as quickly as China did over the same period.[13]

These income gains were crucial in winning people with low incomes away from the right-wing Liberal Front Party (PFL) and the centrist PMDB parties that had previously dominated politics in the north-east. Antônio Carlos Magalhães, the veteran leader of the PFL and a loyal ally of both the military regime and the Cardoso government, had built up a political machine in Bahia, offering financial support to neighbourhood associations, samba schools, and Candomblé (African diasporic religion) churches, as well as – at election time – buying votes with hand-outs of food and drink. That franchise was being transferred more or less en masse to Lula. More than half of the families benefiting from the expansion of the Bolsa Família programme were from the north and north-east. However, the region was home to a little more than a third of Brazil's population. 'The poor have left the PFL and the PMDB and gone to Lula because they've had a big change in their income,' said Marcelo Neri.[14]

The margin of Lula's victory, achieved in a second-round run-off against Geraldo Alckmin, the PSDB candidate, was 60.8 per cent to 39.1 per cent, only slightly less than the 61.3 per cent to 38.7 per cent by which he had defeated Serra four years previously. But Lula's electorate had changed. In 2002 he had won 26 out of 27 states. In 2006 he had secured only 20 of the 27 but had compensated by achieving a much more resounding success in the north-east. Alarmed by the Mensalão corruption scandal, the better-educated and better-off had tended to vote for the opposition. By contrast, those with the lowest incomes either didn't know about the corruption or, for them, it dwindled into insignificance compared with the material improvements in their lives. A March 2006 poll by Fundação Perseu Abramo, a PT think tank, found that 42 per cent of north-easterners knew nothing about the Mensalão. Only a quarter of south-easterners were similarly ignorant.

Polling figures released a few days before the final vote showed that 69 per cent of people who earned up to $324 per month (two minimum wages) and 59 per cent of those earning between $324 and $810 (two to five minimum wages) favoured Lula. On the other hand, anyone earning over five minimum wages was more likely to back the opposition. It seemed that Porto Alegre, capital of the southernmost state of Rio Grande do Sul, and a bastion of support for the PT since 1989, had voted for the opposition.

Another 2006 study showed that those benefiting from government programmes were much more likely to want to re-elect the president. Among interviewees benefiting from a government programme, voting intentions in favour of Lula rose to 62 per cent, compared to an average of 39 per cent.[15]

FROM LABOURISM TO LULISMO

As Brazil began to digest the results of the 2006 election, it was clear that a significant shift had occurred in the politics of Lula and his Workers' Party. The party's core support had shifted from the declining manufacturing centres of the south and south-east to the poorer north-east of the country, where the social policies of the Lula government were having the greatest impact. European-style labourism was being replaced by what the political scientist André Singer termed 'Lulismo', a phenomenon similar in some respects to the populism so frequently found elsewhere in Latin America. Like Argentina's Juan Domingo Perón, Lula provided strong charismatic leadership and a direct appeal to the poor. In 2009, Cardoso, Lula's old rival, described Lulismo as a kind of sub-Peronism.[16]

However, there was a marked difference between Lulismo and the more confrontational populist styles being developed at the time by Néstor and Cristina Kirchner in Argentina, Evo Morales in Bolivia, and most markedly by Venezuela's Hugo Chávez. Lula's commitment to keep inflation under control and his cautious approach towards change marked Lulismo off from more classic populist formulas. Economic stability was central to Lula's approach, partly because the experience of rampant inflation in recent years had been so punishing for Brazil's poor. As Singer put it, 'economic stability was the lever for Lulismo' and the basis for extending Bolsa Família and other income-transfer schemes. Lulismo, he said, was a process of 'reform without rupture'.[17]

The rise of Lulismo also marked the end of the prospect for a more European-style of progressive social democracy. With its strong trade union base and growing experience of local government the PT had once resembled the labour or social-democratic parties that had sprung up in Europe at the beginning of the twentieth century. These centre-left parties in Germany, Sweden, France, and Britain, underpinned by the support of industrial unions, enjoyed their heyday in the first three decades after the Second World War, assuring the political stability that underpinned economic growth, the development of social welfare, and the extension of economic opportunities. The parties associated with these labour movements – the British Labour Party and the German Social Democrats, for example – had led demands for the expansion of the franchise and after the Second World War spearheaded the creation of welfare states. The way that organized labour had struck a deal with elites had 'enabled the development of democracy', as the American political scientists Darren Acemoglu and James Robinson put it.[18]

Until the 1990s it seemed the same process could be about to happen in Brazil. The wave of strikes in the late 1970s had sparked a big increase in unionization and triggered the formation of a working-class party, the first such party of 'classical dimensions' to be created since the Second World War, as the British Marxist Perry Anderson put it.[19] The PT had barely entered the political stage before the conditions that had led to its creation began to change. Across the developed world, the number of workers employed in industry decreased as manufacturing became increasingly capital-intensive. The Asian growth economies were an exception, but this same process of deindustrialization now began to happen in large parts of the developing world. In Brazil, businesses had struggled in the 1980s and were exposed to fierce international competition when the Collor government began to lift tariff barriers in the early 1990s. That process intensified during the 1990s and 2000s. Brazil was experiencing in a very extreme form a version of a Latin American disease that the Harvard-based economist Dani Rodrik has described as 'premature deindustrialisation'.[20]

As jobs disappeared, trade unions lost members and became weaker. In the 1980s more than 30 per cent of Brazilian workers were in unions, but membership halved in the subsequent decade. Brazil had become well known for its labour militancy (the 1,962 strikes registered in 1989, for example, was the second highest number in the world behind Spain), but during the 1990s and 2000s disputes became less frequent. 'Nobody is combative anymore . . . They all spend their time lobbying' said a founder of the PT, Francisco Weffort.[21] With Lula in government many senior members of the Workers' Party were now more interested in the well-paid state jobs that they could obtain. Union leaders spent their time on the boards of significant pension funds formed by Brazilian state companies, such as Banco do Brasil, Caixa Econômica, and Petrobras, and were more concerned about the rates of return on their investments than grassroots organizing. The 'signature of Lula's rule had been demobilisation,' lamented Anderson. 'Now all but completely detached from the working class', he added, this layer of senior officials and managers had been 'inexorably sucked into the vortex of financialisation engulfing markets and bureaucracies alike'.[22]

The 2006 election seemed to show support for Lula, and the PT was now more rooted in the poorest sectors of society and guaranteed by the raft of economic and social policies introduced since 2003. It was an inversion of the pattern that had obtained in 1989 when Lula had first fought a presidential campaign. Then, Lula's support had been heavily concentrated in the industrial states of the south-east, from where the PT had been launched nine years before. But Lula and the PT had made relatively little progress in the poorest parts of the country in the north-east. 'The bitter truth is that those who have defeated us are the least educated and favoured in society,' Lula had said at the time.[23] His electoral base had come to resemble not just that of Collor but also that of Arena, the right-wing party created by the military regime, according to Wendy Hunter and Timothy Power.[24]

Lulistas were less ideologically defined than the kind of people who had supported Lula 20 years before. They did not necessarily support left-of-centre policies backed by the PT but liked Lula for pragmatic reasons or because they identified with his life story. These voters might vote for Lula, but they would not necessarily class themselves as left-wing, nor would they automatically vote for PT candidates, as pointed out by the American political scientist David Samuels.[25]

THE RISE OF LULISMO

During Lula's second mandate, as the government relaxed austerity and extended the reach of social policies, Lulismo became more embedded. As Lula paved the way for the victory of his designated successor, Dilma Rousseff, he increasingly presented himself as a father of the poor, a paternalistic figure who would maintain stability and slowly reduce inequality. Campaign managers presented the 2010 contest as a kind of plebiscite. 'You were for or against him (and his chosen candidate); for or against his record compared with that of his predecessor FHC; for or against "Nosso Projeto" [our project]; ultimately, for or against the people [*O Povo*],' wrote the British political scientist Leslie Bethell.[26] 'The election was not essentially about Dilma, nor the PT, it was about Lula and his extraordinary empathy with the mass of the Brazilian people.'

If the elite who had driven Getúlio Vargas to suicide, forced Jânio Quadros to resign, and ousted João Goulart in a coup, wanted to confront him, said Lula, they would find him on the street with the *Povo Brasileiro*. It was the kind of rhetoric that would be deployed – as we will see – with ever greater frequency after the confusions of Lava Jato, the impeachment of Dilma Rousseff, and Lula's imprisonment eight years later. Still, Lula continued to doggedly insist on maintaining economic stability. There were also other elements to his political programme that went beyond demagogic populism. The environmental policies of Lula's government and its approach toward the problems of the Amazon opened new political ground. That will be the subject of our next chapter.

11

Green Brazil

On 15 October 1994 the editors of *O Estado de São Paulo* deemed fit to feature on their front page news of the election of a previously obscure young left-wing politician from the Amazon region. To everyone's surprise, a few days earlier, voters in the tiny conservative state of Acre in western Brazil had selected a 33-year-old black female history teacher as one of their three senators. And they had done so overwhelmingly, with Marina Silva finishing in first place, well ahead of her more established traditional rivals. As the daily newspaper put it, her 'gentle and firm style had captivated rich and poor alike'. Now, the newly elected senator promised that she was 'going to cause some noise. I'm not just there for the ride.'[1] Marina Silva was true to her word. Less than a decade later, the former rubber tapper, who had been illiterate until the age of 18, had become Minister for the Environment. During the first five and a half years of Lula's first two governments, she was one of the shining stars. The impressive decline in Amazon deforestation achieved under her watch was arguably as big an achievement as the reduction in inequality and poverty. Silva was emblematic of the government's green credentials and helped Lula win international credibility. In the 1990s, Goldman Sachs had awarded her its international environmental prize, and in the 2000s she won additional honours. She had done all this while dealing with a series of chronic illnesses. Even now, it is hard to think of a living Brazilian politician, other than possibly Lula himself, who enjoys such global prestige. Her return to the job in 2023 was the cause of celebration among environmentalists around the world.

Following her decision to support Lula's 2022 election campaign, Marina's recent return to the ministry also represented a significant reconciliation between the two leaders. In 2008, after a series of clashes with other ministers over policy in the Amazon, Marina left the government and subsequently the PT. She was particularly at odds with the decision to prioritize economic growth at the expense of environmental protection. Clashes with Dilma Rousseff, who championed the construction of several controversial hydroelectric dams, were bitter and Marina became one of her firmest political opponents, twice running against her in presidential elections. The break was acrimonious. Many PT members, particularly those on the left, came to detest Marina. Her conversion to evangelical Protestantism (in 1996 she had become a member of one of Brazil's largest Pentecostal churches, the Assemblies of God) had in any case distanced her from many younger PT members who in the last 20 years have become increasingly influenced by Anglo-Saxon identity politics.

But viewed from afar, the rift was surprising given the many parallels between Marina's story and that of Lula. Just as Lula was a product of the factory and the trade union movement of manual workers, Marina's radical politics evolved from the collective experiences of the rural workers of the rainforest, the so-called *seringueiros*, who harvest rubber. Acre, the state where she was born, is one of the most remote in Brazil, certainly as poor and isolated as Pernambuco was during Lula's childhood. Also, like Lula, Marina entered politics as a radical grassroots activist and union leader. In the late 1970s and early 1980s, just as Lula's metalworkers' union was flexing its muscles in São Bernardo, in Acre Marina's rubber-tappers' union was organizing blockades to expel land-hungry cattle ranchers from the forest. Radical clerics were as crucial to their campaigns as they had been for the wage battles of Lula's metalworkers. One of the first places the Workers' Party established itself after its launch in São Paulo was in Acre, and party militants still regard Chico Mendes, the founder of the rubber-tappers' union who was assassinated by a rancher in 1988, as a hero. Marina, like Lula, also made the transition from activism to electoral politics and reform. Her championing of a new approach to conservation and sustainability mirrored that of Lula's party in social policy. Reforms like the protected extractive reserves and the Bolsa Família were also first tried at a local level. Marina's biography has also involved a political journey towards moderation very similar to Lula's own, so much so – in fact – that she has seemed at times like an ideal successor, particularly because the political salience of her area of expertise – the protection of the Amazon and the fight against global warming – has increased so markedly over the past decade and a half. Therefore, it is worthwhile examining this history and the life of a woman who has often seemed to offer so much to Lula and the promise of Brazil's social transformation.

MARINA'S STORY

Acre had been at the centre of Brazil's rubber industry for more than 100 years when Marina Osmarina da Silva was born in 1958 in the village of Breu Velho, about 45 miles north of Acre's capital, Rio Branco. Rubber trees and the latex they produce[2] had long been valued by indigenous groups but became much sought after during the industrial revolution as a material from which bottles, shoes, waterproof clothing, and tyres could be made. Rubber plantations therefore became an attractive commercial though labour-intensive proposition. Business owners found the workers they needed in the poor north-east of Brazil, which as we saw in Chapter 1 was prone to drought. Manaus – an Amazon city 800 miles to the north-east of Acre – became the leading centre of the trade, and for a time one of the most prosperous cities in the world. Competition from Malaysia and other Asian countries triggered a long decline which was interrupted by the Second World War when Brazil revived rubber production as part of a wartime agreement. The United States provided loans and other financial assistance and a guaranteed five-year market for the rubber. It had also agreed to help Brazil start a steel industry. In return, Brazil in 1943 sent 25,000 troops to Europe. But it also agreed to recruit thousands of poor migrants to become 'rubber soldiers' (*soldados de borracha*), and one of those making the arduous 30-day riverboat journey paid for by the government was Marina's father, Pedro, a black Brazilian then aged 19, who had grown up in a rural area of Ceará.

Even at the best of times rubber tapping is skilled and tiring work. Trees must be cut in precisely the right way to yield enough sap; they produce their best yield early in the day; they grow best at a distance from each other and are often hundreds of yards apart. Typically, each tapper would be responsible for between 100 and 150 trees and would cut the bark of the first of these well before dawn, hang a small can under the incision and later return to collect the dripped sap. After covering ten to fifteen miles a day, the tapper would resume work in the early evening, roasting the latex over a smoky fire until it slowly accumulated in a shape like an oversized rugby ball. The way the trade was organized in Brazil made the work harder still. The plantations were privately owned. Rubber tappers sold their rubber to the estate owner and received supplies (food, clothes, and tools) in exchange. But because the owners overcharged for the supplies and underpaid for the rubber, the tappers typically ended up owing money. To make matters even worse, when the American agreement came to an end, prices fell and the industry struggled even more, with many owners eventually abandoning their estates.

It took time for Marina's father, Pedro, to adapt to this rigorous and testing routine. He met his wife, Maria Augusta, the daughter of a mixed Portuguese and African family, and managed to raise his offspring. Marina was one of 11 children born in steady succession during the 1950s and 1960s. The family lived in a shack made from palm-tree wood and straw, built on stilts, with other relatives living nearby. Pedro, like other tappers supplementing their diets, gathered Brazil nuts, culled wild boar and other animals for meat, and cultivated beans and cassava on tiny plots.[3]

Marina remembers her father as a curious man who listened avidly each evening to the Portuguese-language news on the BBC World Service and Voz de América, broadcast on a precious battery-powered radio. She told a biographer that he would spend hours poring over copies of weekly magazines that arrived from time to time from Rio Branco, but which were often months or even years out of date. Marina recalled one evening in 1968 how the family sat around on the earth floor of their shack as Pedro read aloud news reports from the radical weekly *Manchete* about the assassination of John F. Kennedy that had taken place five years earlier.

In this very restricted environment, one of the strongest early influences was folk wisdom and elementary Christian myths. Marina's grandmother, Júlia, with whom she began living at the age of five, taught her New Testament stories gleaned from a tattered catechism that she had brought from Ceará. The cousin of Marina's father, Pedro Mendes, who had lived with indigenous groups in Acre, introduced her to native rituals and magic. In the community, the oral tradition of improvised verse (known as *cordeis*), which developed across the north-east in the eighteenth and nineteenth centuries, had survived and prospered among the immigrant tapper communities.

Even so, material conditions were desperate and the poverty at times was overwhelming. There were no schools or clinics nearby. Although Marina's father could read, her brothers and sisters, as well as most of her other relatives, were illiterate. Diseases were rife. As a child, Marina suffered regular bouts of malaria, hepatitis, tetanus, and leishmaniasis (a disease transmitted by sandfly bites). At the age of six she was infected – probably from contaminated water – by mercury.

Just as it had for Lula and his family back in the 1940s and early 1950s, the reality for the tapper communities was that emigration offered the best hope for social advancement. In 1965, Pedro took his young family 1,000 miles north to the city of Manaus, where he managed a bar for several months before moving again to the east and the Amazonian city of Belém. Neither effort was successful, and Pedro borrowed money from his last employer to make the journey back to Acre, tail between his legs. With the family heavily indebted, Marina, then 11, began working on the *seringal*, rising before dawn, her way lit by the kerosene lamp contained within her *poronga* helmet. Within months, wrote her biographer, Marina had developed the skills of a proficient tapper.[4]

Tapper communities such as Marina's needed extraordinary resilience to survive in these harsh conditions. However, those conditions were about to become much more testing as the military government intensified its drive to develop and settle the Amazon. This push was not entirely new. Back in 1940, Getúlio Vargas, the then president, had announced a 'March to the West' to 'conquer and dominate the valleys of the great equatorial torrents, transforming their blind force into disciplined energy'. For much of the next 30 years, Brazil made sporadic efforts to open up the forest to absorb the poor population struggling to survive in the 'backlands' of the north-east or the expanding peripheries of Brazil's huge Atlantic coastal cities. But this was nothing compared with what was to come in the 1970s.

Military theorists at the country's war college saw the occupation of the rainforest as a security question. The best way to secure the country's borders and maintain control over its natural resources was to bring in settlers, and where better to find them than in the impoverished north-east? General Golbery do Couto e Silva, the military regime's chief political strategist, urged the country to 'flood the Amazon Forest with civilisation'. In 1970 the military government launched a plan to 'integrate so as not to surrender' the Amazon. The scheme's architects also invoked an old slogan that Zionists had popularized back in the nineteenth century. The Amazon, like Palestine a century before, was described 'as a land without people for a people without land'. Cattle were pivotal to this drive, so much so that one Minister of the Interior described the 'steer' as the 'pioneer of the decade'.[5]

The expanding urban population ensured that the demand for beef and dairy products was growing. The authorities offered tax relief and subsidies to would-be settlers. Hence, the typical hump-backed Zebu breed of cattle, whose metabolism had adapted to tropical conditions, began to appear across the region. To integrate these new agricultural zones, the state invested in thousands of miles of new roads. Back in 1960, there were only 200 miles of roads in the entire Amazon. However, the military began to construct enormous highways linking the Amazon to the south-east and the coast. The 1,250-mile BR-010 from Brasília to Belém; the 2,700-mile BR-364 from the south-east to the far west; and the 2,500-mile BR-230 – the so-called Trans-Amazonian Highway – that stretched from the north-east to the far west. On the lands along the new roads, thousands of families established small farms. Alongside the Trans-Amazonian Highway, for example, the military lured thousands of families with plots of land, prefabricated houses, and temporary social benefits. And for every official settler, four others followed in their wake. The Amazon's population, which had numbered only 2.5 million in 1960, quickly increased.[6]

As the pace of road building accelerated, Marina and her fellow rubber tappers found themselves on the front line of a conflict. By the early 1970s, construction crews arrived in Acre to extend the BR-364 highway northward from Rondônia. They brought with them epidemics of malaria and measles. Marina and other family members fell ill. Marina's maternal grandmother died, as well as several of her brothers, sisters, cousins, and other relatives. She caught malaria for the fifth time. And on this occasion it nearly killed her. Marina already had hepatitis, and the medicine she took to attack the malaria parasite damaged her liver badly. Unable to eat basic foods such as nuts, beans, and cassava flour, Marina weakened, her stomach swelled up, and she was unable to work. Leaving the plantation was now a matter of life and death. 'I knew I was going to die if I didn't go to the city', she said.[7] Wearing cheap plastic sandals and carrying a change of clothes and a hammock in a sack, Marina, aged 17, embarked on the uncomfortable six-hour bus journey to Rio Branco.

Once in the capital, where Marina stayed with an aunt, there was more bad news. At the hospital, doctors told her that her condition was terminal. The literacy course run by an agency set up a few years previously was two-thirds complete, and ostensibly, it was too late for her to start. And then how was she to survive financially? Prescribed medicines and changes in diet stabilized her health. Although Marina had never learned the alphabet, she had learned basic arithmetic, an essential skill if tappers were not to be cheated by the middlemen who bought their rubber. That, and her native ability, allowed her to make up lost ground. She found a job minding the children of teachers who were friends of another relative. Within months she had funds to buy bedding and the uniform she needed to satisfy an ambition nurtured since the age of five. She joined the Catholic Order of Maria Reparadora.

Marina did not remain a nun for very long, though, because the world to which she had moved was changing quickly. Acre's governor, Wanderley Dantas, a pro-dictatorship conservative, shared the military government's enthusiasm for cattle. Like them, he thought there was no future in rubber. Acre, fertile and inviting, promoted itself as the 'filet mignon of the Amazon' and – echoing the Palestinian theme – as 'a new Canaan'. Dantas welcomed ranchers from the wealthy southern states of São Paulo, Paraná, and Minas Gerais. The land was cheap. Several of the better-off ranchers began to charter aircraft to ship their cattle northward. Poorer settlers advanced in their wake, and conflict with tapper communities was inevitable. Hundreds of tappers were expelled from their homes as gangs moved in with chainsaws.

Inside the Catholic Church, which Marina Silva was about to enter, there was a good deal of sympathy for the cause of the rubber tappers, many of whom were struggling to survive in an industry that had been abandoned by its owners and was largely moribund. Dom Moacyr Grechi, a Brazilian cleric of Italian descent, was appointed archbishop of Acre and Purus in 1971 and was typical of the new wave of liberation theologians, spending much of his time in poor rural areas.[8] Another radical priest, Otávio Destro, was sent to Acre in 1975 to set up base communities on the rubber plantations. Church missions had supported a new trade union confederation that spread across rural areas in the early 1970s. One of the keenest students at the union's organizing workshops was a young rubber tapper called Chico Mendes. Except for the fact that he was 14 years older, Mendes had a background almost identical to that of Marina. His father, like hers, had been a 'rubber soldier', an immigrant from Ceará. Like Marina, he had been illiterate in his youth. His education and political awakening began in an unexpected way. In the early 1960s he had met by chance an exiled Brazilian communist who had been imprisoned following the unsuccessful Communist Party-led insurrection of 1935. Euclides Fernandes Távora, a former army officer, had spent the rest of his life almost permanently on the run. In the 1950s he had crossed back into Brazil from Bolivia and lived quietly, earning a living from tapping. He met the adolescent Mendes, recognized the boy's keen mind and spent weekends teaching him to read.

By the end of 1975, the year Marina Silva arrived in Rio Branco, organizers had set up two branches of the union. Increasingly, the mood among the tappers favoured confrontation. The tactic adopted was the *empate* in which the union members and their families physically surrounded their rubber trees and blocked access to chainsaw gangs who wanted to cut them down. Tappers would try to dismantle the loggers' camps and break up their machinery or threaten violence to dissuade the invaders. These blockades invariably involved a lot of organization, involved the tappers' families and sometimes lasted for several days. As the union increased its numbers, reaching 30,000 by 1978, and established a state-wide organization, such actions became more common, with an average of four a year between 1976 and 1988.

Marina had met Chico Mendes early in 1977 at a leadership course held by the Church, just as this movement was gaining momentum. The idea of living life as a spiritual recluse was already losing its appeal, and impatient with the conservatism of fellow novices, Marina had left the convent and was becoming familiar with the ideas of liberation theology. Meeting with Mendes hardened her convictions. 'It made me sad. People like Chico Mendes were criticized as being bad, but they were the ones defending the tappers, especially those who had been pushed off their land, and I thought, well if they are communists, the communists must be good because they are fighting for justice.'[9]

Marina started working for the union full-time in 1975, just as Acre's politics began to become more polarized. Frustrated by the defensive abilities of the tappers, ranchers and their supporters started gunning for its leadership. The death toll of tappers and small independent farmers gradually increased in the late 1970s, rising from 39 in 1975 to 51 in 1977 and more than 100 in 1980, when one of the casualties included the union's leader, Wilson de Souza Pinheiro.

Marina, meanwhile, having learned to read very quickly, was studying to enter university and getting involved in radical left-wing politics, including a theatre group where she encountered, for the first time, the ideas of Lenin and the Marxist German playwright Bertolt Brecht.

By 1979 she was working during the day in base communities, taking part in the theatre group on weekends, and studying for university at night. Around the same time, Marina became a member of the clandestine Revolutionary Communist Party, a national organization with a few thousand members that had been closely aligned with the Maoist Communist Party of Brazil and the disastrous guerrilla episode in the Araguaia (see Chapter 3). Like Chico Mendes and Arnóbio 'Binho' Marques, a Trotskyist she had met at the theatre group, Marina was given the code name 'Sara'.[10] A black-and-white photograph taken in 1982 captures this combative figure, sporting an enormous mane of Afro hair, striding confidently at the head of a line of tappers and their families, her face full of determination.

THE ROAD TO *SOCIO-AMBIENTALISMO*

With all this political radicalism, direct action, and violence, it might have been expected that this was only going to end one way, especially since in 1979 the victory of the Sandinista guerrillas in Nicaragua and the apparent imminence of revolutionary insurrections in El Salvador and Guatemala seemed to have given a new lease of life to the old Guevarist certainties about the 'armed struggle'. Acre seemed to have all the ingredients. Facing increasingly aggressive groups of ranchers, there was a radical union movement backed by an activist Church and led by Chico Mendes, a man, who thanks to Távora's endeavours, had been thoroughly schooled in the catechisms of Marxist-Leninism. But that is not the way things turned out.

There were many reasons why Acre avoided more bloodshed. First, based on their experience building up the rubber-tappers' union, Mendes and Marina began to develop a distinct kind of socialism that integrated concern for the environment with a more traditional left-wing set of priorities. Rather than being a subsidiary to the weighty matters of growth, income distribution, and the reduction of poverty, the protection of the environment and in the Amazon – the conservation of the forest – was at the forefront. The people who lived and worked in the forest – indigenous groups as well as groups of tappers themselves who had migrated to the region – would be at the centre of this socio-ambiental movement. This was heretical for many within the PT, particularly those attached to more traditional Marxist notions of class struggle. 'Some people saw the new focus as flirting with American capitalism,' Marina Silva told Rocha de Barros. She and Chico Mendes 'fought a battle with the left so that the people of the forest were not just considered poor peasants'. They had to convince them that the struggle of rubber tappers 'was about keeping the forest intact'.[11] During the 1980s, Mendes and his union persuaded fellow left-wingers to back their demands for changes to Brazil's agrarian reform rules.[12] Soon Mendes and the tappers began demanding that the rubber plantations become part of specially created and legally protected 'extractive' reserves. By 1988, the rubber tappers had succeeded in presenting themselves as the 'genuine defenders of the forest'.

Second, Mendes linked up with Lula just as his plans to form the Workers' Party were coming to fruition. In early 1980, Mendes and a senior colleague travelled down to São Bernardo to meet Lula. The meetings were positive. Acre was the first state outside the south-east heartland where the PT had a serious presence, and the bond between the two leaders was strengthened when both became involved in a long legal battle. After the assassination of Wilson de

Souza Pinheiro, Lula had travelled to Acre to attend his funeral. He gave a fiery speech, using much of the same imagery deployed the year before in São Bernardo to go on the attack. Subsequently, a group of tappers had taken the instruction literally and killed the suspected assassin, a ranch manager, and Lula – along with Mendes and others – were arrested for murder. The case took its time to wind through the courts before, in 1984, a military court absolved Lula, Mendes, and their colleagues.

The rubber tappers made more striking progress, however, in a third area. Backed by NGOs, sympathetic journalists and academics, the union attracted support for their cause in the United States and eventually was able to reduce the flow of funds from the multilateral banks to development projects in the Amazon. This represented a significant new dimension to the PT's approach to politics, allowing it to build alliances with groups who would not have been overly-sympathetic to a more traditional class-based socialist message.

Key figures in this campaign included Mary Helena Alegretti, a Brazilian anthropologist, Tony Gross, a British academic who headed up Oxfam's projects in the Amazon, and the conservationist Simon Cowell, whose films helped publicize the importance of deforestation and its links to climate change. Allegretti, who had been researching a remote rubber plantation, met Mendes and began to raise funds for much-needed schools for the children of the rubber tappers. Oxfam supported these efforts and helped establish a cooperative that would allow the tappers to bypass the commercial intermediaries that had traditionally been exploitative. Allegretti, who had formed an NGO, also took up the rubber-tappers' case in Brasília, creating a lobby to counter the influence of the landowners' association formed by ranchers in 1985. Gross, the British filmmaker Cowell, and Allegretti also took their campaign to Washington by persuading American lawmakers to block flows of subsidised multinational finance to damaging Amazonian projects. During the 1970s loans from the World Bank and the Inter-American Development Bank had supported road building, settlement, and energy schemes. But Mendes and these supporters successfully lobbied for environmental safeguards to be attached to all future loans. The campaigns raised the profile of indigenous populations and groups, such as the rubber tappers, whose fate had previously attracted little interest, either within or outside Brazil. By the late 1980s, Chico Mendes was being lauded as a leader of a new environmental movement, winning prizes from the United Nations and the Better World Society, a short-lived initiative launched by the American media magnate Ted Turner. The attention established Mendes's reputation as an icon of the new movement, a status only enhanced after his assassination in December 1988.

Marina really came into her own in electoral politics. Along with the rest of the party, the PT in Acre had begun to contest local elections in the mid-1980s but had made little progress. That was in part because in the 1980s many of the *seringueiros* who would naturally have been sympathetic to Mendes were illiterate and therefore unable to vote. But Marina also adapted to the challenge more successfully than her mentor. Her colleagues judged her to be the better communicator of the two. 'Chico (Mendes) always did it his way but it was never quite right. Marina was more flexible. When people didn't turn up to electoral meetings, Marina would go out in the middle of the day and give speeches to captive audiences at bus stops. She was compelling. People would even miss their bus to hear her finish,' Jorge Viana (who would become governor of Acre) told Camargo César.[13] Or as Francisco Afonso, another member of the same group, put it: "People began to see her as a game-changer. She was poor, black, a woman, and physically frail but she spoke with such empathy and connected with people."[14]

Only a month before Mendes's death, in November 1988, Marina had been elected as a councillor for the PT in Rio Branco, achieving one of the highest votes, as a proportion of the population, in Brazil. In the press conference afterwards she had surprised local journalists by openly discussing the financial benefits of elected office and returning the special payments habitually made by local councils to *vereadores* or councillors. This gained her a reputation for honesty and openness, increasing her popularity among city dwellers who did not necessarily support the rubber tappers. Afonso claimed that Marina's competence, humble origins, and daring 'won the sympathy of the middle class, that historically had voted for conservative candidates', a position consolidated by the strength of her vote in the 1990 elections for state senator and for her triumph in 1994 which – as we have seen – marked her entry onto the national political stage. With Chico Mendes a martyr to the cause and her own international reputation as an environmentalist growing, Marina in 2002 was a natural choice to be the new minister in Lula's government. But during her first years in office she faced significant challenges. Soaring demand from China had increased the prices of soya, meat, and minerals, and increased the incentives to cut down or burn virgin rainforest and put the land to agricultural use. Indeed, in the first two years of the PT government, with the ministry still refining its plans and commodities booming, deforestation rose close to record levels, with 26,130 square kilometres of forest lost in the 12 months to August 2004.

But then Marina put in place a series of measures that gradually began to take effect. The government gave IBAMA (*Instituto Brasileiro do Meio Ambiente e dos Recursos Naturais Renováveis*, or Brazilian Institute of the Environment and Renewable Natural Resources), the ministry's agency responsible for monitoring deforestation, the authority to levy fines and block credits to ranchers who breached the forest codes that required them to maintain tree cover. Regulators began to confiscate the equipment of illegal miners and loggers. In the first year of Marina's tenure in the ministry, the number of fines levied against those responsible for illegally clearing rainforests rose by 50 per cent. Brazil had been monitoring the destruction since 1988, with high-resolution images taken annually from the Landsat satellite. But in 2004 a new system known as Deter (Real Time Deforestation Detection System) was brought into action, providing data on a monthly rather than an annual basis, allowing regulators to act more quickly. Brazil also stepped up the creation of protected reserves and parks, launching in 2007 a new government agency – the Chico Mendes Institute for Biodiversity Conservation – to oversee them. Under Marina's stewardship, the ministry created 25 million hectares of conservation areas at the federal level. Regulators made particularly impressive progress in stemming the advance of deforestation in areas such as southern Pará, with the creation of a big new park straddling the BR-193 highway. The government demonstrated that it was prepared to back up these powers with force. In 2008, for example, Lula sanctioned the dispatch of troops to Tailândia, the logging capital of Pará, after angry sawmill workers kicked out regulators. Deforestation rates began to decline from 2005 onwards, reaching a low of 4,000 square kilometres by 2012. Between 2003 and 2008 the Lula government was responsible for the creation of nearly three-quarters of all the world's new protected areas. More than 700 people were sent to jail for environmental crimes. The Intergovernmental Panel on Climate Change praised Brazil's efforts, stating that no other country had made a more significant contribution to combating global warming.

Given this progress, it was surprising when rifts emerged between Marina and the government, and in May 2008 she unexpectedly resigned from her job. The immediate cause was Lula's decision to hand over responsibility for the strategic development of the Amazon not to Marina, as she had wanted, but to a left-wing Harvard philosophy professor, Roberto Mangabeira Unger. Critics view Mangabeira as something of an out-of-touch romantic and he had also not endeared himself to the PT, by describing – shortly before his appointment – the Lula government as 'the most corrupt in Brazilian history'.[15] Mangabeira, who only lasted two years in the position, criticized Marina's vision of the Amazon strategy as one of 'primitive and artisanal extractivism'. Subsequently, in 2015, with Dilma Rousseff now president, he was given the same job again, suggesting that Lula's successor regarded him as an essential ally, although his second stint in Brasília lasted only a few months.

However, behind the scenes, tensions had been growing between Marina and several of Lula's ministers, particularly his chief of staff, Dilma Rousseff. Marina was unhappy about the way regulators approved the use of new transgenic seeds, but she found the presidential palace impervious to protest. 'The presidential palace was committed at all costs to the transgenics,' a member of Marina's advisory team told the journal *Piauí* in 2010.[16]

The big crunch came in the second term, though, when Lula asked Dilma Rousseff, to coordinate a build-up in infrastructure spending, consolidating on the stability and social progress achieved in his first four years. Lula ignored Marina's opposition to plans to asphalt a major road and build three sizable new hydroelectric dams planned for the Amazon. Environmentalists judged that the BR-163 road, which links the central-western agricultural belt with the Amazonian port of Santarém, could become a potential vector for deforestation. 'She was outraged because these projects are not meant to bring electricity to rural families, but rather to supply energy-intensive industries that will sell steel, pulp, aluminium, and cement outside of Brazil,' said one former advisor.[17] One commentator later graphically claimed that the project 'has been stuffed down Marina's throat'.[18]

Lula, it seemed, was happy to garner international praise for his minister's achievements, but, as his attention turned to 2010 and attempts to secure his legacy and maintain his party, so jobs, incomes, and living standards were what mattered most. As Gilberto Carvalho, the minister we met in Chapter 6, told the weekly magazine *Veja* in 2008, 'The president thinks preservation is important but not decisive. What is decisive is the economy.'[19]

In any event, the rift with the PT widened particularly during the 2014 election campaign, when at one point Marina – running as a candidate for the Socialist Party *Partido Socialista Brasileiro* or PSB) – looked capable of defeating Rousseff, the incumbent president. Her criticism of the PT's corruption and her support for Rousseff's 2016 impeachment also underlined the depth of the chasm separating the two women. It is to Rousseff's career that we now turn.

12

The Dilma Dilemma

Under a burning mid-morning sun, Dilma Rousseff smiled discreetly as President Luiz Inácio Lula da Silva beckoned her from her second-row seat to the front of an improvised stage. 'I want to thank our Dilma Rousseff. She is the mother of our infrastructure programme,' Lula told the crowd that had been gathering since sunrise in the centre of the sprawling Rio de Janeiro slum of Complexo de Alemão.

It was 7 March 2008 and Brazil's leader was announcing an expensive investment programme in a vast, heavily populated slum area that stretches across rocky hillsides in the north of the city. The government planned to construct asphalt roads, build new houses, clinics, and schools, and improve water and sewage systems. A brand-new transport system, a futuristic cable car linking the Complexo to the better off districts where many residents worked, was to be installed.

'We have to get rid of this idea that these areas are all about crime and you can't do anything,' said Lula. Back in the 1990s, Rio's state government had begun paving roads and introducing electricity connections through its Favela-Bairro programme, and now the federal government was throwing more resources into the mix.

Rousseff had won a fearsome reputation as a hard-working energy secretary and chief of staff since the corruption scandals of 2005. Her efficiency would help allay any fears that these ambitious ideas might not materialize. 'She will look after all these projects and make sure everything is up to speed,' said Lula. 'And she will make sure all those responsible are on their toes. The other ministers will be answerable to her.'[1]

But this was about something bigger than public works. By 2008, Lula was convinced that Rousseff's loyalty and technical capacity were exactly what was needed if the Workers' Party was to build on the successes of his first term and a half in office. Under the constitution, Lula could not run for a third consecutive mandate, and Rousseff seemed like an ideal successor. Journalists covering the event in Complexo had figured this out, and although Rousseff dismissed their questions as impertinent, insiders now knew where things were heading. As a minibus carrying the official entourage wound its way down the steep, narrow streets towards the city's airport, Franklin Martins, the communications minister, turned to Rousseff and said: 'So, that's it. You are the candidate.'[2]

For Lula and the Workers' Party government, it seemed logical. In his first administration, Lula had stabilized the economy and begun to improve living standards. Now, he wanted to build on those achievements and address the shortcomings that held back the country's development and stopped it from growing more quickly. There were many deficiencies, but the country's weak infrastructure remained one of the biggest. Poor roads, inadequate ports, and unreliable energy supply all added to business costs, making companies think twice about investing in the country and leaving more distant regions isolated.

Rousseff had done well as Minister of Mines and Energy. In 2004 she revamped the regulatory system with reforms that won widespread approval. By 2006, Brazil was attracting fresh investment, and capacity was increasing at a rate of more than 4 per cent a year. Standard & Poor's, the American credit-rating agency that Brazil did not always find it easy to please, praised the new system's more straightforward rules and emphasis on long-term planning, noting that Brazil had recovered from the 2002 crisis. Rousseff had performed equally strongly as chief of staff, steadying the government in the wake of the *Mensalão* affair. Basking in the rising popularity that followed his 2006 re-election, Lula attributed a significant part of his success to the work that she was doing as his chief of staff.

Even so, Rousseff's emergence was still a big surprise. For the public, she was an unknown. She had been part of Lula's government from the beginning but had never once, as Brazilian journalists often pointed out, stood for election. That morning in Complexo, dressed in a sober blue blouse and dark slacks and carrying a smart shoulder bag, she looked every inch like a professional civil servant busy behind the scenes rather than a political campaigner battling it out on the front line. One cynical member of the Workers' Party had criticized her lack of charisma and public presence. 'It would be like trying to get a lamppost elected,' he said.[3]

These concerns subsided somewhat after 2010. After all, with Lula's backing, Rousseff proved that she could win votes. She triumphed in 2010 and more narrowly in 2014, but the doubters in the end proved to be right. In government, her lack of political experience and know-how proved to be crippling weaknesses that paved the way for her isolation and impeachment. Her mismanagement and political clumsiness eventually wasted all the political capital that the PT leader had built. As Lula was told by Marta Suplicy, another senior PT woman leader, his decision early in 2014 not to insist that she relinquish her candidacy in his favour was the worst of his life.[4] Where Dilma Rousseff came from and what exactly went wrong are, therefore, essential parts of our story and will be the focus for the rest of this chapter.

DILMA'S IDEALISM

Dilma Rousseff's background could not have been more different to Lula's own. Whereas Lula grew up in a poverty-stricken broken home, Dilma – just two years his junior – came to adulthood surrounded by domestic comforts and intellectual stimuli. Her family was well-off. Pétar Russév, her father, was born in Gabrovo in Bulgaria in 1900, studied engineering in Germany, graduated in law, and then worked for a textile business before fleeing to Paris in 1929 and then emigrating to South America. According to some accounts, Russév was a member of the Communist Party.[5]

By 1945, with a new Brazilian Christian name and his surname Frenchified, Pedro Rousseff settled in Belo Horizonte, married Dilma Jane da Silva Vania, a young schoolteacher, and began working as a steel contractor and in real estate. Dilma was born in 1947. Along with her older brother Igor and her younger sister Zania Lúcia, she grew up in a comfortable house with a swimming pool and an orchard. There were three servants. The family was a member of the local tennis and country clubs, and the children attended private schools, receiving additional lessons at home in piano and French. When Pedro Rousseff died of a heart attack in 1962, he left his dependants with more than a dozen properties.

Dilma's father was also an important intellectual influence. Under his guidance she had developed sophisticated tastes. Her father took her to the opera in Rio de Janeiro and São Paulo and encouraged her to read literature. By the time she was 12, Rousseff had devoured *Germinal*, Émile Zola's tragic novel of striking French mine workers. In her teens she read nearly the entire series of Honoré de Balzac's nineteenth-century realist novels, *La Comédie humaine* (*The Human Comedy*), and discovered the challenging works of Fyodor Dostoyevsky. 'Dilminha was always with some book or other,' Igor told one journalist.[6] She was also developing a social conscience. In the late 1950s, as Rousseff entered adolescence, the Catholic Church was urging its members to care for the underprivileged. Each Sunday, Rousseff – along with fellow students at her conservative convent school, Colégio Sion, was taken to the *Moro de Papagaio favela* and, under the direction of the nuns, helped organize residents' meetings and taught people simple rules of hygiene, such as why, for example, it was so important to boil drinking water. Rousseff, however, was soon wanting to do more. 'I remember her saying this is all very well, but it is not going to change anything at all,' a school friend of Rousseff's told Ricardo Amaral.[7] 'It really left an impression on me. She was only 12 or 13 years old at the time.'

Pedro's death set the stage for a new phase in Dilma's development, a fact she openly admitted some years later. 'When my father died, I lost my super-super ego.'[8] In March 1964, at the age of 16, Rousseff entered a new, less conservative school, the Colégio Estadual, to prepare for her university entrance exams. Even before the military coup, the school, designed by the Communist modernist architect Oscar Niemeyer, was already a hive of political and cultural activity. Dilma quickly made friends with the more radical. Each Saturday a group of girls – still wearing their uniforms of white blouses, green ties, and grey skirts – started to visit a boarding house owned by a friend's mother, where they were offered the *feijoada* (Brazil's classic bean and pork stew) prepared for guests, and where they could continue their excited discussions about music, modernism, and Marxism. Amaral describes how the group would interrupt earnest political debates to play records featuring John Coltrane and Miles Davis, critique the novels of Jean-Paul Sartre and Simone de Beauvoir, and discuss the films of directors Jean-Luc Godard, Federico Fellini, and Michelangelo Antonioni.

As the debates (which we described in Chapter 3) raged among Brazilian leftists about how to respond to the military coup, the sympathies of Dilma and her friends were clear. Pragmatism and caution were dull and out of fashion. Dramatic action was very much in vogue. The revolution could not wait. Already many of the group had sympathies for the Catholic left. But the organizer of these get-togethers was already involved in another group, known as Workers' Politics (Polop or *Política Operária*), formed by dissidents of the Communist Party and which was in some respects close to the ideas of Leon Trotsky.[9] By 1965, the Saturday *feijoada* group had become a branch of Polop.

Rousseff started studying economics at the Federal University of Minas Gerais, but Polop began to absorb more of her time. Dilma worked on its paper *O Piquete* (*The Picket*) and gave classes in Marxism to fellow activists. By the age of 20, having cut her hair stylishly short, she had married the group's leader, Claudio Galeno, a former soldier and journalist three years her senior.

As the dictatorship continued to restrict further democratic freedoms, the young activists began to explore how they might launch some kind of armed action. A debate had raged about the advisability of this. Dilma had initially been cautious. But inspired by Ho Chi Minh's Vietcong and the Cuban revolutionary leaders Fidel Castro and Che Guevara, she threw her lot in with the radicals and, by the end of 1967, was part of a group that joined forces with a handful of ex-soldiers to form the National Liberation Command (*Comando de Libertação Nacional* or Colina). 'The prolonged popular war offered by Ho Chi Minh seemed to take too long, and the Cubans had changed things so quickly,' wrote Amaral.[10]

Colleagues interviewed by one writer said the group had been seduced by Guevara's ideas of the guerrilla *foco* popularized by the French Marxist Régis Debray. This was the notion, as we explained in Chapter 3, that a determined, well-trained group of fighters could outmanoeuvre a much larger standing army and stimulate a broader social revolution. Dilma herself was sceptical. 'Dilma wasn't entirely sure about the "twelve men in the mountains",' wrote Amaral, referring to the established caricature of the way Cuban guerrillas had overthrown Batista. And because she had become a very visible figure in the Belo Horizonte student movement, it made no sense for her to take part directly in the actions planned by Colina. But she went along with the idea anyway. 'It seemed obvious [to her] that you couldn't defeat a military dictatorship without weapons,' wrote Amaral.[11] By the end of 1968, members of Colina had stolen a few cars, robbed four banks, and launched a couple of bomb attacks on the homes of local military leaders. Dilma's partner, Claudio Galeno, was the group's leader. He had started to experiment with making bombs from materials he found in his father's pharmacy.[12] The former Air Force sergeant, João Lucas Alves, who provided the young activists with weapons training, stayed in the apartment where Galeno and Rousseff lived.

The military was soon on the group's trail, and early in 1969, Dilma and Galeno were forced to leave the city and move to Rio de

Janeiro. In mid-year Dilma organized the merger between Colina Carlos Lamarca's VPR (which we encountered in Chapter 3). A romantic interlude followed. The organization despatched Galeno to the city of Porto Alegre. In his absence, Dilma met and fell in love with another Colina militant who had also arrived in Rio, Carlos Araújo. With Araújo, Dilma helped organize the most significant action involving VAR-Palmares, the July 1969 robbery of $2.5 million from the safe box of a corrupt Rio politician. Araújo took the metalworker who blew open the safe from Porto Alegre to Rio, and he and Rousseff helped shift the money. The theft kept the group going for a while longer, but it counted for little. As we saw in an earlier chapter, VAR-Palmares was quickly broken up by army intelligence. During the second half of 1969, Rousseff had kept a stash of arms and munitions under her bed in the boarding house where she had stayed in São Paulo as the group sought to preserve some semblance of organization. She was picked up in January 1970 and held in the notorious dungeons of the Doi-Codi, where for three weeks she was hung from a device known as the parrot's perch, beaten, and electrocuted. The experience, followed by three years in the women's wing of the Tiradentes prison in São Paulo, left Dilma with a malfunctioning thyroid and some other health issues, but with her fierce commitment undimmed.

The picture of her that emerges during these years is of a strong and utterly devoted Marxist revolutionary. Maklouf's interviews with fellow militants tend to confirm Dilma's prominence within the group. Jorge Nahas, who participated in Colina's first armed action, said Dilma had a 'great natural capacity for leadership. She knew how to impose herself in a meeting that was naturally made up of bossy men.' Indeed, her captors were sure they had caught an extremely big fish, with the military prosecutor labelling her the 'Joan of Arc of the guerrilla movement'. Even in prison, Dilma won a reputation for being a formidable organizer, providing economics classes for fellow inmates, arguing that to study was a 'revolutionary duty', and rigorously insisting on regular attendance at the classes she gave. However, there was also a sense in the biographical accounts that she epitomized the impractical utopianism of the movement. Carlos Lamarca, who had spent more than a decade in the army and had been part of a United Nations peacekeeping contingent in Gaza, was famously dismissive of the students and suggested that the *foco* they espoused was *floco* (soft and flaky). One militant interviewed by Maklouf described Dilma as 'aggressive but a little bit fragile. I got the impression that Lamarca saw her as a stuck-up intellectual.'

Lula, as we saw in an earlier chapter, held student radicals in contempt and would surely have held that view of Dilma had he met her at the time. Even when she began to explore reformist politics, Rousseff remained on a very different track from the man who she would succeed as president of the country three decades later. At the time of her release in 1973, Araújo was still serving time at a prison in his home city of Porto Alegre in the south of Brazil. After briefly reconnecting with her own family, Dilma travelled south, stayed with Araújo's parents, and eventually set up a home in the city. The couple had a child.[13] Dilma resumed her university studies and – as Brazil slowly democratized – she began to re-engage with left-wing politics, choosing to work with the more traditional Democratic Labour Party (PDT) of the left-wing populist Leonel Brizola rather than the embryonic PT. It was not surprising in any way. Brizola, who had been governor of Rio Grande do Sul at the time of the coup, remained a powerful and influential figure in the state. Although the PDT was very hierarchical and frequently subject to Brizola's whims, the adopted party might have been viewed as a better bet for the cause of socialist reform than the untried PT. Araújo had been close to Brizola before the coup and subsequently became a state senator for the party, serving from 1982. Dilma worked as an adviser for the PDT's state assembly legislators and was an enthusiastic campaigner when her husband sought election as mayor of Porto Alegre. But the alignment meant the couple found themselves frequently competing with the PT for members and votes.[14] These tensions declined in the

1990s. The PT and the PDT combined forces to support Dutra's successful gubernatorial campaign to become state governor in 1998, and Dilma was one of several PDT members who worked for his administration, taking over as energy secretary. Shortly afterwards, Rousseff switched to the PT.

ROUSSEFF MOVES CENTRE-STAGE

It was during these years, when she played roles in the state government of Rio Grande do Sul and the municipality of Porto Alegre, that Rousseff established a reputation as an effective manager. As energy secretary, she had quickly licensed the construction of several new generators, which meant that the state avoided the blackouts that affected much of the rest of the country during 2001 and 2002. As he prepared his team for the 2002 election, the achievement caught Lula's eye. Rousseff was called upon to participate in discussions of energy policy. Her grasp of detail impressed him. 'She always appeared with her laptop at hand. She was different to the other advisers because she had more practical experience,' he said later. 'In a meeting of 15 people, she stood out because of her objectivity and knowledge of the sector.'[15]

During the transition period that followed the October 2002 election, Lula's convictions became firmer. Rousseff's willingness to learn and to listen to business leaders impressed the rising Antônio Palocci and even won plaudits from members of the outgoing Cardoso team. It was no surprise when Lula gave her the job of Minister of Mines and Energy, preferring her over long-time PT militants who had stronger claims to the position. Following the crisis of the liberalized model introduced under Cardoso, many within the PT favoured the renationalization of the sector. Rousseff would have none of it. Instead, she maintained the mixed system but revamped regulations and adjusted the rules for auctions in a way that encouraged bidders to offer lower prices, thereby reducing costs for consumers. A new agency was established to facilitate long-term planning.

SUPPLY STEADILY EXPANDED

Overall, Rousseff seemed to exemplify the quiet competence that helped underpin investor confidence. By the mid-2000s, her ministry had won a reputation for expertise at a time when Lula was losing his most important allies in the party to the *Mensalão* corruption scandal. In July 2005, with Lula's poll ratings sinking following the resignation of José Dirceu, Lula asked Dilma to be chief of staff because, in the words of the Minister of Communications, Franklin Martins, 'she made things work and got things moving'[16].

In her new position, the minister continued to excel. 'She did everything much more quickly and more efficiently than I thought possible,' said Lula in an interview published later. 'If I asked for something on a Saturday night, by Monday morning, it was ready. The main PT leaders [Dirceu and Palocci] had fallen by the wayside. Dilma, when I made her chief of staff, did such exceptional work that it left me feeling completely calm.' Along with three other senior women – Graça Foster, Miriam Belchior, and Tereza Campello – Rousseff was 'worth [her] weight in gold'.[17]

As chief of staff Dilma was now at the heart of government. Gilberto Carvalho, one of the founders of the PT who we met in Chapter 6, was by now Lula's private secretary and was constantly with the president. He told Maklouf in 2009 that Dilma's ability to 'face up to difficult situations', as well as her technical capacity, marked her out. As chief of staff and head of the infrastructure programme, Dilma saw more of Lula than any other adviser. Between June 2005 and July 2009 (when Maklouf wrote his piece for *Piauí*), Rousseff met with Lula almost every day and had private meetings with the president three times a week on average.

Martins suggested there was something familial about Lula's relationship with his heir apparent. Lula was only two years older than Dilma, but 'they were like father and daughter. [Lula was] a father immensely proud of his daughter. He admired her profoundly.' Dilma's performance as the 'mother of the PAC' reinforced the bond. Progress was bumpy, primarily due to the complexity of the country's planning system and the lengthy environmental approval process. Even so, by 2010, R$440 billion of new road, railway, energy, and other projects were underway, and over a third were more than three-quarters complete. Federal investment had risen by more than a quarter during Lula's two terms in office. In his account of the PT, Rocha de Barros said party activists sometimes despaired about the sluggishness of projects, but the programme could be judged a 'reasonable success'.[18]

As we saw in the previous chapter, however, there were some concerns about Rousseff even at this time, especially among fellow PT members and environmentalists. One of the projects, in particular, a R$40 billion plan to build a dam at Belo Monte on the Xingu River in Pará, became a cause célèbre. The case was a significant one because it highlighted the government's growing determination to drive through developments irrespective of their environmental impact, and it illustrated the downside of Rousseff's management style.

Belo Monte, the largest of five Amazonian dams built during Rousseff's presidency and opened in 2016, diverted the Xingu River away from an 85-mile stretch on which three indigenous groups, as well as traditional fishing communities, depended for their livelihoods, and prompted a flood of litigation. The scale of construction work involved sucked in vast numbers of migrants to the town of Altamira, swelling its population at one point by up to 50 per cent, putting massive pressure on local resources and contributing to a crime wave that has made the town one of the six most dangerous in Brazil.[19] The plant was designed to generate power from the natural flow and elevation drop of a river (on a so-called run-of-the-river basis). That need not necessarily have made it less efficient than conventional plants that store water in a large dam. But at Belo Monte the seasonal variations in the river's depth and flow have been greater than expected, and output has regularly fallen well short of targets. Transmission lines linking the plant to Atlantic coast cities can be used for only five months of the year. 'Project designers appear to have seriously underestimated the Xingu River's flow rates and fluctuations between wet and dry seasons, while also not accounting for reductions in flow due to deforestation caused by rapidly expanding cattle ranches and soy plantations far upriver in Mato Grosso state,' wrote one reporter early in 2020.[20]

Critics had warned that this might happen, but Rousseff, with her disdain for the windy, long-drawn-out, and consensus-seeking style traditionally preferred by the PT, rode roughshod over them. Antônia Melo, an experienced and respected PT activist from Altamira, remembers meeting Rousseff in 2004 to express her concerns about Belo Monte and being treated with utter disdain. 'When we got there, it was a while before Dilma appeared. Then, there she was with officials on either side as if she was a queen surrounded by her courtiers.' Melo and a friendly PT deputy, Zé Geraldo, had said that they wanted the study of the plant's viability to be serious. 'Dilma punched the table. And simply said, "Belo Monte is going ahead." And then she got up and left.'[21]

Rousseff supporters would have cause to question her claims of efficiency and clear thinking on more than one occasion in the years to come. Back in Complexo do Alemão, for example, the futuristic R$250 million cable-car system – the centrepiece of a R$750 million investment programme that Lula had announced that morning – was delivered in 2011. However, within five years, it had closed, having proved to be completely unviable. Nearly ten years later, it remains out of action, having been open for just five years.

For the moment, though, as Lula and his campaign team began to consider how to make Rousseff electable, these doubts were very much in the background. The steady improvement in Brazil's circumstances had emboldened Lula. The global financial crisis of 2008–9 had relatively little effect in Brazil. Lula dismissed it as a 'little wave'. The success of Brazil's bids to host the 2014 World Cup and the 2016 Olympic Games were seen as markers of the country's newly acquired status. The discovery in 2006 of plentiful new reserves of oil 120 miles off the coast of Rio de Janeiro confirmed Lula's sense that the country was living what he repeatedly described as 'a magic moment'. The discovery of the oil, known as pre-salt because exploration teams had found it below thick layers of salt, offered enormous future potential. As Clara Ant, another senior adviser close to the president, told Maklouf in 2009, Dilma Rousseff seemed to be Lula's political equivalent of the new-found oil wealth. When journalists first started talking about Dilma's candidacy, cynics had doubted her electability. But by 2010, with Lula hugely popular, the economy growing at its fastest rate for 40 years, and millions of Brazilians enjoying unprecedented access to consumer markets, Dilma's election was inevitable. What could possibly go wrong?

DILMA'S DIFFICULTIES

Elected with a sizeable majority, Dilma Rousseff began her first term in office amid some considerable optimism. In the run-up to the 2010 election, the Lula government had spent quite heavily, the economy was overheating, and public finances were stretched. Rousseff soon announced measures to bring things under control, to allow the Central Bank to reduce interest rates, lower the cost of credit, and enable the private sector to invest. Antônio Palocci, who had been working as a consultant since his resignation in 2006, returned to serve as chief of staff, reassuring the markets that the ebullient mood of 2010 remained in place. One investment bank referred to Dilma as 'Tropical Maggie', a comparison with the British Conservative Prime Minister who had orchestrated a series of far-reaching liberal reforms in the 1980s.

Soon enough, though, events blew the government off course. The international economy began to slow down as the shockwaves stemming from the 2008–9 financial crisis continued to ripple around the world. During 2011 several smaller European countries, notably Greece, were unable to repay or refinance their debts. China began to grow at a slower pace, triggering a fall in commodity prices. Brazil's top two exports, soya and iron ore, fell by 13.5 per cent and 22 per cent respectively in 2011. US monetary policy weakened the dollar, prompting a surge of speculative capital into emerging markets, such as Brazil, where interest rates were higher. Brazil's currency, the *real*, strengthened to such an extent that it made it difficult for local manufacturers to compete. Cheap Chinese imports flooded the country. Economists began to suggest that Brazil was suffering from a form of Dutch disease, so-called because of the way, in the 1960s, the strength of Dutch gas exports had damaged the rest of the Netherlands' economy. Guido Mantega, who continued as Finance Minister when Rousseff became president, claimed that Brazil was fighting a 'currency war'.[22]

As Dilma and her economic team began to address this new situation, they started to diverge from the cautious macroeconomic approach of the Cardoso and Lula governments. As we saw in Chapter 8, at the heart of the stability ushered in during the later 1990s, the *Plano Real* had been a trio of policies: a floating exchange rate, an inflation target set by the Central Bank, and a fiscal balance that allowed the country to meet its financial obligations comfortably and avoid any increase in its debt burden. In mid-2011, under pressure from the new president, the Central Bank began cutting interest rates despite inflation ticking upward. Alarmed by the impact on businesses of the currency's strength, the government began offering tax breaks. At the end of 2012, Marcio Holland, a senior official in the Ministry of Finance, gave a name to this new, more interventionist and heterodox approach, describing it as a 'new economic matrix'. But as he admitted in an interview with Carlos Rocha,[23] it was in fact a 'post facto rationalisation of what had already been done' rather than a coherent set of measures.[24]

Worried by signs of slowing growth, Dilma and her ministers began to respond to every business demand, conceding easier loans and reducing energy prices at a stroke, a move that pushed the electricity companies to the brink of bankruptcy. Worse still, in 2012 the government had quickly begun to backpedal on its commitment to tighter fiscal policy. Spending was increasing, but the tax breaks were eroding revenue (by R$46.4 billion in 2012, R$78.6 billion in 2013, and R$99.4 billion in 2014). 'You couldn't loosen monetary and fiscal policy at the same time,' Holland told Rocha de Barros. 'From mid-2012, there was no economic strategy in Brazil, in the sense of one policy anchoring another.'[25]

The second mistake that Rousseff made, though, made matters far worse and eventually led to her impeachment. As we saw in Chapter 10, after the disaster of the Mensalão scandal, Lula, like previous democratic presidents, formed a coalition and ceded control of several ministries to the PMDB and various smaller parties. This alliance remained intact during the election campaign, helped Rousseff win the presidency, and party managers renegotiated it when she came to office. Rousseff, though, was never comfortable with such arrangements.

Her 'ethical clean-up' (*faxina ética*) started with the ministries. Press reports, often based on deliberate leaks, would expose cases of petty corruption. In one case a minister had used a private jet owned by a businessman who had recently struck a deal with government officials; in another a minister was paying his maid and private hotel bills from a government account. Rousseff sacked those responsible. By the end of her first year, she had dismissed six ministers, most of whom had served happily and untroubled in the government of Lula. In five cases the parties involved were from allied parties. A sixth, Antônio Palocci – who had initially come back into government as Rousseff's chief of staff – was sacked following controversies about the amount of money he had made from private consultancies.

His replacement, Gleisi Hoffmann, was criticized by Nelson Jobim, the Defence Minister, because she 'did not know Brasília'. Jobim's insubordination led him to also bite the dust. This crusade was popular. Dilma ended her first year with strong ratings. In February 2012 the president extended the drive to Petrobras, the country's largest public company, which politicians had long used as a source of party funding. The company's president, Sergio Gabrielli, a founder of the PT and an academic economist, was replaced by Graça Foster, an austere engineer and long-time Petrobras executive who had worked closely with Dilma during the 2000s. Foster caused waves, summarily removing from their positions several of the company's directors who had been appointed by parties in the government alliance and who, as it soon emerged afterwards with the onset of the Lava Jato corruption investigation, had been channelling money to their political patrons. The private sector and local and international media all welcomed this as a necessary shift to a more technical style of governance, marking the beginning of a new era, sometimes referring to it as 'Delulafication'.

For Dilma's supporters within the PT, it exemplified a new republicanism, an experiment in ethical politics that took the Workers' Party back to its origins and brought it closer to the people it was supposed to represent. The problem, though, was that it was politically flawed. 'Republicanism' was only feasible through carefully crafted reforms that made political financing more transparent and elected representatives to genuinely respond to the interests of voters. Dilma Rousseff was effectively undermining her political base and damaging a painstakingly established coalition. She turned away potential allies and sowed resentment. As one senior Petista told Celso Rocha, 'A clean-up was excellent, but what was she going to put in its place?'[26] Unwittingly, at a time of greater economic uncertainty, Rousseff was undermining governability. At precisely the same time, the president and an increasingly narrow circle of advisers exacerbated the problem by meddling with the successful economic recipes of Cardoso and Lula, introducing new imbalances and unsettling investors and business leaders. Dilma's idealism distanced her from the messy world of practical politics. And – as we will see in the next chapter – her presidency would soon start to crumble because of that.

13

The Fall

When Dilma Rousseff won her second term of office in October 2014, her celebrations were distinctly muted. Lula, who was with her after the results were announced, picked up on his protégé's sombre mood. 'I am convinced it was the first time I saw someone win an election and be sad about it,' he told a small group of sympathetic journalists sometime later. 'She didn't enjoy winning. She told us that she never wanted to take part in a debate again.'[1]

There was quite a bit for Rousseff to be gloomy about. For a start, the election had been a bruising contest. Four years previously, Rousseff had won by a majority of 12 million votes over her main rival from Cardoso's PSDB. Yet in 2014 she was only 450,000 votes ahead of her primary challenger. The margin was so narrow that the defeated PSDB candidate, Aécio Neves, the grandson of former president-elect Tancredo Neves, felt able to contest the result, questioning the integrity of Brazil's electronic voting system and foreshadowing the tactics that Jair Bolsonaro was to adopt eight years later. The electoral court rejected Neves's challenge just as it would Bolsonaro's, affirming the reliability of arrangements. The aggressive stance of Neves and the PSDB reflected the more radical anti-government mood evident in opposition protests towards the end of the campaign.

Even before that, the campaign had been marked by gutter politics and mudslinging. In the first round, the PT resorted to the dirtiest of campaigns to denigrate Rousseff's main rival and former left-wing ally, Marina Silva. As we saw in Chapter 11, Marina had left the government and the party after a series of clashes with Rousseff (and Lula) over policy towards the Amazon. She had run against her former comrade in 2010 for the Green Party, winning more than 19 million votes on a platform that emphasized environmental sustainability and transparent and accountable government. Still, she failed to make the second-round run-off.

Marina was developing a political approach, as she later told Rocha de Barros,[2] that aimed to integrate the legacies of Cardoso and Lula, combining the PSDB's market-friendly third way with the greater emphasis on social reform and environmental sustainability associated with the PT. It was a seductive mix. On Marina's campaign team were market-friendly economists, such as André Lara Resende, one of the architects of Cardoso's *Plano Real*, and the influential former diplomat Rubens Ricupero, who had served as Minister of the Environment in 1993 and 1994.

But it was not easy. Marina had formed a new party called Rede Sustentabilidade (known as REDE or Network). Conscious of her popularity and potential, the PT and its allies blocked its registration. Marina had been campaigning as candidate for deputy president to Eduardo Campos, a reformist social democrat whose Socialist Party (*Partido Socialista* or PS) is, for historical reasons, the leading left-wing organization in the state of Pernambuco.

But following Campos's death in a helicopter accident in August 2014, the PS invited her to be their candidate and she surged in the polls. Fearful that Dilma might be beaten in a run-off, the PT intensified its campaigning and was accused of spreading fake news, alleging, for example, that Marina planned to end social programmes, privatize Petrobras, and – in line with her Evangelical Christian faith – restrict LGBT rights. As a result, Marina's campaign lost ground, and although she won more than 22 million votes, she again finished third.

In the end, Rousseff held on, but the PT saw its representation shrink, losing 13 of its 82 seats in the lower house of Congress and three of its 15 senators. She began her second term in office under challenging circumstances. By 2015, the economic optimism of

Lula's last years in office had evaporated, partly because, as we have seen, conditions on international markets became less favourable to Brazil. The price of oil, the one export commodity that had remained buoyant for the first three and a half years of Rousseff's presidency, began falling sharply in June 2014. Heavy spending had bolstered support in the new heartlands of the north-east but could not mask the growing malaise among much of Brazil's population. That had been brought home by an unexpected series of mass demonstrations in June 2013, only a year and a half earlier.

At the time, the protests were sudden and wholly unexpected, taking Rousseff and the governing Workers' Party entirely by surprise. As the press secretary in Lula's first government put it, 'they were a bolt from the blue', and he suggested that 'something seemed to be happening in the bowels of society that could get out of control'.[3]

A small, left-wing campaign for free public transportation, which had been ongoing for several years, provided the initial spark. The Free Pass Movement, the group that organized it, had been formed mainly by young people, inspired by the style of the anti-globalization movements of the late 1990s and early 2000s, as well as the protests of the US Occupy Movement and the demonstrations associated with the so-called Arab Spring.

On the evening of 6 June 2013, in protest at a modest increase in bus fares, a group of young demonstrators wearing masks and hoodies began to block traffic in the run-down centre of São Paulo. The actions, which had led to chronic traffic jams, were repeated over successive nights, with demonstrators also vandalizing bars and news kiosks, burning rubbish, and daubing public buildings with graffiti. Attacks on police officers called out to quell the disturbances prompted an angry response from the media and promises of firm action by both the governor of São Paulo state and the city mayor.

On 13 June, a week after the original disturbances, military police units attacked the protesters, injuring dozens of people. From short range, police had shot two journalists in the face with plastic bullets. It was this repression that now triggered a series of much bigger mobilizations. As public opinion swung against the police, the city's TV and newspaper outlets became sympathetic to the demonstrators. Within days, thousands of people who had criticized the Free Pass Movement's early excesses were on the streets themselves, raising all manner of grievances.

As André Singer put it, 'People started to go out on the streets in different cities and for different motives, which were not always clear, often organized through social media. There were a surprising criss-cross of classes and currents.'[4] Corruption was one concern. Court cases against politicians involved in the 2005 Mensalão scandal had been televised and had concluded only a few months prior. Others complained about poor education, deficient healthcare services, or the excessive amounts of money that Brazil was spending on its new football stadiums ahead of the 2014 World Cup. Many were simply angry about police violence.

Conservatives worried that sexual permissiveness, particularly around gender and sex education, had gone too far. Radicals, in particular those influenced by North American theories of social justice and the radical identitarian critique of traditional approaches to the family, thought it had not gone nearly far enough. For other demonstrators, the primary concerns were high taxes and unnecessary red tape. By 20 June 2013, the movement had spread to different cities and had metamorphosized into an attack on the entire political class. It was, as Thomas Traumann, Rousseff's head of communications, put it in a piece written in 2019, 'a national catharsis'.[5]

Rousseff, who at the beginning of 2013 had been riding high in opinion polls, saw her ratings plummet. In March, 65 per cent of interviewees rated her government as good or excellent. By the beginning of July – after the protests – the number had fallen to 30 per cent. On 15 June at the opening game of the 2013 Confederations Cup, an international soccer tournament that served as a dry run for the big event a year later, the president was booed.

Rousseff and the entire PT establishment struggled to come to terms with the reversal. Government and party leaders tended to congratulate themselves on the reductions in poverty and inequality, assuming that this would automatically translate into rising political support. The sudden spread of protest was puzzling.

'It is easy to look in the rearview mirror and analyse everything that happened,' said Gilberto Carvalho, who by now was working very closely with Rousseff. 'But let's be clear, at the time, we were really lost.'[6]

Free Pass and its supporters certainly had an agenda beyond bus fares. This new generation of activists advocated an 'autonomist' rejection of staid old representative democracy and argued instead for a much more radical shake-up of the entire political, social, and economic system, which they believed could be achieved by direct action and, if need be, physical attacks on property and its protectors. But for them the reasons for action didn't seem to matter much anyway. As the Free Pass leader Marcelo Hotimsky acknowledged: 'The intensity on the streets is much larger than we imagined. It's not something we control, or something we even want to control.'[7]

The autonomists, though, were a minority and as their prominence faded, all sorts of theories began to emerge. One of the most common ideas on the left was that new right-wing political movements had hijacked the marches and were aiming to destabilize a popular left-wing administration. These groups had launched audacious actions to publicize the injustices of the tax system and overbearing government. They had, for example, briefly persuaded petrol-station owners to suspend the collection of fuel taxes. They were now winning support among university students and became as adept at using social media tools as their left-wing autonomist and identitarian equivalents.

More mainstream thinkers suggested that Brazil was suffering a crisis of expectations, like that which had afflicted North America and Europe a generation earlier. Back in the 1970s, the American social scientist Ronald Inglehart had written about 'a post-materialist shift'. Since the Second World War, full employment and consumer prosperity had led to rising living standards; however, people had become increasingly preoccupied with their freedoms and lifestyles. Perhaps a similar transition was now underway in Brazil.[8]

Whatever the roots of the difficulties, though, a perplexed administration panicked and made concession after concession to placate protesters. Decisions taken to boost the economy and intensify the campaign against corruption misfired. Rousseff's government quickly began to unravel.

DILMA SKIDS INTO TROUBLE

Following the protests, the government began to disregard already loosened spending restrictions. Rousseff ploughed money into new training schemes and building projects, and offered generous tax exemptions to companies that retained their workforce. She encouraged state governments and municipalities to borrow billions of dollars to construct subways and new bus lines. And she funded a scheme to send 10,000 Cuban doctors to help public healthcare in remote areas. Within a year, the country's fiscal deficit had risen from 3.1 per cent to 6.3 per cent of GDP. Guido Mantega, then the Finance Minister, told Thomas Traumann in a book written in 2018, 'The demonstrators wanted better public services. They asked for a bigger state. And we gave them a bigger state.'[9]

With public accounts out of kilter, in 2015 Dilma Rousseff suddenly changed course by appointing a banker and free-market liberal, Joaquím Levy, as Finance Minister. As we shall see, this about-turn damaged her political base. The corruption measures, though, had a longer-term impact, helping turbocharge the Lava Jato investigation that was about to get underway, alienating the PT's most prominent congressional ally, the PMDB, and creating the momentum that in 2016 was to lead to Rousseff's impeachment.

Back in 2013, no one had taken much notice of the measures nestled in the fine print of an organized-crime bill. However, the reform allowed prosecutors to use plea bargains, offering prisoners the possibility of reduced sentences in exchange for providing information about other suspects. The legislation also provided investigators with two additional tools to combat corruption and organized crime: exemplary, ultra-long prison sentences and preventive arrests.

In March 2014 federal police stumbled upon, by accident, a transaction involving the Petrobras director Paulo Roberto Costa and the political fixer and money-market dealer Alberto Youssef. Armed with the new legal powers, police and investigators uncovered a vast scheme of bribes offered in return for contracts with state companies, paid by the country's huge construction companies and channelled to political parties. The construction companies would typically expect a margin of up to 20 per cent on any business with Petrobras. They would also generally agree to pay a further 1–3 per cent on top of that to the political party involved. In the Lava Jato case, four political parties that were all members of the government's coalition – the Workers' Party, the PMDB, the *Partido Progressista* (Progressive Party or PP), and the PTB – obtained cash in this way.

Shortly after Rousseff's re-election in 2014, prosecutors arrested four presidents and 15 other top executives of major construction companies in a series of spectacular dawn raids, sparking celebratory demonstrations of support in several Brazilian cities. Rousseff signalled that the investigators had her full support, even though there was little sign that the anti-corruption efforts had helped her party win any votes. Rousseff carried on regardless, dedicating a good part of her interviews in the days and weeks after her win to the need to fight corruption. 'I will do what it takes, no matter how difficult it is, to tackle corruption,' she told an interviewer at the end of October 2014.[10]

DILMA DOUBLES DOWN

Rousseff spent about a third of her 2015 inauguration speech on corruption. She saw no reason whatsoever to censure or rein in the Lava Jato investigation. Instead, the probe would be different from all the others in Brazilian history. It would get to the bottom of things. In her second government, this would be what Rousseff would be remembered for; it would be her brand.[11]

Within a couple of years, after the Lava Jato prosecutors had turned their fire on the PT and Lula himself, the party would be alleging that Lava Jato was an imperialist plot cooked up in

Washington and designed to destroy Brazil's engineering industry. But as Dilma settled into her second term in office, she was developing an approach towards corruption that was almost identical to that of the Lava Jato prosecutors. 'There was a harmony in the discourses. It is striking. It leaps out at you,' wrote Fernando Limongi, whose book on the impeachment covers in detail all the political intrigues that eventually led to Rousseff's downfall.[12]

Rousseff, during her first term in office, had alienated much of the business sector, which distrusted the more interventionist approach that she had championed. Brazilian society had become increasingly polarized, with a growing number of people angry about corruption and the poor quality of public services. This combination of circumstances would have been challenging for even the most gifted politician to manage. However, by doubling down on her anti-corruption campaign, Rousseff began to destroy her political base. As the Lava Jato investigators began to dismantle the cartel formed by the construction companies, it was clear that the government's main allied parties in Congress and in the Workers' Party itself would soon come under scrutiny.

By attacking the right, the left, and a good deal of the centre at the same time, Rousseff left herself isolated and vulnerable. It is easy to see her undoing as a Greek tragedy, in which she could be cast as a brilliant and courageous hero unable to deal with a dramatic change of circumstances, and sunk by a fatal flaw: her lack of political abilities combined with her unwillingness to take advice from the one man who might have been able to help her survive: Lula.

A TANGLED WEB

Rousseff may have seen herself as the champion of an anti-corruption campaign, but the public gave her little credit for it. As the scale of the protests against corruption began to grow, Rousseff found herself simultaneously targeted by demonstrators for alleged involvement in bribery and criticized by her political allies for not doing enough to protect them from the probe.

On 15 March 2015 – just two months into her second term – more than two million people demonstrated against corruption in the Workers' Party and called for Rousseff's impeachment. It was the largest mobilization since the return to democracy in 1985, larger than the marches that had called for the return of direct presidential elections or the impeachment of Fernando Collor, and even bigger than the enormous protests that had shaken the country two years previously. As momentum gathered, the new right-wing movements that had emerged since 2013 became prominent. *Vem pra Rua* (which had developed close links with the PSDB since the disputed 2014 election) and *Movimento Brasil Livre* (MBL) stepped up the pressure, forming an umbrella organisation led by a politician who would later assume prominence as a leading supporter of Jair Bolsonaro. There were new, well-attended demonstrations that focused all their fire on the PT. There was nothing at all subtle about their slogan: 'Fora corruptos, Fora Dilma, Lula nunca mais.' ('Corruption Out, Dilma Out, No More Lula').

Rousseff's membership in the Workers' Party meant that, in the public mind, she was closely associated with PT leaders such as José Dirceu, who the courts had found guilty in the Mensalão. As Minister of Mines and Energy, Rousseff had served as president of the board of Petrobras, the state company most ensnared by the emerging Lavo Jato investigation. Every appearance by the president on television prompted angry residents to bang pots and pans on their balconies. It mattered little to these demonstrators that Dilma had promoted reforms in the state oil company (discussed in the last chapter), or that within the PT itself, she was distant from the majority faction (Constructing a New Brazil) most involved in political horse-trading and most under fire for its involvement in corruption. Neither were the political nuances of the PT's factional politics of much consequence to demonstrators. Who cared that José Eduardo Cardozo, the Minister of Justice, was a member of a small group, Message to the Party, which was entirely behind Rousseff's ethical republicanism?

Rousseff's anti-corruption drive had already led to tensions with her political allies both inside and outside the PT, and early in her second term things came to a head in this respect as well. After the Mensalão scandal, Lula, as we saw in Chapter 10, returned to the kind of coalition that had been typical of Brazilian democracy. Rather than buying the votes of allied parties, as the PT had done during his first two years in office, the government offered ministerial positions to its partners. Of these, the most important was the PMDB. Shortly after the coup in 1964, the MDB was formed as an opposition party, grouping together the most moderate opponents of military rule. After the late 1970s, when exiled left-wingers returned to Brazil, the party radicalized, incorporating figures such as Fernando Henrique Cardoso, and led the push for the fastest possible transition to democratic government. In 1988, these social democrats left the party to form their own PSDB. The PMDB then became a much more pragmatic and self-interested grouping interested less in putting forward its ideas and policies than in securing the fruits of office at both a regional and federal level. The PMDB ran state governorships and municipalities and provided support for every one of Brazil's democratically elected presidents in return for jobs and control of ministries, state agencies, and public companies. And it became quite fragmented, with factions lining up behind competing leaders. By 2010, the party was divided into three groupings: federal senators associated with Renan Calheiros, federal deputies led by Michel Temer, and a faction close to the former mayor of Rio de Janeiro and presidential candidate Anthony Garotinho and led by the increasingly powerful Rio deputy Eduardo Cunha.

After securing only three ministers in the first Lula government, the PMDB increased its tally to six in the second. In the campaign to elect Rousseff, it became the PT's dominant partner, with Temer serving as deputy president. As we saw in the last chapter, relations between Rousseff and her PMDB allies deteriorated once she was in government, and they took a sharp turn for the worse after the 2014 election. Cunha, a bright, ruthlessly ambitious, and corrupt figure, was a vitally important player in this process. He had worked hard on Rousseff's campaign and expected her to reward him with positions in government. Instead, the president had sacked one of his allies when she launched her ethical clean-up in February 2011.[13] When another PMDB politician close to Cunha was purged from Petrobras early in 2012, the relationship soured further. Early in 2015 things came to a crisis when Cunha won the presidency of the lower house of Congress, defeating a PT politician backed by Rousseff.

The position gave Cunha immense power. It allowed him to assist or block the government's legislative agenda or even launch proceedings to force the president (or any other minister for that matter) out of office. Cunha promptly declared his independence from the administration. He was, as one recent account of the crisis puts it, 'a remarkably tough rival. He was a master of backroom negotiation, already renowned for his clientelism in a Congress that was hardly a paragon of ethics and venerated by his peers for his quiet ability to squeeze whatever he needed out of the governments of the day.'[14] Arguing, as he did repeatedly, that Rousseff was not prepared 'to share power with her allies',[15] Cunha was already intent on revenge. When the Lava Jato investigation revealed that he had secret bank accounts and the government took no action to quash his indictment, Cunha went on the offensive. After PT members of the Chamber of Deputies ethics committee voted to take immediate action against him, Cunha unleashed an impeachment petition against the president.

ACCOUNTANCY MANOEUVRES

A minor accounting manoeuvre designed to disguise the extent of overspending triggered Rousseff's downfall. Cunha had initially dismissed the tricks involved – the so-called *pedaladas* that pushed the registration of spending items from one year to another – as a potential cause for impeachment. 'I think it's a bad practice to delay the registry of payments to achieve artificial primary surpluses,' said Cunha. 'But governments have been doing this for the last ten to fifteen years. It is not enough for an impeachment.'[16] Under both Cardoso and Lula, the government had delayed payments to the Caixa Econômica, and the publicly owned bank had been in the red for about six months. The Rousseff administration made significantly more use of the tactic, especially after spending increased in the wake of the 2013 demonstrations, and the deficits persisted for a total of 21 months, spanning from August 2013 to September 2014. In 2013, Nelson Barbosa, then a treasury official but subsequently Minister of Planning and then Minister of Finance, resigned from the government because he disagreed with such practices. However, in 2015, when Cunha had a change of heart and Congress established a committee to examine Rousseff's impeachment, these violations couldn't be considered. During Rousseff's second term, there were only two minor irregularities. When the lower house of Congress voted to oust Rousseff in April 2016, there was an element of the Kafkaesque about the procedure. Not one deputy justified their votes in the trial by referring to the accounting errors. As Celso de Barros wrote: 'The juridical basis of the impeachment was effectively irrelevant.'[17]

Rousseff's supporters have argued that a reactionary group of politicians had conspired to force her from office. 'The government made mistakes but not enough to bring her down. She was a person of unshakeable honesty who was sacked more for her virtues than for her errors,' José Eduardo Cardozo, her Minister of Justice, told me.[18] As we will see in the next chapter, the PT soon began to describe the ouster of Rousseff – and the subsequent imprisonment of Lula – as tantamount to a slow-motion coup d'état; they argued the links between the Lava Jato prosecutors and the US Justice Department indicated that the plot enjoyed the backing of the United States. According to this view of events, the funding provided by US Republican supporters to the campaigns to overthrow Rousseff and Lula was further evidence of external meddling. But the more you look at Rousseff's strategy, the more naive it seems. Her plan to forge a cleaner and more accountable politics was – and is – a worthy and necessary objective. But Rousseff surely knew that to achieve success, she would require support not just from the PT but also from its allies in the PMDB and the mishmash of other parties whose very existence depended on the financing schemes

Rousseff had now decided to attack. Moreover, she was launching this strategy at a time when the PT's corrupt involvement in the Mensalão was the subject of public outrage. One perhaps more logical approach would have been to champion the cause of political reform through the introduction of smaller constituencies, an end to the open-list system of proportional representation, and a system of public financing of political parties.

Rousseff, however, was singularly ill-equipped to navigate this complex political process, which would have required an extraordinary level of skill and expertise. Lula's trade union experience made him extremely adept at the kind of backroom dealing that was inevitably part of this approach. Attracted by Rousseff's abrasive, no-nonsense toughness, Lula knew full well that his protégé was not a people person. When Lula left office in 2010, both he and his followers had assumed that he would return to the presidency in 2014. Rousseff would effectively be a stop-gap candidate, limiting the potential damage any mistakes might cause. Moreover, Lula had assumed that Rousseff's intelligence would enable her to navigate the complex world of politics just as easily as she seemed to dominate abstract economic ideas and intricate technical details. 'I had learned, so I thought she ought to be able to learn as well,' Lula told an interviewer in 2018, reflecting on his journey from trade union official to national politician. 'She was educated and experienced; she knew a lot more than I did, so she should have been able to learn easily. In any case, there was the party, and many experienced people there [to help].'[19]

Lula had been sadly mistaken in this judgement. Rousseff hated congressional politics. 'The art of politics is to converse, to talk with your opponents [but] Dilma didn't even want to speak with Eduardo Cunha,' Lula lamented.[20] She allowed political divisions to become too personal.

Cardozo, who worked with Rousseff as closely as anybody, recognized her shortcomings explicitly. 'You had to have a dialogue, but Dilma had a problem. She didn't want to negotiate with members of Congress. It irritated her to receive a deputy. She would cancel meetings. She didn't want to do them [and was always] invent[ing] excuses.'[21]

Rousseff not only lacked these skills, but she was also not particularly interested in acquiring them. For most of her term in office, she sought to distance herself from Lula and his political style. In 2018, Lula attributed part of the blame to João Santana, the public-relations guru who had advised her to develop an image quite separate from that of Lula's. 'Dilma told me in 2010 that they wanted her to stand on her own two feet and break her dependency on the Lula administration.'[22] In 2014 campaign organizers had signalled an even sharper break in style from that of Lula with the slogan *Muda Mais* ('Change More').

'She made a lot of mistakes in politics because she didn't want to deal with it. A lot of the time, she didn't do things that would have been simple to do,' lamented Lula. 'In the government, there was a joke. Ministers used to say that they enjoyed two things. First, it was great to get a meeting with the president. But second, it was even better when the meeting was cancelled.'[23]

'I got to the point where I would say to her. "Look, you are going to end up as the only president in history that not even the ministers will defend." Ministers would come to me, and I'd ask them. "Why isn't this happening? Why isn't that happening?" They'd say to me, "You know how she is."' Rousseff, it seems, was not prepared to listen. 'I was the only person who could tell Dilma this was the way things were. She listened, but because she had such a strong personality, she must have thought, "This guy doesn't understand anything."'[24]

To make matters worse, Rousseff even began to lose the support of her party and its allies. As we saw, Rousseff in 2013 had dispensed with the cautious fiscal and monetary approach that underpinned stability during Lula's government, throwing aside controls on spending. But in 2015 she suddenly adopted the most draconian orthodoxy. Lula had wanted to appoint Henrique Meirelles, a conservative banker who had been his reliable Central Bank chief throughout his two terms in office. Rousseff, though, thought she knew better. After seven years of Guido Mantega, the low-key, quietly spoken PT economist, it would have been hard to imagine a more radically different Finance Minister than Joaquim Levy, a hard-headed banker educated according to the Chicago School of Economics. Levy sliced billions from spending, raised taxes on fuel and electricity tariffs, and eliminated the panoply of tax breaks, plunging Brazil into recession, with output shrinking by 3.5 per cent during 2015. Having alienated the business sector through her earlier economic meddling and the political class through her anti-corruption drive, Rousseff now lost the support of the grassroots. As we saw in the last chapter, she was never comfortable dealing with the trade unions and social movements, whose leaders were quickly alienated by her closed and impatient style. Lula described the abrupt economic turn as 'a disaster for our militants. We won the election with one set of proposals, we mobilized people [from] the periphery [and] the social movement and to block the right, and then we got Levy to be minister of finance. We lost a lot of credibility.'[25]

Rousseff had effectively made enemies on all sides of the political spectrum and her popularity plummeted, falling to as low as 10 per cent in April 2016. The atmosphere when the lower house of Congress met to consider impeachment charges on 17 April was frenzied. Groups of deputies paraded through the modernist corridors of Congress like gangs of football supporters, carrying flags and placards and shouting slogans. '*Tchau Querida!*' chanted the right. '*Democracia!*' responded a much smaller band of left-wingers. In the end, 367 of the 513 deputies condemned Rousseff, with only 137 – just over a quarter of the total – sticking with the embattled president. Four months later, 61 of 81 senators voted to confirm her impeachment. Filmed as she left the first of these sessions, Rousseff looked bewildered and said she felt like Joseph K, the character in Kafka's *The Trial* who is arrested and eventually executed for an unspecified crime.[26] But worse, much worse, was to follow for the PT. Within two years, the party's iconic leader himself would be caught up in the Lava Jato probe. That is the story of our next chapter.

14

The Fall 2: Lula Bites the Dust

Strutting back and forth across an improvised stage opposite the metalworkers' union building in São Bernardo do Campo, Lula was in an angry mood. Clad in jeans and a blue T-shirt and back in the place where his political career had begun, the former president slipped easily into the rabble-rousing style of his younger days. 'I am a dream maker. I dreamed it was possible to stop infant mortality. I wanted the poor to be able to buy a house, a car, to take a flight and to go to university,' he said, punching the air with his right hand as he made his points. 'It is for these crimes that I have been sentenced. If these are crimes, then I am going to go on being a criminal.'[1]

It was Saturday, 7 April 2018, two days before Judge Sérgio Moro had ordered the immediate enforcement of a lengthy prison sentence, to which Lula had been condemned a few months earlier for corruption and money laundering. Much of the country had been astonished when the news of the order had been received. Surely there would be one more twist in the country's famously long-winded legal process that would save the former president from immediate detention. Instead, Lula was given 24 hours to hand himself in to federal police and had retreated to his stronghold. Protected by thousands of trade unionists and militant activists, he was considering his options.

Lula's closest political allies – Fernando Haddad, the PT's former mayor of São Paulo; Gleisi Hoffmann, the party's president;

Dilma Rousseff, his impeached successor, and other PT leaders – surrounded him on the platform, urging him to resist. So did Guilherme Boulos, the radical young leader of the Homeless Movement. In an uncanny historical echo, several thousand of Boulos's members had just ended a triumphant six-month-long occupation of the disused Scania factory, the site of the first strike in 1978, and had joined the crowds of militant trade unionists and party members who had been milling in and around São Bernardo do Campo for the last day and a half.

Boulos had met with Lula over breakfast on that Saturday morning and told him that 'the best way to respond is to challenge our enemies. What are they going to do – shoot thousands of people in the street?' Another influential figure, Luiz Eduardo Greenhalgh, a PT lawyer who back in the 1980s had handled Lula's legal defence against a murder charge in Acre, had suggested he defend himself from exile, quoting the example of Juan Domingo Perón, the Argentinian leader, who after being overthrown in a military coup in 1955, had spent 18 years in Madrid. During a trip to the southern border town of Santana do Livramento to meet the veteran former Uruguayan guerrilla leader and president, José 'Pepe' Mujica, the idea had cropped up again. 'People said to me, "Lula, pretend that you are going to buy a whisky, cross the road and stay in Uruguay under Mujica's protection. Or go and stay in the Bolivian or the Russian embassy [in Montevideo],"'[2] he told an interviewer.

Lula ignored these calls. Security advisers worried that with hundreds of riot police – armed with tear gas and plastic bullets – assembled nearby, there was little chance the battle could be won on the streets, and the human cost of a fight could be high. Lula emphatically denied the corruption charges, but, advised by his lawyers, opted to continue his fight from prison and prove his innocence. 'I must be the only man in the world who has been tried for owning an apartment that was not mine, but the federal police lied, and the prosecutors lied. I am sure that none of them can sleep at night,' he told the crowds in São Bernardo as they begged him not to hand himself over. 'Não se entrega [Don't give yourself up!], não se entrega, não se entrega!' they chanted.³

Lula was furious, railing against the prosecutors and the media that had tried to crush him. There had been constant editorializing against him by the influential news programmes of Record, Bandeirante, and especially O Globo, Brazil's biggest terrestrial channel, for which Lula reserved a particular scorn. Newspapers and magazines such as *Veja*, a popular news weekly, had not hesitated to condemn him in front-page stories. The better-off middle classes and those less well-off, whose living standards had declined during the recession, readily bought into the story.

'This is a consumer dream for them. It began with the coup against Dilma and will end when they stop Lula from being a candidate for the presidency in 2018,' insisted Lula. 'Globo and the rest of the media want a photograph of Lula going to jail. They are going to have multiple orgasms when they get that picture. But the more they attack me, the closer my relationship with the people becomes. The more days I stay in prison, the more Lulas will be born in this country.'⁴

As Lula processed his anger, a theme began to emerge, which would colour the next few years of Brazilian politics and exercise a crucial, radicalizing influence on the politics of the Workers' Party. Lula saw his imprisonment as part of what he called a slow coup, organized by the far-right, supported by the Brazilian media, the business establishment, and backed by the United States. It would become clearer as Lula focused relentlessly on the politics of his imprisonment from his cell in Curitiba, capital of the state of Paraná in southern Brazil. The former president believed that his adversaries had instigated 'lawfare' against him and his party: a neologism that combined old-style anti-democratic conspiracies with the spurious politicized use of the law. Effectively, Lula and his supporters argued that corruption cases, such as Mensalão and Lava Jato, lacked a solid foundation. Instead, they had been designed to destroy the reputation and delegitimize the arguments of progressive governments, such as those led by Lula and Rousseff.

THE CASE AGAINST LULA

Lula had first been targeted two years before his arrest in 2018. At six in the morning on 4 March 2016, dozens of federal police agents, accompanied by tax auditors, knocked on the doors of the former president's apartment in São Bernardo do Campo and systematically rifled through his possessions. Police hauled Lula off to answer questions. And they quizzed his wife, sons, and daughter-in-law about multiple cases of alleged corruption.

There were more than 20 cases in all. Cases where Lula had ostensibly traded political contracts to win business for Brazilian and international companies. There were other cases involving construction companies. In exchange for contracts from state companies or the government, the builders had carried out improvements at a ranch regularly used as a weekend retreat by the former president. And in the most notorious case, OAS, one of the construction companies targeted, had reserved a luxury apartment for Lula and his wife in the seaside town of Guarujá, again apparently in payment for services rendered.

So far, since its inception in March 2014, the Lava Jato investigation had focused most of its attention on the businessmen and civil servants involved in this type of bribery case. Dozens had been arrested and were serving prison time. Other politicians and ministers were in the sights of investigators, but under Brazilian law anyone who had been elected had to be tried by their peers.[5]

Lula was vulnerable because, since leaving the presidency, he held no elected office. He had been happy to respond to the charges, all of which he and his lawyers vehemently denied. However, fearing that Lula would soon be appointed a minister in the Rousseff government and therefore be beyond the reach of investigators, Judge Sérgio Moro had taken an unusual step, issuing a bench warrant. This document usually authorizes the arrest of an individual who has failed to appear in court or has committed contempt of court and cannot be found.

For the task force, this was a logical step. The PT had been the governing party for the last 13 years. It was strongly associated in the public mind with corruption due to the Mensalão case. This was particularly so because, although the scandal dated back to 2004 and 2005, the usual delays in the slow-moving Brazilian legal system meant that the trials of those involved had only just concluded when the chief prosecutor established the Lava Jato team.

However, a growing number of critics believed that the investigation had become too partisan, too sympathetic to the anti-PT mood sweeping the country, and increasingly prone to arguing that Lula and the Workers' Party were at the root of the country's problems. Until 2016, the conservative prejudices of Moro and the Lava Jato team may have been incidental to their legal qualifications. Now, as Brazil's ideological climate became more polarized, Moro was increasingly seen by his supporters as their saviour. As Celso Rocha writes, 'There was no legal justification [for the bench warrant]. Moro was entering the [political] game.'[6]

Legally questionable or not, Moro's action fuelled opposition campaigning against the government. Nine days after the authorities questioned Lula, enormous demonstrations demanded Rousseff's impeachment. Behind the scenes, Moro was secretly and illegally monitoring communications in and around the presidential palace. When Rousseff, on 28 March, told Lula during a phone call that she planned to take him out of the line of prosecutorial fire by designating him as her chief of staff, the investigators illegally recorded them. Then they leaked the tape, again breaking the law, to the press. Amid a media storm and public outrage, Rousseff had to abandon the plan.[7]

Rousseff's impeachment during mid-2016 took the pressure off Lula for a moment, but the team in Curitiba was steadily pushing ahead with their case. In September 2016 the task force launched formal charges against Lula in connection with the Guarujá apartment. At a press conference, Deltan Dallagnol, the lead prosecutor, made much of an alleged broader conspiracy involving Rousseff, Guido Mantega, Antônio Palocci, and the PT treasurer, João Vaccari Neto, headed by Lula and centred on Petrobras.

Despite his new investigatory powers, Dallagnol had provided little to substantiate these claims. Presenting the case at a press conference, he stood before a PowerPoint slide consisting of an incongruous and unconvincing series of bubbles and arrows that led the eye to a central bubble labelled Lula. It was a ludicrously poor effort. In the weeks that followed, the presentation was widely trolled. For weeks, WhatsApp groups were filled with ironic images of PowerPoint slides establishing preposterous links. One, for example, centred on the song-writing efforts of soccer star Neymar da Silva Santos and Brazil's traumatic seven-one defeat to Germany in the 2014 World Cup semi-final. For the public at large, the PowerPoint 'devalued the credibility of the evidence against the president, raised hackles among the legal community that was already chafing at the newfound use of legal doctrines such as dominio de facto [de facto control] and its seemingly vague burden of proof'.[8]

In the 1960s the German jurist Claus Roxin had systematized the legal concept of de facto control, which had first been deployed during the Nuremberg trials of Nazi war criminals some 20 years before. Roxin claimed Brazilian prosecutors and judges misused the idea. The jurist argued that it was not enough for those accused simply to occupy a position in a hierarchy. There had to be specific proof that illegal commands had been issued, something that was lacking in the Brazilian case.[9]

There were other weaknesses in the prosecution's case, too, particularly those related to the apartment in Guarujá. Back in 2005, Lula's wife, Marisa Letícia, had bought an apartment in the same Guarujá building where the three-storey unit identified by prosecutors was located. For four years, while the building was under construction, she had paid for it in monthly instalments. Then, the credit union responsible for financing the project went out of business, and OAS, a construction company targeted by Lava Jato, took over ownership. Lula said that his wife had once considered exchanging the apartment she owned for a larger one in the same building, but the couple had never signed a contract or been given a key. Lula's lawyers were confident that the case was far too weak.

'There is no way this case is going anywhere. It is ridiculous and is going to be stopped,' Lula had been told by one of his advisers.[10]

However, Moro and the prosecutorial team had the bit between their teeth. For weeks the chief executive of OAS, Leo Pinheiro, had denied that either the apartment or the improvements, valued at just R$3.7 million, had anything to do with Lula. Dozens of other witnesses had confirmed his testimony. But under intense pressure from prosecutors, Pinheiro had been advised by his lawyers to change his account. Prosecutors claimed that the company had reserved the apartment on its information system and that documents found during the search of Lula's house proved the former president and his wife had planned the exchange, even though precise details had been erased.

So, on 12 July 2017, Moro ruled that Lula had been guilty of corruption and money laundering and sentenced him to nine years and six months in prison.[11]

Early in 2018 the appeal court confirmed the ruling, increasing the sentence to 12 years and one month, and in early April the 11 members of the Supreme Court ruled that Lula could be sent to prison before the exhaustion of all his legal remedies, a precedent that judges had established only two years before and would soon reverse. That set the scene for Lula's imprisonment. By the evening of 7 April, after a short helicopter ride to Congonhas airport and an hour-long flight to Curitiba, Lula was asleep in a makeshift cell, apparently beginning a long period of seclusion.

PRISON AND A HARDER MOOD

For most of those condemned to spend their lives in them, Brazil's jails are dirty, overcrowded, and violent hell holes run by criminal gangs. Like other well-off or celebrity detainees, Lula was at least insulated from this mayhem. So, in a way, he got off lightly. His cell was a room on the fourth floor of the police headquarters building in Curitiba, normally set aside for visiting police officers who needed to stay overnight in the city. Directly underneath the flat roof from which helicopters took off, the space was approximately 160 square feet in size, containing a single bed, a table, and chairs, with a curtained-off area at one end housing a shower and toilet. Lula was allowed to use a laptop, and a television was attached to the wall. However, he was deprived of internet access and had no telephone. Two barred windows high up on the wall allowed daylight through opaque glass. Into what Lula's biographer described as a 'dark and humid kitchenette', his jailers brought in food and drink, although prison rules prohibited alcohol. Lula had access to books and pen drives (USB flash drives) containing films, TV documentaries, and talks. Eight federal policemen watched over Lula, but the former president got along well with his jailers, so well that one of them, Paulo Rocha Gonçalves Jr, also known as Paulão, joined Lula's security team after Lula began campaigning in the 2022 election.[12]

Visitors arrived regularly. Two of the most important were retired left-wing lawyers, Luiz Carlos da Rocha and Manoel Caetano, who lived in Curitiba and became the local representatives of Lula's São Paulo-based legal team. As such, they were allowed regular access during working days. Da Rocha and Caetano managed to persuade the prison to permit Lula to use a treadmill, on which the former president quickly resumed his morning exercise routine. There were regular visitors too from abroad. Among them were North American trade unionists, left-wing intellectuals such as Noam Chomsky, and Hollywood celebrities. There were sundry European and Latin American left-wing leaders. There was, however, a sense that many of these figures were somewhat tired relics of the past and not the kind of people at the cutting edge of progressive thinking. Former presidents such as Argentina's Eduardo Duhalde and Colombia's Ernesto Samper, as well as Mexico's Cuautémoc Cárdenas, a former mayor of Mexico City, had long been absent from front-line politics.

A few years before, when he had been in his pomp, Lula had kept different company. Back in 2009, former US President Barack Obama had been a massive fan of a president he described as 'the most popular politician on earth'. But in his 2020 memoir

A Promised Land, Obama took a different view, suggesting Lula 'had the scruples of a Tammany Hall boss'. Obama's distance typified that of many friends and erstwhile allies who had kept away from Lula because of the revelations of Lava Jato. 'Everyone is frightened,' Lula told journalists shortly before beginning his imprisonment. 'Who is mad enough to want to say they will come and see me? Even discreet meetings away from the attention of the press are difficult.' And it underlined the value of the deeper ideological connections that had been forged with the left. 'I know that my long-term friends will remain my friends. The temporary ones will disappear. It is a lesson of life.'[13]

Outside the police building, activists maintained a constant vigil to protest Lula's imprisonment. Within weeks, trade unions had banded together to rent a property directly opposite the building, installing a giant collective kitchen and a coffee stall there. Rooms in the property on the site were available to house visitors overnight, and a garage was equipped with an internet connection and transformed into a media centre. Like clockwork, every day at 9 a.m., 2:30 p.m., and 7 p.m., demonstrators shouted out their greetings to Lula: 'Bom dia, Presidente!'; 'Boa tarde, Presidente!'; 'Boa noite, Presidente'. It was a commitment that served to reinforce Lula's connection to the more ideological wing of his party and movement. 'I am eternally grateful to them for this. It cheers me up and strengthens my will to bear this ordeal,' Lula told his interviewers in 2019.[14]

Still Lula railed against the imposed restrictions, which sometimes seemed exceedingly petty. When his oldest surviving brother Vavá died of cancer in January 2019, the courts forbade Lula from attending the funeral (although a month later he was allowed to attend the funeral of his seven-year-old grandson Arthur who had died from meningitis). Until April 2019 judges had prohibited Lula from giving press interviews. More importantly, they also thwarted his efforts to run in the 2018 presidential election at a time when, as we shall see, opinion polls had indicated he was in the lead.

Lula soon had a new love interest to boost his spirits. He had lost his wife, Marisa Letícia, early in 2017. She had been diagnosed with an aneurism seven years previously, and as the legal pressure on the family increased, her condition slowly deteriorated. 'She got more and more tense, was no longer good-humoured, she never wanted to go out,' explained Lula in 2018. 'Every time there was something against one of her sons, it really hit her. My detention and all the violence surrounding it was the last straw.'[15] On 3 February, Maria Letícia suffered a stroke and at the age of 67 she died.

Nearly a year later, Lula had met Roseangela da Silva, a 50-year-old sociologist, at a celebrity football match organized to raise party funds. Roseangela, known as Janja, had joined the PT as a teenager and lived in Curitiba, where she had worked for the last 17 years at the headquarters of Itaipu Binacional. This large hydroelectric plant straddles Brazil's border with Paraguay and was completed in 1984. Janja was responsible for supervising the settlements where families displaced by the development were housed. With Lula in prison, Janja was listed as a family member and brought him food each evening and took his clothes home to wash. The two regularly wrote letters to each other.

Even so, for a man who was famously gregarious, not overly fond of the written word, and well-known for absorbing information through conversations and meetings, this was a time of unusual introspection. Lula watched an awful lot of TV news and devoured films, documentaries, and talks that friends made available on USB drives. And he read a lot more than he usually would have, averaging more than a book a week, predictably favouring radical and often left-wing writers and novelists. Among authors singled out in a 2019 interview, Lula mentions Gregorio Bezerra, whose autobiography details the life of a communist army officer from Lula's home state of Pernambuco, Raduan Nasser, a Brazilian writer whose most famous work is a short novel called *Um Copo de Cólera* (translated into English as *A Cup of Rage*), and the Havana-based Cuban writer Leonardo Padura. *El Hambre* (*Hunger*) by the Argentine journalist Martín Caparrós, and *The Prize: The Epic Quest for Oil, Money, and Power*, Daniel Yergin's 1990s book on the geopolitical importance of oil, both figure on Lula's list, as do two recent and very long books on Brazilian slavery: a popular three-volume history by the journalist Laurentino Gomes, and *Um Defeito de Cor* (*A Colour Defect*), a prize-winning novel by a black Brazilian writer, Ana Maria Gonçalves. In his first week in detention Lula read *A Elite do Atraso* (*The Backward Elite*), a dense treatise written in response to the Lava Jato scandal, which would have reinforced his sense that he had been subject to a vindictive right-wing. Its author, Jessé Souza, was a Brazilian sociologist who, in opposition to the subtleties of Brazilian historiography proposed by left-wing writers such as Celso Furtado, Raimundo Faoro, and above all Sérgio Buarque de Holanda, advanced a more Manichaean vision.[16]

Lula liked the black-and-white emphasis of Souza's analysis. He discovered a course on the nineteenth-century messianic religious leader, Antônio Conselheiro, that taught how the utopian experiment of Belo Monte (based on the current town of Canudos in Bahia) had been crushed by federal troops (as we saw in Chapter 1). Just as Souza had taken on Buarque de Holanda and other establishment figures, the academic who gave the course, Pedro Vasconcellos, a professor from the north-eastern state of Alagoas, took aim at another Brazilian intellectual great, the journalist, sociologist, and author Euclides da Cunha, whose book *Os Sertões* (*The Backlands*) is regarded as a classic and is a set text on school curricula. Vasconcellos claimed the book was an elite account that falsely characterized Conselheiro as a fanatic and had written his impoverished adherents out of history. Lula's supporters had pointed out distant family links between one of the judges in his appeal court ruling in January 2018 and a military officer killed in the attack on Canudos: the connection piqued Lula's interest. In April 2019 an interviewer asked him about his life behind bars. Lula mentioned the course and said he had suggested 247, a pro-PT media channel, do a follow-up encompassing all 'social struggles'. Vasconcellos, meanwhile, expanded on his teaching and in a book published in March 2020 drew an explicit – though at times tortuously abstract – connection between Conselheiro and Lula.[17] 'We understand how the Belo Monte of Antônio Conselheiro and Lula's

Brazil have much in common,' read the preface by Mauro Lopes, the journalist whose channel had organized the original course. 'Both are in the dreams of the poor and are hated by the elites.'

This kind of reflection was symptomatic of a more radical mood inside Lula's Workers' Party. The year 2016 had been a particularly depressing one. After the fall of Dilma Rousseff and the launch of the case against Lula, the party lost control of dozens of mayoralities at the 2016 municipal elections, abruptly reversing its steady expansion in local government over the previous fifteen years. With several of its other historic leaders languishing in prison, there was a general feeling within the party that it was being unfairly targeted for practices that had been standard in Brazilian politics for decades. Correspondingly, the party began to distrust the independence of the judiciary and the fairness of the media. Radicals on the Marxist-influenced left of the party, who had always believed that faith in institutions was misplaced, gained ground. At its conference in May 2016 the party approved positions more uncompromising than any contemplated since the 1980s. A document issued after the meeting said the PT should have done more to prevent the 'conservative sabotage' of the federal police and the public prosecutor's office, directly contradicting the autonomy guaranteed in its previous policy. The party also regretted not using the federal state's advertising budget to pressure the 'communication monopolies', which it believed had acted against its interests.

As Rocha de Barros put it in his history, the 'general tone' was in favour of 'Boliviarianism', the radical and explicitly partisan approach to media and institutions introduced in Venezuela by Hugo Chávez and favoured by other followers of so-called twenty-first-century socialism in countries such as Bolivia, Ecuador, and Nicaragua. As Rocha de Barros also points out, this bias did not necessarily affect the party's performance when it held or was contesting office. PT state governors, for example, might voice the party's belief that Michel Temer, the new president, had taken office through a 'coup d'état', but they continued to work with his administration on a day-to-day basis. Similarly, in 2018, PT local politicians often fought the election in alliance with centrist or even right-wing allies who had voted in favour of Rousseff's impeachment. 'While the militants tried to deal with the trauma of the fall, the institutional PT tried to stay in the game,' wrote Rocha de Barros.[18]

Even so, no doubt stunned by the attacks to which they had been subject, many moderates were having second thoughts about their embrace of social-democratic politics. During the 1990s, José Genoíno more than anyone had personified that shift. After participating in a disastrous guerrilla offensive in the Araguaia (see Chapter 3), Genoíno abandoned his beliefs in violent revolution and became an enthusiastic parliamentarian. In 1999 he spearheaded the PT's move to the centre, forging links with Cardoso's PSDB. As president of the PT, however, Genoíno was embroiled in the Mensalão scandal and was one of those sentenced to a prison term. For him, the experience was emotionally devastating, and in reaction he now advocates a much more uncompromising, hard-line approach. 'I thought the transformation of Brazil would go through the institutions,' he told *Piauí* in 2022.[19] 'But this is too limited. A bourgeoisie that is inherently authoritarian, patriarchal, violent and has a slave-owning mentality will not accept our demands.' Inevitably, perhaps, this move to the left has been accompanied by a revival of anti-Americanism that seemed to be dissipating during the 2000s, when Lula even became friendly with President George W. Bush. Many in the PT believe that American geopolitical interests lie behind Lava Jato and the attacks on the party. A 2022 cartoon book for militants portrays the corruption probe as a mission to 'destroy industry and attack our sovereignty' and seize control of Brazil's new-found oil wealth.[20]

Lula himself has frequently expressed the same view. Shortly before he was imprisoned in 2018, he told journalists that the 'coup' was planned 'from the outside in' (*fora para dentro*). 'A part of the Brazilian elite, allied to the international financial system and multinational interests, wanted to take apart the Brazilian financial system, especially the public banks, and give Petrobras to foreign capital. The media was the flagship for all this. We got to the point where the headlines of all the papers were the same.'[21] Or even more bitterly in his first interview from prison, 'It was a staged farce, set up here and in the US Department of Justice.'[22]

'The day I get out of here, they know I will be out there, together with the people, head held high and not letting them give Brazil to the Americans,' he continued. 'Does anyone reckon that the US is going to favour Brazil? Americans tend to think about themselves first, second, third, fourth, and fifth, and there is still time for them to think of themselves. And there are still these Brazilian lackeys who think the Americans will do something for us. We must do things for ourselves.'

ASSESSING THE IMPACT OF LAVA JATO

It was a simple argument that was hugely appealing to Lula's supporters. However, the legal scandals had a much more complex origin, and, as we saw in the last chapter, it was Lula's own designated successor, Dilma Rousseff, who had created some of the conditions that allowed Lava Jato to flourish. Several changes, introduced gradually since the return to democracy in 1985, have improved the judicial system and made the government more transparent and accountable. The public prosecutor's office was given a greater degree of independence. The selection process for judges was made more meritocratic, introducing a new generation of technically capable officials who were freer than their predecessors from political ties. And as we have seen, Rousseff hastily introduced legislation built on that foundation but dramatically expanded the powers available to prosecutors and judges.

Certainly, the US Justice Department had cooperated with Brazilian legal authorities. In 1997, Brazil had been a signatory to the Organization for Economic Cooperation and Development's Anti-Bribery Convention. That agreement had been modelled on the 1977 Foreign Corrupt Practices Act, a US law that prohibits bribery by American companies operating abroad, and in 1998 it was extended to foreign companies doing business in the United States or making dollar transactions. Under the convention, the Department of Justice offered training and technical assistance. Several judges and prosecutors had attended courses in

America under the programme. The department also acted against Petrobras, which lists its shares and raises capital in the US and is therefore subject to the FCPA. In September 2018, as part of a broader global resolution over violations of the act linked to Lava Jato, Petrobras agreed to a $680 million settlement with the Brazilian public prosecutor. Half of the money was controversially earmarked for a foundation proposed by Deltan Dallagnol, one of the Lava Jato prosecutors, further reinforcing the sense that Lava Jato and the department were acting in tandem.[23]

But much of the thinking behind the Lava Jato approach had been developed in Italy in the early 1990s. Italian judges, such as Giovanni Falcone, served as a model for reformers. With their *Mani Pulite* (Clean Hands) probe, the Italians had brought down powerful politicians, such as Prime Minister Bettino Craxi. They had sought to influence public opinion, arguing that an anti-corruption campaign could only succeed if it had popular backing. The Lava Jato unit, established in 2014 in Curitiba, Paraná, where prosecutors had experience in handling money-laundering cases, was modelled on a similar Italian unit formed to combat the mafia. Moro himself had carefully studied the experience and copied Italian precedent by establishing close links with sympathetic journalists.[24]

In its early days the Lava Jato investigation appeared to be fairly even-handed as it cut a swathe through the entire Brazilian establishment. High-flying company executives who sanctioned the payment of bribes and politically appointed officials at Petrobras and other public companies that received them, as well as the middlemen who oiled the wheels, were all successfully targeted. Testimony from the plea bargains highlighted the involvement not just of the Workers' Party but of all its allies in the coalitions that had backed the Lula and Rousseff governments.

But just as they had done in 1964, the Marxist left exaggerated the power of Washington for ideological reasons, and, as we shall see in the next chapter, underestimated the domestic roots of reaction. Of course, the US administration had an influence on events during the 2010s, but most Brazilians favoured reforms that would bring about cleaner government. Compared to their counterparts in other developing countries, Brazil's institutions were relatively strong. Still, they also had some fundamental flaws, not least because of their susceptibility to pressures from private interest groups. In 1997, Brazil, which wanted to reduce the costs of corruption to its economy, was a willing signatory to the OECD convention. Washington's support for these efforts partly stemmed from self-interest. If it became more difficult for their competitors to win business by offering bribes, it was more likely that American companies could compete more effectively in overseas markets. However, Odebrecht and other privately held construction companies, not subject to the governance standards of the stock markets, rather than the PT and the left, were the targets. Moreover, PT governments had shown every sign of supporting these efforts. Lula's first two governments had backed several piecemeal reforms that had improved levels of transparency and made institutions like the public prosecutor less subject to political influence. As we saw in the previous chapter, President Rousseff had prioritized the fight against corruption throughout her six years in office, advocating an approach very much in line with that of the Lava Jato team.

The impact of Lava Jato on Brazilian party politics was also more complicated than the more conspiratorial accounts suggest. The PT were certainly big losers. It is hardly disputable. The economic downturn and the Mensalão scandal had already begun to erode the party's popularity in elections before Rousseff's impeachment. In 2010 the party had won 88 seats in the lower house of Congress and 19 in the Senate. Two years later came the high-water mark of its political representation when it won control of 637 municipalities, up from 553 in 2008 and only 189 in 2000. However, from 2014, those numbers began to decline, with the quantity of lower house seats dropping to 69 in 2014, then 54 in 2018, while in the Senate only 12 members represented the party's interests in 2014 and just six in 2018.

But Lula seemed to be immune to this political shift. You might expect that as he languished in prison, Lula's political career was approaching its end. But something curious happened as he sat out his dull days of incarceration. His popularity rose. A poll conducted in November 2015 showed that Gerardo Alckmin, the

THE FALL 2: LULA BITES THE DUST

governor of São Paulo and the most likely candidate for the PSDB, would have defeated Lula by a margin of 57 per cent to 43 per cent. After Rousseff's impeachment, the gap shrank to 51 per cent to 49 per cent. By December 2016, Lula had regained the lead, with 53 per cent to 47 per cent, and by April 2017, eight months after corruption proceedings had been launched against him, Lula was ahead in the polls by 20 percentage points. In prison, Lula continued to gain, and when in August 2018 the electoral court ruled 12 to 1 that Brazil's Clean Slate law prevented him from running, Lula was leading in the polls. 'Ironically, from the perspective of public opinion, the coup turned out to be a good thing for Lula, and also for the PT,' wrote two political scientists in 2022.[25]

At least as important was the way the Lava Jato scandal wiped out Brazil's political centre. In some ways the immediate political beneficiaries of the 2016 action against Rousseff were more severely affected than the victims. When he took over, Michel Temer, Rousseff's vice-president, relied heavily on his own PMDB (which in 2017 reverted back to the original MDB name as part of a rebranding exercise) and other allied parties, including Cardoso's PSDB. Fifteen parties in total formed a legislative coalition to back Temer, with his own MDB given 10 and the PSDB four of the 28 cabinet positions. Shortly ahead of the impeachment, Romero Jucá, a leading adviser to Temer and Planning Minister in the new government, had told a colleague that a change of government was needed to rein in the Lava Jato investigators. 'This shit has to be fixed,' he had told a colleague in April 2016. 'The government needs to be changed to staunch the bleeding.' The comments, caught on a police wiretap, exposed congressional duplicity in the impeachment and served as a good indication of the direction of travel under Temer.[26]

Sure enough, the pace of the inquiry slowed from 2016, with several officials close to Temer appointed to the independent agencies involved. Congress blocked efforts by the Lava Jato investigators to introduce legal reforms that would have increased accountability. However, Lava Jato was still popular and maintained momentum. Prosecutors made progress and soon had Temer and his MDB confidants in their sights. Eduardo Cunha, the president of Congress, was quickly jailed after Rousseff's removal.

Geddel Vieira, Temer's chief of staff, was forced out by a series of scandals, culminating in the discovery of an apartment filled with unexplained cash, and subsequently sentenced to a lengthy prison term. Jucá was forced to resign from his position as Planning Minister when the press published details of his secretly taped admission. Three other Temer ministers also fell. Henrique Alves was forced to resign, too, because of his links to the Petrobras scandal: Eliseu Padilha was indicted by the prosecutor general, and Moreira Franco was investigated and detained. Temer himself was soon entangled in the Lava Jato net when tapes of discussions about hush-money payments to Cunha were released to the press. Temer survived the affair, managing to fend off impeachment on two separate occasions, but his popularity dived towards single figures. By May 2018 more than 82 per cent of Brazilians disapproved of his government. The PSDB was also affected, with several PSDB governors caught in the web of investigations. In 2018, Eduardo Azeredo, a former PSDB governor of Minas Gerais, was sentenced to a 20-year prison term for political financing misdemeanours that dated back to the late 1990s. Beto Richa and Marconi Perillo, respectively the former governors of Paraná and Goiás, were briefly detained. The most significant casualty was Aécio Neves, one of the party's grandees and its unsuccessful presidential candidate in 2014, who was charged in 2017 with taking bribes from the JBS meatpacking group, and allegedly attempting to obstruct justice. It would take him six years to clear his name.

All of this badly damaged the electoral prospects of the two parties, which had been dominant players in Brazilian politics for the last quarter-century. Running for a Senate seat in Goiás, Perillo was leading the race when details of his case came to light. He ended up finishing fifth. 'The allegation made in 2018 killed my chances . . .' said Perillo.[27]

In 2014 the PSDB and the MDB, together, had won 132 of the 513 seats in the lower house of Congress and 31 of the 81 positions in the Senate. That fell to 69 and 19, respectively, in 2018. There were also significant losses in local government. Between them the two parties controlled nearly half of the state governorships in 2014. That number had fallen to just six in 2018. That was part of a broader trend, contributing to the political earthquake, which, as we will see in the next chapter, led to the 2018 election of a political outsider, Jair Bolsonaro. As Alberto Almeida and Tiago Garrido put it, the political system had been knocked down with a punch from a 'knuckleduster'.[28]

15

Bolsonaro

Paulo Romes Junqueira seemed like an unlikely supporter of Jair Bolsonaro. When I met him in July 2019, Junqueira was running his family-owned company based in the growing city of Uberlândia in the centre of Brazil. Junqueira had been a progressive in his youth, had disliked the military regime, and, back in 1984, had identified with the pro-democracy demonstrators. He had been a supporter of Cardoso's PSDB and in the early 2010s had even served as a commercial secretary for Uberlândia's PT mayor when the party, during the heyday of its municipal power, briefly took control of what had traditionally been a fairly prosperous city, a bastion of conservatism typical of the kind of city where Bolsonarismo has thrived in recent years.

However, when Bolsonaro visited Uberlândia during the 2018 election campaign, Junqueira had been among the welcoming committee set up by local businessmen, had dinner with the controversial candidate, and was impressed by what he found. 'He was relaxed and good-humoured. He appeared such a simple, straightforward person,' recalled Junqueira. 'These meetings made us see that he was an ideal candidate for Brazil at that moment. We needed someone radical to resolve the issues of the moment. It needed strong remedies, not just something to dull the pain.'

Junqueira's company, Junco, like much of the rest of Uberlândia's business sector, had prospered amid the consumer boom that seemed to be transforming the country during Lula's first two terms in office. Demand for the company's paper hats and other novelty party products was soaring as more and more poor Brazilians began to celebrate their newfound prosperity.

However, since 2014, the company's expansion had stalled. Investment plans had been on hold since the recession, and Junqueira and his business colleagues believed the PT and, in particular, the government of Dilma Rousseff were to blame. 'I never liked the way the PT managed the economy. They always liked to be generous with other people's money. They were not very consistent or coherent. We were worried that the left would continue governing the country. They ran things for themselves. I do not doubt that the PT government was a government for itself, with bad, disastrous levels of corruption.'[1]

Fabio Pergher, another of the city's self-made men, shared Junqueira's enthusiasm for the new right. Start Chemicals, his company, had begun from scratch in 1987, by packaging detergents and undercutting multinational giants such as Unilever. The range had been expanded to agricultural supplies such as seeds, as well as food and drinks. The company even sold its own brands of rum and other spirits. Pergher employed 3,500 people and had built up sales of over R$1 billion. But he, too, was frustrated by the way the size of the Brazilian state had grown under the PT. "The alligator has huge jaws,' he claimed. 'All the money that the state has is badly spent. The way we were going, we were going to become like Cuba or Venezuela, so when Bolsonaro won, it gave real energy to the business class. The clouds began to clear.'[2]

When the Uberlândia businessmen met Bolsonaro, the candidate had still been a long shot for the presidency. Incarcerated in Curitiba's police headquarters, Lula was way ahead in the polls and intended to contest the elections. Many commentators still thought Geraldo Alckmin, the candidate of Cardoso's PSDB, was better placed to harvest the anti-PT vote, even though his campaign at that point had been unimpressive. Alckmin was a colourless candidate and was trailing in the polls, but party managers had secured the support of several moderate and right-wing parties. Alckmin would have the lion's share of TV advertisements when campaigning started heating up a few weeks ahead of the election. But Brazilian politics were changing rapidly, and it wasn't just a result of the recession and the corruption scandal.

For most of his three-decade-long career in the Brazilian Congress, Bolsonaro had been an eccentric outsider that no one took seriously. After a career in the army in which he rose to the rank of captain, Bolsonaro had fallen foul of the military hierarchy. His strident advocacy of the demands of junior officers and the rank and file had alarmed his superiors, and Bolsonaro had been obliged to quit. In civilian life he had made a political career by representing soldiers and their families, pressing their demands for better conditions and pensions. In 1989, Bolsonaro was elected as a councillor in Rio de Janeiro. A year later, he became a federal deputy. At a time when Brazil was embracing democracy and even the military's commanders were trying to distance themselves from the 1960s and 1970s, Bolsonaro defended what had been done and suggested that the dictatorship had failed because it had not been sufficiently ruthless with its opponents.

Hosts of TV talk shows would regularly invite him to appear because they knew he would not shrink from making hugely controversial, incendiary comments that would increase their ratings. He was openly, unapologetically contemptuous of democracy. 'Elections won't change anything in this country,' an angry Bolsonaro told an interviewer on the programme Câmara Aberta, broadcast by TV Band in 1999. 'It will only change on the day that civil war starts here and we do the job that the military regime didn't do, and kill 30,000 people. If we kill some innocent people, that's fine [because] in every war, innocent people die.'[3] Bolsonaro went on to say that if he became president, he would dissolve Congress on his first day in office, and he defended the use of torture. 'I'm in favour of torture. You know that, and the people are in favour as well.'

During the 2000s, Bolsonaro began to expand his range into a much broader attack on liberalism. As Brazil under Cardoso, Lula and Dilma embraced new global human rights norms and international standards on environmental protection, the former army captain lined up behind the domestic reaction. He began to rail against issues such as gay marriage and plans to improve sex education. His pronouncements on sexuality and violence were so inflammatory and outrageous that they seemed designed to tweak liberal sensibilities. 'I've got five kids, but on the fifth I had a moment of weakness, and it came out as a girl,' he told an audience at the Clube Hebraica in São Paulo in April 2017.[4]

Three years earlier, in an angry exchange, he told the PT congresswoman Maria de Rosário that 'she was too ugly to rape', prompting Rosário to press criminal charges, and the left-wing publication *The Intercept* to describe Bolsonaro as 'the most misogynistic, hateful elected official in the democratic world'.[5] In rural areas, many Brazilians were unhappy with the crackdown on deforestation and the expansion of conservation areas and indigenous reserves characteristic of Lula's first two terms in office, arguing that the drive was affecting their ability to make a living. Farmers, big and small, land speculators, illegal miners and loggers were guaranteed to win a sympathetic hearing from Bolsonaro, who had, during his military service, used holidays to prospect for gold. When the PT government sponsored an effort to tighten gun control, Bolsonaro actively campaigned to defeat the measure. When police officers lambasted the idea that they should respect the rights of criminals, Bolsonaro supported them.

During the 2000s, Bolsonaro defended the way in which off-duty policemen in Rio de Janeiro were participating in militias formed to fight the growing influence of organized crime groups such as Comando Vermelho in poor areas. In 2003, when the lower house of Congress debated death-squad killings in the north-eastern state of Bahia, Jair Bolsonaro was as provocative and belligerent as ever. 'A little while ago, I heard a legislator criticize the death squads. I want to say that as long as the state does not dare to adopt the death penalty, the crime of extermination, as far as I am concerned, is a very welcome thing.'[6]

In Uberlândia, both Junqueira and Pergher had told me how Bolsonaro's stance on these kinds of questions had resonated with voters. 'There is a small, noisy group of activists that defends this idea of gender theory, that you have absolute freedom to be what sex you want to be. I am not saying it is right or wrong, just that those who back this idea are really a tiny minority,' Junqueira had told me. 'The majority of Brazilians support the idea of the traditional family.' In a city that is one of the safest in the country, security and policing were another reason why many had supported Bolsonaro, said Junqueira. 'When [he] said that we have to stop treating criminals like artists and allow people to own and use guns to defend themselves, it got him a lot of votes. People thought that by backing Bolsonaro, they were increasing their security.'[7]

BEEF, BIBLE, AND BULLETS

Several significant, longer-term trends fuelled these concerns during the 2000s. The expansion of organized crime, the growing power of agribusiness, and the extraordinary growth of the Protestant Church. The agricultural boom in soya and beef exports had increased the prosperity and the political weight of the farming lobby. Prosperity had drawn more people to smaller towns and cities like Uberlândia that served this vast rural hinterland. The boom in commodity prices drew people to the less populated north, where land was cheaper. It encouraged speculation and illegal deforestation. IBAMA, the agency most associated with environmental control, clashed with local farming interests. In the smaller, least populated corners of the Amazon there were constant conflicts between ranchers, illegal miners – known locally as *garimpeiros* – and officials from IBAMA and ICM Bio, another agency tasked with protecting the environment.

Roraima, nestling in the far north of the Brazilian Amazon and bordered by Venezuela and Guyana, was one of the states where I had found tremendous local support for these populist right-wing arguments. When I travelled there towards the end of 2019, I found a kind of mythical cowboy-and-indian territory of Hollywood films. Local settlers felt bitter about the way their farms had been expropriated to create the Raposa Serra do Sol indigenous reserve.

Farmers were angry about the interference of IBAMA. *Garimpeiros* were extolled as brave frontiersmen. There was even a statue of one in the main square of Boa Vista, the state's capital.

At the same time, another issue was increasingly propelling voters to the right. In the poorer areas of Brazilian cities, organized-crime groups – their power based on extortion and the distribution and export of cocaine and other illegal drugs – had over the last two or three decades become powerful players, with clashes with the police leading to relatively high death rates. From 2015 onwards, two of the largest groups, the Rio de Janeiro-based Comando Vermelho and the Primeiro Comando do Capital (from São Paulo), began to fight each other for control of the business, drawing on the support of local gangs with names that seemed to have been culled from video games.

Bonde do Maluco (The Madman's Tram) took root in the slums of Salvador. Guardiões do Estado (State Guardians) linked up with the PCC and battled for control of the peripheral districts of Fortaleza. In hitherto relatively peaceful corners of the northeast, such as Aracaju and Maceió, which happened to be on drug routes, there were seemingly endless episodes of ultra-violent tit-for-tat killing. The gangs took control of poorly administered parts of the prison system, which were also wracked by the same factional clashes. Crime rates had fallen steadily in the more developed south-east, but during 2016 and 2017 sensationalist media coverage of prison massacres and neighbourhood shoot-outs in the north and north-east created the impression that the country was at war. Calls for the police to be given the necessary weapons and the authority to intervene and resolve issues became increasingly popular. A survey by the Brazilian Forum of Public Security, an NGO, found that these fears directly translated into support for authoritarianism.

And finally, there was another, even more profound social trend that was fundamentally changing the attitudes of ordinary Brazilians. Across Brazil, the Protestant Church had made tremendous advances. Since the Catholic Church had retreated from its left-wing stance of the 1960s and 1970s, most of its base communities – that as we saw were so fundamental to the formation of the PT – had disappeared, to be replaced by all manner of radical Protestant churches, espousing the conservative social values based on the family, self-sacrifice, personal responsibility, and individual ambition. Numbering only 6.7 per cent of Brazil's population in 1980, more than 27 per cent were Protestant by 2022. Aggressive, home-grown churches, such as the Igreja Universal do Reino de Deus (Universal Church of the Kingdom of God), and local factions of the Assemblies of God, seemed to be ubiquitous in the poorer districts of Brazilian cities and the more remote areas of the Amazon. In 2018 two out of every three evangelicals voted for Bolsonaro, attracted by his opposition to homosexuality, abortion, and liberal sex education. As one Methodist churchman told me in July 2019, 'he showed the kind of thinking that evangelicals were looking for'.[8]

Perhaps Bolsonaro's anti-liberalism resonated more broadly. The small towns of provincial Brazil, located away from the huge coastal-belt cities such as São Paulo and Rio de Janeiro, which locals sometimes refer to as the *interiorzão* or the big interior, are socially conservative. Steve Bannon, the right-wing ideologue who advised Donald Trump, saw liberal ideas about human rights, gender, and climate change as part of a broader ideological trend which he labelled 'cultural Marxism'. Bolsonaro's hard-line supporters made the same argument.

All of these trends were represented politically by cross-party lobbies of legislators set up to press for legislation that favoured their interests. During the 2000s, the size of these lobbies expanded, and their influence increased. One of the oldest lobbies, or Frente Parlamentar Agropecuária, was the one that brought together farming interests and was known as the Ruralistas. It had been formed in 1987 to head off demands for agrarian reform during the debates about the new constitution, but now members routinely argued in favour of easing environmental standards.

Both the security and evangelical lobbies – nicknamed bullet and bible – had been launched by members of Congress in 2003. Those two and the agricultural front, labelled beef, saw their numbers grow steadily during the 2000s, and especially from 2010 onwards. The security front had lobbied to stop the tightening of gun laws in 2004, for example. The evangelicals united over an opposition lobby that opposed gay marriage and sex education in schools, and blocked any relaxation of restrictions on *abortion*. By 2016, each of these fronts had more than 200 members among the 513 deputies in the lower house of Congress. Conservatives, who could be members of any one of a dozen parties and would frequently flit from one party to another, were often linked to all three lobbies. Indeed, in 2015, the PT legislator Erika Kojay coined the term 'BBB' in an internal meeting of the PT to label the potential threat that it represented to minorities and human rights.

Even so, at the beginning of August, just two months before the first round of the 2018 election, Bolsonaro – despite support and an increasingly active presence on social media, coordinated by the second of his three most politically active sons, Carlos – was lagging in second place in the polls. Two events within a space of seven days were to change that.

First, as we saw in the last chapter, the electoral authorities voted by a narrow margin to exclude Lula, who, despite his imprisonment, had been the consistent front-runner in the race. The decision made under the *fichas limpas* law – under which politicians facing or found guilty of criminal charges cannot participate in elections – was no real surprise. However, Lula was determined to run, if possible, and his party had not done enough to prepare the ground for an alternative candidate. The replacement, Fernando Haddad, had been a relatively successful mayor of São Paulo and had done well as Minister of Education. Still, he was not well known nationally and could not hope to match Lula's charisma and presence. Then on 6 September, Bolsonaro, shortly after his visit to Uberlândia, was campaigning a few hundred miles to the south-east when he fell victim to an assassination attempt. Out among supporters in the city of Juiz de Fora, Bolsonaro was being carried shoulder high through the crowds when a fist reached out and drove a kitchen knife into his stomach. Bolsonaro spent several days in intensive care and survived the attack, but it removed him from the debates where rivals could have challenged his ideas. And it made many neutrals more sympathetic to him than they otherwise would have been, particularly since the attacker, Adélio Bispo de Oliveira, a 40-year-old bricklayer, had once been a member of the far-left Socialism and Liberty Party (PSOL). By mid-September, Bolsonaro had established a substantial poll lead, while more moderate conservatives failed to make any inroads. Anxious to avoid another PT government, more and more better-off Brazilians began to think along the same lines as Paulo Junqueira and Fabio Pergher. In the end, Bolsonaro secured nearly 58 million votes, almost 10 per cent more than Haddad. His party, the Social Liberals – the latest of a string of small, right-wing parties adopted by Bolsonaro over the previous 30 years – had been expected to disappear but was now the second-largest force in Congress, with 52 of the 513 deputies.

AN UNWIELDY ALLIANCE

In government, Bolsonaro selected a cabinet that reflected this broad range of support which his campaign had received. The governing coalition comprised both far-right-wing parties and mainstream liberal conservatives with close ties to the business sector. Among the most prominent radicals were the Foreign Minister, Ernesto Araújo; Damares Alves, an evangelical Christian who became the Minister of Women, Families, and Human Rights; Abraham Weintraub, the Minister of Education; and General Augusto Heleno, a military hard-liner who advised the president on security questions. At the same time, Sérgio Moro, the well-known judge in the Lava Jato case, became Minister of Justice. Paulo Guedes, a former banker well known for his laissez-faire views, became a kind of economic super-minister, charged with implementing liberal reforms and slashing red tape. Another liberal conservative, Rodrigo Maia, a deputy for a liberal conservative party called the Democrats, was elected president of the lower house of Congress and thereby became the most important government politician in the legislature. Mainly during 2019, Maia functioned as an effective prime minister, successfully piloting through the legislature the administration's most important reform: a pension law that reduced benefits for public-sector workers and eased the impact of pension spending on government accounts.

It proved to be an unstable mix. There were repeated clashes between the radicals and liberal conservatives throughout 2019 and early 2020. Bolsonaro's three oldest sons – Flávio, Carlos, and Eduardo – worked as a kind of radical ginger group, linking Bolsonaro to his most fervent right-wing supporters and urging their father to stick to the agenda he had promised during the campaign. They were particularly critical of Maia for representing what they described as the 'old-fashioned politics' of congressional deal-making and attacked the chief of the lower house relentlessly on social media. Various senior military officers who had urged moderation and pragmatism also came under attack from the same source. The government secretary, General Carlos Alberto Santos Cruz, for example, was sacked in mid-2019 after he found fault with Bolsonaro's three sons. During the campaign, Bolsonaro had criticized China and said that he wanted Brazil to pursue a much more pro-American agenda, a vision that his Foreign Minister shared. But China was by far Brazil's biggest trading partner, and cooler heads realized that it made no economic sense for Brazil to create frictions in this way. General Hamilton Mourão, the deputy president, headed a committee that tried to improve relations between the two countries but was constantly at odds with Bolsonaro's sons.

These tensions came to a head in the first half of 2020. First, public prosecutors in Rio de Janeiro state stepped up their investigations into corruption involving deputies in the state's legislative assembly. Bolsonaro's oldest son, Flávio, who had been a state representative for 18 years, was among those targeted. In April, in a move widely seen as designed to protect Flávio from further investigation, Jair Bolsonaro sacked Maurício Valeixo, the director general of the federal police. Valeixo had been a close ally of Sérgio

Moro, and as a result of the affair, Moro resigned towards the end of April 2020.

There was also increasing dissonance within the governing alliance regarding other issues. Radical support for conservative changes to social norms foundered on the rock of institutional and judicial opposition. Despite opposition from socially conservative legislators, the Supreme Court made homophobia a criminal offence. Congress threw out efforts to give police officers greater leeway to use their weapons and refused to back efforts to reduce the age of criminal responsibility to 16, a measure that would have allowed courts to jail young gang members and other offenders. At the same time, following the 2019 pension reform, the pace of economic reform slowed markedly, disappointing the hopes of business people such as Junqueira. Then, from February 2020 onwards, Bolsonaro's government came unstuck. The issue at the root of the problem was the government's management of the coronavirus pandemic.

In February 2020, when the first cases of coronavirus were detected in Brazil, Health Minister Luiz Henrique Mandetta, a low-key orthopaedic surgeon from the rural state of Mato Grosso do Sul, had suggested that the government implement rules recommended by the World Health Organization. Mandetta, another member of the more liberal wing of the government, urged the use of hand gels and masks, and suggested that social isolation was the best way to inhibit the spread of the disease, in effect embracing the internationally accepted conventional approach. This infuriated Bolsonaro. Like Donald Trump, the Brazilian president was a denialist who believed the international health authorities were pursuing a liberal agenda that had ulterior motives. Like Trump, Bolsonaro advocated the use of chloroquine and its cousin, hydroxychloroquine, anti-malaria treatments that at the beginning of the epidemic were seen as drugs that could alleviate the symptoms of the COVID-19 virus. Subsequently, when the first jabs became available towards the end of 2020, Bolsonaro remained an unrelenting sceptic, exaggerating the risks and delaying by several months the country's eventual deployment of a mass-vaccination strategy.

All this brought him into constant conflict with more moderate voices. Mandetta and his immediate successor were dismissed for doubting the efficacy of alternative treatments. Local mayors and governors who implemented quarantines were criticized. João Doria, the governor of São Paulo, who had supported Bolsonaro in the second round of the election, was dismissed as a 'shit' for advocating that the state's residents work at home during the pandemic. Wilson Witzel, elected to the governorship of Rio de Janeiro with the backing of the Bolsonaro clan, was derided as a 'piece of dung' for recommending the same approach. Judges upholding the rights of local authorities in this respect also came under attack, with Bolsonaro threatening to have them arrested. Tensions became especially acute early in 2021 when the death rate from COVID-19 began to accelerate rapidly. At the end of 2020, 500 people were dying from COVID-19 each day in Brazil. On some days in March and early April more than 4,000 deaths from the disease were recorded. The hum of private-sector dissatisfaction with mismanagement of the disease reached a crescendo in the middle of that month, when 1,500 business leaders, banks, and senior economists signed a letter condemning Bolsonaro's approach: 'We have no more [time] to lose in sterile debates and false news . . . The government is using the resources at its disposal badly in part because it ignores or gives little weight to scientific evidence.'

By then, however, the politics of the Bolsonaro government had already been transformed. With liberal conservatives out of the government and Bolsonaro vulnerable to impeachment, the president stitched together a congressional coalition with a group of small, middle-of-the-road or conservative parties known as the Centrão, or the Big Centre. It was a remarkable volte-face for him, because during the campaign and in his first year in office Bolsonaro had claimed that he intended to break with the horse-trading in politics, which had been exposed by corruption scandals of the 2000s and 2010s. Now as the mood in congress became angrier and more critical, it was precisely to those self-interested politicians that Bolsonaro turned for survival.

The Centrão held about 220 seats in the highly fragmented Congress. To ensure the support of his new allies, Bolsonaro needed to supply these deputies with funds. The government was able to do this by handing over control of three public institutions (resources destined for education, drought prevention, and urban transport) that were responsible for spending more than R$70 billion, then about 2 per cent of the federal budget. In February 2021 this unusual alliance was consolidated when with Bolsonaro's backing the lower house of Congress elected as their head Arthur Lira, whose Progressive Party (PP) was an important force within the Centrão. Lira, who had faced multiple corruption allegations, mainly tied to Car Wash investigations, promised to shield Bolonsaro from possible impeachment charges in exchange for cabinet appointments and jobs for his allies and greater control over federal funds. The alliance with the Centrão could protect Bolsonaro, but it couldn't ensure that he would win again.

The reality of a possible defeat that would leave him open to legal prosecution began to dawn on Bolsonaro in March 2021 – almost as soon as Judge Edmar Fachin of the Supreme Court annulled the Guarujá rulings against Lula and cleared the former president to run again at the upcoming election in 2022. From then on until the election took place at the beginning of October, Bolsonaro trailed Lula in virtually every opinion poll.[9]

March – with the escalation of the death rate – had been a bad month anyway for Bolsonaro, and a long-running congressional inquiry, which ended only in October, provided an ongoing focus for public dissatisfaction with the president. The committee's report highlighted allegations of corruption in the purchase of vaccines, as well as the promotion of 'early remedies' that were controversial.

As his ratings fell, Bolsonaro repeatedly campaigned against the alleged unfairness of the electronic voting system. The allegations were groundless. Bolsonaro favoured a paper voting system simply because it would be easier for him and his supporters to fraudulently influence the results, said his critics. The idea led nowhere: congressmen voted it down, and two senior judges ruled that there was no basis for any change. Bolsonaro and his hyperactive social-media team, coordinated by his son Carlos from the presidential palace and nicknamed by journalists the 'cabinet of hate', intensified their attacks on the courts and top judges. There was dark talk that Bolsonaro's supporters in the higher echelons of the armed forces were preparing a coup.

16

Lula 3 Takes Shape

Sundays in Brasília, the modernist capital carved out of remote scrubland in the late 1950s, are usually extremely quiet. The city is a bit of a bubble, somewhat remote from the lives of most Brazilians. Governmental, congressional and legal business, its raison d'être, is heavily concentrated during the week. Every Thursday or Friday, most of the 612 legislators fly back (at enormous cost to the public purse) to their home states.

Sunday, 8 January 2023 was an exception, however. Shortly after three o'clock in the afternoon, hundreds of Bolsonarista demonstrators breezed past police cordons, brushed aside hapless security details, and furiously attacked the empty headquarters of the country's Presidency, Congress, and Supreme Court.

The protesting supporters of former president Jair Bolsonaro rampaged through the wide corridors, smashing glass, setting fires, and wrecking computers. Desks were destroyed. Plaques and pictures celebrating democracy were trashed, and fire extinguishers and sprinklers were set off, flooding various sections of the complex. Artworks were not spared. One demonstrator, a hairdresser, used her lipstick to daub the words *'perdeu mané'* ('you've lost, sucker') across the chest of the judge represented in Alfredo Ceschiatti's modernist sculpture *A Justiça*. A vast canvas, *As Mulatas*, painted in Cubist and Expressionist style in the 1920s by Emiliano di Cavalcanti, was repeatedly slashed. Maybe the work's theme – Brazil's multi-racial identity and history of miscegenation – stuck in the craw of the predominantly white protesters.

Generally, this was an action that mimicked the assault carried out by Trump supporters in Washington, two years before. Journalists seemed to be stunned. 'They are throwing chairs out of the windows,' said one bewildered GloboNews commentator. 'They are destroying public buildings.' 'What we are witnessing is a terrorist attack,' the news anchor Erick Bang announced on the GloboNews television network as word of the upheaval spread. 'The three buildings have been invaded by coup-mongering terrorists.'[1]

It was over soon enough. Within an hour or so, the demonstrators were surrendering to federal police units sent in to clear up the damage and being driven away in police buses. At the time, I thought it was all political theatre, an afternoon tropical storm whose brevity belied some of the more hyperbolic establishment reactions. After all, it was tame stuff compared to some of the insurgent attacks I remembered from covering Latin America in the 1980s: the Guatemalan police invading the occupied Spanish embassy in 1980, setting off fires that led to the incineration of three dozen peaceful protesters; the Colombian army in 1985 blowing apart the Supreme Court building in Bogotá to dislodge guerrilla units of the M19; or the bloody occupation of the Japanese embassy in Lima by the Túpac Amaru Revolutionary Movement (*Movimiento Revolucionario Túpac Amaru* or MRTA) a few years later.

In Brasília, the police and army units had simply let the attacks happen. Six people had been killed during the 2021 Capitol attacks in Washington, but no one had even been injured in Brasília. Yet though the anti-democratic movement had ended in a whimper, it had been marked by serious intent. I had been in Brazil for the election, and in the weeks that followed the tensions were palpable.

In the Jardins district of São Paulo, where we were staying in a hotel next door to the apartment we used to rent, the mood was becoming quite ugly. Our friendly reunions with the cab drivers we remembered from the neighbourhood taxi rank soured when the conversation turned to politics. I remember one afternoon, eating lunch in a local café, when the atmosphere suddenly cooled as groups of grumpy middle-class Brazilians sporting the canary yellow shirt of the Brazilian national football team came in. All had attended an opposition rally on the same avenue where we had watched Lula's victory celebrations a few days before.

A little later, staying in the gated middle-class community where my sister-in-law lives in the conservative central Brazilian city of Uberlândia, every other house seemed to be advertising their support for Bolsonaro by flying the Brazilian flag, And at a barbecue a day or so afterwards, where everybody seemed to have voted for the defeated candidate, I remember someone confidently telling me that Lula would be assassinated before he could take office. A Brazilian friend, who had voted neither for Lula nor Bolsonaro, told me that social unrest would escalate to such an extent that the military would be compelled to intervene solely to restore order and would then remain in place.

Brazilian lorry drivers, whose business association had always strongly supported Bolsonaro, launched blockades of the country's highways. Instead of crime reports, TV news programmes were full of aerial images of articulated trucks jack-knifed across one highway or another. Throughout November and December, Bolsonaro supporters had been camping out across Brazil. Groups, mainly older, better-off Brazilians and often retirees, had pitched tents in front of military barracks, where again soldiers were sympathetic to their cause. In these camps, the air was thick with conspiracy theories. Lula, these people believed, had won by a fraud subtly engineered by 'the system'. The occupant of one camp, a stone's throw from Ibirapuera Park in São Paulo, told the BBC that 'there is a group of people, parties, businessmen, media, judges – that want to control society to the detriment of ordinary people'.[2]

Equally, many protesters seemed to believe that Lula had already been deposed and that General Augusto Heleno, perhaps the most hard-line of Bolsonaro's military allies, was already running things.

In this parallel world, the smallest detail of camp organization had to be carefully monitored. Supplies were to be paid for in cash, rather than through the more easily tracked Pix electronic-transfer system, and food deliveries were to be tightly controlled, lest PT operatives secretly contaminate them with laxatives or rat poison. And after Lula's inauguration on 1 January 2023, they prepared for a final push. In the week after Lula's inauguration, activist groups began to bus their supporters into Brasília, swelling the size of the camp next to the central barracks of the Brazilian army. With farmers and other well-off businessmen footing the bill, organizers offered free trips, providing all with food and shelter. Messages circulated on the preferred social media platforms WhatsApp and Telegram, warning darkly of a possible need to confront police and asking retired policemen and soldiers to bring their weapons. Their plan, according to another message, was to take control of government buildings and establish a camp inside. Outside, lorry drivers would step up their blockades, with the aim of isolating oil refineries, starving the country of fuel and provoking chaos. All this, the Bolsonaristas believed, would trigger military intervention. 'Some of the farmers called me and now they have contracted 3,000 buses from different parts of Brazil,' said one of the protest organizers in an audio produced on 4 January 2023. 'We are going to take power.'[3]

Bolsonaro himself watched this plan crumble from the comfort of a borrowed home in Orlando. He had fled to Florida to avoid the constitutional necessity of having to appear at the inaugural ceremony and hand over the green and yellow sash of office to his successor. Subsequently, it emerged that his closest associates had been urging him and military commanders to move much more decisively ahead of Lula's inauguration. According to an 800-page police dossier, whose contents became known two years later in November 2024, it was only the refusal of the army's General Marco Antônio Freire Gomes and of Lieutenant-Brigadier Antônio Carlos Moreno, head of the air force, that frustrated a coup. According to prosecutors, a group of conspirators had formed a plan to kill Lula, Geraldo Alckmin, the deputy president-elect, and Alexandre de Moraes, a Supreme Court judge who had been a particular bête noire for Bolsonaristas. Court proceedings against Bolsonaro himself and seven other senior associates began in June 2025 and in September they were all sentenced to long prison terms.[4]

In January 2023, however, the swift suppression of the intrigue presented the newly elected president with an opportunity. The courts, which had clamped down on the protests of the Bolsonarista lorry drivers and ordered police to dismantle the blockades, also instructed Bolsonaro supporters to disperse their camps in front of army barracks. Hundreds of those arrested were jailed. Less than two weeks after the attacks, Lula moved to replace the head of the army. He also brought in a new officer to head the presidential security force, which had been unable to prevent the violence taking place.

Immediate international responses invited Lula to position himself on the side of democracy and against authoritarianism, whether of the right-wing Trumpist or Bolsonaro variety, or the more left-wing kind being promoted by Xi Jinping, Putin, or, closer to home, Venezuela's Nicolás Maduro. The US Secretary of State, Antony Blinken, said: 'We condemn the attacks on Brazil's Presidency, Congress, and Supreme Court today. Using violence to attack democratic institutions is always unacceptable. We join @LulaOficial in urging an immediate end to these actions.' Emmanuel Macron, the French president, tweeted: 'The will of the Brazilian people and the democratic institutions must be respected. President @LulaOficial can count on the unconditional support of France.' This accorded with the broader sense at the time that Lula's Brazil would lend new dynamism and momentum to the climate change movement. But the defeat of the conspiracy also allowed Lula to reinforce the democratic alliance that had been launched during the campaign itself. As we've seen he had won in October 2022 by the narrowest of margins. The Workers' Party had only 68 seats in the lower house, and to govern they would need to make alliances with a ragtag set of centre and right-wing groupings. The presidents of the lower house and the Senate, Arthur Lira and Rodrigo Pacheco, leaders, respectively, of the right-wing Progressive and Social Democratic parties, had both worked with Bolsonaro. In 2021, in return for money and jobs, they had helped him avoid impeachment. These politicians, however, largely condemned the coup attempt and they both moved without hesitation to defend their institutions and effectively align with the government. Early on Monday, 9 January 2023, judges, congressional leaders, and the president signed a note rejecting 'terrorism, vandalism, criminality' and calling for a 'calm response'. Pacheco described the demonstrators as an 'anti-democratic minority that represented neither the Brazilian people nor the will of the Brazilian people. This minority would not be allowed to impose their will by barbarism, force and criminality.' A vote to transfer responsibility for security from the federal district – whose governor was a Bolsonarista – to the federal government was overwhelmingly carried by the Senate. 'There was no ambiguity at all about their response,' Sérgio Abranches, a political scientist, told Portugal's *Público* magazine. 'The democratic coalition is strong and united.'[5]

As the consensus shifted in favour of the newly elected administration, all the right-wing parties hurried to distance themselves from their most discredited activists. Valdemar Costa Neto, leader of Bolsonaro's Liberal Party (*Partido Liberal* or PL), said the coup movement 'had been an embarrassment for us. It doesn't represent the PL or Bolsonaro.' Altineu Côrtes, another PL congressional leader, said the party should expel those responsible for the attacks summarily. Meanwhile, individual members of these parties, who, in the excitement of the riot, had filmed themselves participating in the destruction, were having second thoughts. Some deleted their social-media posts.

On the night of 9 January, Lula met with all of Brazil's recently elected state governors in Brasília. Among them were several close allies of Bolsonaro, most notably Tarcísio de Freitas, the former president's Minister of Infrastructure and now the elected governor of Brazil's largest state, São Paulo. Tarcísio had planned to skip the meeting, but after speaking with the Supreme Court president, Rosa Weber, he decided to attend. Weber had insisted on the need for a dialogue between the states and Brazil's federal institutions.

Later that day, Tarcísio seemed to draw a line between himself and the radicals. 'The opposition has to be responsible and *show* the way forward. Demonstrators lose legitimacy as soon as there is violence, destruction and infringement of rights,' read his post on Twitter. 'We are not going to permit this in São Paulo.'[6] On that evening of 9 January, with Tarcísio among the group that walked down the ramp of the Planalto palace to view the destruction at the Supreme Court building, Lula took the chance to drive home his advantage. 'They want a coup, but there is not going to be a coup,' he told journalists. 'They have to learn that democracy is a complicated thing to build. It demands that people support one another, it demands that we live with people whom we don't like, with people whom we don't get on with, but it is the only system that gives everyone a chance to govern the country.'[7] It seemed a propitious moment, but within weeks strains and tensions within Lula's alliance were apparent.

THE CHALLENGE OF GOVERNING

As the dust settled, the real problem that Lula faced was how to govern effectively. Polarization was undoubtedly part of the problem. However, since his first two presidential terms, Brazilian politics had also undergone a more subtle change. The office of the president had become much less powerful, and over the previous decade or so, power in Brazilian society, already dispersed among state and municipal governments, had become even more diffuse.

For one thing, Brazilian judges had begun to play a much more direct role in politics. Back in the 2010s, the judiciary's support for Lava Jato had fatally wounded Lula and the PT. More recently, the Supreme Court decisions to support local authority-imposed quarantines in the pandemic and then reaffirm the integrity of the country's electronic voting system had weakened Bolsonaro. And by allowing Lula's release from prison and restoring his political rights, the rollback of the Lava Jato judgements paved the way for Bolsonaro's defeat in the 2022 election.

Congress, too, had gained more sway over the executive, especially on budgetary matters. The rivalry between Bolsonaro and Lula may have split the country in two. Still, the peculiarities of the election system and political party organization meant that Congress was very fragmented, notwithstanding a fall in the number of parties represented.[8]

The big difference, though, was that Lula in 2023 had a much smaller group of congressmen who would provide reliable backing for his programme than in his first two governments, or that Dilma Rousseff had in her own two. Not only was the hardcore of PT and other left-wing party representatives smaller than it had been before, but the support of allied parties was less reliable.

No government since Brazil returned to democracy in 1985 had such a small base of consistent support among deputies in the lower house of Congress. Even Fernando Collor, the president impeached for corruption in 1992, could rely on more votes. Back in the late 2000s, when Lula was in his pomp, government managers could depend on the votes of 291 of the 513 deputies. After Dilma Rousseff was elected in 2010, what the Brazilians call the 'allied base' became even stronger, with the support of 351 legislators guaranteed. Now, beginning his third mandate, Lula had only 140 votes assured.

Back in the 1990s and 2000s, the three big centre-right and conservative parties – the PMDB, the PFL (subsequently relabelled the Democrats and then Brazil Union) and the PSDB – had formed part of stable government coalitions, first led by Cardoso's PSDB and then with the PT of Lula and Rousseff. As we saw in Chapter 10, political scientist Sérgio Abranches had labelled this arrangement 'coalitional presidentialism'.[9]

But now the system was beginning to break up. Since the 2010s these big parties that were such an essential component of political stability, had been riven by internal divisions, with local state-based bosses gaining ground at the expense of national leadership. As a result, it was more difficult for presidents to negotiate coalitions. 'Congress today is formed by invertebrate parties . . . You can't build a coherent coalition [with them],' Abranches told the weekly news magazine *Veja* in June 2024.[10]

The stable terrain of coalitional presidentialism had been replaced by a political quicksand in which a big group of newer, smaller, self-interested centre-right and right-wing Centrão parties came into their own. The Centrão had come to Bolsonaro's support in 2021, helping him survive the threat of impeachment. But in 2023 it backed Lula, who in return gave three cabinet positions each to the centre-right Social Democratic Party and the right-wing Brazil Union, as well as one to the right-wing Progressive Party.

However, deputies from these parties voted only occasionally for the government, leaving it to negotiate support on a case-by-case basis. The Brazil Union was a particularly unreliable ally. Even though it had been given three ministries, its deputies backed the government in fewer than half the votes. The Progressive Party (*Progressistas* or PP), which had one ministry, voted with the government in 52.1 per cent of votes. Even the Social Democratic Party (PSD), a party that had formed numerous local alliances with the PT in the north-east and had three cabinet positions, wasn't a reliable supporter when it came to legislating, with only six out of ten votes cast in favour.[11]

Underpinning the influence of the Centrão was its control over the key leadership positions in Congress and its ability to direct a growing body of funds, known as congressional amendments, to supporters. All this was relatively new and something that Lula had not had to deal with in his first two terms in office, even though the origins of the problem lay in the utopian ambitions of the politicians who drafted a new constitution in 1988. That document had allocated fixed amounts to health, education, and social welfare. By the early 2000s, more than 90 per cent of spending was already earmarked. There were always battles between the executive and the legislature over how the remainder of the budget was to be spent, but during the 2000s, as the economy prospered, revenues generally exceeded expectations and the government could usually direct enough money towards the projects favoured by loyal congressmen. That began to change in the 2010s as the economy slowed, money became increasingly scarce, and – as we saw in Chapter 12 – President Rousseff began to clamp down on traditional party-funding practices.

In 2013 congressional leaders compelled the government to agree to new arrangements, whereby they would have exclusive control over a portion of these funds. Eduardo Cunha, the leader of the PMDB and then president of the lower house in Congress, introduced various types of congressional budget amendments. Since then, Congress has appropriated larger amounts of the available funds. By 2024, congressional leaders had control of approximately R$49 billion (just under $10 billion), three times more than in 2015, and an amount equivalent to more than 20 per cent of discretionary funds.[12]

Since 2020, politicians from the Centrão have controlled the leadership of both the House and the Senate, which has given these parties an unprecedented degree of power. In the past, individual members of Congress who sought to secure funding were more reliant on their relationships with the president and his ministers. The displacement of financial power away from the executive towards Congress has changed that. Deputies on the lookout for money are now just as likely to look to the congressional authorities who control funding as they are to the president and his ministries.[13]

THE RISE OF HADDAD

Another factor complicating Lula's third term in office was that the president could not always rely on automatic support from his own Workers' Party. That was largely because it was becoming harder to pursue the same Lulista market-friendly but socially progressive approach – what the political scientist Andrés Singer called 'Reform without Rupture' – which had been so successful in his first two terms in office. Lula was as committed as ever to keeping inflation under control, but he had come back to office with big spending commitments. Both he and his party were as determined as ever to improve the living standards of the poorest groups and repair those institutions – like IBAMA, the environmental regulator – that had been underfunded and damaged by the Bolsonaro government. This was a tricky balancing act for several reasons.

First, since Lula had initially come to office two decades before, the pressure on public finances had increased. Brazil's state had swollen in size over the years of PT government, increasing from 32 per cent of GDP to 42 per cent of output by 2015, and under the two succeeding right-wing governments of Michel Temer and Jair Bolsonaro it had continued to expand, reaching the equivalent of 43.5 per cent of output by the end of 2022. As we saw in Chapter 10, the deficit had been kept at a relatively low 2–3 per cent, but under Dilma Rousseff it had risen and after the recession of the mid-2010s and the COVID-19 pandemic, debt had edged higher still. For a developing economy Brazil's spending and tax burdens were already much greater than those in fellow BRICS nations such as Russia and China, and much higher than those of most of its Latin American neighbours.[14] Second, as we have seen, congressmen were taking growing chunks of the budget for their own plans and projects. Third, the PT rank and file and many of its leaders and representatives were becoming more reluctant to sanction austerity or tax rises, partly because the mood in the governing party had shifted to the left due to the impeachment of Rousseff and the imprisonment of Lula himself. Back in 2005, Rousseff had derided the idea of balancing the books as 'economic illiteracy' and – despite the disasters of her government – many of her comrades still thought the same way.[15]

Lula looked to Fernando Haddad, a 59-year-old lawyer and economist, to find a way out of the maze. Over the tumultuous past decade Haddad had become one of Lula's closest and most reliable allies. During Lula's imprisonment Haddad had been one of the few leading figures to stay close to the former trade unionist. 'At the nadir of Lula's fortunes during Lava Jato, his allies could all fit inside a [Volkswagen] Kombi [minibus],' a lawyer close to the PT told a reporter at *Piauí*. 'Haddad was in that bus. Haddad had a relationship with Lula that transcended politics.'[16] Selected as the party's candidate in 2018 when the courts forbade Lula from running, Haddad's campaign slogan, 'Haddad is Lula, and Lula is Haddad', was designed to win over voters likely to vote for Lula but not necessarily the PT. But it also epitomized the bond between the two men, which this same lawyer claimed was 'almost fatherly'.

Haddad was a moderate, a politician whose ideas differed from those of the ascendant hard left within the party. His politics, in fact, were rooted in modern European social democracy. In the student movement of the 1980s, he had led a PT faction critical of both the Communist Party and the Trotskyist Libelu (which became part of the PT). He was clear-sighted about the deficiencies of old-fashioned socialism. He had written critically about the Soviet Union and its economic model. As a philosopher, Haddad had written his doctoral thesis on the ideas of Jürgen Habermas, a contemporary German social theorist who had embraced social democracy. And as a politician Haddad was very much a pragmatist. In a four-year stint in São Paulo town hall, Haddad had sorted out the city's accounts, resisted left-wing demands for spending, and won plaudits from credit rating agencies. His secretary of finance had been a partner at McKinsey, a management consulting firm. Haddad was close to the ideas of the PSDB (Lula once described him as the most Toucan of the Petistas), and expressed admiration for its founder, former president Fernando Henrique Cardoso.

As Lula planned his political comeback, Haddad had played a key role in building bridges with figures from the political centre. In 2021 he made initial contact with Geraldo Alckmin, Lula's former rival for the presidency, who was about to leave the PSDB. 'Haddad thought Lula could only win by stitching together the widest possible alliance on the centre-left and he sounded out Alckmin,' wrote Ana Clara Costa in *Piauí*.[17]

The gambit had paid dividends, strengthening Haddad's position, since Alckmin's presence on the ticket had helped Lula win more votes in São Paulo, the newly elected deputy president's home state. (In 2022, Lula won 4.3 million votes more than Haddad had in São Paulo state back in 2018, votes that in the end helped Lula edge ahead of Bolsonaro.)

In government, though, it was harder for Haddad than it had been for Antônio Palocci, the similarly moderate Finance Minister who faced similarly testing challenges 20 years before. After the bruising experience of Rousseff's governments, investors and fund managers were more sceptical and more demanding. News of Haddad's appointment disappointed hopes that Lula might give the post to Pérsio Arida, who in the 1990s had been one of the architects of the *Plano Real*, or another liberal economist to the job. A wave of selling ensued. 'There was consensus within the financial sector that Haddad would be a front man for Lula, someone worried about turning the economy into an electoral machine,' wrote Thomas Traumann in a profile piece.[18]

And – as Traumann added – Lula did not make things any easier by stating in an interview that 'the finance ministry has its autonomy, but I was the one who won the election. I know what's good for the people and what's good for the market.'[19] The president's uncompromising stance on the need to channel more funds to the lower paid, restoring an expensive formula that increased the minimum wage at a rate well above inflation, had upset investors as well. So did the decision to scrap the rigid ceiling on annual spending in favour of a much looser straitjacket.

Yet at every turn, it seemed Haddad faced opposition from the left of his own party. During the 2022 campaign Lula had promised to reverse many of the changes enacted by his right-wing predecessors, including reforms that had introduced flexibility into the labour market, granted autonomy to the Central Bank, and allowed private capital to invest in the water industry. But lacking a congressional majority, Lula was unable to deliver. In such circumstances Haddad's efforts to restrict public spending led many left-wingers to snipe from the sidelines. At times, Haddad seemed like a lone voice in Lula's cabinet.

Rui Costa, the former governor of Bahia and Lula's chief of staff, was one of Haddad's fiercest critics. Gleisi Hoffmann, the president of the party (until 2025), was especially combative. Hoffmann, who had been Dilma Rousseff's chief of staff and done much to keep the PT together during its crisis of the 2010s, signed off a party statement lambasting Haddad's spending policies which she labelled fiscal 'austericide'. The left, too, were critical of the Central Bank's interest-rate policies – designed to keep a lid on inflation – and not infrequently demanded that the body be brought under government control.[20]

Haddad, however, found a way through. Supported by a team of technical specialists, he negotiated directly with congressional leaders, revealing a talent for deal-making. Rather than rely on Lula or on the ministers specifically appointed to handle coordination with Congress, he was doing it himself. 'Haddad was able to form a surprising alliance with the president of the lower house and head of one of the most important Centrão parties, Arthur Lira, which allowed them to get approval for important tax reforms,' wrote Traumann.[21]

Slowly the mood on Faria Lima, the southern suburb that serves as a kind of Wall Street in São Paulo, began to change. Surveys showed growing support there for Haddad. 'Before, we used to meet with [Guido] Mantega [Finance Minister between 2007 and 2015], and he treated us as if we were class enemies. Haddad goes to São Paulo on Fridays to meet with people in the market, and they like the way he is,' a fund manager told Costa. Another claimed: 'We know where we are going now. We know that there aren't a band of madmen in the ministry who have no commitment to fiscal responsibility. That is at least a comfort.'[22]

At the end of 2023, Haddad achieved a major reform. The 1988 constitution had given the country's 27 states and approximately 5,570 municipalities the right to impose taxes, leaving Brazil with the most complex set of fiscal rules in the world. With five separate indirect taxes charged on sales at different rates in different states, the system was chaotic. For businesses, compliance was expensive and time-consuming, often requiring the services of lawyers. In 2019 the World Bank estimated that companies spent 1,501 hours a year complying with Brazilian tax law, compared with a global average of 234 hours.[23] The *Economist* also pointed out that 'many of Brazil's taxes are cumulative'. This means that companies producing goods must pay tax on each input without securing refunds, as is the case elsewhere. Products that are more complex to make, requiring more technology and inputs, are disproportionately burdened.

The tax legislation was drafted by Bernard Appy, an economist and tax specialist. It had been initially proposed in the early 2000s and was revived during the Bolsonaro government. It simplified the system by introducing a value-added tax charged at a single rate. It wasn't perfect. Even when implemented, it would take several years before the changes took effect, and the probable VAT rate (27.5 per cent) was likely to be one of the highest in the world. But everyone agreed that the new system would be a significant benefit for businesses.[24] Rates – although high – would be lower than before and the costs of compliance would plummet. EY, a professional services firm, calculated that the typical number of hours needed to comply with consumption taxes alone would decrease from 885 per year to 285.

Lula seemed as if he was sometimes unhappy with his Finance Minister, but he usually ended up backing the moderate path. And Haddad emerged as the most Lulista of the PT grandees, perhaps the one most capable of appealing to those groups increasingly at odds with PT collectivism. As individualism swept through Brazilian society, the left-wing Petistas were out of touch. We will examine in greater detail just how much the party has failed to come to terms with social, economic, and demographic shifts. The rise of small-scale self-employment, which Brazilians somewhat optimistically refer to as *empreendedorismo (entrepreneurship)*, both in cities and in the countryside, is the focus of our next chapter.

17

'Welcome to the sacred land of the working class'

At 10 a.m. on a Tuesday the concrete and glass headquarters of the Metalworkers union in São Bernardo do Campo had the feel of one of Brasília's modernist churches that I had visited a few days before: the trade union's nerve centre was completely quiet but awash with colour: fourteen giant portraits of left-wing heroes hung down like icons over the stillness of an empty reception area.

Predictably, Lula and those standard left-wing Latin American heroes – Che Guevara and Fidel Castro – were among those celebrated. As for the rest, there was a curious mix of figures highlighting the political mishmash that has influenced a union closely tied to Lula's Workers' Party since its formation 45 years ago. A portrait of Brazil's most celebrated urban guerrilla leader, Carlos Marighella, rubbed shoulders with Rosa Luxemburg, Chico Mendes, Chico Buarque, and Mahatma Gandhi. Nelson Mandela's portrait sat alongside that of the notorious bandit Lampião and his gangster moll, Maria Bonita, Robin Hood-style figures who had rampaged across the rural north-east during the 1920s.

When I met Moises Selerges, the 57-year-old car worker who is now the president of the union in which half a century earlier Lula had forged his political career, the sensation of otherworldliness lingered. 'Welcome to the sacred land of the working class, where everything began,' he said only half in jest, as he ushered me into an office that provided more evidence of firm ideological convictions.

On the coffee table were the complete works of Xi Jinping and a volume of interviews with Hugo Chávez, the leader of Venezuela's experiment with twenty-first-century socialism. On the wall there was a framed Brazilian football shirt signed 'by your friend Lula'. Curiously, too, for a Brazilian fan, there was a photograph of the Argentinian player Diego Maradona, a legendary hero of Brazil's most bitter sporting rivals. 'Footballers can be so reactionary, and I always liked the things Maradona said. He is dead on politically,' said Selerges, reflecting on Maradona's well-known proximity to Castro and Chávez. Selerges, it turned out, was so passionate about his left-wing sympathies that he had called his youngest daughter Frida, in homage to Frida Kahlo, whose portrait I had also glimpsed earlier. His youngest grandson, Ernesto, had been christened after Ernesto 'Che' Guevara (also an Argentinian).

Lula, though, is the fundamental reference point. A larger-than-life figure, who likes to wear loose-fitting, brightly coloured Hawaiian-style shirts and a cloth cap, Selerges brimmed with self-confidence. His down-to-earth style and charisma bore a striking resemblance to Lula's to such an extent, in fact, that he almost seemed like a younger version of the Brazilian president. Selerges's biography was similar. He, too, had started working at a factory (Mercedes-Benz) in his teens, and like Lula, he had been initially suspicious of unions before being eventually persuaded to get involved. 'I didn't like unions. I thought they were all thieves and that negotiations were simply an excuse to drink whisky with the bosses.'

Also like the president, Selerges is a football obsessive, although the two support different São Paulo teams (Selerges is a member of the Independente fan group of São Paulo FC, whereas Lula watches Corinthians). Selerges had first met the Brazilian leader in 2002 during one of his union visits. Lula had taken a close interest in his career and, in 2017, invited him to live in his apartment, a 20-minute drive away in the south of São Bernardo. 'He came to visit me in our [tiny] flat, and he said, "Look, you are going to become president of the union. You must find somewhere else. You can't have businessmen and bankers come round to your place. And you can't meet at the union." He pressed me a lot.'

When Lula and the PT had fallen from grace, Selerges had remained doggedly loyal. He had looked after Lula when he had been holed up in the union headquarters ahead of his imprisonment. 'We experienced some of the most difficult moments in his life together,' Selerges said, adding that he was regularly in touch with the president. 'Sometimes he'll call, and we'll have a beer together. A lot of the time, we talk about his life, talk nonsense really, about football, about our families. We'll train together. We don't talk politics necessarily. Sometimes I go to Brasília, and I don't see him. I don't mind. I know he has an important job to do. He knows he can count on us.'

The problem, though, is that the trade union's power – and the appeal of its call to collective action – are diminishing. The ideals represented by the displayed icons no longer resonate with most of the population. In working-class suburbs like São Bernardo do Campo, the lure of individualism, social mobility, and what Brazilians call *empreendedorismo* (entrepreneurship) has become a dominant mentality.

Lula can undoubtedly count on the support of leaders such as Selerges, but the trade unions have far less power than they did when Lula himself was sitting in these headquarters. At the beginning of 1980, when he frequented the corridors of this same building, manufacturing and union membership were on the rise. Factories accounted for approximately a third of Brazil's economic output. By the mid-1980s, more than 30 per cent of workers had joined trade unions. Forty years on, industry has shrunk to about 13 per cent of GDP and unions have lost two-thirds of their members. Selerges's union still has 70,000 affiliates but has lost 40,000 since 2012.[1]

Growing numbers of less-educated, unskilled Brazilians are making their living in the burgeoning services sector. Their focus is on getting by rather than on the future. Hundreds of thousands of them drive or cycle for taxi, food delivery or e-commerce platforms, the business behemoths that are to Brazil in 2025 what the car companies were 50 years ago. The three biggest are Uber (in which institutional investors such as BlackRock, Vanguard, and Morgan Stanley have significant stakes); 99 Taxi, owned by China's Didi Chuxing; and iFood, a local startup that has been backed by the big South African publishing and online retail group, Naspers, through its internet finance arm, Protus. Perhaps more than two million Brazilians are contracted as gig workers for these companies' platforms.[2] Researchers found that in August 2021, 485,474 Brazilians were contracted by Uber, 402,453 by 99 Taxi, and 102,000 by iFood. The numbers have likely increased since then, as Brazil was only beginning to emerge from the COVID-19 pandemic at the time. A year previously, for example, iFood's employment roster had been twice the size.

A labour reform introduced by the Temer government in 2017 in the wake of Dilma Rousseff's impeachment is partly responsible for the surge in numbers. The new rules gave employers much greater freedom to introduce flexible labour arrangements. Uber taxis were permitted to compete freely with private taxi drivers and cooperatives, and because of these changes Uber, 99 Taxi, and iFood, which had already established initial operations between 2009 and 2014, increased their investments. The reform also eliminated a labour tax that had been mandatory for union members. Proceeds from it had been used to finance unions' organizational costs, and their capacity to respond, as well as to mobilize politically, was crippled. According to one report, the unions lost R$3 billion in annual income and were forced to lay off staff and take other cost-saving measures.[3]

At the same time, in Brazil's informal sector, where thousands of people have traditionally survived by offering manicures or haircuts, or simply selling home-made snacks or knick-knacks on the streets, digital phones, mobile banking, and better transportation have opened up new possibilities. Brazilians have been able to open accounts with new digital banks, such as NuBank, a start-up that has built a market share of more than 25 per cent among poorer Brazilians in a short time. Pix, a payments system introduced by the Central Bank in 2020, enables money transfers via mobile phone and reduces dependency on cash.

On top of that, the rapidly growing evangelical churches have created support networks and instilled values that help their members face up to the challenges of this precarious world. In his book *O Povo de Deus*, Juliano Spyer describes this aspect of the evangelical movement as one of the most important mass phenomena of the last few decades. 'It is seen as something negative, as fanatic, conservative and intolerant, when it is a spontaneous movement of poor Brazilians that promotes entrepreneurship.'[4]

Working in the digital economy often means long hours and is very insecure, offering little protection against illness, accidents, or old age. However, the money is usually more attractive than what the unskilled would make working in shops and restaurants or on construction sites. It is not easy to measure, but formal sector wages are much lower than they were 50 years ago. Selerges reckoned that when he started at Mercedes-Benz in the mid-1980s, he picked up a wage that was more than 50 per cent higher than a newcomer today would receive. Typically, today's manufacturing workers rarely receive the kind of regular increases that they did in the 1980s.

Against that background, working as an Uber driver or in the informal sector is often perceived to be more attractive than a fixed job in the formal sector. In recent years I have spoken to dozens of Uber drivers and have always been struck by how much better off they consider themselves to be. That is particularly the case if they worked previously as a shop assistant or in a restaurant, where hours are long and wages generally around the legal minimum. Lula's governments have usually increased the minimum wage at a rate above inflation, but as of November 2025 it still amounted to only R$1,518 per month ($280). By contrast, drivers said they earned, after deductions for fuel, car maintenance, Uber or 99 Taxi's sizable commission, and in some cases, a payment to rent or buy their car, up to R$200 per day. Official data from the 2021–2022 period confirmed this advantage. Overall, the workers on the platforms earned an average of R$2,645 a month, 5.4 per cent more than those in the formal sector. But that gain was much greater for less-educated, unskilled workers. Working for the platforms, these workers earned on average 30 per cent more than they did in the formal sector. However, they also tended to work longer hours (46 hours a week, rather than 39.5 hours for workers in the traditional economy) and were much less likely to be insured against illness or accidents or to have pension provision.[5]

An anecdote that Selerges himself told me provided further confirmation of this trend. When he moved into his new home, the apartment in São Bernardo that Lula owns, in 2020, he contracted a *diarista* (a domestic day-rate cleaner) called Aparecida ('Cida' for short) to come once a week. Cida lived in a *favela* a stone's throw away and had other clients in the same building, so she was able to look after two apartments each day, earning as much as R$200 for each of those jobs. She and Selerges had got on well, and the union leader offered to help her get a job with Mercedes-Benz, the motor manufacturer whose employees his union represented, and which, under Brazil's labour laws, still paid his wage. Back in the 1970s, when a factory job was highly sought after and the worker's blue overalls were a symbol of status, prosperity, and security, this would have been a no-brainer. But Selerges said Cida had turned him down flat. 'She told me, "There is no way I want a job at Mercedes, Moises. Being a *diarista*, I can send my daughter to school, buy a car for her, and organize my house in the *favela*. Why am I going to work at Mercedes to get less money?"'

Self-employment offers another advantage that is highly prized: flexibility. In my conversations many drivers told me they appreciated having the opportunity to take time off during the day. It allowed them to drop off or pick up children from school, or simply to enjoy a break from their grinding routine. In addition, some drivers worked to supplement income earned in another job, helping compensate for low pay rates while still retaining social benefits. The apps also offered a rapid way to earn money for those who had lost their jobs in the formal sector, as many thousands of people did during the deep recession of 2015 and 2016. In another survey, four out of ten interviewees reported being unemployed before working with the apps.⁶

Yet another survey, this time by the São Paulo Industrialists Association (*Federação das Indústrias do Estado de São Paulo* or FIESP), found that a majority of those interviewed preferred to work for themselves rather than in a job with all the protection of the labour code. Some 59 per cent of those questioned preferred self-employment, with the reluctance to enter formal work so widespread in the city that nearly 80 per cent of businesses are finding it difficult to contract labour. Another piece of research confirmed the picture. Respondents cited various reasons, but lifestyle factors – such as autonomy and the work atmosphere – were frequently mentioned. A total of 63 per cent of those responding to a survey by Locomotiva, a local research company, thought that formal work offered too little space for their personal lives.⁷

The COVID-19 pandemic added significant momentum to this trend, with thousands of people forced to brave the uncertain world of self-employment for the first time to survive. Among them was Daiane Batista Vieira, a 37-year-old manicurist from Salvador whom I met at my mother-in-law's apartment in the city in July 2023. During the 2010s, Daiane worked as a shop assistant at Cacau Show, an upmarket store whose outlets are mainly located in urban shopping malls, and where the better-off buy fancily wrapped boxes of high-quality chocolates. The hours were long and the pay poor. Working six days a week, Daiane took home less than R$1,500 (about $280 at current exchange rates) for a month's work. She eventually switched to a beauty salon and learned to be a manicurist. But during the pandemic, when the outlet was forced to close, she began operating independently, providing manicures in the homes and apartments of her customers. Daiane had some modest set-up and running expenses, including transport costs, her small bag of nail clippers and other tools, and bottles of gels and varnishes. She had a cheap Samsung Galaxy smartphone on which she could organize appointments and an account with Uber, which provided her transport. Over the course of a day, Daiane found she could comfortably visit her own four or five clients, who were happy to pay her the R$40 or so, slightly less than they would have spent in the salon, but all of which went straight into her account. Payments were often made electronically by the easy-to-use Pix app installed on her phone. Apart from any funds she was able to set aside, Daiane had no protection in the event of illness or accident; however, she reckoned that with an income way above what she earned from the shop, she was far better off. 'It is so much more flexible, and I am earning at least double the amount I used to,' she told me. 'All this would have been very different without my mobile phone and Uber.'[8]

For Selerges and many others on the left, including, it sometimes seems, Lula himself, the answer to all this is simple. First, Brazil needs a policy to create new industries or rebuild old ones shattered by decades of liberal reform. Second, it needs to convince the self-employed that their freedoms are illusory and bind them into new collective organizations. Both objectives are more complicated than they sound, and as of November 2025, the third Lula administration had made only minimal progress towards achieving them.

An active industrial policy certainly makes sense, at least on paper. After all, most governments in developed countries, such as the United States, Great Britain, Germany, France, and Japan, at one time in their history subsidized businesses or protected them from competition, allowing them to grow. In the 1970s and 1980s, South-East Asian economies, such as South Korea and Taiwan, built up competitive export industries in this manner. As globalization advanced in the 1990s and 2000s, the idea of intervention became discredited, with strategists focusing on how developing countries could become part of cross-border 'business clusters' or international 'value chains'. But since the 2008–9 financial crisis there has been a new emphasis on government intervention. Perhaps the best example of this new trend is the way the Biden administration in the United States responded to growing geopolitical competition with China between 2020 and 2024, promoting the development of its microchip industry and reducing dependency on Asian production. Brazil's historical experience of industrial policy was initially very positive. As we saw in Chapter 2, the import substitution policies of President Getúlio Vargas enabled the development of a broad manufacturing sector. But since then, the story has been chequered to say the least. Few businesses were ever able to compete internationally and survived by selling overpriced and often poor-quality products to domestic consumers. Brazil's efforts, under the military government, to produce its own computers were laughable. Frequently, as in the rest of Latin America, these protected sectors survived due to their close relationship with political elites. Policies were often deployed erratically for short-term political goals. The military government's efforts to promote capital goods production were an expensive failure, contributing to a significant build-up in debt and leading to the country's financial isolation for much of the 1980s. As we saw in Chapter 13, the Rousseff government's tax breaks, offered to a varying and bewildering range of manufacturing sectors to help businesses cope with an overvalued exchange rate, did nothing to encourage industrial investment and ultimately increased the extent of the country's fiscal problems.

Early in 2024 the Lula government announced a new industrial policy designed to channel investments of R$300 billion into various sectors. The policy – which aims to integrate developmental and environmental goals – is innovative, being based on an approach pioneered by the Italian American development economist Mariana Mazzucato.[9] As a professor of economics at University College London, and a high-level adviser to several governments in Europe and the developing world, Mazzucato is drawing up plans to capitalize on Brazil's comparative advantages – its agricultural productivity and well-developed base in hydroelectricity and other sources of renewable energy, for example – and establish goals or 'missions', which to be achieved require executive backing and smooth coordination between ministries and state agencies. Selerges and his trade union are enthusiastic supporters. 'We are insisting a lot on industrial policy. We are working hard on it,' he told me. 'We can't just be a country that exports commodities.

We must have a strong industry. We are talking about engineering and food processing, not just cars. We must have a policy to deal with this.'[10]

The schemes, however, have met with considerable scepticism, not least because its reputation for labyrinthine and slow-moving bureaucracy makes the Brazilian public sector an unlikely candidate to become one of Mazzucato's 'enterprising states'. 'It seems a reheating of a lot of developmentalist ideas, sold with a modern branding,' concluded Pedro Cavalcanti and Renato Fragelli of the Fundação Getúlio Vargas business school, in one typically dismissive piece.[11]

Combining union demands for jobs with environmental transformation will not be an easy task. Brazil has seen a surge of investment interest in electric cars. However, these vehicles contain fewer components than traditional vehicles and are easier to build, resulting in fewer jobs being required. Selerges's union would like to see the country become a hub for petrol or diesel-powered car production.

Even a government economist sympathetic to the plan in general terms suggested that its ambitious investment targets sit uneasily with the reality of fiscal restraint, noting that Fernando Haddad, the Finance Minister, had not even been present when the policy was launched. In 2025, Brazil's fiscal deficit was running at very nearly 9 per cent of GDP, and the country's debt was growing. Although the debt-to-GDP ratio remains modest compared to Japan, the United States, and many European countries, it has grown significantly since Lula took office, making it more expensive to borrow money abroad.

Persuading thousands of digital workers to join trade unions seems equally unrealistic. When Lula was elected in 2022, he had promised to introduce legislation improving the working conditions of Uber drivers and other app-based employees. The unions and their lawyers have criticized the long hours and the lack of protection. Accidents among delivery riders are notoriously frequent. Selerges told me that the union had discussed the issue of the app workers and had talked about the idea of creating a rest area at the union where riders and drivers could stop, use the bathroom, take a coffee, and relax for a while. However, the problem, as I have suggested, is that most riders and drivers aren't especially well-disposed to the union or the left in general, tending to see them as interfering busybodies. As Rosana Pinheiro-Machado, a Brazilian anthropologist, put it, 'app workers were belligerent about their ability to do it for themselves'.[12]

Efforts to regulate the sector have predictably foundered. In March 2024, when the Minister of Labour, Luiz Marinho, a former president of the Metalworkers Union, finally presented proposals to limit working hours, establish a minimum wage, and introduce accident insurance and pension provision for app drivers, too, they demonstrated against them. Stoppages were called in various cities. 'Drivers are not going to survive for more than five or six months if this bill is approved,' Eduardo Lima de Souza, president of the Associação de Motoristas de Aplicativo de São Paulo (Amasp; the app motorists association of São Paulo), told a local journalist. Drivers claimed that the minimum hourly rate suggested was too low, but they also defended their autonomy and opposed limiting the working day to 12 hours. Maciel Tomaz Nina, a labour lawyer, told the same newspaper that the idea of controlling a driver's working day was 'unimaginable'.[13]

Initially submitted as urgent legislation that needed to be debated by Congress relatively quickly, the plans were soon downgraded and then quietly dropped. Renan Bernardi, a labour lawyer and professor at the University of São Paulo, who has been lobbying for reform, told me in October 2024 that the government had underestimated the obstacles. 'They had no idea of the scenario they were going to face. Even though people who have been involved in this debate for some time told them that this was going to be difficult, the government did not pay much attention.'[14]

The anthropologist Pinheiro-Machado claimed that the entire business structure of digital platforms is highly individualized, focuses on performance, and exaggerates hyper-liberal tendencies. 'It is a system based on illusion. For them [the app worker] the enemy is the bad worker and the waster [*vagabundo*],' she said.[15]

Yet the appeal of individualism is not confined to the digital world or urban settings. In the next section, we examine how the seductions of mobility and consumerism have undermined one of the most successful environmental reforms of the last 30 years, in the state of Acre. And it has done so in a manner that has important implications for another objective of the Lula government: the effort to reduce deforestation and mitigate climate change.

THE CHARM OF THE COW

Raimundo Mendes did not attempt to disguise the difficulties faced by the rubber tappers' union that he founded with his cousin Chico 47 years ago. The powerful and tall, white-bearded 78-year-old struck a sad – even mournful – note as he described the gradual decline of the Chico Mendes extractive reserve in the western state of Acre, one of the largest and most emblematic protected areas of the Amazon rainforest.

'We are in a lot of trouble here in the reserve,' said Mendes, who is ubiquitously known by fellow tappers as Raimundão (Big Raymond). 'There are so many more cattle in the reserve now than there used to be. The rubber tappers themselves are cutting down trees to make pasture, and some of our members are selling their lots, which, strictly speaking, is illegal. It's a rather embarrassing situation.'[16]

Raimundão reckoned that at least 300 families – 10 per cent of the members of the rubber tappers' union – had left the reserve in recent years. Many others had converted more of their land than they were allowed to into pasture.[17]

It was October 2023, and we were sitting on the balcony of a wooden house on stilts flanked by dense tree cover on three sides. We were an hour's truck ride away from Xapuri, the town from which Chico Mendes had built up the union from the 1970s and where, in December 1988, he was assassinated. Raimundão had worked from this same house since the mid-1970s, and it was there that he received news of his cousin's killing. 'They sent people here to tell me at 3 a.m. It was a shock. It wasn't easy to accept, the loss of Chico,' he said. 'In a way, though, it wasn't too much of a surprise. Chico said to me one day, "It is very difficult for guys like us who start a fight to see it through to the end."'[18]

As we sipped sweetened cashew juice from blue plastic cups, Raimundão lamented the steady erosion of interest among younger members of tapper families, who were seduced by the attraction of the state's flourishing agri-business and the brash cowboy culture that accompanied it. 'The younger people have no direction,' he said. 'The school that Chico set up to help them read and write has done nothing to make them want to preserve the trees. And our union has failed as well, so now we have a load of kids who want to raise cattle and work on farms. Others are getting involved with drugs. So, we have a really serious problem.'[19]

It was a worrying sign for the broader prospects of saving the Amazon. Although Acre has been a small and remote state for much of the last 30 years, it has served as a showcase for Brazil's environmental protection efforts. The protected reserves have been at the core of this model. For Raimundão and his union colleagues, a combination of right-wing politics and organized crime had put this vision at risk. The impeachment of Dilma Rousseff in 2016, the imprisonment of Lula, and Bolsonaro's triumph in Brasília in 2018 were accompanied by the victory of an ally of a right-wing populist in Acre, with the PT losing control of the state government for the first time in 20 years. After 2018, federal and state authorities disregarded the advance of the ranchers, both local and federal protection agencies were deprived of funds, and their staff were intimidated. Organized-crime groups had also begun to extend their tentacles into the state, just as they had in the wider Amazon region. The union reckoned that four-fifths of the 33,000 hectares of forest lost between 2020 and 2022 had been cut down by Red Command, one of Brazil's two largest organized-crime groups. They are increasingly involved in not just drug trafficking but also illegal logging, mining, ranching, and fishing. 'We have very solid evidence that organized crime is inside the reserve,' Raimundão told me.[20]

The longer I spent in Acre, the deeper the roots of the extractive reserves' problems seemed to become. Just as in urban areas the attractions of lowly paid formal employment were paling beside the potential rewards from the gig economy, so in Acre owning a cow seemed to make more economic sense than harvesting rubber or Brazil nuts. Raimundão had suggested as much, and one afternoon in Rio Branco in her stylish office above a supermarket called Barriga Verde (Green Belly), Angela Mendes, Chico Mendes's 51-year-old daughter, told me why she, too, thought things were going wrong.

'Cattle exercise a charm,' said Angela, who now runs an environmental NGO named after her father. It was hard to persuade younger members of the tapper families to support the union and the reserve because it seemed to clash with their aspirations. 'The problem is that people have set their sights higher. They have seen that the ranchers have trucks, and that's what they want. [This newer generation] has no consciousness at all. Even some people from the era of the blockades [*empates*] now have cows. There are only a few who believe in the reserve model. Cattle are so profitable, and you can make money so quickly. It is not so much work, and then, when the animal gets to a certain age, you can sell it.'[21]

The cattle economy in Acre was booming in the 1970s and 1980s, of course, but that had been driven by government subsidies, incentives, and road building, which had all encouraged ranching. However, subsequently, a range of economic and cultural factors emerged, particularly among poorer small farmers. Between 1998 and 2008 the number of cattle in Acre quadrupled, the biggest rise of any Brazilian state. Much of this expansion was driven by smallholders who had no prior experience in raising the animals. According to Jeffrey Hoelle, an American anthropologist who studied the rise of Acre's cattle economy, many of the new cattle farmers were rubber tappers.[22] This advance was all part of a broader trend in the Amazon region. Between 1990 and 2003 beef output in the Amazonian states increased at a rate ten times faster than the rest of the country, driving deforestation higher. Before 1975, less than 1 per cent of the Amazon region had been deforested. Fifty years on, more than 20 per cent of the Amazon has been lost, and as much as 70 per cent of the deforested land is being used as cattle pasture.

Cattle were desired by these groups for various reasons. For a start, cows supply milk, a reliable source of protein. Cattle could be used, albeit in a limited way, for transportation. Many smallholders deployed their animals to help transport nuts and rubber short distances from their homes to roads, from where the produce could be moved by truck. Moreover, as an asset, a cow or bull was a versatile entity. Unlike a rubber or nut tree, it didn't just produce at one time of the year. Owning a cow or two was a helpful way to hold savings, as they could be easily sold in times of need.

Jeffrey Hoelle also found lots of evidence for the growing cultural popularity of the rancher economy. Cattle – either in the simplest form of owning a cow or working on a ranch – were a passport to social mobility. From eating steaks to listening to what Brazilians call *sertanejo*, a particularly brash form of country music, and from wearing cowboy boots, wide-brimmed cowboy hats and plaid shirts to attending rodeos, it was all attractive to most young Acreans. Some 40 per cent of the beef produced in the state was consumed by its residents. The people of Acre ate more beef per head than those of any other state. And just like in the rest of the vast soya and beef belt of the centre-west, in Acre, rodeos rival the national obsession with football. Hoelle interviewed a broad range of agriculturalists and found that nearly as many tappers enjoyed rodeos as did ranchers (50 per cent to 65 per cent of his small sample).

Sertanejo, whose stars typically wear Stetsons and tight jeans secured by wide leather belts and large, showy buckles, is almost universally popular in the state. Hoelle's interviewees viewed cattle culture positively, but associated forest activities, such as rubber tapping or nut gathering, with poverty. Young people from the plantations often wanted to work on the ranches, where, in addition to being protected by the labour code, they could eat meat every day. 'I came to perceive a mutually reinforcing system of positive signs and practices that made cattle raising socially, economically, and culturally more appealing than forest-based or agricultural livelihoods,' he wrote.[23]

For environmentalists, the rise of the cattle economy in Acre was alarming because the local government had made significant efforts to create an alternative. Marina Silva's Senate victory in 1994 (see Chapter 11) was part of a broader pattern of political success for the PT in the state. A small group of activists, linked to a traditional landowning family – the Vianas – and the rubber tappers' union, dominated the state's politics for more than 20 years. Jorge Viana won the mayoralty of Rio Branco, the state capital, in 1993 and was elected governor of the state in 1998 and again in 2002. Marina Silva's friend Binho Marquez, and Jorge's brother, Tião, were subsequently elected governors.

After the establishment of the Chico Mendes Reserve and another reserve at Alto Juruá in early 1990, Acre had become a showcase for environmental protection, setting up five extractive reserves that cover about a fifth of its entire area. In the reserves that the state owns and protects, traditional populations – generally either indigenous groups or rubber tappers – are guaranteed the right to use the land for sustainable activities. Acre pioneered a trend.

In total, Brazil has established 71 extractive reserves, primarily in the Amazon, which cover approximately 2 per cent of the forest. As a result, at least until the recent incursions into the Chico Mendes Reserve. These territories have been seen as something of a buffer zone, helping to limit the inroads of agricultural and mining activities.[24]

THE DECLINE AND FALL OF FLORESTANIA

The Vianas built upon this legacy of socio-ambientalism (see Chapter 10) by promoting sustainable forest-based businesses, such as rubber and nut production. They sought to protect the interests of the tappers and more than a dozen other indigenous groups living in Acre. The state introduced subsidies for rubber and marketed products such as resins and a vitamin-rich Amazonian fruit called *açaí*. As part of this approach, which they labelled Florestania, Acre's government commissioned research looking into other possible products that might be developed from plants found in the forest.

There was some initial success. In 1999 the subsidies attracted 3,000 families back to the rubber plantations that they had abandoned. The government launched public-works programmes and brought order to public finances. But as a sign of its even-handedness and with one eye on jobs and its popularity, the PT also encouraged the cattle ranchers. A vaccination programme enabled farmers to immunize their herds against foot-and-mouth disease. Silos were built to help grain farmers store their crops. Electricity connections were extended to isolated farms. Money was invested in an annual summer fair for farmers that featured big-name country singers contracted from outside the state. 'Jorge Viana's whole approach to politics was very new, and he began to overcome the negative perceptions that the PT faced here in Acre,' Nelson Euclides, a politics professor at the local university, told me.[25]

In 2002, Jorge Viana was re-elected with an increased majority. Slowly, though, the state government began to lose its way. Critics argue that promoting ranching was easy, but protecting and managing timber, plants, fruits, rubber and other resources was much more challenging. Rubber subsidies were eroded by inflation. An annual show for forest producers received little backing. Nothing was done to promote the cultural values of these areas. 'We needed to try and minimize the appeal of the city for young people from rural areas,' said Toinho Alves, the state's former culture secretary and long-time adviser to Marina Silva, Minister of the Environment. 'A few years ago, there were different role models.'[26]

By 2010, as agribusiness continued its relentless advance, the forest-based vision was withering. In his book, Jeffrey Hoelle noted the decline. 'When I first arrived in Rio Branco, Acre, in 2007, the billboards showing Chico Mendes were still fresh and new . . . I returned every year for the next three years, and each time I noticed that the signs were a little more faded and tattered, with older advertisements peeking through Mendes's moustachioed face and the forest behind him. By 2010, many had been painted over by ads for fashion stores, cell-phone carriers, and English schools.'[27]

The PT's vote declined steadily after 2002, and the party finally lost control of the state in 2018, when Gladson Cameli, a supporter of Jair Bolsonaro and a strong advocate of agribusiness, won the election. By then though Florestania was on the ropes. One story that highlighted the difficulties was a seemingly promising state government plan to make condoms from high-quality rubber harvested in the Acrean reserves. The rubber harvested on Acre's high ground is famously of a much higher quality than that produced closer to the Amazon River. 'Denser, stronger and more flexible, it is equally good for medical gloves and aircraft tyres, as well as prophylactics,' Toinho Alves had told me.[28] When it was built in 2007, the factory could count on financial backing from both the state and federal governments, and investment was made available. Once it started activity, the health ministry's HIV AIDS prevention programme meant that there was a ready market for one million condoms a year. The factory struggled, though, and now stands empty, something of a monument to a failed policy. By 2016, when the health ministry, for financial reasons, reduced its orders, the business was already struggling to compete with Asian imports. Costs were high partly because doing business in Acre is expensive. Power is unreliable, and transport connections are weak. State managers did nothing to diversify. An attempt to sell the company to the private sector failed, and the factory, a few miles outside Xapuri, has been mothballed since 2018. When I visited Acre in towards the end of 2023, I met environmentalists who were hopeful that investments in carbon bonds could revive Florestania. The basic idea was a simple one. Companies and funds dedicated to environmental sustainability would channel money to communities and pay them to keep their bit of the forest intact. The saved trees would generate carbon credits that could be used to offset emissions elsewhere and would therefore enhance a company's green credentials and make it easier to attract capital from the funds that specialise in ESG (environment, social and governance) schemes. But the practical obstacles surrounding the implementation of such schemes seemed to be considerable.

In Rio Branco, I met a young team from a small Belo Horizonte-based company, Waycarbon, specializing in carbon bonds. Two of the staff had just spent the best part of two days travelling by rough track and boat to reach the remote riverine communities that could be the site of new carbon protection projects. Waycarbon had identified interest among investors. But to gain the certification from Verra, one of the leading certification agencies, the group would need to demonstrate the 'previous and informed' consent of the communities involved. This would be a time-consuming and very difficult task, Lucas Ribeiro, one of Waycarbon's founders, warned me. Many of the residents in the communities were illiterate, and Waycarbon knew it would take significantly longer than anticipated to involve them in the project. 'The investors get fed up with these delays, but we have to tell them the projects won't work unless we get all these aspects right,' Ribeiro told me.

Isabela Gomes, a colleague of Ribeiro's, said to me that not all companies in the market are as meticulous as Waycarbon. 'Lots of other companies aren't this transparent, and they run amok, cheat and harass the communities. They'll give the communities food baskets, health kits, and ecological ovens, but that is not going to solve the problem,' she said.[29]

The PT's former governor, Jorge Viana, attempted a political comeback in 2022, but the architect of Florestania now presented himself as the candidate best equipped to advance the interests of farmers. Even then he was defeated comprehensively, with Gladson Cameli returning for a second term. It was easy to see why Toinho Alves was so gloomy about the future of the forest. The battle for Acre's environment was essentially lost, he said. 'In 2011, there was still much of the state that wanted to give priority to the forest,' he said. Now, 'the domination of the ranchers was unstoppable. [Acre] was the birthplace of socio-environmentalism. It is also going to be its grave.'[30]

Given the challenges, the fight to preserve the forest and limit climate change would depend to a great extent on the kind of international support that Lula was able to garner in his third term in office. The auguries – as we will see in the next chapter – were good. However, here too, things began to go awry.

18

The Seductions of Celebrity

Even before his inauguration in January 2023, Lula had announced his – and Brazil's – return to the international stage. At the Egyptian resort of Sharm el-Sheikh, host to the 2022 Climate Change Conference, the president-elect was the star of the show. While Bolsonaro's outgoing Environment Minister spent his time diving in the Red Sea, Lula, accompanied by his new wife, Janja, confidently strode the corridors of the conference following his recent election triumph. They were surrounded by a bevy of state governors, officials, politicians, and activists, including several indigenous women with their faces painted and traditional headdresses on show. The walls shook with the noise of joyful chanting, as Lula was given a rock star's reception. 'Brazil is back, and I am here to say that Brazil is ready to join once again the efforts to build a healthier planet,' he roared to cheering crowds. 'We must stop this rush to the abyss. There is no climate security for the world without a protected Amazon. We will do whatever it takes to have zero deforestation. Let's prove once again that it is possible to generate wealth without provoking climate change.'[1]

Everyone seemed to be in a hurry to see him. Joe Biden, the then US president, had been quick to welcome Lula's victory. Now his climate envoy, John Kerry, said he was pleased the president-elect 'talked about, for once and for all, getting it right, pulling people together to preserve the Amazon'.[2]

Germany's Ministry of Development, which had heavily backed a multi-million-dollar Amazon fund that Bolsonaro had frozen, would set up calls immediately after the conference to discuss ways of financing Brazil's transition to a more sustainable economic model. Lula, wearing a stylish casual blue sweatshirt and a smartly cut suit, shook hands meaningfully with China's climate negotiator. After the travails and tribulations of the last few years, he was back in the big time. Back in the old routine. 'Lula has descended gloriously on Sharm el-Sheikh,' commented one Brazilian columnist. 'He is living some of the best days of his life.'[3]

The outlook was excellent. Just as Lula had headed a broad alliance within Brazil to topple Bolsonaro, by embracing former political rivals such as Geraldo Alckmin, he also seemed well-positioned to develop a wide set of partnerships abroad. As one local commentator put it: 'Few leaders could claim on taking office to have induced sighs of relief from both Chinese President Xi Jinping and U.S. President Joe Biden.' Lula had won 'an enormous agenda-setting capacity' on the international stage. Along with India's Narendra Modi, he had become 'the most visible leader of the Global South'.[4]

For a time, too, in the early days of government, the momentum of environmental policy was impressive. Funding for the relevant agencies – IBAMA, which monitors and polices deforestation, and ICM-Bio, which administers parks and reserves – was quickly restored. Spending cuts under Bolsonaro had weakened both organizations. The Ministry of the Environment also relaunched a R$200 million programme known as Bolsa Verde (Green Grant), which provided financial support to low-income families in exchange for their participation in conservation initiatives. Marina Silva, back in government for the first time since 2008, began to liaise with fellow ministers on environmental plans.

The Amazon Fund, supported by Germany and Norway, was unblocked, freeing up R$3 billion for environmental projects. The new administration quickly revoked a move by the Bolsonaro government to allow small-scale mining plots, known as *garimpos*, in indigenous reserves. Then, at the end of January, in a high-profile initiative designed to publicize official commitment, IBAMA's agents and federal policemen were dispatched to the Yanomami reserve in northern Roraima state to break up illegal gold-mining camps. The mining – something of a tradition among the settler community of this tiny northern state – had been tacitly encouraged by the previous government and had led to outbreaks of malaria and mercury poisoning among the 28,000 or so indigenous population. Five hundred children had died in the last year, and the government declared a health emergency.

And then it all started to go wrong. In his first few months in office, Lula, despite advice from his successful and experienced former Foreign Minister, Celso Amorim, seemed to be making a series of mistakes. His comments on the Ukraine war and other foreign-policy issues began to alarm the same Americans and Europeans who had welcomed his return to the presidency and had been eager to speak with him in Sharm el-Sheikh. Lula said Ukraine and those countries that supplied it with arms were as responsible for the war as Russia. In mid-2023, he led a group of countries that initially vetoed the invitation of Volodymyr Zelensky to a summit of European and Latin American leaders. After extending an invitation to the Russian Foreign Minister, Sergey Lavrov, to Brasília, Lula insisted that the meeting's communiqué contain no condemnation of Russian aggression. He had initially criticized Zelensky back in May 2022 in an interview with *Time Magazine*: 'Sometimes I sit and watch the President of Ukraine speaking, being applauded, getting a standing ovation from European parliamentarians. This guy is as responsible as Putin for the war. Because in the war, there's not just one person guilty.'[5]

Biden had welcomed Lula to Washington in February, but after Lula criticized US support for Ukraine, the atmosphere at the meeting soured. He disparaged American sanctions against Venezuela but said nothing about the repression that had brought them about. He welcomed Nicolás Maduro, the country's autocratic leader, to Brazil. He lambasted Israel's bombardment of Gaza, drawing comparisons with the Holocaust.[6] Israel immediately declared

Lula a 'persona non grata' and summoned Brazil's ambassador to the Holocaust Museum in Jerusalem for a reprimand. Hamas, the Palestinian Islamist group which runs Gaza, praised his comments as 'accurate'.[7]

When visiting China, Lula suggested that developing countries should shun the dollar and embrace the yuan or other currencies for their trade. As Brian Winter, editor of the New York-based *Americas Quarterly*, put it in July 2023, more and more people in Washington were beginning to ask whether Lula was 'anti-American? It's the question that won't go away.'[8]

But Lula's stance was not just upsetting Americans. The left-leaning French newspaper *Libération* called him a 'false friend of the West'. In a front-page editorial published ahead of Lula's visit to Paris in June 2023, the paper said, 'we expected a messiah, but his image has been slightly tarnished'.[9]

Chile's Andrés Velasco, who had served as Finance Minister in the centre-left government of Michelle Bachelet, wrote in a piece entitled 'Lula's Dance with Dictators': 'When a former human-rights advocate and working-class hero backs dictators guilty of abominable butchery, shock is followed by abhorrence. That is how I feel watching [Lula] embrace Putin and Nicolás Maduro. Lula's is a moral failure of appalling proportions. Telling the Ukrainians they have to negotiate now is like telling a man who is being attacked by a knife-wielding maniac that he should engage in frank and fruitful dialogue with his assailant.' Lula's defence of Maduro was equally specious. Ignoring well-documented cases of assassination and torture in Venezuela, he had described reports of rights violations and anti-democratic practices as a 'narrative construction'.[10]

Ricardo Kotscho, a Brazilian journalist who in 2003 and 2004 was Lula's press officer, said Lula 'was giving ammunition to his enemies, something that did not happen in his first two mandates. Speaking badly about the US, dividing responsibility for the war in Ukraine and proposing a new international currency without any concrete proposal. It is as if they are coming up with these ideas to hurt themselves.' Instead, there was an opportunity to focus on sustainability and the green economy. 'So many countries want to help Brazil with the Amazon Fund. We shouldn't waste time on other subjects.'[11]

Interviewed in February 2024, another Latin American critic, Matias Spektor, a professor of international relations at the Getúlio Vargas Foundation in São Paulo, said Lula's defence of Putin and is comparison of Israel's attacks in Gaza to the Holocaust had soiled his reputation 'as a democratic leader who can build bridges between the West and the rest of the world. Lula seems increasingly to vindicate dictators. What the devil is Lula doing?'[12]

THE PULL OF THE GLOBAL SOUTH

When Lula first took office in 2003, his foreign policy was built on Brazil's traditional non-aligned stance. Brazil had sought to contain the interests of dominant foreign powers – Britain in the nineteenth century, Germany in the 1930s, and the United States since the Second World War. The country's diplomatic service was experienced and had developed considerable skills in advancing a form of soft power in the region, aiming to insulate Brazil from any instability in neighbours such as Bolivia, Paraguay, and Venezuela. Right-wing military governments had collaborated with the United States on security issues, but they had maintained a certain distance from Washington in other respects. In 1975, for example, as their long independence wars were just starting Brazil was the first country to recognize Angola and Mozambique ahead even of Cuba and the Soviet Union.

Democratic governments elected after 1985 pursued an independent stance on world trade. The Doha Round was a significant milestone in this respect. Brazil and India, for example, worked together to encourage developed countries to reduce trade-distorting domestic support for agriculture. Brazilian diplomacy helped secure exceptions to the rules on trade-related intellectual property (the so-called TRIPS agreement) that gave developing countries easier access to essential medicines, for example.

However, under Lula, the policy took on a new dimension. There was a significant emphasis on regional integration, with several recently elected left-wing governments looking to increase cooperation. Hugo Chávez, a rebel army officer and radical nationalist, had won a landslide victory in Venezuela in 1998. Ricardo Lagos, the Chilean socialist, was elected in 2000, and after Lula's win in 2002, Néstor Kirchner, a left-wing Peronist, took over in Argentina in 2003. In the next two years, what came to be known as a pink tide spread through the region, as Uruguay, Bolivia, and Ecuador all followed suit. With the US efforts to forge a continent-wide free-trade pact, effectively extending the North American Free Trade Agreement, throughout South America, these left-wingers looked to revive regional integration. In 2004 ambitious talks got underway to form a South American economic union – along European lines. This initiative – known as the Union of South American Nations – was designed to exclude the United States, the dominant player in hemispheric blocs and institutions such as the Organization of American States or the Inter-American Development Bank.

Brazil sought to position itself as a leader of the developing world, giving much greater emphasis and importance to its links with African and Asian countries than had been afforded hitherto. It was a stance that appealed to Lula's experience as a trade union leader: just as a union brought together workers and gave them more muscle to win higher wages or better conditions, so poorer countries needed to band together and win concessions from the rich ones that controlled the multilateral banks and institutions of global governance. This approach gained greater momentum towards the end of Lula's second term in office, when Brazil joined forces with three other large developing countries – Russia, India, and China – to set up an institutional framework for what became known as the BRICS.

The group had had a slightly quirky origin. In 2001, Jim O'Neill, an investment banker and then chief economist at Goldman Sachs, had come up with the term in a research paper, 'Building Better Global Economic BRICs'. Reflecting on their rapid recent growth and China's entry that year into the World Trade Organization,

O'Neill concluded that the four countries were on course to rival the large, developed countries such as the United States, Japan, and members of the European Union, and that in consequence, the dynamics of the global economy were changing. Those seeking to coordinate monetary or regulatory policies would need to take these changes into account, and governance structures based on the hitherto overwhelming dominance of the United States and Europe should be amended to reflect them. In 1999 the four BRICs had all become part of an expanded grouping of major countries, known as the G20, whose leaders met regularly. However, in his paper, O'Neill suggested that 'world policymaking forums should be re-organised and in particular, the G7 should be adjusted to incorporate BRIC representatives'.[13]

For Goldman Sachs the idea had a commercial dimension, of course, since it helped BRICs promote the stocks and bonds of these four emerging markets to clients. However, the BRICS countries themselves soon began to utilize the framework for their own political purposes. Senior figures from the Russian government began meeting with their counterparts from China and India in 2003. Three years later, at a meeting of the United Nations, Sergey Lavrov, the Russian Foreign Minister, raised the idea of Brazil joining this group.

Chinese trade and investment with the BRICS and many other emerging markets skyrocketed during the 2000s, helping to insulate them to some extent from the financial crisis of 2008–9. As we saw in Chapter 9, China's entry into the World Trade Organization in 2001 paved the way for a sharp rise in Chinese manufacturing exports and a massive state-directed investment boom. Millions of Chinese families had already moved to cities since Deng Xiaoping began opening the economy in the late 1970s, but between 2000 and 2023 an average of nearly 20 million people every year started living in towns and cities for the first time.[14]

All this set the stage for a significant surge in Brazil's China trade, helping the Lula government pay down debt and build up reserves. In 2008 and 2009, with American and European banks brought to their knees by the lending excesses of the 2000s, the developing world, its economies underpinned by the scale of Chinese expansion and the resulting commodity boom, shrugged off any difficulties.

Underneath the surface, the tectonic plates of the global economy were shifting rapidly. When O'Neill coined the term BRICs in 2001, the gross domestic product of the four BRIC countries amounted to less than 10 per cent of the world total. Ten years later, when the BRICs invited South Africa to become a member (thus becoming BRICS), the group produced 18 per cent of global output. When the actual buying power of local populations was taken into account and the numbers calculated in so-called purchasing power parity (PPP) dollars, the BRICS economies were equal to more than a quarter of the world's total. The hour of the BRICS was at hand.

The trend was unstoppable, with China's economy rising at a faster rate than O'Neill had expected. Despite slowdowns during the COVID pandemic, huge capital investments and a steady expansion of export sectors allowed China to grow far faster than the global average. In PPP terms, barely half the size of the United States in 2001, China's economy had grown to be a fifth larger by 2023 though its nominal GDP remained substantially smaller. When Lula returned to office that year the BRICS were generating nearly a quarter of global GDP and, in PPP terms, more than a third of the world's economic output. On the latter measure, the five BRICS were now larger than the G7 (France, Germany, Britain, Italy, Japan, Canada, the United States).

The entire apparatus of economic, financial, and security institutions founded at the end of the Second World War was now outdated. As Celso Amorim, Brazil's Foreign Minister, told a meeting at the Carnegie Endowment in July 2024, 'it was as if the world at the beginning of the twentieth century was being run by arrangements founded at the Congress of Vienna'.[15]

There was, however, a huge problem. The BRICS group was becoming increasingly critical of the political model – representative democracy, transparency, the rule of law – favoured by the West. China's rapid growth and its emergence as a superpower have been accompanied by increasing political confidence. Rather than simply defending its one-party state and authoritarian governance model, China has begun to promote its model actively. Since 2012, when Xi Jinping became the Communist Party's general secretary, the regime has promoted its system internationally as 'worthy of emulation'. At the nineteenth congress of the Chinese Communist Party in November 2017, Xi suggested that other countries could learn from the Chinese model, particularly those disenchanted with liberal democracy.[16]

This aggressive stance has been accompanied by growing repression and censorship at home, highlighted by the suppression of Muslim Uyghur minorities. In the early 2000s many American and European policymakers and critics had hoped that the country's trade, growth, and prosperity would gradually lead to the emergence of a more institutionalized, responsive, and law-bound system of governance. As one China watcher put it in 2021, 'many proponents of engagement also believed that, as China's economy grew and its expanding middle class demanded a greater voice in its own political and economic future, China's leaders would transform the country's domestic institutions to reflect greater protection for individual political and economic rights and assume more of the economic attributes of a market democracy'.[17]

Authoritarian trends had also begun to be apparent in other BRICS countries. With a population of nearly 1.5 billion, India could still claim to be the world's largest democracy. Still, governments led since 2014 by Prime Minister Narendra Modi have come under fire from international critics. For example, Modi has amended laws to favour Hindus over Muslims and arrested and intimidated government critics. Several international organizations have now marked India as only 'partly free' or as a 'flawed democracy'.[18]

The erosion of democracy was most marked in Russia, particularly since the invasion of Ukraine in February 2022. Media freedoms have been curtailed, and there has been increasingly brutal repression of liberal opposition groups, culminating in the death in prison of Alexei Navalny in 2024. '[Putin's] highly repressive, personalistic autocracy that threatens not just its immediate neighbours but increasingly its own citizens,' wrote one academic expert. The war in Ukraine had 'decisively ended the liberalization of politics within Russia itself, a process that began . . . before the collapse of the Soviet Union in 1991'.[19]

Against this background, Brazil continues to defend its democratic system, a stance strengthened during the 2022 campaign and the aftermath of the election. But Lula also continues to argue more than ever for a shift in power to the poorer countries. The balancing act is more challenging as Brazil becomes a relatively less important player within the BRICS. Back in 2001, it was the second largest economy in the group, with its economy (in PPP terms) more than half the size of China's. By 2023, when Lula returned, it was only one-ninth the size of China and the third largest player. That means it has correspondingly less influence, a weakness that has been highlighted by ongoing battles over the proposed expansion of BRICS.

Keen to maintain its sway within the group, Brazil opposed enlargement. Nonetheless, in 2023, under pressure from China and Russia, the group agreed to accept the membership of four other countries (see below) – none of which are democracies. While China and Russia became more autocratic, Brazil sought to persuade the BRICS to preserve independence and opposed pressure from them to adopt anti-Western language in their declarations. As Oliver Stuenkel, a foreign-policy specialist at the Getúlio Vargas Foundation, put it, 'Russia wants to portray BRICS as a counterweight to the G7. For Lula the BRICS is not "against anyone".' But in 2023, China and Russia ignored Brazil's request not to include Iran in the group, part of an expansion that also saw the adhesion of the United Arab Emirates, Egypt, and Ethiopia. 'The BRICS now increasingly looks like a pillar of Sino-centric order,' wrote Stuenkel.[20]

THE VENEZUELA TEST

Back in the 2000s, Lula was able to be everybody's friend. His Foreign Minister, Celso Amorim, courted Brazil's neighbours and the big developing countries that formalized their BRICS alliance in 2009. No one doubted Lula's commitment to democracy. However, as China has become more dominant within the Global South and more assertive about its authoritarian model, it has become increasingly complex to satisfy these two constituencies: the increasingly autocratic South has often seemed at odds with the democratic North, and Brazil has been caught in the middle. Amorim, rated in 2009 by one review associated with the US foreign-policy establishment as 'Foreign Minister of the year', is now judged by local commentators as being too indulgent towards the Chinese and Russians. His recent calls for greater pragmatism and audacity are now seen, by critics, as evidence of naivety and a lack of principle. Venezuela, Brazil's troublesome northern neighbour, has provided a testbed for the country's foreign policy, both in terms of its democratic commitment and its ability as a regional power to exert real influence.

If Brazil could affect events anywhere, it would be in Venezuela. With a population and economy nearly ten times larger, Brazil has potentially enormous leverage and much to gain from developing good relations with an adjacent oil power. There are economic ties and a mutual interest in clamping down on the illegal mining, logging, and drug running that take place along the shared 1,400-mile border. Since 2014 more than a million Venezuelans have fled to Brazil, most of them trudging for days to reach the dusty frontier town of Paracaima, where, for a while at least, they live in camps run by the Brazilian army. And Lula and the PT have been close to the Venezuelan United Socialist Party, formed by Hugo Chávez and, since his death from cancer in 2013, run by Nicolás Maduro.

Back in the early 2000s, the relationship had been good. Chávez, the leader of what he described as twenty-first-century socialism, was genuinely popular (although the elections and referendums he won were not entirely fair). Oil wealth helped finance an extension in social-welfare programmes and a sharp reduction in poverty and inequality. One of the centre pieces of this effort was *Barrio Adentro* (inside the barrio), a programme in which several thousand Cuban doctors and other healthcare professionals were stationed in impoverished areas of Venezuelan cities. Chávez paid for all this by supplying Cuba with oil. In 2005 I recall spending a day in Santa Eduvigis, one of the numerous sprawling poor neighbourhoods on the western edge of Caracas, accompanying doctors on their daily rounds and watching as dozens of children queued up to see dentists and have their fillings done in an improvised clinic.

But even before Lula left office in 2010, Chávez clashed with the Brazilian leader. Whereas Lula did his best to strike up a good relationship with US President George W. Bush, Chávez attacked Bush as the 'devil' who was trying 'to preserve the current pattern of domination, exploitation and pillage of the peoples of the world'. Chávez irritated Lula by egging on the nationalization of Brazilian assets in Bolivia and Ecuador.

Moreover, the strains inherent in Chávez's economic populism were already becoming apparent.

Much of the money for Chávez's social programmes had come from the investment budget of Petroleum of Venezuela (*Petróleos de Venezuela, S.A.* or PDVSA), Venezuela's state-owned oil company. The productivity of the fields soon began to decline. Venezuelan oil contains impurities such as sulphur, is relatively expensive to process, and needs constant injections of capital to sustain output. Investment faltered during the 2000s. These factors are highlighted in a recent perceptive analysis of Venezuela's downward economic spiral under Chávez and Maduro.[21]

When PDVSA management and technicians protested and took strike action, Chávez sacked them. From 2006 he expanded his offensive against the entire private sector by nationalizing dozens of companies and closing independent newspapers and TV stations.

After Maduro took office in 2013, oil prices continued to fall, dollars became scarce, and the value of the currency, the *bolívar*, collapsed. By 2016, hyperinflation had reached a scale far worse than that which had plagued Latin America thirty years prior. (Most economists rate the inflation as the worst seen in modern times in a country not actually at war.) Price controls simply made the situation worse, further depressing production. By the second half of 2014, life was impossible for many Venezuelans, and thousands began to leave. Over the last ten years, 7.7 million people have fled the country, reducing the population by more than a fifth to 25 million. 'In the last two years, Venezuela has experienced the kind of implosion that hardly ever occurs in a middle-income country like it outside of war,' wrote Moises Naim and Quico Toro in May 2016.[22]

Maduro, who lacked Chávez's charisma, struggled, and under his leadership Venezuela became increasingly authoritarian, with some observers describing it as a dictatorship. The judiciary had effectively lost its independence under Chávez. When the opposition won the congressional election of 2015, the government started to trim its powers and then cracked down on extensive ensuing protests, arresting and detaining activists. American economic sanctions, imposed by the first administration of Donald Trump, deepened the economic crisis, with the government becoming increasingly reliant on support from China and Russia. Ironically, it was the de facto adoption of the US dollar from late 2018 that eventually stabilized the economy. In 2019 the establishment by the now neutered legislative assembly of a parallel government, led by a young deputy named Juan Guaidó, won widespread international recognition but failed to make a significant impact in Venezuela itself. After an unsuccessful coup attempt, it was eventually abandoned. All this paved the way for elaborate mediated negotiations over opposition participation when Maduro contested his third consecutive six-year term. Tempted by the offer of an end to international economic sanctions, the regime agreed, and on 28 July 2024 an election took place.

Maduro's claim of victory (by 51 to 44 per cent) divided international opinion, with China, Russia, Iran and local allies such as Cuba and Nicaragua predictably recognizing the result, and the United States, the European Union, and much of Latin America withholding approval on the grounds of fraud. The claims of malpractice seemed well-founded. Opposition activists managed to collect 80 per cent of the tally sheets (or *actas*) printed directly from the electronic voting machines when the ballots closed. And on that basis they claimed the opposition candidate Edmundo

Gonzalez won the contest by a margin of two to one. These sheets, which contained all their original security features, were published online. An audit by the AP news agency showed that Gonzalez had won more votes than were granted to him in the official result. The Venezuelan government has still to publish tabulated results (at least as of November 2025), a failure for which, in the words of the United Nations, 'there is no precedent in contemporary democratic elections'. Steve Levitsky, an expert on democracy at Harvard University, called the 28 July vote 'one of the most egregious electoral frauds in modern Latin American history'.[23]

Lula and Amorim, acting in consort with Colombia's left-wing president, Gustavo Petro, continued to press Maduro, refusing to recognize the result until voting tallies were published. In October, at a summit of the BRICS in the Russian city of Kazan, Brazil even blocked a bid by Venezuela to join the group. In response, Maduro's crew lashed out, labelling Lula 'a CIA agent' and Amorim 'a messenger of American imperialism'. Initially there appeared to be few practical consequences, with diplomatic relations between the two countries largely unaffected. Mauro Vieira, the Foreign Minister, made it clear that Brazil did not intend to sever connections. The spat even served Lula's public-relations purposes, as polling had consistently shown that the pro-Venezuelan position to be deeply unpopular among the Brazilian public. Between seven and eight out of ten Brazilians surveyed in late August 2025 said Brazil should not recognize the Venezuelan result. Earlier polls had shown that Lula's foreign-policy stances were unpopular. Large majorities believed the president spent too much time on external affairs.[24]

In any event, there was considerable ambiguity about the Brazilian position, not least because of the sympathies of the Workers' Party leadership towards the Venezuelan government. Within hours of Maduro's post-election proclamation, the PT national executive had 'recognized the result' with an anodyne statement, 'saluting the Venezuelan people for a peaceful, democratic and sovereign day'.[25]

A couple of days later, as the regime was rounding up and detaining hundreds of opposition supporters, Lula described the electoral process as 'standard [and] orderly. People who disagree should have the right to express their views and challenge the results, while the government has the right to defend its position.'

By mid-August, Lula appeared more critical, telling a local Brazilian radio station that 'I think Venezuela is living under a very unpleasant regime. It is a government with an authoritarian slant, but it isn't a dictatorship like so many we know in this world,' he said.[26] Towards the end of the year, following the BRICS spat and as it became evident that Brazilian and Colombian diplomatic pressure was not yielding any tangible results, Lula sometimes seemed irritated by the issue. Nicolás Maduro was 'not a problem for Brazilians. I have learned that we must be careful when the talk is about other countries and other presidents. Maduro is a problem for Venezuela, not for Brazil,' said Lula, seeming to admonish a TV interviewer for having the temerity to ask the question. 'I'll look after Brazil; Maduro can look after Venezuela. I can't be worrying about all this. One moment fighting with Nicaragua, the next with Venezuela, then with I don't know who.'[27] Perhaps this inward turn seemed sensible. After all, Lula had a good deal to preoccupy him closer to home. However, it was hardly a stance that enhanced Brazil's international reputation, or that endeared Lula to a world looking for peacemakers and bridge-builders in Ukraine or the Middle East.

Conclusion

A FADING STAR?

At times during the first half of 2025, Lula – now in the second half of his third period of office – seemed like a fading star. Approaching his 80th birthday, the leader had apparently lost his famed political touch. The broad congressional alliance formed in 2023 to back his government was disintegrating. Beset by mistakes and scandals, the popularity of Lula's administration declined and the government's centrist and right-wing allies, never that reliable at the best of times, started to jump ship and dusted off their plans to back an opposition candidate in the upcoming 2026 presidential election.

As I researched this book during 2023 and 2024, it had been clear that trouble was brewing for Lula and his party. The PT's poor performance in the October 2024 municipal elections had been a particularly important setback. Virtually every PT member I talked to in advance of that contest had told me how important it was that the party do well. Local mayors, I was told, could make all the difference in the presidential and congressional campaigns due to take place in October 2026. They would help give the party a stronger position in Congress, and make Lula's fourth term in office more effective than his third. At a local level the PT had been on the slide since 2012 and had done very badly in the last contest in 2020 conducted at the height of a very short-lived COVID

19-related spending boom. But with Lula back at the helm, the Petistas were confident they could recapture some of the glories of the 2000s when they had looked on course to become a natural party of local authority in poorer parts of the country.[1]

But the 2024 local election result was desperately disappointing. With 248 town halls – out of a total of 5,569 – the PT was only the ninth biggest party. In São Bernardo do Campo, the industrial city on the southern periphery of São Paulo, where Lula's political career began in the 1970s, the party's candidate finished third. Back in the 2000s, the party had controlled nine of Brazil's state capitals. In October 2024 it won just one. Its defeat in São Paulo, Brazil's most populous city, had been salutary. At Lula's insistence, the PT had thrown its weight behind Guillermo Boulos, the charismatic leader of the homeless movement and the far-left Socialism and Liberty Party (PSOL). Millions had been ploughed into the campaign. One PT activist had called the contest the PT's 'Stalingrad',[2] referring to the Second World War battle of 1942–3 in which the Soviet army had finally turned the tide against the German invasion force. It made no difference. Lula's man stumbled to defeat, losing by a margin of 20 percentage points, a performance no better than that which Boulos, with a makeshift and poorly resourced fight, had achieved four years before. The election underlined how far the PT was from its traditional supporters in the eastern and southern suburbs of the city, where in the first round Pablo Marçal, a conservative free-marketeer, social media influencer, and fan of Jair Bolsonaro, had won nearly a third of the vote.[3]

In the poor north-east of the country, which since the mid-2000s had become Lula's most reliable source of support and where his party controlled four state governorships, the picture was scarcely much brighter. True, the PT scraped a victory in Fortaleza, the capital of Ceará state. But most of the party's gains were in tiny rural towns. Many of its successful candidates had originally won office with one of the conservative parties. They had been persuaded to switch to the PT only after Lula's presidential victory, undoubtedly swayed by the promise of funding.

CONCLUSION

There too in the heartland of Lulismo there had been serious setbacks. I'd watched the campaign unfold in Lauro de Freitas, a municipality on the northern edge of Salvador, which typified the new urban twenty-first-century Brazil. A mid-size city of 200,000 people, Lauro had expanded on the back of higher levels of consumer spending and the strength of its service sector and job market. According to the most recent census, it was one of the country's fastest-growing towns, and for most of the last 25 years it had been a minor PT stronghold.

But in her four terms as mayor, Moema Gramacho, a former chemical engineer and trade unionist, had struggled to manage the pace of expansion and in October 2024 her successor was swept aside by a right-wing candidate. 'People are fed up with Moema,' Tais Fernanda Reis, a 36-year-old secondary-school teacher and writer, had told me a few days before the vote as she showed us around the city in her white Hyundai HB20. 'There are so many problems. There are potholes on the roads, the traffic is terrible, and many of their promises have not been fulfilled. They said they would install air conditioning in schools, and nothing happened for ages. It is only since the campaign began that they have started,' she said. As is the way with parish-pump politics, a seemingly innocuous dispute about improvements to a public square in the Itinga neighbourhood had angered many locals. The upgrades had been significantly more expensive than initially budgeted. 'People didn't know what had changed when the work was done,' said Tais, who had been a firm supporter of the PT but said she would now vote for the opposition.

In 2025 things for Lula seemed to go from bad to worse. Rapid rises in food prices went down badly among the less well-off. Coffee became so expensive that many consumers turned to a cheaper ersatz mix, nicknamed Cafake. On campaign in 2022, Lula had promised that his supporters would soon be able to afford to eat *picanha*, a favourite cut of beef steak. But in 2024 and 2025 price rises were making the meat even more unaffordable than it had been under Bolsonaro. And then in April, the government stumbled amid a series of public-relations disasters and scandals. Lula's brother Frei Chico, the trade unionist we met in Chapter 4, was one of those caught up in a corruption scandal at a social-security institute. The trade union of which he was a director was one of those accused of skimming thousands of small amounts from the pay cheques of pensioners.[4] Several million *reales* had been lost in the scandal, which had started during Bolsonaro's time in office, but whose scale had increased under Lula.

And then, out of the blue in early July 2025, came salvation for Lula from an unlikely source. President Donald Trump imposed a 50 per cent tariff on Brazilian exports to the United States, threatening to cripple businesses – ranging from producers of orange juice, fruit, and coffee to manufacturers of shoes and aircraft – dependent on the American market. The sanctions, said the US president, would only be lifted if Brazil suspended its legal case against former president Jair Bolsonaro, for his alleged role in a December 2022 plot to kill Lula, his deputy Geraldo Alckmin, and chief justice Alexandre Moraes, and install a military regime (see Chapter 16). The Brazilian court action, raged Trump, was an 'international disgrace', amounting to a 'witch hunt' that should 'end IMMEDIATELY' – the last word capitalized for added emphasis.

Since the late 2000s, the United States had been regularly exporting to Brazil more than it imported, accumulating tens of billions of dollars in trade surpluses. But now, the US leader said, Washington had decided that it needed to refashion a trade relationship that was 'unfair' and 'far from reciprocal'. The measure was an odd one. The United States had once been Brazil's biggest trade partner, but that was 17 years ago. Now, Brazil earned only 12 per cent of its export dollars from US sales, with China, its biggest trading partner, accounting for nearly three times as much. The loss of American sales would hit some sectors hard, but overall economists reckoned that Brazilian output would fall by only half a percentage point at most.

Trump followed this up with another misjudged attack that seemed even more likely to damage his friends than its target: Lula's government. The focus was Pix, an extremely popular electronic transfer system launched in November 2020 by the Brazilian Central

CONCLUSION 303

Bank. Trump alleged that Brazil had blocked efforts by American tech companies to set up similar services and threatened further sanctions. None of this went down well in Brazil. Business leaders hit by the trade measures disparaged Eduardo Bolsonaro in the US, the former president's third son, who had been lobbying for such intervention. Right-wing politicians were divided. This defence of the Pix system seemed to hold the prospect of boosting Lula's image among the vast class of Uber drivers, delivery riders, and other aspiring entrepreneurs from whom he had largely been estranged.

In the first poll conducted after Trump's announcement, in mid-July 2025, Lula's popularity rose, with the gap between his acceptance and rejection rates widening by nine percentage points compared to the previous research two months earlier. The boost to his popularity was especially sharp in the hitherto Bolsonarista strongholds of the south and south-east. It was an extraordinary shift. Rebranding himself as a nationalist, Lula began to wear a blue baseball cap with the words 'O Brasil É Dos Brasileiros' ('Brazil is for the Brazilians') emblazoned across its front. 'Thank You, Mr Trump!' shouted the front cover of the popular news magazine *Veja* a few days later, on 18 July.

Lula's boost in popularity may prove to be short-lived. But as of November 2025 his political brand had been strengthened, and it seemed he might well enter the 2026 election with a significant chance of securing a fourth term in office. Even so, it seemed equally likely that his political career might be coming to an end. If he does win next year's contest, Lula would be 81 when he starts his fourth mandate in 2027. Although he has pronounced himself healthy, associates say he is far less energetic than he was in his first two periods in government, less inclined to spend as much time travelling or involved in the kind of political negotiations for which he has become famous.

Many of his closest associates – trade union and party colleagues who used to see him regularly – enjoy less access than they once did. Diplomats and politicians in Brasília told me towards the end of 2023 that his younger wife, Janja da Silva, protects him, ensuring, for example, that he eats and rests properly. He has suffered health crises. A throat cancer with which he was diagnosed in 2011 was quickly cured but he has been left speaking more hoarsely than he used to. In October 2024, Lula fell in his bathroom and injured his head, requiring several stitches. Two months later he was hospitalized and doctors discovered an intracranial haemorrhage for which he underwent surgery.

So how to assess Lula's career?

Looking back over the past five decades of his front-line involvement in Brazilian politics, the tally of achievements is mixed. As his popularity ebbed during his third mandate Lula's deficiencies were regularly highlighted by Brazil's largely conservative media. For them Lula has presided over the inexorable growth of the state, with private companies labouring under the burden of red tape and a rising tax burden. What's more, insist the critics, Lula's governments have promoted corruption and allied themselves with the world's most closed and authoritarian regimes. As we saw in Chapter 16, for a relatively poor country the Brazilian state is enormous (as a percentage of GDP), larger, much larger in fact than those of its fellow BRICS or its neighbours in Latin America and stands comparison with the most well-equipped states of more prosperous Europe. Much of the money is badly spent and the overall quality of Brazil's education and healthcare provision, and its transport infrastructure, is way inferior to Germany, France, or Italy.

As explained in Chapters 12 and 13, corruption has been a feature of the country's political system for several decades. Lula and his party are in this sense part of a broader dysfunction whose character has been distorted by the judicial system. Backed by Lula's successor, Dilma Rousseff, the Lava Jato task force began to crack down on cronyism and bribery. In its early days the task force – headed by Judge Sérgio Moro – targeted a wide range of politicians and businessmen. But it became politicized and focused much of its energy on Lula and the PT, scapegoating them for a problem that had deeper and more extensive roots. Its nature was twofold. Lula failed to promote a more open and more accountable political system, and when his successor, Dilma Rousseff advanced her ethical clean-up she was so inept and clumsy that she destroyed her political base and fundamentally undermined her ability to govern. Lula's omission in this sense has since been compounded by his international alignments, when he has seemed to court authoritarian leaders ranging from Nicolás Maduro to Vladimir Putin and Ji Xinping and been insufficiently enthusiastic about cultivating his relationships with the democratic world, including most notably, at least until the re-election of Donald Trump, the United States.

Lula's diplomatic advisers would argue that Brazil fights within the BRICS group for the country's own democratic values. The growing trade relationship with Brazil and the BRICS means that any government, irrespective of its political complexion, will necessarily pursue close relations with countries such as China and Russia. The efforts of the Bolsonaro administration to foster closer ties with Asian democracies such as South Korea, Taiwan, and Japan at the expense of China were unsuccessful, for example. Bolsonaro even found himself visiting Russia, under pressure from his own agribusiness supporters to secure access to fertilizers, many of which came from Russia or Belarus. Trump's aggression towards Brazil simply underlines the good sense of the government's drive to develop a wide range of international trading partners.

Even so it is hard to avoid the impression that in both these areas Lula has accommodated his stance to that of his beloved Workers' Party, whose profound anti-Americanism and – at least as far as some of its most recalcitrant left-wing factions are concerned – anti-capitalism are still very evident during conversations with grassroots activists or even on the most casual acquaintance with TV 247, the PT-aligned podcast and media outlet. This identity is rooted in the anti-imperialist assumptions of the 1960s and 1970s and the emotional attachment of many older militants to the PT's political crusades of the 1980s.

Lula's legal travails between 2016 and 2018, and his depressing experience in the police cell in Curitiba tended to reaffirm his suspicions of the United States. It does seem that, in line with this leftward shift, Lula has been insufficiently critical sometimes of the steadily increasing authoritarianism of China and Russia. Quizzed by interviewers about the growth of anti-democratic movements, he tends to focus on examples associated with the populist right, rather than the cases of Russia, China, or Venezuela, and tends to speak in hyperbolic terms. In an interview conducted in June 2025 he lambasted the lack of democracy in Hungary under Viktor Orbán, in America under Trump, and Argentina under Javier Milei, before comparing the state of Brazil at the end of Bolsonaro's government to the bombardment suffered by the people of Gaza.[5]

Lula and his foreign adviser Celso Amorim have tended to see the BRICS as members of a club of poor countries battling the dominance of the West rather than as burgeoning authoritarian powers whose expansionism represents a threat to the democracies of Ukraine or Taiwan. To European diplomats, Lula's claim to be a potential peacemaker in Ukraine seems naive, a perception strengthened by his failure to influence political events in neighbouring Venezuela, a smaller country with which Brazil has a shared border and many common interests. Blaming Volodymyr Zelensky for the war in Ukraine was equally shocking. Moreover, Lula was the only leader from a Western democracy to attend, in May 2025, the 80th anniversary of the Soviet victory over Germany in the Second World War, which earned him particularly scathing criticism from many European leaders.

But set against that Lula has overseen significant progress. The most striking advances have been achieved in two areas: the reduction of deforestation, and sharp falls in levels of inequality and poverty. A large part of these improvements was achieved in Lula's first two periods in government between 2003 and 2010. Under Marina Silva's stewardship between 2003 and 2008, Brazil was a global leader in rainforest protection. Since she returned as Minister of the Environment in 2023, the rate of deforestation has again started to fall, although the path has been bumpy, not least because temperatures have been increasing, and in 2024 several Brazilian states were badly hit by drought.[6]

More striking still is the dramatic decline in poverty and inequality. During his first two terms in office, Lula presided over an expansion of the consumer economy, in which millions of people started to eat better food, won access to further education and improved healthcare, and enjoy greater leisure.

Overall, under Lula, Brazil has become fairer and less unequal. During the 2000s, the rise of what Brazilian statisticians have labelled Class C – the middle-income group earning in 2024 between R$3,400 and R$8,100 a month – was the most dramatic domestic manifestation of Brazil's improved fortunes, with 40 million people making the transition upwards into this group by 2012. During the PT-led governments between 2002 and 2014 the number of those living in poverty (defined as those living on income of less than $3.50 per day) fell by more than 31 million (or from 28 per cent to 9.2 per cent of the population). At the same time, inequality fell markedly, with a pronounced reduction from the mid-1990s – the years when Cardoso's counter-inflationary *Plano Real* came into effect – until 2014, when Dilma Rousseff completed her first term in office. The GINI coefficient (an often used measure of a nation's inequality, in which 1 equals maximum inequality and 0 perfect equality) reached about 0.6 in 1995 but fell to about 0.5 in 2012.

Some of those gains were reversed over the following eight years, mainly because of Brazil's recession and the COVID-19 pandemic, but since Lula's return to office in 2023 levels of poverty and inequality have both fallen again. In 2024, for example, 22 per cent of the population were living in poverty, down from 30 per cent at the height of the pandemic. And the GINI fell to 0.506, compared to 0.54 in 2021, and was at its lowest since 2012.[7] Tax reforms introduced by Fernando Haddad in 2025 seem set to reinforce this latter trend significantly. Under changes to be fully introduced in 2026 those earning less than R$5,000 per month will no longer pay income tax. (The income-tax threshold was increased from R$1,800 to R$3,000 in 2025.)

Meanwhile, the United Nations Food and Health Organization (FAO) announced in July 2025 that fewer than 2.5 per cent of

Brazil's population were undernourished in 2024, compared to 3.9 per cent in 2023. The improvement took Brazil off the World Hunger Map for the first time since 2019. For a man who grew up in some privation in the drought-stricken north-east and who made the elimination of hunger a priority of his first government in 2003, this was an important achievement and one that 'made him the happiest man in the world'.[8]

Critics will argue that much of the foundation for all this progress was laid by the economic stabilization programmes championed by the preceding government of Fernando Henrique Cardoso, and originally opposed by Lula. In addition, China's rapid economic expansion after it joined the World Trade Organization contributed to a remarkable increase in Brazilian exports, and for a while at least ended the external account problems that had dogged governments in previous decades. Lula was lucky to inherit the stability bequeathed by his predecessor and fortunate too to be blessed by the China dividend. But unlike some of his more leftwing peers elsewhere in Latin America, most notably in Venezuela and Argentina, where the fruits of a commodity boom were squandered, Lula and his ministers had the pragmatic sense to build on these legacies. In this sense Lula's decision to pursue social reforms while maintaining institutional and economic stability – what the political scientist André Singer describes as 'reform without rupture' – has been the right decision. It also seems reasonable to claim that Lula's patient incremental approach towards social improvement has contributed to the resilience of Brazilian democracy, in the face of the challenges to which it has been subjected over the last decade or so. Brazil – as explained at various points in this book – is politically polarized and many of its institutions stand in need of reform, but the country would be in a much worse position if Lula had taken the advice of his left-wing critics and pursued a more confrontational approach to social change.

For at root Lula – for all his occasional flights of populist fancy – is a practical politician, generally disposed to find ways to do things that seem useful, and if necessary, to change his mind. It is for that reason that he has always distanced himself from the far-left activists who contested his control of the metalworkers in the 1970s, and why he backed the PT's transformation from a grassroots movement-oriented party to an electoral force in the 1980s and 1990s. That is also why he was so intent on maintaining low inflation during his first two terms. And that is why too – at least until November 2025 – Lula has been so loyal to his moderate Finance Minister, Fernando Haddad, against pressure from many of his party's leaders. Prison radicalized Lula to a degree, but he remains as pragmatic as he ever was.[9] In a world seduced by the idea of the quick fix and by ideological obsession, Lula's pragmatism offers some welcome relief. And at a time when few democratically elected politicians can hope to complete more than one term in office, it may help Lula manage a potential fourth term as president. For much of the last three years that has seemed unlikely. But Lula has regularly defied expectations before. It would not be wise to dismiss his chances of doing so again.

Acknowledgements

Early in November 2022, shortly after Lula won his third term in office, Tomasz Hoskins, an editor at Bloomsbury in London, contacted me and suggested I write a book on the newly elected president. The idea seemed a very good one. After all, Lula's story and particularly his return from the political dead is extraordinary by any standards, and I seemed to be in a good position to write it. I'd been living in Brazil for much of his first two periods in office (2003–2011) and had visited the country regularly in the years since. What's more, I'd recently concluded a book on the rise of the former right-wing president, Jair Bolsonaro, Lula's nemesis. I think it is fair to say, though, that this book was challenging to write, not least because the fortunes of Lula in his third term in government have been so up and down. Sometimes it was difficult to separate out the signal of long-term trends from the noise of day-to-day events. At no time was that truer than in July and August 2025 when I was racing to meet a final deadline for the text. Early in July, Donald Trump's administration imposed 50 per cent tariffs on Brazilian products to pressure the government to intervene and make the courts drop the trial on conspiracy charges of Bolsonaro and his associates on the far-right. The tariffs damaged the interests of Bolsonaro's business supporters and allowed Lula to present himself as a champion of Brazilian sovereignty. The clash has worked to Lula's advantage. His poll ratings, which were declining steadily in the first half of 2025, have started to rise and his chances of seeking a fourth term in office in the elections due to take place in October 2026 seem good. Things can change, of course, but at present (November 2025) in the wake

ACKNOWLEDGEMENTS

of Bolsonaro's condemnation to a long prison term in September 2025, right-wing parties in Brazil seem fractious and divided.

Lula's life story is well documented, and I have made extensive use of two Portuguese-language books in particular. Fernando Morais's still uncompleted multi-volume biography of the Brazilian president is long and detailed, but also extremely readable with a store of colourful anecdotes based on extensive access to Lula himself. Denise Paraná's *Lula: O Filho do Brasil* is a valuable social history of Lula's childhood, trade union and early political career, and is based on conversations that took place with Lula and his closest family members in 1993 and 1994. I also found immensely helpful a more recent and superbly researched book by John French, which is especially good on Lula's rise through the trade union movement, his relationship with his brother Frei Chico and his mentor in the metalworkers union, Paulo Vidal. French's title *Lula and the Politics of Cunning* seemed especially appropriate at a time when Lula was seeking to divide and weaken his enemies on the right of the political spectrum. Finally, a set of interviews with Lula conducted by Brazilian journalists in 2018 and 2019, and published as *Lula: A Verdade Vencerá*, were also extremely helpful, especially in understanding Lula's relationship with his successor in 2011, Dilma Rousseff, and her downfall. Richard Bourne's *Lula of Brazil* (2nd Press, 2007) and *Brazil After Bolsonaro* (Routledge, 2024), a set of essays edited in the wake of Lula's 2022 win, were also useful. So was Michael Reid's seminal *Brazil: the Troubled Rise of a Global Power*. In addition, I'd like to draw attention to two other works in Portuguese that were essential to my research. As far as I am aware, Elio Gaspari's monumental five-volume work on the Brazilian dictatorship, and Celso Rocha de Barros's brilliant history of the Workers' Party, remain untranslated.

In addition to these publications, I read more widely. I tracked down out-of-print histories, accumulated online biographies, and dived into newspaper and other archives. It is worth singling out the following: Brian Winter's inspired translation and adaptation of Fernando Henrique Cardoso's *A Arte da Política*, which provided the basis for my chapter on the rivalry between Lula and Cardoso. Autobiographies by José Dirceu and Antônio Palocci were important for chapters 9 and 10. The work of Ricardo Amaral and Luiz Maklouf Carvalho on Dilma Rousseff and Marília de Camargo César, and Ana Clara Costa on Marina Silva, provided essential background on Brazil's two leading left-wing women and helped underpin chapters 11–13. The political scientist Fernando Limongi's superb analysis of the events leading up to the 2016 impeachment of Rousseff, and Luciano da Ros and Matthew Taylor's comprehensive study on governance and anti-corruption reforms since the return to democracy, were essential background for my analysis of Lava Jato, which figures in chapters 13 and 14.

I reported some of the events of the 2000s for *The Financial Times*. Subsequently as editor of the specialist *FT* publication, aimed at investors and called *Brazil Confidential*, I followed in great detail the rise and fall of the Rousseff administration and was often in Brazil. After retiring from the *FT* in 2015 I kept in touch with Brazil, continued to visit, and for this book made several reporting trips during 2023 and 2024, to São Paulo, Brasília, Rio de Janeiro, Salvador, Uberlândia and Rio Branco, and neighbouring communities in the Amazonian state of Acre, interviewing people who knew or had worked with Lula, as well as many grassroots leaders of the Workers' Party. My interviews with Gilberto Carvalho, a PT founder, and Moises Selerges, head of the metalworkers' union of São Bernardo, were especially insightful. I discussed the ideas in this book with numerous people from London, where I now live, as well as in Brazil, and elsewhere.

Thanks to Richard House, Brian Winter, Elizabeth Johnson, Graham Hillyard, Colin Henfrey, Taís Reis, Tony Pereira, Tony Danby, Maria 'Cuca' Abbott, Helena Vieira, John Rumsey, Jonathan Wheatley, and Phil Gunson for reading, commenting, and in the case of Graham Hillyard editing in some detail various drafts of the text. In addition to my 'readers', other friends provided ideas and contacts. I'd like to thank – among others – Thomas Traumann, Leslie Bethell, Tony Gross, Chris Albi, Wilber Colmerauer, Peter West, John Kolodziejski, Andrés Velasco, Jon Lee Anderson, Michael Reid, Andrew Downie, Felipe Krause, Celso Rocha de Barros, Duncan Green, Russell Southwood, Steve Fidler, David Owen, Daniel Lansberg-Rodriguez, Antônio Patriota, João Fellet, Alberto Almeida, Gabriel Penna, Paulo Melvino, Michael Pooler, Ana Lankes, Yana Marull, Lucinda Elliot, Ricardo Amaral, Tony Boadle, Marcos Palacios, Sérgio Gabrielli, Leo Bichara Rocha, Michael Barzelay, Cristovam Buarque, Mark Langevin, Otaviano Canuto, João Silvio Cerqueira Monteiro, Ricky Monteiro, Chris Sabatini, Felipe Krause, Sandro Torres Avelar, Clauder Diniz, Carlos Alberto Júnior, Fabiana Moreira, Lilian Chagas, Eriel Araújo, Milton Júlio Carvalho,

ACKNOWLEDGEMENTS

James Sinclair, Sayuri Carbonnier, Tereza Cruvinel, Helena Chagas, José Maria and Redu Trindade, Cynara Menezes, Luciana Martins, Maria Maia, Teresinha Froes and Paul Burnham, Emiliano José, Nildon Pitombo, Walter Takemoto, Jerry Matalauê Pataxó, Sergio Gabrielli, Georges Souto Rocha, Jesse Alves, Cecilia Tornaghi, Alexandre Aroeira Salles, Kevin Ivers and Chris Whitehouse.

During the years I was researching this book I wrote a regular monthly report for Aurora Macro Consulting, a political-risk advisory co-founded by Daniel Lansberg-Rodriguez, and that helped keep me in touch with day-to-day events. My wife Fátima provided support throughout the process and accompanied me on the reporting trips. The retired Reuters journalist Tony Boadle and his wife Fiona Murphy introduced us to many friends and contacts in Brasília. My brother-in-law Guto Carvalho drove us to the battlefields of Canudos in northern Bahia. Fábio Pontes and Angela Mendes helped orient us in Rio Branco. Taís Reis took us around Lauro de Freitas, near Salvador, and introduced us to several local politicians. My sister-in-law Núbia Carvalho, her husband Rogério Silva, and my nephew Henrique Carvalho hosted us in Uberlândia. My mother-in-law Lia Carvalho made us feel at home during our several visits to Salvador, providing a typically warm Bahian welcome. My sister-in-law Michelle Magalhães and my niece Sophia Magalhães transcribed several dozen taped interviews.

Sadly, two of my British friends who shared my love of Brazil died in March 2025 as I was completing the book. I was at school with Chris Whitehouse, who spent four years in São Paulo in the early 1980s and worked for a trade union information centre there. When I stayed with Chris in Sheffield to talk about his memories, he and his wife Linda Whitehead were generous hosts. During 2023 and 2024, after renewing contact with my Liverpool University teacher Colin Henfrey, I visited him and his wife Claire Dove several times at their home in Liverpool and we spent many hours in Colin's beautiful garden, talking amid the hydrangeas and the azaleas about his research in rural areas of the north-east and the Amazon. Both Chris and Colin are much missed.

Finally, thanks to Tomasz, Fahmida Ahmed and their colleagues at Bloomsbury for shepherding this work to publication, and to Richard Mason for his invaluable editing work.

Notes

INTRODUCTION

1 This was the second-round run-off between Lula and Bolsonaro on 30 October, the two candidates who had finished first and second in the first round held three weeks previously.
2 Lucas Font, 'El Lulismo se adueña de las calles de Brasil', *El Periódico de España* (30 October 2022).
3 Patrizia Antonini, 'Lula "ressuscita" no silêncio perturbador de Bolsonaro', *Ansa* (31 October 2022); https://noticias.uol.com.br/ultimas-noticias/ansa/2022/10/31/lula-ressuscita-no-silencio-perturbador-de-bolsonaro.htm (accessed 4 June 2025).
4 See Leslie Derfler, *Political Resurrection in the Twentieth Century: The Fall and Rise of Political Leaders* (London: Palgrave Macmillan, 2012). Derfler lists eight cases of return: Pierre Trudeau (Canada, 1968–79, 1980–4); Winston Churchill (Great Britain, 1940–5, 1951–5); Charles de Gaulle (France, 1944–6, 1958–69); Juan Domingo Perón (Argentina, 1946–55, 1973–4); Olof Palme (Sweden, 1969–76, 1982–6); Indira Gandhi (India, 1966–77, 1980–4); Yitzhak Rabin (Israel, 1974–7, 1992–5); Olusegun Obasanjo (Nigeria, 1976–9, 1999–2007). He provides a detailed analysis of three of them (Trudeau, Perón, and De Gaulle).
5 Author interview with Gilberto Carvalho, Brasília (3 November 2023).
6 Juliano Spyer, Povo de Deus: Quem são os Evangélicos e por que eles importam (São Paulo: Geração Editorial, 2020), Kindle Edition (Portuguese Edition), p. 22.

7 Felipe Nunes and Thomas Traumann, *Biografia do Abismo* (London and New York: HarperCollins, 2023), p. 12. The authors acknowledge that the term 'calcification' had been used by the political scientists John Sides, Chris Tausanovitch, and Lynn Vavreck in their analysis of the 2020 Biden-Trump race, *The Bitter End: The 2020 Presidential Campaign and the Challenge to American Democracy* (Princeton, NJ: Princeton University Press, 2022).

8 See Ricardo Batista Amaral, *A Vida Quer é Coragem* (São Paulo: Primeiro Pessoa, 2011), p. 129.

9 Fernando Cervantes, *Conquistadores: A New History* (Harmondsworth: Penguin, 2021), esp. pp. 206–9. In Brazil the Jesuits were especially influential. In 1549 – nine years after they had been formed by Ignatius of Loyala – they were invited by the Portuguese authorities to be part of a broader effort to establish and consolidate colonial rule in the region. They set up ten so-called 'reductions', community projects that aimed to save local populations from enslavement and convert them to Christianity.

CHAPTER 1: A MAN FROM THE BACKLANDS

1 She obtained the equivalent of $18,000, much of which was spent on the journey.

2 Sérgio Miguel Buarque and Inês Campelo, 'A viagem que mudou o Brasil', *Saiba Mais* (31 December 2022); https://saibamais.jor.br/2022/12/marco-zero-a-viagem-que-mudou-o-brasil (accessed 30 June 2025).

3 Buarque and Campelo, op. cit.

4 Denise Paraná, *Lula, o filho do Brasil* (São Paulo: Editora Fundação Perseu Abramo, 1996), pp. 194–5.

5 Quoted in Monia de Melo Ferrari, *Migração Nordestina para São Paulo (1951–4)* (São Carlos University, 2005). Downloaded MA thesis (13 September 2023); https://www.researchgate.net/publication/333781700_Migrantes_Nordestinos_na_Regiao_Metropolitana_de_Sao_Paulo_caracteristicas_socioeconomicas_e_distribuicao_espacial (accessed 30 June 2025).

6 De Melo Ferrari, op. cit.

7 Paraná, op. cit., pp. 194–7.

8 Paraná, op. cit., p. 57.

9 Paraná, op. cit., pp. 194–7.

10 See Livraria do Folha, Conheça, 'A História de Lula: O Filho do Brasil', que Originou Filme na Mira do Oscar, *Folha de São Paulo* (23 September 2010); https://www1.folha.uol.com.br/folha/livrariadafolha/803531-conheca-a-historia-de-lula-o-filho-do-brasil-que-originou-filme-na-mira-do-oscar.shtml.
11 Interview with Maria Ferreira Moreno, in Paraná, op. cit., pp. 268–9.
12 Celso Furtado, *Formação Econômica do Brasil* (São Paulo: Companhia Editora Nacional, 2005), pp. 67–72. In recent years Furtado's account has been contested as digitalization has allowed researchers to access a broader range of sources and more comprehensive data. Jorge Caldeira, a São Paulo-based social scientist, believes that the interior was always more dynamic than Furtado claimed.
13 John French, *Lula and his Politics of Cunning: From Metalworker to President of Brazil* (Chapel Hill, NC: University of North Carolina Press, 2020), p. 34.
14 Eve Elizabeth Buckley, 'Drought in the Sertão as a Natural or Social Phenomenon: Establishing the Inspetoria Federal de Obras Contra as Secas, 1909–1923', published by the Boletim do Museu Paraense Emílio Goeldi, Ciências Humanas 5:2 (January 2010).
15 Buckley, op. cit.
16 Euclides da Cunha, *Os Sertões*, 1902, translated as *Backlands: The Canudos Campaign* by Elizabeth Lowe (Harmondsworth: Penguin, 2010).
17 Roger Bastide, *Brasil Terra de Contrastes* (São Paulo: Difusão Europeia do Livro, 1971), p. 87.
18 Bastide, op. cit., p. 87.
19 Maria Isaura Pereira de Queiroz, *O Messianismo no Brasil* (São Paulo: Universidade de São Paulo, 1965).
20 Pereira de Queiroz, op. cit., pp. 200–1.
21 In 1907, Cicero was elected deputy-governor of the state of Ceará, and even today, nearly a hundred years after his death, he is widely venerated. A giant statue erected to his memory in the 1960s stands 100 feet high in the centre of the city, overshadowing everything around it.
22 Pedro Vasconcellos, *Belo Monte: Canudos de Antonio Conselheiro a Lula da Silva* (Curitiba: Kotter Editorial, 2020), p. 247.

23 Da Cunha, op. cit., p. 203.
24 Da Cunha, op. cit., pp. 137–8.
25 Paraná, op. cit., p. 193.

CHAPTER 2: THE CITY AND THE FACTORY

1 Paraná, op. cit., p. 69.
2 Paraná, op. cit., pp. 205–6.
3 Paraná, op. cit., p. 50.
4 Eliane Brum, 'Pai Pedrasto', *Época* (12 October 2002); http://web.archive.org/web/20050309202833/https://revistaepoca.globo.com/Epoca/0,6993,EPT359275-1659-1,00.html (accessed 2 July 2025).
5 Luís Eduardo Leal, 'Lula muda de endereço à procura de empregos', *Folha de São Paulo* (2 October 1994); https://www1.folha.uol.com.br/fsp/1994/10/02/cotidiano/13.html Accessed 2 July 2025.
6 Daniel Ignácio Franco, 'Vila Carioca – Ilha dos Sapos, Portal do Ipiranga'; https://www.independenciaoumorte.com.br/vila-carioca-ilha-dos-sapos (accessed 2 July 2025).
7 Paraná, op. cit., p. 61.
8 Fernando Morais, *Lula*, vol. 1 (São Paulo: Companhía das Letras, 2021), p. 267.
9 Morais, op. cit., p. 268.
10 Morais, op. cit., p .267.
11 Morais, op. cit., p. 324.
12 Paraná, op. cit., p. 263.
13 Morais, op. cit., pp. 273–4.
14 Lula 1981 interview with Mário Morel quoted in French, *Lula and his Politics of Cunning*, op. cit., p. 43.
15 Paraná, op. cit., p. 87.
16 Quoted in Mercedes S. Hinton, *The State on the Streets: Police and Politics in Argentina and Brazil* (Boulder, CO: Lynne Rienner, 2017), p. 159.
17 Leslie Bethell, ed., *The Cambridge History of Latin America, Volume IX: Brazil since 1930* (Cambridge: Cambridge University Press, 2008), p. 108; see Bethell for the best account of the Vargas period.
18 John Humphrey, *Capitalist Control and Workers' Struggle in the Brazilian Auto Industry* (Princeton, NJ: Princeton University Press, 1982), p. 14.

19 Humphrey, op. cit., p. 15.
20 Bethell, op. cit., p. 64.
21 Quoted in Sheldon Maram, 'Juscelino Kubitschek and the Politics of Exuberance, 1956–1961', *Luso-Brazilian Review* 27:1 (Summer 1990, 2013).
22 Morais, op. cit., p. 277.
23 Quoted in French, op. cit., p. 146.
24 Morais, op. cit., p. 228; also see French, op. cit., esp. ch. 3.
25 Paraná, op. cit., pp. 88–9.
26 Paraná, op. cit., pp. 315–27.

CHAPTER 3: SOLDIERS AND GUERRILLAS

1 Morais, op. cit., pp. 283–4.
2 Elio Gaspari, *Coleção Dictadura* (Kindle Edition) (São Paulo: Intrínseca, 2002, 2014), p. 62.
3 Morais, op. cit., pp. 283–4.
4 'What is the Mann Doctrine?', *The New York Times* (21 March 1964); https://timesmachine.nytimes.com/timesmachine/1964/03/21/118654911.html?pageNumber=24 (accessed 1 July 2025).
5 Gaspari, op. cit., p. 125.
6 José Dirceu, *Zé Dirceu: Memórias*, vol. 1 (São Paulo: Geração Editorial, 2018), p .39.
7 See Jon Lee Anderson, *Che Guevara: A Revolutionary Life* (New York: Bantam Books, 1997), pp. 544–5.
8 Anderson, op. cit., p. 587.
9 Gaspari, op. cit., p. 94.
10 Dirceu, op. cit., p. 40.
11 Fernando Gabeira, *O Que É Isso, Companheiro* (Sao Paulo: Estação Brasil, 1979; Kindle Edition, 2016), pp. 37 and 43.
12 Gabeira, op. cit., p. 97.
13 Dirceu, op. cit., pp. 33–4.
14 Gaspari, op. cit., p. 233.
15 Gaspari, op. cit., p. 250.
16 Denise Rollemberg, *O Apoio de Cuba à Luta Armada no Brasil: O Treinamento Guerrilheiro* (Rio de Janeiro: Mauad, 2001).
17 Gaspari, op. cit., p. 312.
18 See the testimony of Domingos Fernandes in Rollemberg, op. cit., p. 38.

19 Testimony of Osawa in Rollemberg, op. cit., p. 96.
20 Gaspari, op. cit., pp. 1355–1418.
21 See Julia Sweig, *Inside the Cuban Revolution* (Cambridge, MA: Harvard University Press, 2002), p. 2.
22 Sweig interview with Ricardo Alarcón, former Cuban Foreign Minister, op. cit., p. 2.
23 Timothy J. Power, 'The Brazilian Military Regime of 1964–1985: Legacies for Contemporary Democracy', *Iberoamericana* 16:2 (2016), pp. 13–26, quoted in Richard Lapper, *Beef, Bible and Bullets: Brazil in the Age of Bolsonaro* (Manchester: Manchester University Press, 2021), p. 31.
24 Flávio Tavares, *Memórias do Esquecimento*, 3rd ed. (São Paulo: Globo, 1999), quoted in Rollemberg, op. cit., p. 24.
25 Rollemberg, op. cit., pp. 23–31.
26 Rollemberg, op. cit., p. 24.
27 Gaspari, op. cit., p. 1,267.

CHAPTER 4: THE RELUCTANT TRADE UNIONIST

1 Teresa Camarão and Bruno Amaral de Carvalho, 'A democracia mais plena no Brasil foi nos governos de Lula e Dilma', *Voz Operário* [Portugal] (19 July 2021); https://vozoperario.pt/jornal/2021/07/19/a-democracia-mais-plena-no-brasil-foi-nos-governos-de-lula-e-dilma (accessed 25 January 2024).
2 Ibid.
3 Morais, op. cit., p. 300.
4 The relationship between the two is well-documented. The American historian John D. French, in a biography that contains a magisterial account of Lula's trade union career, lists 16 separate interviews (ten with Lula and six with Frei Chico) conducted between 1976 and 2008 (French, op. cit.).
5 French, op. cit., p. 80; also see the interview with Frei Chico by Carlos Alberto Almeida; https://www.youtube.com/watch?v=pUrGOONgzDE Live Canal Carlos Alberto Almeida (17 May 2021 (accessed 25 January 2024).
6 Morais, op. cit., p. 299.
7 French, op. cit., p. 114.
8 See the interview with Marcos Andreotti, cited in French, op. cit., p. 98.

9 French, op. cit., p. 106.
10 Paraná, op. cit., pp. 97–8.
11 French, op. cit., p. 170.
12 The term *pelego* describes the sheepskin cloth that cowboys placed on their saddles to cushion their ride.
13 Paraná, op. cit., p. 99; see also French, op. cit., p. 206.
14 Interview with Paulo Vidal, 'Homem que lançou Lula no sindicalismo, abre o coração e revela a ingratidão do petista', *Crusoé* (13 May 2018); https://crusoe.com.br/edicoes/lula-sem-pre-gostou-de-dinheiro/#google_vignette?utm_source=site_CR&utm_medium=organic&utm_campaign=paywall_stake (accessed 3 October 2025).
15 Morais, op. cit., p. 318.
16 Between the late 1960s and the end of 1972 the unionized workforce in the ABC towns had risen from 20 per cent to 50 per cent of the total labour force. The union's membership increased from 7,000 to 30,000 between 1969 and 1978. Morais, op. cit., p. 310. See also Agência Brasil, interview with Paulo Vidal (18 April 2005); whttps://memoria.ebc.com.br/agenciabrasil/noticia/2005-04-18/ex-presidente-do-sindicato-dos-metalurgicos-destaca-conquistas-da-categoria (accessed 28 January 2024).
17 French, op. cit., pp. 225–6.
18 Morais, op. cit., pp. 323–4.
19 French, op. cit., p. 188.
20 French, op. cit., p. 236.
21 Gaspari, op. cit., pp. 4,099–4,101.
22 Bethell, op. cit., pp. 201–2.
23 Morais, op. cit., pp. 338–58.
24 Testimony to the National Truth Commission; https://nsarchive2.gwu.edu/NSAEBB/NSAEBB496 (accessed 30 July 2025).
25 French, op. cit., p. 231.
26 Paraná, op. cit., p. 129.
27 Lula won by an overwhelming majority. See Jorge Araújo, 'Mais light, Lula se aproxima do irmão', *Folha de São Paulo* (30 June 2002); https://www1.folha.uol.com.br/fsp/brasil/fc3006200216.htm (accessed 7 February 2024).
28 Morais, op. cit., p. 325.
29 French, op. cit., pp. 126–7.
30 Morais, op. cit., pp. 325–6.

CHAPTER 5: ALL OUT

1 Author interview with Juno Rodrigues Silva (9 November 2023).
2 Morais, op. cit., p. 407.
3 The *cruzeiro* was Brazil's currency between 1942 and 1986.
4 Author interview, São Paulo (November 2023).
5 Author interview with Paulo Okamotto (8 November, 2023).
6 Valdir dos Santos, *O Estado de São Paulo* (13 May 1978); https://www.estadao.com.br/acervo (accessed 15 February 2024).
7 Humphrey, op. cit., p. 169.
8 *Latin American Newsletter* (30 March 1978), accessed via https://www.latinnews.com.
9 John D. French, 'The Creation of a Myth. Charisma's Birth from the Bottom Up: Lula, ABC's Strikes and the Social History of Brazilian Politics', *Journal of Latin American Studies* 54:4 (November 2022), pp. 705–29; https://www.cambridge.org/core/journals/journal-of-latin-american-studies (accessed 7 February 2024), Latam Studies.
10 Dos Santos, op. cit.
11 Humphrey, op. cit., p. 162.
12 Gaspari, op. cit., p. 4,229.
13 Paraná, op. cit., p. 93.
14 *Latin American Newsletter* (2 June 1978).
15 Morais, op. cit., p. 406.
16 Bourne, op. cit., p. 39.
17 Author interview with Okamotto, op. cit.
18 Bishop Hummes used his speech at the 30 March 1980 rally to place ABC's fight within a broader Latin American context. Less than six days earlier, he noted, the archbishop of El Salvador, Oscar Romero, had been gunned down by right-wing assassins in the cathedral of his nation's capital. In July 1980, Frei Betto accompanied Lula, just one month after his release from prison, on a trip to Managua to celebrate the victory of the Nicaraguan Revolution.
19 Gaspari, op. cit., p. 4,267.
20 The ministry's role in industrial disputes was formally reduced in 1988 to simply ensuring that the paperwork was in order. The constitution also recognized public servants' freedom of association and guaranteed all workers the right to strike. Finally, unions in the private sector won the right to establish representatives in the

workplace in companies with 200 or more employees. However, unions have faced significant difficulties overcoming employer resistance to their presence in the workplace. (Karen Lang and Mona-Josée Gagnon, Brazilian Trade Unions: In (In)Voluntary Confinement of the Corporatist Past in Relations Industrielles/ Industrial Relations 64:2 (Spring 2009), pp. 250–69; https://www.jstor.org/stable/23078279 (accessed 15 February 2024).

21 Interview with De Souza in *Peões* (2004), dir. Eduardo Coutinho.
22 Peter Robb, *A Death in Brazil* (London: Bloomsbury, 2005), p. 133.
23 Ricardo Kotscho, *De Golpe ao Planalto Companhía das Letras* (2006), quoted in French, *Creation of a Myth*, op. cit.
24 *Playboy*, Brazil edition (July 1979).
25 Gaspari, op. cit., p. 4,235.
26 Juan de Onis, 'Strikes, Once Repressed, Return to Brazil', *The New York Times* (22 June 1978); https://timesmachine.nytimes.com/timesmachine/1978/06/22/110872456.html?pageNumber=75 (accessed 8 July 2025).
27 Björn Kumm, 'A Trade Union Man Who Hates Extremes', *Globe and Mail* (22 July 1978), accessed via the Factiva database.
28 'Brazil: Lula's Triumph', *Latin American Weekly Report* (10 August 1979).
29 Interview in *Isto É* (19 September 1979), quoted in Humphrey, op. cit., p. 192.

CHAPTER 6: THE WORKERS' PARTY ARRIVES

1 Author interview with Gilberto Carvalho, Brasília (3 November 2023).
2 Celso Rocha de Barros, *PT, Uma História* (São Paulo: Companhía das Letras, 2022), pp. 79–80.
3 Margaret Keck, *The Workers' Party and the Democratization of Brazil* (New Haven, CT: Yale University Press, 1992), p. 69.
4 Rocha de Barros, op. cit., p. 7.
5 Author interview with Carvalho, op. cit.
6 For the Balaam story see Plínio Fraga, 'Os ouvidos do planalto', *Piauí* (September 2011); https://piaui.folha.uol.com.br/materia/os-ouvidos-do-planalto (accessed 10 September 2024).
7 Luiz Fernando Emediato, 'Dos rebeldes ao destino incerto', *O Estado de São Paulo* (3 October 1978; accessed 2 March 2024).

NOTES 323

8 Rocha de Barros, op. cit., p. 152. The first editions of Gramsci's *Prison Notebooks and Letters* were published in Italian in 1947 and in Portuguese in partial form in the late 1960s: https://www.scielo.br/j/rbcsoc/a/z99XqSHV7Fpr79vhJgxDJhS/#:~:text=A%20edi%C3%A7%C3%A3o%20completa%20dos%20Cadernos,S%C3%A9rgio%20Henriques%2C%20editor%20da%20revistaalthough.
9 See 'Brazil Gaining in Drive to Eradicate Illiteracy', *The New York Times* (20 August 1975; accessed 28 February 2024).
10 Rocha de Barros, op. cit., p. 89.
11 Margaret Keck, op. cit., pp. 100–110.
12 Rocha de Barros, op. cit., p. 104.
13 Rocha de Barros, op. cit., pp. 120–222.
14 Rocha de Barros, op. cit., pp. 127–9.
15 Rocha de Barros, op. cit., p. 127.
16 The name 'Articulation' subsequently became synonymous with the party's majority faction to which Lula belonged.
17 The biggest mentioned by Dirceu were Socialist Convergence (*Convergencia Socialista* or CS), Genoíno's Revolutionary Communist Party (*Partido Revolucionária Comunista* or PRC), the Movement for the Emancipation of the Proletariat (*Movimento da Emancipação do Proletariado* or MEP), Socialist Democracy (*Democrácia Socialista* or DS), and the International Socialist Organization (*Organização Socialista Internacional* or OSI).
18 José Dirceu, *Ze Dirceu, Memória*, vol. 1 (São Paulo: Geração, 2018), pp. 252–4.
19 Author interview with Walter Takemoto, Salvador (7 July 2023).
20 Rocha de Barros, op. cit., p. 174.
21 Robb, *Death in Brazil*, p. 149.
22 Rocha de Barros, p. 217.

CHAPTER 7: THE ODD COUPLE

1 Fernando Henrique Cardoso with Brian Winter, *The Accidental President of Brazil: A Memoir* (Public Affairs, 2007), p. 137.
2 Rocha de Barros, op. cit., p. 288.
3 Cardoso, op. cit., p. 41.
4 Cardoso, op. cit., p. 65.
5 André Gunder Frank, *Capitalism and Underdevelopment in Latin America: Historical Studies of Chile and Brazil* (Monthly Review Press, 1967).

6 Eduardo Galeano, *The Open Veins of Latin America* (Monthly Review Press, 1970), Kindle Edition, p. 2.
7 Isabel Allende, foreword to Galeano, *The Open Veins of Latin America*.
8 André Gunder Frank, *Latin America: Underdevelopment or Revolution: Essays on the Development of Underdevelopment and the Immediate Enemy* (Monthly Review Press, 1969).
9 Fernando Henrique Cardoso and Enzo Faletto, *Dependencia y Desarrollo en America Latina, Siglo XXI* (1969), was translated as *Dependency and Development in Latin America*, but not published in English until 1979 (Berkeley, CA: University of California Press).
10 Fernando Henrique Cardoso, Dependent Capitalist Development in Latin America, New Left Review, July-August 1972.
11 Andrés Velasco, *Foreign Policy* (9 November 2009), web reference (accessed 22 March 2024).
12 Quoted in Felipe Antunes de Oliveira, 'Bourgeois Dependency Theory and the Forgotten Roots of Neodevelopmentalism, *Latin American Perspectives* 49:1; https://journals.sagepub.com/doi/full/10.1177/0094582X211037341is (accessed 8 July 2025).
13 Timothy J. Power, 'The Brazilian Military Regime of 1964–1985: Legacies for Contemporary Democracy', *Iberoamerica* 16:2 (2016), and Scott Mainwaring, *Rethinking Party Systems in the Case of Brazil* (Stanford University Press, 1999). Both quoted in Richard Lapper, *Beef, Bible and Bullets: Brazil in the Age of Bolsonaro* (Manchester University Press, 2021).
14 Cardoso, op. cit., p.166–7.
15 Cardoso, op. cit., p.166–7.
16 Rocha de Barros, op. cit., p. 132; see also, for example, Sérgio Buarque de Holanda, *Roots of Brazil* (Kellogg Institute Series on Democracy and Development, 2012), trans. G. Harvey Summ.
17 Cardoso, op. cit., p. 169.
18 See Rosemary Thorpe, *Progress, Poverty and Exclusion: An Economic History of Latin America in the Twentieth Century* (Inter-American Development Bank, 1998).
19 Cardoso, op. cit., p. 183.
20 Richard House, 'President Collor's First 100 Days in Power', *The Independent* (26 June 1990).
21 James Brooke, *The New York Times* (14 March 1991).
22 Stephen Fidler, Edward Mortimer, and Christina Lamb, '"Determined Driver of the Last Train to Modernity", Brazil's President

NOTES

Collor Talks to *FT* Writers about the Earth Summit and the Challenges of Economic Reform', *The Financial Times* (15 May 1992).
23 Cardoso, op. cit., pp. 179–80.
24 Edmar Bacha, 'Brazil's Plano Real: A View from the Inside: Development Economics and Structuralist Macroeconomics: Essays in Honor of Lance Taylor', ed. Amitava Krishna Dutt and Jaime Ross (Cheltenham: Edward Elgar, 2003), pp. 181–205; http://Users/richardlapper/Downloads/040623RealTaylor.09.51.pdf (accessed 28 March 2024).
25 Cardoso, op. cit., p. 187.
26 Cardoso, op. cit., p. 199.
27 Cardoso, op. cit., p. 193.

CHAPTER 8: THE TIDE TURNS

1 The biggest changes included in the US the repeal of withholding tax on foreign borrowing in 1984, and in the UK the stock market Big Bang reforms of 1986.
2 Richard Lapper, 'Slow-Motion Dominoes', *The Financial Times* (17 August 1998).
3 Lapper, op. cit.
4 Cardoso, op. cit., p. 244.
5 Richard Lapper and Geoff Dyer, 'Hopes Still Waiting to Reach Fulfilment – President Cardoso is on the Defensive as the Nation Seeks to Restore Financial Confidence', *The Financial Times* (21 December 1998).
6 Richard Lapper and Geoff Dyer, 'Brazil's Unenviable Choices', *The Financial Times* (5 February 1999).
7 Antonio Carlos Seidl, 'Goldman Sachs recomenda privatizar Petrobrás, CEF e BB', *Folha de São Paulo* (25 January 1999). Elio Gaspari, 'O governo capturou o especulador', *Folha de São Paulo* (7 February 1999).
8 'Planalto nega Leme em diretoria do BC', *Folha de São Paulo* (7 February 1999).
9 Cardoso, op. cit., p. 243.
10 Richard Lapper and Raymond Colitt, 'Cardoso Keeps a Cool Head', *The Financial Times* (19 April 2002).
11 Geoff Dyer, 'Brazil Picks Hedge Fund Poacher as Economic Game Keeper', *The Financial Times* (3 February 1999).

12 *Gazeta Mercantil* (3 February 1999).
13 *Folha de São Paulo* (3 February 1999).
14 See José Maria Mayrink, 'Lula/Armínio Fraga', *Agência Jornal do Brasil* (2 February 1999).
15 Jenny Anderson, 'Buy, Buy Brazil', *Institutional Investor* (1 November 2000).
16 Anderson, op. cit.
17 See Geoff Dyer, 'Deregulation Fails to Deliver – Brazil: The Weather is Being Blamed for Shortages, but the Real Culprit is Under-Investment', *The Financial Times* (30 April 2001). According to the Economist Intelligence Unit, during the 1990s electricity consumption increased by 45 per cent compared to a 28 per cent rise in electricity generation (EIU, 18 May 2001).
18 Alberto Carlos Almeida and Tiago Garrido, *A Mão e a Luva: O Que Elege um Presidente* (Editora Record, 2022).
19 Lucilene Cardoso, 'Em minha opinião', *Jornal do Comércio do Rio* (16 August 2001).

CHAPTER 9: 2002 A DECISIVE YEAR

1 See *Folha de São Paulo, O Globo, O Estado de São Paulo,* 2 March (3 March 2002).
2 Author interview with Armínio Fraga (24 July 2023).
3 See Richard Lapper, 'Pessimism Trap Puts a Damper on Growth', *The Financial Times* (26 September 2000).
4 Ariel Wilkis and Mariana Luzzi, 'The Dollar: How the US Dollar Became a Popular Currency in Argentina' (Albuquerque, NM: University of New Mexico Press, 2023). The authors point out that the dollar has been widely used in Argentina since the late 1930s and particularly since the 1960s.
5 Dirceu, op. cit., pp. 396–7.
6 Rocha de Barros, op. cit., p. 309.
7 Dirceu, op. cit., p. 410.
8 Paulo Markum, *O Sapo e O Príncipe* (São Paulo: Objetiva, 2004), p. 315.
9 Markum, op. cit., p. 320.
10 Rocha de Barros, op. cit., p. 313.
11 See Patrice M. Jones, 'Presidency in View: Brazil's Leftist Tries to Burnish Image', *Chicago Tribune* (20 May 2002).

12 Alberto Carlos Almeida and Tiago Garrido, *A Mão e A Luva: O Que Elege Um Presidente* (Editora Record, 2022), p. 104.
13 Antônio Palocci, *Sobre Formigas e Cigarros* (2007), chapter 2.
14 Ibid.
15 Author interview with Armínio Fraga, op. cit.
16 Ibid.
17 Ibid.
18 Ibid.
19 4th volume, as reported in *Exame* (10 October, 2019).

CHAPTER 10: THE RISE OF LULISMO

1 Richard Lapper, 'Piling on the Pressure: Leftist Radicals are Reshaping Brazil's Election Agenda, but they Offer Few Answers to the Problems of the Country, or the Continent', *The Financial Times* (28 October 2002).
2 Intervención del Comandante Presidente Hugo Chávez, en el encuentro Solidaridad con la Revolución Bolivariana con Venezuela en el marco del primero *Foro Social Mundial* (26 January 2003); https://web.archive.org/web/20190421083237/http://www.todochavez.gob.ve/todochavez/1481-intervencion-del-comandante-presidente-hugo-chavez-en-el-encuentro-solidaridad-con-la-revolucion-bolivariana-con-venezuela-en-el-marco-l-foro-social-mundial (accessed 30 July 2025). The World Forum is a movement established as a counterweight to the business conference the World Economic Forum held in Davos every year.
3 Palocci, op. cit., pp. 97–8.
4 Interest rates were increased to 26.5 per cent in the first weeks of the new government and remained above 15 per cent until July 2006.
5 Palocci, op. cit., pp. 109–18.
6 Palocci, op. cit., p. 119.
7 Rocha de Barros, op. cit., p. 352.
8 Luigi Mazza, 'Quero ser rebelde', interview with José Genoíno, *Piauí* (November 2022); https://piaui.folha.uol.com.br/materia/quero-ser-um-rebelde/Genoino (accessed 28 July 2025).
9 Quoted in Rocha de Barros, op. cit., pp. 358–9.
10 Rocha de Barros, op. cit., p. 369.
11 Rocha de Barros, op. cit., pp. 313–14.

12 Richard Lapper and Jonathan Wheatley, 'Lula Set to Collect Rich Reward for Poverty Relief Effort', *The Financial Times* (29 September 2006).
13 See Alberto Almeida and Tiago Garrido, *A Mão e a Luva* (Editora Record, 2002), esp. pp. 113–51.
14 Lapper and Wheatley, op. cit.
15 See the research by Yan de Souza Carreirão, 'Evolução das opiniões do eleitorado durante o governo Lula e as eleições presidenciais brasileiras de 2006' (2007), www.waporcolonia.com (accessed 30 August 2009), quoted in André Singer, 'Raízes Sociais e Ideológicos do Lulismo', *Cebrap Novos Estudos* (November 2009), pp. 82–102.
16 Fernando Henrique Cardoso, 'Para onde vamos?', *O Estado de São Paulo* (1 November 2009).
17 André Singer, *Os Sentidos do Lulismo* (São Paulo: Companhia das Letras, 2012), p. 77.
18 Darren Acemoglu and James Robinson, *Economic Origins of Dictatorship and Democracy* (Cambridge: Cambridge University Press, 2009), quoted in Danni Rodrik, 'Premature Deindustrialisation', Harvard University (November 2015; accessed 27 May 2024).
19 Perry Anderson, *Brazil Apart: 1964–2019* (London: Verso, 2019).
20 Dani Rodrik, 'Premature Deindustrialization', NBER Working Paper no. 20935 (January 2015); https://drodrik.scholar.harvard.edu/files/dani-rodrik/files/premature_deindustrialization.pdf (accessed 28 July 2025).
21 Karen Camacho, 'Sindicalização Cai pela Metade', *Folha de São Paulo* (12 May 2008).
22 Anderson, op. cit., pp. 68, 79.
23 Quoted in Leonardo Boff, *Sem Medo de Ser Feliz* (São Paulo: Editora Atica, 1989).
24 Wendy Hunter and Timothy Power, 'Rewarding Lula: Executive Power, Social Policy, and the Brazilian Elections of 2006', *Latin American Politics and Society* 49:1 (Spring 2007), pp. 1–30.
25 David Samuels, 'Sources of Mass Partisanship in Brazil', *Latin American Politics and Society* 48:2 (Summer 2006). In his research Samuels found that PT voters were typically active in politics, knowledgeable about it, identified as left of centre, supported clean government, and believed that their vote could make a difference. None of this necessarily applied to Lula voters.

26 Leslie Bethell, *Brazil: Essays on History and Politics*. Institute of Latin American Studies, School of Advanced Study (London: University of London, 2018), p. 193.

CHAPTER 11: GREEN BRAZIL

1 Marco Uchôa, 'Serengueira promete surpresas no senado', *O Estado de São Paulo* (15 October 1994); https://acervo.estadao.com.br/pagina/#!/19941015-36886-spo-0001-pri-a1-not (accessed 12 July 2025).
2 A white fluid contained in a network of tubules contained just beneath smooth bark helps protect the tree by gumming up the mouthparts of invading pests.
3 For details of the rubber industry and life in the *seringal* see Andrew Revkin, *The Burning Season* (London: Houghton Mifflin, 1990). For these details of Marina's early life based on interviews with Marina Silva, see Marília de Camargo César, *Marina: A Vida Por Uma Causa* (São Paulo: Mundo Cristão, 2012).
4 Camargo César, op. cit., Location, loc. 612–20.
5 For details of this drive see Revkin, op. cit., p. 105.
6 By 2021, more than 30 million people lived in the Amazon, while roads stretched more than 14,000 miles. Adding in the many tens of thousands of tracks and roads, the transport network is even more dense, with 40 per cent of the Amazon less than six miles away from a connection; see https://news.mongabay.com/2022/09/road-network-spreads-arteries-of-destruction-across-41-of-brazilian-amazon (accessed 30 July 2025).
7 Camargo César, op. cit., loc. 612–20.
8 Moacyr Grechi's role was far-reaching. In 1977, with the local media very much at the beck and call of conservative landed interests, the bishop loaned money to a group of journalists, which allowed *Varadouro*, an alternative newspaper, to get off the ground (effectively, the money was gifted, since the loan was never repaid). *Varadouro* served as a focal point, enabling the tappers to build links with urban professionals and students living in Rio Branco and other small urban centres.
9 Camargo César, op. cit., loc. 816–19.
10 Camargo César, op. cit., loc. 1,287: Chico Mendes was Santos, and Binho Marques, Ricardo.

11 Rocha de Barros, op. cit., p. 112.
12 The agrarian reform agency (INRA) increased the size of plots handed out to the rubber tappers. The 120–250 acre limit, typically distributed to small farmers benefiting from the reform, were too small for tapping to be economically viable.
13 Camargo César, op. cit., loc. 1,486–1,552.
14 Francisco Afonso quoted in Camargo César, op. cit., loc. 1,515–22.
15 John Paul Rathbone, 'Lunch with the *FT*: Roberto Mangabeira Unger', *The Financial Times* (3 October 2014; accessed 15 July 2024).
16 Daniela Pinheiros, *Piauí, A Verde* (January 2010); https://piaui.folha.uol.com.br/materia/a-verde (accessed 12 July 2025).
17 Pinheiros, op. cit. (January 2025).
18 Marcelo Leite, 'Lula, Dilma e Mangabeira abortaram adaptação à mudança climática', *Folha de São Paulo* (18 May 2024); https://www1.folha.uol.com.br/colunas/marceloleite/2024/05/lula-dilma-e-mangabeira-abortaram-adaptacao-a-mudanca-climatica.shtml (accessed 15 September 2024).
19 Gilberto Carvalho, *Veja* (2008), quoted in Pinheiros, op. cit.

CHAPTER 12: THE DILMA DILEMMA

1 For details see 'Em favela do Rio, Lula diz que Dilma é a 'mãe do PAC', *Folha de São Paulo* (8 March 2008), 'Lula lança obras em favelas do Rio e diz que Dilma é a mãe do PAC', *O Estado de São Paulo* (8 March 2008), 'Ministra-chefe da Casa Civil, possível candidata do PT à sucessão, vai para a frente do palanque', *O Globo* (8 March 2008).
2 Ricardo Batista Amaral, *A Vida Quer é Coragem: A Trajetória de Dilma Rousseff, a Primeira Presidenta do Brasil* (Rio de Janeiro: Primeira Pessoa, 2011), p. 176.
3 Ibid.
4 Rocha de Barros, op. cit., p. 445.
5 Luiz Maklouf Carvalho, 'As armas e os varões, a educação política e sentimental de Dilma Rousseff', *Piauí* (April 2009), and Mares Nunca Dantes Navegados, 'A trajetória de Dilma Rousseff da prisão ao poder – e como ela se tornou a candidata do presidente Lula à sua sucessão', *Piauí* (July 2009). In the first of these two articles Maklouf Carvalho in *Piauí* states definitively that Russév

had joined the Communist Party in 1924 and left for South America in the late 1930s. Ricardo Amaral [op. cit.] claims there is no confirmation of Russév's political affiliation and that he left France only in 1944.
6 Maklouf Carvalho, op. cit.
7 Amaral, op. cit., p. 28.
8 Amaral, op. cit., p. 29.
9 The founder of Polop was Eric Sachs, an Austrian communist who had been active in the German Communist Party.
10 Amaral, op. cit., pp. 44–5.
11 Amaral, op. cit., p. 47; Maklouf Carvalho, op. cit.
12 Maklouf Carvalho, op. cit.
13 Paula Rousseff was born in March 1977.
14 Araújo was twice defeated in elections for mayor of Porto Alegre by PT leaders, first by the bank workers' organizer, Olívio Dutra, and then by Tarso Genro.
15 Maklouf Carvalho, op. cit.
16 Maklouf Carvalho, op. cit.
17 Luiz Inácio Lula da Silva, *A Verdade Vencerá* (São Paulo: Boi Tempo Editorial, 2018), p. 121.
18 Maklouf Carvalho, op. cit.; Rocha de Barros, op. cit., p. 392.
19 Two indigenous peoples – the Juruna (at Paquiçamba) and the Arara – live along the 'Big Bend', and a third – the Xikrin – on a nearby tributary, also depending on the fish and turtles in this stretch of the river. Four other dams were opened, two on the Madeiros River and two on the Tapajós. Opponents submitted twenty-two separate legal actions, with one already ruling in favour of an aggrieved indigenous group.
20 Tiffany Higgins, 'Belo Monte Boondoggle: Brazil's Biggest, Costliest Dam May Be Unviable', *Mongabay* (17 January 2020).
21 Eliane Brum, 'Brasil construtor de ruinas', *Arquipélago Editorial* (2019), p. 58.
22 For the background to this period see André Singer's *O lulismo em Crise: Um Quebra-Cabeça do Período Dilma (2011–16)* (São Paulo: Companhía das Letras, 2018), and Claudia Safatle, João Borges, et al., *Anatomia de um Desastre* (São Paulo: Companhía das Letras, 2016).
23 Rocha de Barros, op. cit., p. 428.

24 The government had initially introduced tax breaks with a precise aim: that of compensating for currency overvaluation. In 2012 officials extended them erratically to sectors such as construction that had not been directly affected by the strong *real*.
25 Rocha de Barros, op. cit., p. 428.
26 Rocha de Barros, op. cit., p. 417.

CHAPTER 13: THE FALL

1 Lula da Silva, op. cit., p. 46.
2 Interview with Marina Silva, in Rocha de Barros, op. cit., p. 406.
3 Quoted in André Singer, *O Lulismo em Crise* (São Paulo: Companhía das Letras, 2018), p. 28.
4 Singer, op. cit., p. 125.
5 Thomas Traumann, 'What Brazil's 2013 Protests Tell Us About Chile 2019', *Americas Quarterly* (27 October 2019).
6 Angela Alonso, *Treze: A Política da Rua de Lula e Dilma* (São Paulo: Companhía das Letras, 2023), p. 4.
7 Simon Romero and William Neuman, 'Sweeping Protests in Brazil Pull in an Array of Grievances', *The New York Times* (20 June 2013); https://www.nytimes.com/2013/06/21/world/americas/brazil-protests.html (accessed 15 July 2025).
8 See Ronald Inglehart, *The Silent Revolution: Changing Values and Political Styles Among Western Publics* (Princeton, NJ: Princeton University Press, 1977).
9 Traumann, op. cit.
10 Dilma Rousseff, interview with TV Globo (28 October 2014).
11 See Fernando Limongi, 'Operação Impeachment', *Todavía* (2023), pp. 49–50.
12 Limongi, op. cit., p. 50.
13 From a position in Furnas, an energy company, located in Minas Gerais.
14 Luciano da Ros and Matthew Taylor, *Brazilian Politics on Trial: Corruption and Reform Under Democracy* (Boulder, CO: Lynne Rienner, 2022), p. 117.
15 Limongi, op. cit., p. 92.
16 Limongi, op. cit., p. 101.
17 Rocha de Barros, op. cit., p. 484.
18 Author interview with José Eduardo Cardozo (30 March 2023).

19 Lula da Silva, op. cit., pp. 41–7 and 123–7.
20 Lula da Silva, op. cit., p. 150.
21 Author interview with Cardozo, op. cit.
22 Lula da Silva, op. cit., p. 150.
23 Lula da Silva, op. cit., p. 43.
24 Lula da Silva, op. cit., p. 44.
25 Lula da Silva, op. cit., p. 126.
26 Lapper, *Beef, Bible and Bullets*, pp. 99–100.

CHAPTER 14: THE FALL 2: LULA BITES THE DUST

1 Quoted in Fernando Morais, *Lula: Biografía*, vol. 1 (São Paulo: Companhía das Letras, 2021), pp. 71–3.
2 Morais, op. cit., p. 44.
3 Morais, op. cit., pp. 21–4.
4 Morais, op. cit., p. 73.
5 Under Brazilian law, they enjoyed a privileged forum, providing them with some protection.
6 Rocha de Barros, op. cit., pp. 475–8.
7 Rocha de Barros, op. cit., pp. 476–8.
8 Da Ros and Taylor, op. cit., pp. 147–52.
9 Anderson, op. cit., pp. 159–60.
10 Lula da Silva, op. cit., p. 83.
11 See Estelita Hass Carazzai and Felipe Bachtold, 'Lula é condenado a 9 anos e 6 meses de prisão por tríplex em Guarujá', *Folha de São Paulo* (12 July 2017), https://www1.folha.uol.com.br/poder/2017/07/1900580-lula-e-condenado-a-9-anos-por-corrupcao-no-triplex.shtml (accessed 3 September 2024); and Talita Bedinelli, Gil Alessi, and Heloísa Mendonça, 'Lula é condenado a 9 anos de prisão por Sérgio Moro em caso do tríplex', *El País* (12 July 2017), https://brasil.elpais.com/brasil/2017/07/12/politica/1499879326_453878.html#?rel=mas (accessed 3 September 2017).
12 Morais, op. cit., p. 111.
13 Lula da Silva, op. cit., p. 94.
14 Lula da Silva, op. cit., p. 201.
15 Lula da Silva, op. cit., pp. 144–6.
16 Buarque de Holanda explored how the hazy distinction between private and public interests had led Brazilian elites to treat the state as if it were private property, coining the term 'patrimonial-

ism'. The concept of the cordial man, introduced by Buarque de Holanda, helped clarify how informal, family-style relations permeated public life, contributing to some of the country's cultural charm while also hindering its development. For Souza, these concepts disguised the fundamental class and race inequalities rooted in the nineteenth-century experience of slavery. Formally, slavery may have been abolished long ago. However, the mass of the population were still stuck in an impoverished and desperate servitude, and the country's backward elites were determined to keep them there. The writers being attacked were no reactionaries: Furtado's economic analysis had influenced generations of left-wing thinkers. Buarque de Holanda had been an opponent of the military government, a founder of the Workers' Party, and his son Chico had become one of the country's most prominent progressive cultural icons, the singer and novelist (and PT member) Chico Buarque.

17 Pedro Vasconcellos, *Belo Monte: Canudos de Antônio Conselheiro a Lula da Silva* (Curitiba: Kotter Editorial, 2020), p. 247.
18 Rocha de Barros, op. cit., p. 490.
19 Luigi Mazza, 'Quero Ser Um Rebelde', *Piauí* (November 2022); https://piaui.folha.uol.com.br/genoino-lula-quer-harmonia-eu-quero-conflito (accessed 1 September 2024).
20 Rônei Rodrigues, Vitor Teixeira, Bira Evaristo, and Carolina Rieger, *Lula da Perseguição à Esperança Renovada: Uma História em Quadrinhos* (Brasilia: Partido dos Trabalhadores, 2022).
21 Lula da Silva, op. cit., p. 137.
22 Monica Bergamo and Florestan Fernandes, *Folha de São Paulo* and *El País* (17 April 2019); https://www1.folha.uol.com.br/poder/2019/04/lula-fala-sobre-prisao-moro-bolsonaro-e-stf-veja-versao-completa-de-entrevista.shtml (accessed 30 July 2025).
23 Da Ros and Taylor, op. cit., p. 151.
24 See Vladimir Netto, *The Mechanism* (Harmondsworth: Penguin, 2017), p. 37.
25 Alberto Almeida and Tiago Garrido, *A Mão e a Luva: O Que Elege um Presidente* (Editora Record, 2022), p. 19.
26 'Brazil Leaked Tape Forces Minister Romero Jucá Out', BBC (24 May 2016); https://www.bbc.co.uk/news/world-latin-america-36365781 (accessed 16 July 2025).

27 Diogo Magri, 'Livre da Lava Jato, Marconi Perillo pode tentar o quinto mandato em Goiás', *Veja* (17 May 2022); https://veja.abril.com.br/coluna/maquiavel/livre-da-lava-jato-marconi-perillo-pode-tentar-o-quinto-mandato-em-goias (accessed 7 September 2024).
28 Almeida and Garrido, op. cit., pp. 173–207.

CHAPTER 15: BOLSONARO

1 Author interview with Paulo Romes Junqueira, Uberlândia (3 July 2019).
2 Author interview with Fábio Pergher, Uberlândia (2 July 2019).
3 Quoted in Lapper, *Beef, Bible and Bullets*, p. 25.
4 Lapper, *Beef, Bible and Bullets*, p. 28.
5 Ibid.
6 Quoted in Bruno Paes Manso, 'A República das Milicias; dos Esquadróes da Morte à Era do Bolsonaro', *Todavía* (2000), loc. 249.
7 Author interview with Junqueira, op. cit.
8 Lapper, *Beef, Bible and Bullets*, p. 168.
9 Of 247 opinion polls listed in Wikipedia, Lula was ahead in all but 16.

CHAPTER 16: LULA 3

1 Tom Phillips and Andrew Downie, 'Jair Bolsonaro Supporters Storm Brazil's Presidential Palace and Supreme Court', *The Guardian* (8 January 2023).
2 João Fellet, 'A rotina do acampamento em SP onde bolsonaristas pedem intervenção militar', BBC Brasil (26 December 2022); https://www.bbc.com/portuguese/brasil-64042482 (accessed 1 July 2025).
3 Levy Teles and Marcelo Godoy, 'Extremistas Bolsonaristas articulavam invasão de sedes dos três poderes nas redes desde 3 de Janeiro', *O Estado de São Paulo* (8 January 2023); https://www.estadao.com.br/politica/extremistas-bolsonaristas-articulavam-invasao-de-sedes-dos-tres-poderes-nas-redes-desde-3-de-janeiro/?srsltid=AfmBOooHGh5M16j5VJCFFr42CYqTlqlmJFC-VicYntkl8jVx4oab32oaV (accessed 3 October 2025).

4 Breno Pires, 'O Golpista', *Piauí* (December 2024); https://piaui.folha.uol.com.br/materia/o-golpista-as-digitais-de-bolsonaro (accessed 16 July 2025).
5 João Ruela Ribeiro, 'Para Lula, insurreição pode ajudar a cimentar unidade política', *Público On Line* (9 January 2023).
6 Carolina Linhares, *UOL* (9 January 2023).
7 'Lula se reúne com Tarcísio de Freitas', *O Globo Tempo Real* (11 January 2023; accessed through Factiva, 23 June 2025).
8 Political reforms made it harder for parties to form coalitions and required parties to obtain a minimum number of votes to retain their registrations. Eleven smaller parties had disappeared as a result, with the number of parties represented falling to 19 in 2022.
9 For an excellent analysis of the term, see Timothy Power, 'Optimism, Pessimism, and Coalitional Presidentialism: Debating the Institutional Design of Brazilian Democracy', *Bulletin of Latin American Research* 29:1 (January 2010), pp. 18–33; https://www.jstor.org/stable/27805077 (accessed 18 November 2024).
10 Valmar Hupsel Filho and Laisa Dall'Agnol, 'Terreno Movediço', *Veja* (13 June 2024).
11 Filho and Dall'Agnol, op. cit.
12 At the end of 2022, the Supreme Court ruled on one category of these funds, a particularly opaque category that had been left in the hands of the so-called *rapporteurs*, deputies who coordinate the pieces of legislation, and it was known as the secret budget. But three other categories – those allocated by the elected congressional leadership to individual legislators, those channelled to deputies through the caucuses (*bancadas)* of their party, and those channelled through cross-party commissions formed to monitor policy areas – are still being paid.
13 In an academic study a political scientist from Bahia quizzed no fewer than 379 political scientists about which parties constituted the Centrão, and they found a range of opinion but generally agreed that four parties, the Progressive Party (PP), the Republicans, the Social Democratic Party and Podemos (We Can), were at the centre of things, but were often able to bring on board deputies from the PMDB, the Liberals, the UB (*União Brasil,* or Brazil Union), and the tiny Avante (Advance)

and the Democratic Renewal Party (*Partido Renovação Democrática* or PRD). The labels increasingly meant very little. What united the Centrão was self-interest, money for their party organizations and the districts that had elected them, jobs for their party colleagues and their families, and security for their future.
14 In 2025, Brazil's public sector was expected to absorb 47 per cent of output, compared to 27 per cent for Mexico, 32 per cent for South Africa, 35 per cent for Turkey, 34 per cent for China, and 37 per cent for Russia. The average for the 20 countries of the OECD was expected to be 42 per cent. Source: Statista.
15 See Richard Lapper, *Beef, Bible and Bullets*, p. 78.
16 Marco Aurélio de Carvalho quoted in Ana Clara Costa, 'Fernando Haddad, a Ascensão', *Piauí* (August 2023); https://piaui.folha.uol.com.br/materia/o-ministro (accessed 18 November 2024).
17 Costa, op. cit.
18 Thomas Traumann, 'Fernando Haddad: Still the Odd Man Out', *Americas Quarterly* (18 January 2024); https://www.americasquarterly.org/article/fernando-haddad-still-the-odd-man-out (accessed 16 November 2024).
19 Teo Cury, Carol Raciunas, and Marcelo Tuvuca, 'Ministro da Fazenda terá autonomia, mas terei inserção nas decisões econômicas, diz Lula', CNN Brasil (2 December 2022); https://www.cnnbrasil.com.br/politica/ministro-da-economia-tera-autonomia-mas-terei-insercao-nas-decisoes-economicas-diz-lula
20 This friction began to end in 2025 when Campos Neto stepped down. His replacement, Gabriel Galípolo, was a private-sector banker who agreed with the current policy but was also a PT supporter and was close to both Lula and Haddad.
21 Traumann, op. cit.
22 Costa, op. cit.
23 'Can Lula Fix Brazil's Fiscal Mess', *The Economist* (29 January 2024); https://www.economist.com/the-americas/2024/01/29/can-lula-fix-brazils-fiscal-mess (accessed 18 November 2024).
24 *The Economist*, op. cit.

CHAPTER 17: 'WELCOME TO THE SACRED LAND OF THE WORKING CLASS'

1. When the Brazilian statistical institute first published figures in 2012, 16 per cent of the labour force were union members. By 2023, that had dropped to 8.4 per cent, with the biggest unions mainly in the public sector, among teachers or the state-owned banking groups.
2. 'Teletrabalho e trabalho por meio de plataformas digitais', Investigacoes Experimentais, Pesquisa Nacional por Amostra de Domicílios Contínua, Instituto Brasileiro de Geographia e Estatistica (2023); https://biblioteca.ibge.gov.br/visualizacao/livros/liv102035 informativo.pdf (accessed 30 October 2024).
3. See Marlene Bergamos, 'Sindicatos temem perda de até R$ 3 bilhões com fim de imposto', *Folha de São Paulo* (15 October 2017); https://www1.folha.uol.com.br/mercado/2017/10/1927150-sindicatos-temem-perda-de-ate-r-3-bilhoes-com-fim-de-imposto.shtml (accessed 21 October 2024). Under the rule, which had been in place since the 1940s, workers had been obliged to direct one day's wages each year toward the unions.
4. Juliano Spyer, *O Povo de Deus: quem são os evangélicos e por que eles importam* (São Paulo: Geração Editorial, 2020), p. 24.
5. 'Teletrabalho e trabalho por meio de plataformas digitais 2022', op. cit.
6. Wesley Gonsalves, 'Brasil tem 1,66 milhão de pessoas trabalhando como motoristas de aplicativos ou entregadores', *O Estado de São Paulo* (11 April 2023); https://www.estadao.com.br/economia/trabalhador-de-aplicativo-tem-mais-de-30-anos-e-pardo-ou-negro-e-pertence-a-classe-c-aponta (accessed 30 October 2024). Sidnei Machado and Alexandre Pilan Zanoni, *O Trabalho Controlado por Plataformas Digitais: dimensões, perfis e direitos* (Clínica Direito do Trabalho, Universidad Federal do Paraná, 2021).
7. Maeli Prado, 'Rejeição à CLT impulsiona apagão de mão de obra na indústria', *Folha de São Paulo* (22 June 2025); https://www1.folha.uol.com.br/mercado/2025/06/rejeicao-a-clt-impulsiona-apagao-de-mao-de-obra-na-industria.shtml (accessed 2 July 2025).
8. Author interview with Daiane Batista Vieira (13 July 2023).
9. Mariana Mazzucato, 'Innovation-Driven Inclusive and Sustainable Growth: Challenges and Opportunities for Brazil', published

NOTES 339

        by the UCL Institute for Innovation and Public Purpose, policy report no. 2023/06.
10. Author interview Moises Selerges, op. cit.
11. Pedro Cavalcanti and Renato Fragelli, 'A velha nova política industrial', *Valor Econômico* (25 January 2024); https://valor.globo.com/opiniao/coluna/a-velha-nova-politica-industrial.ghtml (accessed 1 November 2024). Paulo Kliass, 'Política industrial: heresia ou solução?', *Correio do Brasil* (25 January 2024); https://www.correiodobrasil.com.br/a/politica-industrial-heresia-solucao (accessed 1 November 2024).
12. Fernanda Canofre, 'Trabalho por app pode estar empurrando pessoas para a direita, diz antropóloga', *Folha de São Paulo* (21 March 2022); https://www1.folha.uol.com.br/mercado/2022/03/trabalho-por-app-pode-estar-empurrando-pessoas-para-a-direita-diz-antropologa.shtml (accessed 17 July 2025).
13. Lívia Azevedo, 'Motoristas de aplicativos: sem acordo com governo sobre projeto de regulamentação, categoria mantém protestos', *Brasil 61* (28 March 2024); https://brasil61.com/n/motoristas-de-aplicativos-sem-acordo-com-governo-sobre-projeto-de-regulamentacao-categoria-mantem-protestos-bras2411360 (accessed 17 July 2025).
14. Author interview with Renan Bernardi (24 October 2024).
15. Canofre, op. cit.
16. Author interview with Raimundão Mendes, Chico Mendes Extractive Reserve (21 November 2023).
17. The tappers enjoy a legal right to work plots of trees, and under the terms of the legal agreement by which the reserve was set up, they can farm up to 10 per cent as pasture.
18. Mendes, op. cit.
19. Ibid.
20. Detailed research based on police figures and published in 2022 by the Igarapé Institute, a Rio de Janeiro-based NGO, showed a growing relationship between trade in illegal drugs, which had brought organized crime to the region, and environmental crimes. See Laura Trajber Waisbich, Melina Risso, Terine Husek, and Lycia Brasil, 'Illicit Rainforest Economies in Brazil', Igarapé Institute (April 2022); https://igarape.org.br/wp-content/uploads/2022/04/The-ecosystem-of-environmental-crime-in-the-Amazon.pdf (accessed 21 November 2024). I had been made painfully aware

of this in June 2022 when a close friend and colleague, Dom Phillips, who was writing a book on the Amazon, had stumbled upon gang involvement in the illegal trade of a protected fish in a remote corner of Amazonas state and was shot down in cold blood. Dom had been working on a story with Bruno Pereira, a former official of Funai, Brazil's indigenous affairs agency, in the Javari Valley in Amazonas state. Pereira was also killed. The valley is home to several indigenous groups, including the Kanamari, Kulina, Korubo, Marubo, Matis, Mayoruna, and Tsohom-dyapa. Phillips's book, *How to Save the Amazon: A Journalist's Deadly Quest for Answers*, completed with the assistance of colleagues, was published by Ithaka in June 2025. Both Red Command and its main Brazilian rival, Primeiro Comando da Capital (PCC) – as we saw in Chapter 15 – evolved in Brazil's chaotically organized prison system in the 1980s and 1990s. By the mid-2010s, however, their business had grown, and they were starting to operate along with local affiliates in the Amazon.

21 Author interview with Angela Mendes, Rio Branco (16 November 2023).
22 Jeffrey Hoelle, *Rainforest Cowboys: The Rise of Ranching and Cattle Culture in Western Amazonia* (Austin, TX: University of Texas Press, 2015).
23 Hoelle, op. cit., p. 4.
24 There are five extractive reserves in Acre, but the Chico Mendes and Cazumbá-Iracema reserves are among the biggest in the country, between them accounting for more than 10 per cent of the total land area given over to this class of reserve. Most reserves have been set up by the federal government, but states created 26, the bulk of these being relatively small areas set aside in the mid-1990s in the state of Rondônia.
25 Author interview with Nelson Euclides (22 November 2023).
26 Author interview with Toinho Alves (20 November 2023).
27 Hoelle, op. cit., p. 1.
28 Alves, op. cit.
29 Author interviews with Lucas Ribeiro and Isabela Gomes, Waycarbon, Rio Branco (17 and 24 November 2024).
30 Alves, op. cit.

CHAPTER 18: THE SEDUCTIONS OF CELEBRITY

1 Salma El Wardany, Oliver Crook, and Laura Millan, 'Lula's Pledge to Save Amazon Wins Hero's Welcome at COP27', *Bloomberg* (16 November 2022); 'Lula Says "Brazil is Back" as he Vows to Reverse Amazon Deforestation – as it Happened', Live Blog, *The Guardian* (16 November 2022); https://www.bloomberg.com/news/articles/2022-11-16/brazil-s-lula-offers-to-host-cop30-stresses-amazon-s-importancehttps://www.theguardian.com/environment/live/2022/nov/16/cop27-paris-agreement-deal-nature-biodiversity-brazil-lula-live?page=with%3Ablock-6374be6e8f08341844537004&filterKeyEvents=false#liveblog-navigation (accessed 17 July 2025).

2 'Brazil's Lula Vows to Halt Rampant Deforestation', *Al Jazeera* (16 November 2022); https://www.aljazeera.com/news/2022/11/16/at-cop27-brazils-lula-vows-halt-to-rampant-deforestation#:~:text=On%20Tuesday%2C%20Lula%20met%20with,front%20of%20Lula%20remains%20massive (accessed 17 July 2025).

3 Elio Gaspari, 'Lula nos dias de encantamento', *Folha de São Paulo* (15 November 2022); https://www1.folha.uol.com.br/colunas/eliogaspari/2022/11/lula-nos-dias-de-encantamento.shtml (accessed 3 October 2025).

4 Matias Spektor, 'What Happened to Lula?', *Foreign Affairs* (28 February 2024); https://www.foreignaffairs.com/brazil/what-happened-lula Stuenkel (accessed 3 October 2025).

5 Ciara Nugent, 'Lula talks to *Time* about Ukraine, Bolsonaro, and Brazil's Fragile Democracy', *Time Magazine* (4 May 2022); https://time.com/6173232/lula-da-silva-transcript (accessed 1 July 2025).

6 On 18 February at a meeting of the African Union, Lula said, 'What is happening in Gaza and to the Palestinian people has not existed at any other time in history', adding 'actually, it has existed: when Hitler decided to kill the Jews.'

7 https://www.bbc.co.uk/news/world-latin-america-68332821 (accessed 30 July 2025); James Gregory, 'Israel Condemns Brazil's Lula Likening Gaza War to Holocaust', BBC News (19 February 2024); see https://www.bbc.co.uk/news/world-latin-america-68332821 (both accessed 3 October 2025).

8 Brian Winter, 'Is Lula Anti-American?', *Americas Quarterly* (23 July 2024); https://americasquarterly.org/article/is-lula-anti-american (accessed 3 October 2025).

9 'Jornal francês chama Lula de "decepção" e "falso amigo do Ocidente"', CNN Brasil (23 June 2023); https://www.cnnbrasil.com.br/internacional/jornal-frances-chama-lula-de-decepcao-e-falso-amigo-do-ocidente (accessed 3 October 2025).

10 Andrés Velasco, 'Lula's Dance with Dictators', *Project Syndicate* (1 August 2023); https://www.project-syndicate.org/commentary/why-lula-consorting-with-putin-and-maduro-by-andres-velasco-2023-08 (accessed 12 November 2024).

11 Ricardo Kotscho, 'Para evitar novos ruídos, foco da política externa deveria ser a Amazônia', *UOL Opinião* (31 May 2023); https://noticias.uol.com.br/colunas/balaio-do-kotscho/2023/05/30/para-evitar-novos-ruidos-foco-da-politica-externa-deveria-ser-a-amazonia.htm (accessed 12 November 2024).

12 Giuliano Guandalini, 'Que diabos Lula está fazendo?' O Brasil e a diplomacia da corda esticada', *Brazil Journal* (24 February 2024); https://braziljournal.com/que-diabos-lula-esta-fazendo-o-brasil-e-a-diplomacia-da-corda-esticada (accessed 12 November 2024).

13 Jim O'Neill, 'Building Better Global Economic BRICs', *Goldman Sachs Research* (30 November 2001); https://www.goldmansachs.com/insights/goldman-sachs-research/building-better (accessed 29 September 2025).

14 China's population increased from 981.2 million in 1980 to 1,411 million in 2023, with the rate of urbanization rising from 18.39 per cent to 66.16 per cent over this same period; https://www.statista.com/statistics/270162/urbanization-in-china (accessed 12 November 2024).

15 A Conversation with Celso Amorim, Carnegie Endowment for International Peace (18 July 2024); https://carnegieendowment.org/people/celso-amorim-2024/?lang=en (accessed 29 September 2025).

16 Elizabeth Economy, 'The Chinese Model: Unexceptional Exceptionalism', The Hoover Institution (2020); https://www.hoover.org/sites/default/files/research/docs/prosperityproject economy.pdf (accessed 1 July 2025).

17 Elizabeth Economy, 'China's Assertive Authoritarianism', *Democracy: A Journal of Ideas*, Special Issue (2021); https://democracyjournal.org/author/elizabeth-economy (accessed 6 November 2024). The

same writer added, 'in the mid-1980s, and then again beginning in the mid-1990s through the 2000s, such a transition appeared to be underway. There were experiments with grassroots democratic elections, the development of an activist Chinese civil society that protested for change around issues such as environmental protection, and a small but robust group of intellectuals who called for democratic transition.'

18 In the US-based non-profit Freedom House, India was downgraded from a free democracy to a 'partially free democracy'; the Sweden-based V-Dem Institute said India had become an 'electoral autocracy'; and the Economist Intelligence Unit described India as a 'flawed democracy'; https://www.intelligencesquared.com/events/narendra-modi-is-the-biggest-threat-to-indias-democracy-since-independence-online (accessed 22 October 2024).

19 Kathryn Stoner, 'The Putin Myth', *Journal of Democracy* 34:2 (April 2023); https://www.journalofdemocracy.org/authors/kathryn-stoner (accessed 5 November 2024).

20 Oliver Stuenkel, 'Brazil's BRICS Balancing Act Is Getting Harder', *Americas Quarterly* (21 October 2024); https://www.americasquarterly.org/article/brazils-brics-balancing-act-is-getting-harder (accessed 3 July 2025).

21 Noah Smith, 'How Maduro and Chávez Wrecked Venezuela's Economy', Noah Opinion Substack Blog (1 August 2024); https://www.noahpinion.blog/p/how-maduro-and-chavez-wrecked-venezuelas (accessed 3 October 2025).

22 Quoted in Smith, op. cit.

23 Quoted in Julie Turkewitz, 'What Happened to Venezuela's Democracy?', *The New York Times* (30 July 2024); https://www.nytimes.com/2024/07/30/world/americas/venezuela-election-maduro-chavez.html?searchResultPosition=1 (accessed 14 November 2024).

24 Igor Gielow, 'Datafolha: Economia, política externa e imagem pessoal prejudicam Lula', *Folha de São Paulo* (22 March 2024); https://www1.folha.uol.com.br/poder/2024/03/datafolha-economia-politica-externa-e-imagem-pessoal-prejudicam-lula.shtml; 'Pesquisa Genial/Quaest: para eleitores de Lula, presidente se dedica 'mais do que devia' à agenda internacional', *O Globo* (25 October 2023); https://oglobo.globo.com/blogs/pulso/post/2023/10/pesquisa-quaest-para-eleitores-de-lula-presiden-

te-se-dedica-mais-do-que-devia-a-agenda-internacional.ghtml; Paulo Freitas, 'Pesquisa mostra que 71% dos brasileiros querem que Lula defenda democracia da Venezuela', *Veja* (29 August 2024); https://veja.abril.com.br/mundo/pesquisa-mostra-que-71-dos-brasileiros-querem-que-lula-defenda-democracia-da-venezuela (all accessed 15 November 2024).

25 'O PT saúda o povo venezuelano pelo processo eleitoral ocorrido no domingo, dia 28 de julho de 2024, em uma jornada pacífica, democrática e soberana'; https://pt.org.br/nota-da-executiva-nacional-do-pt-sobre-eleicoes-na-venezuela (accessed 1 August 2024).

26 Tom Phillips, 'Lula Criticises Maduro's "authoritarian" Regime amid Venezuela Election Dispute', *The Guardian* (15 August 2024); https://www.theguardian.com/world/article/2024/aug/16/lula-criticizes-maduro (accessed 3 October 2025).

27 'Lula diz que Maduro é "problema" da Venezuela, não do Brasil', *Agência Globo* (11 November 2024).

CONCLUSION

1 In 2004 the party had won nine of Brazil's 27 state capitals (and 409 of its 5,500 mayors). As late as 2012, with Lula's designated successor Dilma Rousseff in office, it held 637 town halls, including four state capitals.

2 Ana Clara Costa, 'Foro de Teresina', podcast of *Piauí* (11 October 2024).

3 Marçal had been beaten into third place by Boulos and the eventual winner, Ricardo Nunes, with the centre-rightist winning the run-off.

4 In 2024, Frei Chico had become vice-president of the Sindicato Nacional dos Aposentados, Pensionistas e Idosos da Força Sindical (Sindnapi), one of the organizations involved.

5 See the interview with the Brazilian rapper Mano Brown, Mano a Mano Podcast (19 June 2025).

6 In July 2025, Congress approved legislation that would, if eventually implemented, significantly relax environmental controls. One activist described it as the biggest setback for environmentalism in Brazil for 40 years.

7 IBGE, Desigualdade cai ao menor nível desde 2012, indica IBGE (8 May 2025); https://agenciagov.ebc.com.br/noticias/202505/

desigualdade-cai-ao-menor-nivel-desde-2012-indica-ibge (accessed 3 October 2025).
8 Idiana Tomazelli, 'Brasil sai do Mapa da Fome após queda na população em risco de subnutrição', *Folha de São Paulo* (28 July 2025); https://www1.folha.uol.com.br/mercado/2025/07/brasil-sai-do-mapa-da-fome-apos-queda-na-populacao-em-risco-de-subnutricao.shtml (accessed 29 July 2025). Brazil had first left the map in 2014 but was back on it by 2022, after the pandemic and the dismantling of some food security programmes.
9 As Lula told the rapper Mano Brown in a recent podcast. 'Since I was a trade unionist, I was never one of those "everything or nothing" guys. If you ask for everything, the chances are you'll get nothing. I used to demand what it was possible to win in accordance with the forces at our disposal and we won a lot.'

Index

ABC da Greve (film) 85
Action (magazine) 58
Alckmin, Geraldo 3, 159, 228–9, 234–5, 258, 259, 284
Alegretti, Mary Helena 176
Alencar, José 141, 150, 154
Alexander VI, Pope 21
Alfonsín, Raúl 135
Aliança Renovadora Nacional 68
Allende, Isabel 108
Allende, Salvador 8, 85
Almeida, Alberto 231
Alternative in Eastern Europe, The (Bahro) 67
Alves, Damares 241
Alves, Henrique 230
Alves, João Lucas 186
Alves, Toinho 279, 280, 281
Amaral, Nazareth 143
Amaral, Ricardo 184, 186
Amorim, Celso 285, 290, 296, 306
Anderson, Jon Lee 48
Anderson, Perry 161, 162
Ant, Clara 193
Appy, Bernando 147
Araújo, Carlos 187, 188–9
Araújo, Ernesto 241
Argentina 88, 120, 122, 134–8, 288
Arida, Pérsio 259

Arrães, Miguel 58
Atatürk, Kemal 35
Azeredo, Eduardo 230

Bacha, Edmar 116
Bachelet, Michelle 109, 286
Bahro, Rudolf 67
Balaam's Donkey: An Experience of a Brazilian Favela (Kunz and Bouchard) 92
Balzac, Honoré de 184
Banco do Brasil 126, 138, 162
Bannon, Steve 239
Baran, Paul 107, 108
Barbosa, Nelson 208
Bardella, Cláudio 86
Barelli, Walter 72, 81
Bastide, Roger 24, 25
Batista, Fulgencio 45, 55
Beauvoir, Simone de 58
Belchior, Miriam 190
Belo Monte dam 191–2
Benário, Olga 49
Bernardi, Renan 273
Bethell, Leslie 69, 163
Bezerra, Gregorio 222
Biden, Joe 283, 284
Blair, Tony 112
Bolivia 125, 224, 288

INDEX

Bolsonaro, Carlos 242, 246
Bolsonaro, Eduardo 242, 303
Bolsonaro, Flávio 242–3
Bolsonaro, Jair
  in 2018 presidential election
    1, 233–5, 240–1
  loses 2022 presidential election 1
  during COVID pandemic 2–3,
    243–4
  in prison 6
  as political outsider 235–7
  as president 241–6
  and protests after 2022 elections 250
Bom, Djalma 85
Bouchard, Joseph 92
Boulos, Guilherme 214
Boulos, Guillermo 300
Brasilia 38, 247–8
Brazil
  growth in conservatism in 4–6,
    237–40
  millenarianism in 7–8, 25–8
  as Portuguese colony 21–7
  from early to mid–twentieth century
    34–8
  coup in 1964 43–4, 49, 51, 52,
    57, 62
  in Cold War period 46–7, 48–59
  radical politics in 48–59
  during 1973 oil crisis 70, 72–3
  reactions to Scania strike 80–1
  and 1998 constitution 110–11
  hyperinflation in 112–14
  under Fernando Collor de Mello
    114–15, 120, 122
  Plano Real in 115–18, 120, 121,
    122, 129, 134, 194, 198, 307
  under Fernando Cardoso 120–1,
    122, 123–31
  Lula's first term as president 149,
    150–7
  Lula's second term as president
    160–3

development of Amazon in 1970s
    170–1
  under Dilma Rousseff 193–211
  judicial reform in 226–8
  under Jair Bolsonaro 241–6
  protests after 2022 elections 247–53
  changes in patterns of employment
    265–71
  Lula's third term as president
    250–61, 271–4, 283–97, 299–304
Brazil: The People and the Power
  (Arrães) 58
Brazilian Communist Party (*Partido
  Comunista Brasileiro*/*PCB*)
  crackdown of under Vargas 35
  under Luís Carlos Prestes 48–9, 59
  and 1964 coup 49, 52
  support for Lula's trade union
    election campaign 66–7
  military crackdown on 68–9
  in 1974 elections 69
  and Fernando Cardoso 105–6
Brazilian Democratic Movement
  (*Movimento Democrático Brasileiro*/
  MDB) 66, 67, 68, 69, 87, 97, 103,
  206, 229–31
Brazilian Democratic Movement
  Party (*Partido do Movimento
  Democrático Brasileiro*/*PMDB*)
  97, 111, 120, 141, 153, 158–9,
  206–7, 229, 254
Brazilian Labour Party (*Partido
  Trabalhista Brasileiro*/*PTB*) 46, 90,
  104, 120, 153–4, 203
Brazilian Social Democracy Party
  (*Partido da Social Democracia
  Brasileira*/*PSDB*) 103–4, 112, 139,
  140, 153, 197, 205, 225, 229–31,
  254, 255
Brecht, Bertolt 174
BRICS 288–9, 290, 292, 293, 296,
  2997
Brizola, Leonel 51, 56–7, 87, 88, 90

Buarque, Chico 83
Bush, George W. 225, 294

Caetano, Manoel 220
Caixa Econômica 126, 162, 208
Caldera, Rafael 126
Calheiros, Renan 206
Cambão – The Yoke (Julião) 58
Cameli, Gladson 278, 281
Campello, Tereza 190
Campos, Eduardo 198
Caparrós, Martín 222
Capitalism and Underdevelopment in Latin America (Gunder Frank) 108
Cardenal, Ernesto 96
Cárdenas, Cuautémoc 220
Cardoso, Augusto Inácio do Espírito Santo 104
Cardoso, Fernando Henrique 9, 10
  supports Lula in 2022 presidential election 3
  pragmatism of 10
  relationship with Lula 103–4, 112, 118, 147–8
  early life and career 105–9
  changing political views 109–12
  financial reforms as Finance Minister 115–18
  as president of Brazil 120–1, 122, 123–31
  in 2002 presidential election 147, 148
  and Dilma Rousseff 189
Cardoso, Joaquim Inácio Batista 104, 105
Cardoso, Leônidas 104, 105
Cardoso, Lucilene 131
Cardozo, José Eduardo 20, 208
Carlos, Roberto 41
Carter, Jimmy 81, 95
Carvalho, Fátima 9
Carvalho, Gilberto
  suspicions of Lula 67
  and formation of Worker's Party 89, 90, 91–3, 94, 95, 96
  and *Mensalão* corruption scandal 156
  on Lula's Amazon policies 180
  and Dilma Rousseff 190, 201
Carvalho, Maklouf 187, 188, 190, 193
Casaldáliga, Pedro 92
Castro, Celso 69
Castro, Fidel 8, 46, 51, 52, 55, 86
Cavalcanti, Pedro 272
Cavallo, Domingo 135–6, 137
Centrão (The Big Centre) 244–5, 255, 256
César, Camargo 177
Ceschiatti, Alfredo 247
Chão da Fábrica (film) 85
Chávez, Hugo 119–20, 126, 149–50, 224, 288, 293–4
Chile 8, 9, 120, 122, 288
China 288–91, 292, 293
Chomsky, Noam 220
Churchill, Winston 3
Cícero, Father 7, 26, 27
Clemente, Telma 1–2
Clinton, Bill 112
Coelho, Paulo 142
Collor, Pedro 115
Collor de Mello, Fernando 102, 112, 114–15, 120, 122, 154, 155, 254
Columbia 248
Communist Party of Brazil (*Partido Comunista do Brasil/PCB*) 51, 54, 57, 92, 174
Conniff, Ray 41
Conselheiro, Antônio 7, 26–7, 223–4
Convergência Socialista (Socialist Convergence) 90
Costa, Ana Clara 258
Costa, David Sebastião 158
Costa, Rui 260
Coutinho, Eduardo 85

INDEX

COVID pandemic 2–3, 6, 243–4, 269–70
Cowell, Simon 176
Craxi, Bettino 227
Cruz, Carlos Alberto Santos 242
Cuba 45–6, 47, 48, 51–2, 54–5
Cunha, Eduardo 206–7, 208, 209, 230, 256

Da Cunha, Euclides 24, 25, 27–8
Da Rocha, Luiz Carlos 220
Da Silva, Aristides 17, 18–19, 20, 28, 29–31, 32
Da Silva, Erudinha 100
Da Silva, Jaime 18, 20, 28
Da Silva, José Ferreira (Frei Chico)
  childhood of 18, 20–1, 30, 31, 32
  in Brazilian Communist Party 59, 61
  part in Lula's trade union activity 61–2, 63, 65, 66, 67
  kidnap and torture of 68–71
  in corruption scandal 301–2
Da Silva, José Inácio (Zé Cuía) 18, 20
Da Silva, Maria Baixinha 18, 33
Da Silva, Marinete 18, 20, 39
Da Silva, Roseangela (Janja) 222, 283, 303
Da Silva, Tiana (Ruth) 18, 28
Da Silva, Vavá 16, 18, 19, 20, 21, 28, 31, 32, 221
Dallagnol, Deltan 217–18, 227
Daniel, Celso 139, 144, 155, 156–7
Dantas, Wanderley 172
Darien scheme 8
De Aguilar, Otávio Medeiros 81
De Barros, Celso Rocha 91, 98, 99, 101, 102, 104, 140, 144, 154, 156, 157, 191, 194–5, 196, 198, 208, 217, 224
De Beauvoir, Simone 106
De Freitas, Tarcísio 252–3
De la Rúa, Fernando 136, 137

349

De Lozada, Gonzalo Sánchez 120
De Melo, Sérgio 20
De Melo, Otília Ferreira 17
De Né, Jorge 16
De Né, Zé 16
De Oliveira, Adélio Bispo 241
De Onis, Juan 87
De Queiroz, Maria Isaura Pereira 25
De Rosário, Maria 236
De Souza, Joaquím Lima 85, 273
Death in Brazil (Robb) 102
Debray, Régis 58, 186
Delfim Netto, Antônio 72, 73
Demaria, Emilio Bonfante 67
Democratic Labour Party (*Partido Democrático Trabalhista/PDT*) 188–9
Dependency and Development in Latin America (Cardoso and Faletto) 109
Di Cavalcanti, Emiliano 247
Dieese 72, 81
Dirceu, José
  resistance to 1964 coup 44, 57
  on Cuban revolution 47
  in Brazilian Communist Party 49
  at university 50
  and initial troubles in Worker's Party 99–100
  changes in the Worker's Party 140–1, 144, 145, 146
  and *Mensalão* corruption scandal 153, 154, 155, 190, 205
Direct Elections Now Movement (*Diretas Já*) 103
Dom Pedro II, King 104
Dominican Republic 45
Dona Lindu (Eurídice Ferreira de Melo) 15, 17–20, 29, 30–1, 32–3, 39–40, 62
Dos Santos, Jacinto Ribeiros (Lambari) 41
Dos Santos, Silvestre José 25
Dos Santos, Valdir 80

Dostoyevsky, Fyodor 184
Duhalde, Eduardo 138, 220

Ebrick, Charles 57
Ecuador 224, 288
Egydio, Paulo 67
Eisenhower, Dwight D. 45
Erundina, Luiza 155
Estenssoro, Victor Paz 125
Euclides, Nelson 279
Everisto Arms, Paulo 84

Fachin, Edmar 245
Falcone, Giovanni 227
Faletto, Enzo 109
Ferrador, João 73, 79
Ferreira, João 25–6
Financial Times, The 9–10, 119, 120, 124, 126
Florestania 278–81
Fontenele, Maria Luiza 98
For the Liberation of Brazil (Marighella) 58
Foster, Graça 190, 195–6
Fraga, Armínio 124, 127–8, 134, 145, 146, 147, 150
Fragelli, Renato 272
Franco, Gustavo 123, 124
Franco, Itamar 115, 116, 127
Franco, Moreira 230
Free Pass Movement 199–200, 201
Frei Chico *see* Da Silva, José
Freire, Paulo 46, 94–5, 96
Freyre, Gilberto 36
Frota, Silvio 69
Furtado, Celso 23

Gabeira, Fernando 49–50, 57
Gabrielli, Sergio 195
Galeano, Eduardo 108
Galeno, Claudio 185, 186–7
Gandhi, Indira 3
Garotinho, Anthony 147, 206

Garrido, Tiago 231
Gaspari, Elio 47, 52, 58, 68, 82, 84, 86–7
Geisel, Ernesto 68–9, 80
Genoino, José 54, 99, 140, 145, 146, 154, 225
Geraldo, Zé 192
Germinal (Zola) 184
Getúlio Vargas Foundation 73, 157–8, 292
Globe and Mail 87
Godard, Jean-Luc 58
Gomes, Ciro 147
Gomes, Isabel 281
Gomes, Laurentino 223
Gonçalves, Ana Maria 223
Gonçalves Jr, Paulo Rocha (Paulão) 220
Gonzalez, Edmundo 295–6
Gordon, Lincoln 47
Gorostiaga, Xavier 96
Goulart, João 43, 44, 46–7, 106
Gramacho, Moema 301
Gramsci, Antonio 94, 101
Grande, João 17, 19
Grechi, Dom Moacyr 172
Green Party (*Partido Verde/PV*) 198
Greenhalgh, Luiz Eduardo 155, 214
Gross, Tony 176
Guaidó, Juan 295
Guatemala 45, 248
Guatemala – Another Vietnam (Melville & Melville) 58
Guerrilla Warfare (Guevara) 58
Guevara, Che 8, 45, 51, 54–5, 58, 186
Gunder Frank, André 107–8
Gurría, José Ángel 123
Gushiken, Luiz 146, 154

Haddad, Fernando 10, 213, 240, 257–61, 272, 309
Heleno, Augusto 241

INDEX

Henfrey, Colin 8–9
Herzog, Vladimir 69
Hirszman, Leo 85
Hitler, Adolf 35
Hoelle, Jeffrey 276, 277, 279
Hoffmann, Gleisi 195, 213, 260
Holland, Marcio 194–5
Homeless Movement 214
Hotimsky, Marcelo 201
Hoxha, Enver 54
Human Comedy, The (Balzac) 184
Hummes, Cláudio 84
Hunter, Wendy 162

IBAMA 236–7, 257, 284, 285
Indústrias Villares 40, 63
Inglehart, Ronald 201
Institutional Investor (magazine) 130
Intercept, The (magazine) 236
Intergovernmental Panel on Climate Change (IPCC) 179
International Monetary Fund (IMF) 116, 130, 143, 147, 152
Israel/Gaza conflict 285–6, 287
Isto É (newspaper) 88

Jefferson, Roberto 153–4
Jobim, Nelson 195
John III, King 21
John XXIII, Pope 50
Johnson, Lyndon B. 47
Jornal do Brasil (newspaper) 49
Jucá, Romero 229, 230
Julião, Francisco 58
Junqueira, Paulo Romes 233, 236–7

Kennedy, John F. 45, 46, 48, 169
Kerry, John 283
Kertész, Mário 142
Khrushchev, Nikita 46, 47–8
Kirchner, Cristina 6, 288
Klein, Alcides 80
Kotscho, Ricardo 86, 286

Kubitschek, Juscelino 36, 37–8, 46, 112–13
Kumm, Björn 87
Kunz, Fredy 92

Lagos, Ricardo 288
Lamarca, Carlos 53, 188
Landless Workers' Movement (*Movimento dos Trabalhadores Rurais Sem Terra*/MST) 149
Latin America
  rise of conservatism in 6
  Utopian thought in 7–8
  Cold War period 44–6
  guerilla insurgencies in 51
  and developmental theory 107–9
  market reforms in 119–20, 122
  1997/98 financial crisis in 123
Latin American Newsletter 9, 88, 96
Latin America: Underdevelopment or Revolution (Gunder Frank) 108
Lava Jato scandal 154, 163, 196, 202, 203–4, 207, 208, 211, 213–19, 221, 223, 225–31, 253–4, 258, 304
Lavrov, Sergey 285, 289
Leme, Paulo 126
Lenin, Vladimir 174
Les Temps Modernes (magazine) 58
Letícia, Marisa 75, 97, 143, 218, 222
'Letter to the Brazilian People, A' 145–6
Levitsky, Steve 296
Levy, Joaquim 147, 202, 211
Libânio Christo, Carlos Alberto (Frei Betto) 92
Liberal Front Party (*Partido da Frente Liberal*/PFL) 141, 158–9, 254
Liberal Party (*Partido Liberal*/PL) 141
Libération (newspaper) 286
liberation theology 50–1, 91
Limongi, Fernando 204
Lira, Arthur 245
Lisboa, Marcos 147

Llosa, Mario Vargas 9
Lopes, Francisco 124, 128
Lopes, Mauro 224
Lourdes Ribeiro, Maria de 41, 62, 65, 77
Luís, Washington 34–5
Lula
  in 2022 presidential election 1–2, 3
  political odyssey of 2–3
  in office after 2022 4–6
  childhood of 15–21, 28, 29–34
  early working life 32–4, 38–40
  marriage to Maria de Lourdes Ribeiro 41, 62, 65
  view of 1964 coup 43–4, 62
  early trade union activity 61–8, 71
  and kidnap of Frei Chico 70–1
  role in 1979 strikes 75–88
  marriage to Marisa Letícia 75
  media attention on 84–8
  and formation of Worker's Party 87, 89–91
  in 1982 local elections 98
  initial troubles in Worker's Party 99, 100
  in 1989 presidential election 102, 112
  relationship with Fernando Cardoso 103–4, 112, 118, 147–8
  and Franco presidency 116
  in 1998 presidential election 120
  on appointment of Armínio Fraga 127–8
  shift in strategy and style 138–47
  in 2002 presidential election 134, 147
  first term as president 149, 150–7
  and *Mensalão* corruption scandal 157–8
  in 2006 presidential election 157–60
  second term as president 160–3, 179–80
  and Marina Silva 175–6, 179–80
  and Dilma Rousseff 181, 189, 190–1, 197, 209, 210
  and Lava Jato scandal 203, 213–19
  corruption charge against 213–19
  in prison 219–24, 225–6
  relationship with Roseangela da Silva 222, 283, 303
  popularity of whilst in prison 228–9
  and 2018 presidential election 240
  and protests after 2022 elections 250–3
  and Fernando Haddad 257–61
  third term as president 250–61, 271–4, 283–97, 299–304
  and Moises Selerges 264–5
  health concerns 303–4
  assessment of political career 304–9
Lunus scandal 133–4
Luxemburg, Rosa 108–9

Maduro, Nicolás 285, 286, 293, 294, 295, 297
Magalhães, Antônio Carlos 127, 142, 143, 158–9
Maia, Rodrigo 241–2
Malan, Pedro 127, 128, 129, 145, 147
Maluf, Paulo 142
Mandetta, Luiz Henrique 243, 244
Mann, Thomas 46
Mantega, Guido 128, 145, 147, 194, 202, 210–11, 217
Mao Zedong 48
Maradona, Diego 264
Marçal, Pablo 300
Marcílio, Benedito 90
Marighella, Carlos 51, 58
Marinho, João Roberto 145
Marinho, Luiz 273
Markum, Paulo 142
Marqeuz, Binho 278
Márquez, Gabriel García 8–9
Martins, Franklin 190
Martins, João 17

INDEX

Mazzucato, Mariana 271, 272
Meirelles, Henrique 150, 210
Melo, Antônia 190
Melville, Thomas and Marjorie 58
Mendes, Angels 276
Mendes, Chico 166–7, 172–3, 175–7, 178, 274–5
Mendes, Pedro 169
Mendes, Raimondo 274–5, 276
Mendonça, Duda 142–3
Menem, Carlos 120, 122, 134–6
Menezes, Gilson 98
Mensalão corruption scandal 152–7, 182, 190, 205, 216–17, 225
Mercadante, Aloizio 147
Metalúrgica Independência 39
Mexico 120, 122
Miró, Joan 58
Moçinha 18
Modi, Narendra 284, 291
Moraes, Mário de 16
Morais, Fernando 32, 63, 65, 66, 72–3
Morales, Evo 6
More, Sir Thomas 8
Moro, Sérgio 213, 216, 219, 227, 241, 242–3
Mourão, Hamilton 242
Movimento Brasil Livre (MBL) 20–5
Mujica, José 'Pepe' 214
Mussolini, Benito 35

Nahas, Jorge 187
Naim, Moises 295
Nasser, Raduan 222
National Liberation Action (*Ação Libertadora Nacional/ALN*) 52, 58, 92
National Liberation Command (*Comando de Libertação Nacional/Colina*) 186–7
National Renovation Party (*Arena*) 68, 69, 87

National Revolutionary Movement (*Movimento Nacional Revolucionário/MNR*) 51, 56
National Service of Industrial Apprenticeships (Senai) 32–3, 34, 38–9
Neves, Aécio 197, 230
Neves, Tancredo 101, 114, 197
New Left Review 109
New York Times 87
Nicaragua 45, 95–6, 174, 224
Niemeyer, Oscar 185
Nina, Maciel Tomaz 273
Nixon, Richard 45
Nunes, Felipe 5

O Cruzeiro (magazine) 16, 17
O Estado de São Paulo (newspaper) 76, 80, 81, 93, 165
O Journal (magazine) 35
O Povo de Deus (Spyer) 267
Obama, Barack 220–1
Odebrecht, Norberto 143
Okamotto, Paulo 79–80, 81, 82, 83, 131
Olavo 41
O'Neill, Jim 288, 289, 290
Open Veins of Latin America, The (Galeano) 108
Os Sertões (*The Backlands*) (da Cunha) 24, 27–8
Osawa, Shizuo 53

Padilha, Eliseu 230
Padura, Leonardo 222
Palme, Olaf 3
Palocci, Antônio
  changes in the Worker's Party 139, 144, 145, 146, 147
  as Finance Minister in Lula's first government 150–1, 259
  and Dilma Rousseff 189, 190, 195
  corruption charges against 217

Panama Canal 45
Parafusos Marte 34, 38–9
Paraguay 45
Paraná, Denise 16, 18, 19, 29, 31, 33, 40, 64, 67
Pedagogy of the Oppressed, The (Freire) 95
Peixoto, Floriano 104
Pelé 76
Peões (film) 85
Pereira, Silvio 153
Pergher, Fabio 234, 236–7
Perillo, Marconi 230
Perón, Eva 135
Perón, Juan Domingo 3–4, 88, 135, 160, 214
Peru 45, 120
Petrobras 37, 162, 195, 198, 203, 205, 207, 217, 225, 227, 230
Piłsudski, Józef 35
Pinheiro, Leo 219
Pinheiro, Wilson de Souza 174, 175–6
Pinochet, Augusto 8, 9
Pinto Neto, Luiz Ribeiro 87
Plano Real (*Real Plan*) 115–17, 120, 121, 122, 129, 134, 194, 198, 307
Playboy (magazine) 86, 87
Pochmann, Mario 131
Popular Action (*Ação Popular/AP*) 51, 61
Portugal, Murilo 147
Power, Timothy 162
Prebisch, Raúl 107
presidential elections
 1989 102, 112
 1998 120, 123
 2002 134, 147
 2006 157–60
 2010 163, 198
 2014 197–8
 2018 1, 233–5, 240–1
 2022 1–2, 3

Prestes, Luís Carlos 35, 48–9, 59, 71
Prison Notebooks and Letters (Gramsci) 94
Progressive Party (*Progressistas/PP*) 255
Promised Land, A (Obama) 221

Quadros, Jânio 46

Rede Sustentabilidade (*REDE/Network*) 198
Resende, André Lara 198
Revolution in the Revolution (Debray) 58
Revolutionary Communist Party (*Partido Revolucionária Comunista/PRC*) 99, 174
Revolutionary Popular Vanguard (*Vanguardia Popular Revolucionária/VPR*) 53, 187
Ribeiro, Lucas 281
Richa, Beto 230
Ricupero, Rubens 198
Robb, Peter 102
Rocha, Carlos 194
Rodrik, Dani 161
Rodrigues Silva, Juno (Gijo) 75, 76, 77–8, 79, 82, 84
Rollemberg, Denise 52, 53
Rousseff, Dilma 4, 104
 resistance to 1964 coup 44
 on truth commission 70
 and Gilberto Carvalho 89
 and *Mensalão* corruption scandal 156, 182
 in 2010 presidential election 163
 and Marina Silva 166, 179–80
 in Lula's first government 181–3, 189–92
 early life and career 183–9
 as president 193–211
 in 2014 presidential election 197–8
 impeachment of 202–11, 228
 and corruption charges against Lula 213–14, 217

INDEX

Rousseff, Igor 184
Rousseff, Pedro 183–4, 185
Roussell, Zania Lúcia 184
Roxin, Claus 218
Russell, Sam 48
Russia 291–2
Ryan, Thiago 93

Samper, Ernesto 220
Samuels, David 162
Sandino, César Augusto 95
Santana, Helenita 158
Santana, João 210
Santos, Ivandro 158
Sarney, José 114, 133
Sarney, Roseana 133–4
Sartre, Jean-Paul 58, 106
Scania strike 80–1
Sebastianism 7, 25
Selerges, Moises 263–5, 268, 272–3
Serene Ones 26
Serra, José 111, 133–4, 147, 157
Silva, Maria Augusta 168
Silva, Marina 165–74, 197–8, 278, 279, 306
Silva, Pedro 168–9
Singer, André 200, 256–7, 308
Singer, Hans 107
Singer, Paul 81, 82
Soares, Ayrton 97
Soares, Delúbio 153
Social Liberal Party (*Partido Social Liberal/PSL*) 241
Socialism and Liberty Party (*Partido Socialismo e Liberdade/PSOL*) 300
Socialist Internationalist Organization (*Organização Socialista Internacionalista/OSI*) 144
Socialist Party (*Partido Socialista/PS*) 198
Socialist Party (*Partido Socialista Brasileiro/PSB*) 180
Socrates 82

Sombra, Sérgio 156
Somoza, Anastasio 95
Soros, George 127, 128, 145
Souza, Jessé 223–4
Spektor, Matias 287
Stalin, Joseph 47
Stédile, João Pedro 149
Suplicy, Eduardo 127, 155
Suplicy, Marta 183
Sweezy, Paul 107

Takemoto, Walter 100
Távora, Euclides Fernandes 173
Temer, Michel 206, 224, 229–30, 266
Thatcher, Margaret 8, 193
Tordesillas Treaty 21
Toro, Quico 295
Traumann, Thomas 5, 200, 259
Tribuna Metalúrgica (newspaper) 64, 73, 79
Trump, Donald 243, 295, 302–3

Ukraine 285, 286, 287, 291–2, 306
Unger, Roberto Mangabeira 179
Uruguay 288
Utopia (More) 8

Vaccari Neto, João 217
Valeixo, Maurício 242–3
Valério, Marcos 153
Vargas, Getúlio 4, 35–6, 37, 46, 49, 56, 104, 170, 271
Veja (magazine) 58, 180, 215, 255, 303
Velasco, Andrés 109–10, 286
Vem pra Rua movement 205
Venezuela 6, 45, 119–20, 149–50, 224, 285, 288, 292–7
Viana, Jorge 177, 278, 279, 281
Viana, Tião 278
Vidal, Paulo 64, 65–6, 67
Vieira, Geddel 230
Voltaire 8

Weber, Max 111
Weber, Rosa 253
Weffort, Francisco 94, 97, 106, 139
Weintraub, Abraham 241
Wind from the East (film) 58
Winter, Brian 286
Worker's Party (*Partido dos Trabalhadores/PT*)
  formation of 7, 87, 89–96
  influence of 1964 coup on 44
  initial troubles in 96–102
  shift in strategy and style 138–47
  and *Mensalão* corruption scandal 152–7, 216–17
  and Marina Silva 175–6
  alignment with PDT 188–9
  in 2014 Congressional elections 196–7
  and Lava Jato scandal 203, 228
  in 2016 municipal elections 224–5
  continued decline in support for 280, 299–300
Workers' Politics (*Política Operária/Polop*) 185–6
World Trade Organization (WTO) 151

Xi Jinping 284, 291

Yergon, Daniel 222–3

Zanone, Sebastião 31
Zedillo, Ernesto 120, 122
Zelensky, Volodymyr 285, 306
Zola, Émile 184